QUEEN
ELIZABETH
II

~ · ~

AND THE

Royal Family

QUEEN
ELIZABETH
II
AND THE
Royal Family

SECOND EDITION

Senior Art Editor Mahua Mandal	**Senior Editors** Peter Frances, Dharini Ganesh
Managing Art Editors Sudakshina Basu, Michael Duffy	**Editors** Hannah Westlake, Ishita Jha
Picture Research Manager Taiyaba Khatoon	**Managing Editors** Angeles Gavira, Rohan Sinha
Senior Picture Researchers Sumedha Chopra, Surya Sankash Sarangi	**Production Manager** Pankaj Sharma
Jacket Designer Tanya Mehrotra	**Design Development Manager** Sophia MTT
Senior Jacket Designer Suhita Dharamjit	**Production Editor** Kavita Varma
Senior DTP Designer Shanker Prasad	**Production Controller** Laura Andrews
DTP Designer Ashok Kumar	**Pre-production Manager** Balwant Singh
Design Head Malavika Talukder	**Editorial Head** Glenda R. Fernandes
Art Director Karen Self	**Design Director** Phil Ormerod
Associate Publishing Director Liz Wheeler	**Publishing Director** Jonathan Metcalf

FIRST EDITION

DK UK

Senior Art Editors Sharon Spencer, Amy Child	**Senior Editor** Rob Houston
Design assistance Alex Lloyd	**Editors** Constance Novis, Helen Fewster
Managing Art Editor Michael Duffy	**Managing Editor** Angeles Gavira Guerrero
Jacket Design Development Manager Sophia MTT	**Producer, Pre-production** Francesca Wardell
Jacket Editor Claire Gell	**Producer** Mary Slater
Jacket Designer Mark Cavanagh	**Picture Researcher** Sarah Smithies
Art Director Karen Self	**Publisher** Liz Wheeler
	Publishing Director Jonathan Metcalf

DK DELHI

Art Editors Shreya Anand, Upasana Sharma	**Senior Editors** Sreshtha Bhattacharya, Anita Kakar
Jacket Designer Suhita Dharamjit	**Editors** Vibha Malhotra, Priyaneet Singh
DTP Designers Jaypal Chauhan, Nand Kishore Acharya	**Managing Jackets Editor** Saloni Singh
Picture Researcher Sakshi Saluja	**Production Manager** Pankaj Sharma
Pre-production Manager Balwant Singh	**Managing Editor** Rohan Sinha
Managing Art Editor Sudakshina Basu	

This edition published in 2021
First published in Great Britain in 2015 by
Dorling Kindersley Limited
DK, One Embassy Gardens, 8 Viaduct Gardens,
London, SW11 7BW

The authorized representative in the EEA is
Dorling Kindersley Verlag GmbH. Arnulfstr. 124,
80636 Munich, Germany

Copyright © 2015, 2016, 2021 Dorling Kindersley Limited
A Penguin Random House Company
10 9 8 7 6 5 4 3 2 1
001–323124–June/2021

A CIP catalogue record for this book
is available from the British Library.

ISBN 978-0-2414-8743-3

MIX
Paper from responsible sources
FSC™ C018179

This book was made with Forest Stewardship Council ™ certified paper – one small step in DK's commitment to a sustainable future. For more information go to www.dk.com/our-green-pledge

Printed and bound in China

For the curious
www.dk.com

CONTENTS

1

THE BRITISH MONARCHY

400–1911 8

Introduction and Timeline 10

The First English Kings 12
From Alfred the Great onwards, these early monarchs fashion Anglo-Saxon and Norse kingdoms into a realm called England.

■ **THE BAYEUX TAPESTRY** 14

The Normans 16
Thanks to William the Conqueror's victory at Hastings, England gains a new foreign ruling class from Normandy.

The Plantagenets 20
The longest-ruling royal house, the Plantagenets endure everything from the Black Death to the Hundred Years' War.

■ **THE PEASANTS' REVOLT** 22

Lancaster and York 24
Two warring families within the Plantagenets embark on a long period of civil strife as they fight bitterly for the throne of England.

■ **THE WARS OF THE ROSES** 26

The Tudors 28
The first modern royal dynasty, the Tudors try to assume control of the Church and send the kingdom hurtling between Protestantism and Catholicism.

■ **ELIZABETH I** 32

Monarchs of Scotland 34
A series of dynamic and ambitious monarchs forges Scotland into a nation.

■ **HOLYROODHOUSE** 36

The Stuarts 38
Under the Stuarts, the role of the sovereign changes from that of God-appointed ruler to constitutional monarch.

Britain's Civil Wars 40
Wars between royalists and parliamentarians lead to the only period of republican rule in Britain's history.

■ **THE RESTORATION** 42

■ **WINDSOR CASTLE** 44

The Hanoverians 48
The desire for a Protestant monarch leads the people to invite a royal relation from Germany to rule Britain.

■ **QUEEN VICTORIA** 50

Victoria becomes Queen 54
A young Victoria accedes to the throne on the death of her uncle, William IV.

■ **OSBORNE** 56

■ **THE GREAT EXHIBITION** 58

Victoria after Albert 60
Queen Victoria mourns the loss of her beloved husband and trusted advisor Prince Albert.

■ **EMPRESS OF INDIA** 62

From Empire to Commonwealth 64
The dominions of Britain's vast empire gradually gain some self-determination.

Victoria's Jubilees 66
The public rediscovers its love of the Queen as the people help her celebrate first 50, then 60 years on the throne.

■ **THE CROWN JEWELS** 68

■ **END OF AN ERA** 70

■ **EDWARD VII** 72

2

THE HOUSE OF WINDSOR
1911–1947 74

Introduction and Timeline 76

■ **GEORGE V** 78

The Royals in Wartime 80
The Royal Family finds itself the focus for national unity and patriotism during the deadliest conflict in the country's history.

■ **BUCKINGHAM PALACE** 84

■ **THE FIRST KING'S SPEECH** 88

■ **EDWARD VIII** 90

Edward VIII's Abdication 92
The burden of the monarchy sits heavily on the shoulders of the new king, and he gives up the throne to marry the woman he loves.

The Unexpected King 94
Although unprepared to be king, George VI discharges his duties unflinchingly at the most difficult of times, as Britain is again drawn into world war.

■ **GEORGE VI** 96

Elizabeth and Margaret's Childhood 98
As Princess Elizabeth is born to the Duke and Duchess of York, she is third in line to the throne. When her father is crowned King George VI, she is 11 years old.

The Royal Family in World War II 102
Following his father's example in World War I, George VI takes on the task of boosting the nation's morale.

Elizabeth's Teenage Years 106
War breaks out when Princess Elizabeth is 13 years old. In a foreshadowing of her future role, she addresses the country's children on the radio.

■ **FAMILY PETS** 108

■ **QUEEN ELIZABETH, THE QUEEN MOTHER** 110

■ **THE FIRST TOUR IN AFRICA** 112

Elizabeth and Philip 114
The young princess meets an exuberant and outspoken exiled Greek prince. The Royal Family warms to him and Elizabeth and Philip are engaged to be married.

3

ELIZABETH II
1947–1960 116

Introduction and Timeline 118

The Wedding of Elizabeth and Philip 120
Amid the grey austerity of post-war Britain, the wedding of Princess Elizabeth to Philip Mountbatten offers a flash of colour.

■ **CLARENCE HOUSE** 122

■ **THE DUKE OF EDINBURGH** 124

The Births of Charles and Anne 126
Within a year of their marriage, Princess Elizabeth and Prince Philip celebrate the arrival of their first son.

■ **ELIZABETH II, THE EARLY YEARS** 130

Elizabeth becomes Queen 132
The unexpected death of her father propels Elizabeth to the throne at the age of 25.

The Queen in Parliament and Politics 134
The Queen opens Parliament for the first time and takes on her role in politics.

■ **CARRIAGES AND COACHES** 136

The Coronation 140
A global audience tunes in to an event that combines tradition, reverent solemnity, and genuine joy.

■ **THE CORONATION CEREMONY** 142

■ **CORONATION DRESS** 144

■ **SANDRINGHAM** 146

The Queen as Head of the Church 150
The Queen takes on her role as head of the Anglican Church worldwide and commits to ensure freedom to worship for all.

Travel and State Visits 152
Elizabeth II embarks on a gruelling tour of Commonwealth countries within a year of her Coronation. During her entire reign, she maintains a busy regime of overseas visits.

Margaret's Doomed Romance 154
Princess Margaret is forced to choose between her life in the Royal Family and her love for a divorcee, Peter Townsend.

■ **THE FIRST TELEVISED CHRISTMAS MESSAGE** 156

4

QUEEN AND MOTHER
1960–1980

Introduction and Timeline   160

The Childhood of the Princes and Princess   162
The education and early years of Queen Elizabeth's four children, and how their schooling shaped their personalities.

■ THE PRINCE OF WALES   166
■ THE LAUNCH OF THE QE2   168

Charles is Invested as the Prince of Wales   170
An ancient ceremony is updated for the television age, as Prince Charles pledges his loyalty to the Queen as Prince of Wales.

■ ROYAL FAMILY   172
■ THE PRINCESS ROYAL   174
■ THE ROYAL WALKABOUT   176

The Prince's Trust   180
How a radio interview inspired Prince Charles to found his personal charity, and help thousands of young people.

The Silver Jubilee   182
National and international celebrations mark Queen Elizabeth II's 25 years on the throne.

■ PRINCESS ANNE'S EQUESTRIAN CAREER   186
■ PRINCESS MARGARET   188
■ ST JAMES'S PALACE   190

The Assassination of Lord Mountbatten   192
The Irish Republican Army strikes at the heart of the British establishment with the murder of the Queen's cousin.

The Decolonization of Africa and the Caribbean   194
Dismantling the British Empire creates new international bonds when the Commonwealth of Nations is formed.

5

QUEEN AND GRANDMOTHER
1980–2000

Introduction and Timeline   198

The Marriage of Charles and Diana   200
The world is invited to the fairy-tale royal wedding at St Paul's Cathedral in London through the magic of television.

■ VISITING THE VATICAN   202
■ COMMEMORATIVE STAMPS   204
■ DIANA, PRINCESS OF WALES   206

The Caring Princess   208
Diana's easy nature and empathy wins hearts and raises cash for charities, as the role of Royal Patron evolves.

■ KENSINGTON PALACE   212
■ PRINCE ANDREW IN THE FALKLANDS   216
■ THE DUKE OF YORK   218

The Marriage of Andrew and Sarah   222
The nation celebrates the wedding of a popular modern couple and relations with the media undergo dramatic change.

The Queen's 60th birthday   224
Queen Elizabeth II marks another milestone greeting the crowds and collecting daffodils on a rainy day at Buckingham Palace.

■ DIANA'S DRESSES   228

Charles and Diana Divorce   230
A royal soap opera unfolds when the Prince and Princess of Wales become publically estranged.

The Annus Horribilis   234
A devastating fire at Windsor Castle caps a turbulent year for the monarchy but ushers in an era of financial change.

■ BUCKINGHAM PALACE OPENS TO THE PUBLIC   236

Wartime Anniversaries   238
World leaders and royalty gather to commemorate acts of valour from past conflicts.

■ DIANA: A STAR IS BORN   240

The Death of Diana   242
Tragedy strikes, and the nation reacts with an unparalleled outpouring of grief.

■ FAREWELL TO DIANA   244
■ BALMORAL CASTLE   246
■ THE EARL OF WESSEX   250

6

TODAY'S ROYAL FAMILY
2000–PRESENT — 252

Introduction and Timeline — 254

The Duchy of Cornwall — 256
How Prince Charles funds public, private, and charitable activities through successful management of the Duchy estate.

Two Royal Farewells — 258
The Royal Family mourns the deaths of the Queen Mother and Princess Margaret.

The Golden Jubilee — 260
A national and international party starts to celebrate Queen Elizabeth's 50th year on the throne.

■ **BACK TO SCHOOL** — 262

The Marriage of Charles and Camilla — 264
A campaign to win over public support for Camilla comes to fruition with her marriage to Charles in 2005.

■ **THE DIAMOND WEDDING** — 266

■ **THE DUKE OF CAMBRIDGE** — 268

■ **STATE VISIT TO IRELAND** — 270

The Pilot Prince — 272
Prince William takes to the skies as his career takes off, flying military and civilian helicopters.

The Wedding of William and Catherine — 274
Huge celebrations follow the marriage of the new Duke and Duchess of Cambridge.

■ **ROYAL MEMORABILIA** — 276

■ **THE DUCHESS OF CAMBRIDGE** — 278

The Diamond Jubilee — 282
Spectacular shows mark the 60th year of the Queen's reign.

■ **OPENING THE OLYMPICS** — 284

■ **PRINCE HARRY** — 288

Harry in the Army — 290
Prince Harry's decade of military service, including life on the frontline in Afghanistan.

The Marriage of Harry and Meghan — 292
Harry and Meghan marry amid increasing strain from an intrusive media.

Royal Ambassadors — 294
Younger royals step up to fill the Queen's shoes and become ambassadors for Britain.

The Queen's Grandchildren — 296
Queen Elizabeth's relationship with her children's children.

■ **ELIZABETH II, THE LATER YEARS** — 298

■ **THE INVICTUS GAMES** — 300

The Queen as Patron — 302
How the Queen supports more than 600 charitable causes.

The Royal Working Life — 306
Queen Elizabeth's dedication to duty, and a typical day at the office.

The Queen's 90th Birthday Celebrations — 310
As the Queen turns 90, the special events begin at Windsor.

■ **THANKSGIVING SERVICE AT ST PAUL'S CATHEDRAL** — 312

The Queen's Official 90th Birthday — 314
A weekend of official celebrations climaxes with the Patron's Lunch on the Mall.

Elizabeth's Long Reign — 318
How the world has changed during the Queen's record-breaking reign.

INDEX — 322

ACKNOWLEDGMENTS — 327

CONSULTANT

Joe Little has been managing editor of *Majesty* magazine for 17 years. He has travelled extensively reporting on royal tours since his first overseas assignment covering Queen Elizabeth II's historic state visit to Russia in 1994. He was also in Ireland in 2011 to witness the warmth of the welcome for the Queen and Prince Philip. On many of the big royal occasions Joe assists the BBC in an advisory capacity; among the projects he has been involved with were the wedding of the Prince of Wales to Camilla Parker Bowles in 2005, the Queen's 80th birthday celebrations in the following year, Prince William and Catherine Middleton's nuptials and, most recently, Trooping the Colour.

AUTHORS

Susan Kennedy formerly worked in publishing as an editor of encyclopedias and historical atlases. She has contributed to more than 15 books for adults and younger readers, and has a particular interest in history and modern culture.

Stewart Ross is a teacher, lecturer, and prizewinning author of historical books for adults and students. His books on British kings and queens include *The British Monarchy From Henry VIII*, *Monarchs of Scotland*, and *The Stewart Dynasty*.

R G Grant is a history writer who has published more than 30 books, many of them dealing with aspects of military conflict. He has written on the American Revolution, World War I, World War II, and the Vietnam War. He is author of DK's *Battle*, *Flight*, *Battle at Sea*, and *Soldier*.

Joel Levy is an author and journalist with a broad experience in writing about the past. Among his many books on history are the titles *History's Worst Battles*, *History's Greatest Discoveries*, and DK's *History Year by Year*.

Ros Belford is the author of numerous travel titles for DK, which combine her interest in history, geography, and biography with a love of travel. She is particularly interested in tracing the history of women – from ancient matriarchs to contemporary monarchs.

1

THE BRITISH MONARCHY
400–1911

« Gold coin of Elizabeth I picturing
a galleon and a Tudor rose

THE BRITISH MONARCHY
400–1911

400	1000	1100	1200	1300	1400

410
Rome abandons Britain; Romano-Britons must now defend themselves against Anglo-Saxon invaders as best they can.

597
St Augustine arrives in the Kingdom of Kent with a mission to convert the southern English to Christianity.

793
Viking assaults on the English mainland begin.

≈ The Alfred jewel, late 9th century

871
Accession of Alfred to throne of Wessex, the only English kingdom not in Viking hands.

973
Coronation of Edgar as King of the English lays foundations of modern coronation ceremony.

≈ Cnut the Great

1016
On death of King Ethelred the Unready, Cnut becomes first Norse King of England.

1018
Malcolm II, King of Scots, establishes his southern frontier on the River Tweed.

1042
Anglo-Saxon royal line returns with accession of Edward the Confessor.

1066
After slaying King Harold at Hastings, William Duke of Normandy takes the English crown.

1086
Results of survey of the realm are presented in the *Domesday Book*.

« Facsimile copy of the *Domesday Book*

1100
Accession of Henry I, who unites England and Normandy.

1135
After crown left to Queen Matilda, daughter of Henry I, Barons revolt in favour of King Stephen.

1154
Accession of Henry II, the first Plantagenet king, whose wife Eleanor brings him vast lands in France.

1170
Row between the Church and the State leads to the murder of Archbishop Thomas Becket in Canterbury Cathedral.

1189
Crusading and chivalrous hero Richard I, Lionheart, takes the crown.

1215
King John puts his seal to the *Magna Carta*, placing the crown beneath the law.

» The final version of the *Magna Carta*, issued in 1225

1265
Simon de Montfort invites "common" people to meet at the same time as Lords – the first Parliament.

1272
Accession of Edward I, "Hammer of the Scots", whose son will become first Prince of Wales.

1290
Death of Margaret "Maid of Norway" leaves Scottish throne vacant; Edward I asked to adjudicate, leading to the Scottish Wars of Independence.

1314
Scotland's Robert I (the Bruce) crushes the English army of Edward II at Bannockburn.

1337
Edward III attacks France, launching the series of conflicts known as the Hundred Years' War.

» Henry V of England

1381
Boy-king Richard II faces off with rebels in the Peasants' Revolt that followed labour shortages caused by the Black Death.

1399
Position of crown seriously undermined when Richard II is deposed and murdered by his cousin, Henry Bolingbroke, who becomes Henry IV.

1415
Henry V startles Europe with a remarkable victory over the French at Agincourt, paving the way for his son to be claimed King of France.

1455
Ineffective and incompetent government of Henry VI leads to outbreak of conflict known as Wars of the Roses between the houses of York and Lancaster.

1461
Edward of York becomes King Edward IV.

1485
Yorkist King Richard III is killed at the Battle of Bosworth, and Henry Tudor accedes to the throne as Henry VII.

Britain's monarchy stretches back further than almost any other similar institution. Over 1,500 years, between the Early Middle Ages and the early 20th century, its history was at best chequered. The position of British kings and queens of this period – some rogues, some quite normal, a few genuinely heroic – rose from that of exalted tribal leaders to rulers appointed by God. Their role then changed slowly, and at times painfully, into that of living symbols, politically neutral personifications of their realm. This long and extraordinarily diverse tale mirrors that of the nation itself. Its keynote is the triumph of pragmatism – survival through adaptability.

1500   1600   1700   1800

1553
Accession of Henry VIII's daughter Mary I, who takes England back to Roman Catholicism.

1603
Crowns of England and Scotland are united with the accession of Scotland's James VI of the house of Stuart as James I of England.

1660
Restoration of Charles II ends 11 years of republican rule.

1714
Protestant George I, elector of Hanover (Germany), accedes to the British throne.

1832
William IV gives his assent to the Reform Bill, which expands the electorate.

« Gold Renaissance medal showing Henry VIII, 1545

⤒ Commemorative beaker for Victoria's coronation, 1837

1509
Beginning of Henry VIII's reign, one of the most momentous in British history.

1513
James IV of Scotland, married to Henry VIII's sister Margaret, is killed in crushing Scottish defeat at Flodden.

1558
Start of long reign of Elizabeth I; England returns to Protestantism and basks in new-found national pride.

⤒ Elizabeth I in her coronation robes

1628
Conflict between Charles I and Parliament leads to Parliament drawing up the Petition of Right.

1685
Accession of Roman Catholic James II, who plans to make the monarchy a continental-style absolutism.

1745
Bonnie Prince Charlie leads the last serious attempt by the exiled house of Stuart to regain British crown.

1637
Scottish rebellion erupts when Charles I and Archbishop Laud try to force an English-style Prayer Book on Scotland.

1688
Mary II and her Dutch husband William III arrive in England; James II flees.

1689
Bill of Rights lays foundations of constitutional monarchy.

1760
George III comes to the throne determined to play a major role in politics.

1775
American colonies begin their successful rebellion against the British crown.

1837
Beginning of long reign of Queen Victoria, during which British power is at its height.

1642
Outbreak of British Civil Wars between King and Parliament.

1694
Foundation of Bank of England ties the monied classes to the new regime.

1793
Beginning of long Revolutionary and Napoleonic Wars with France.

1861
Victoria becomes reclusive after the death of Prince Albert; rise of republicanism.

1901
Death of Queen Victoria marks the end of an era.

1534
Parliament makes Henry VIII Supreme Head of the Church of England.

1547
Beginning of six-year reign of Edward VI, during which the Church of England becomes Protestant.

1587
Execution of Elizabeth I's Roman Catholic cousin, Mary Queen of Scots, a prisoner in England.

1588
Spanish invasion fleet, the Armada, is defeated by the Royal Navy and the weather.

1649
Execution of Charles I: England becomes a republic.

» Portrait of Charles I and Henrietta Maria of England

1910
Death of popular Edward VII in the middle of a constitutional crisis over the powers of the House of Lords.

The **First English Kings**

Between the accession of King Alfred in 871 and the Norman invasion of 1066, Anglo-Saxon and Norse monarchs forged several small kingdoms into a prosperous, orderly realm called England. It became one of the most tempting targets in Western Europe.

Following their invasion of 43 CE (see p.10), the Romans were the first to govern a unified England. Unity collapsed, however, when the legions departed at the beginning of the fifth century and southern Britain was invaded by Germanic tribes of Angles, Saxons, and Jutes.

Over the next three centuries, the many small Anglo-Saxon kingdoms coalesced into just a handful, the most prominent being Wessex, Mercia, and Northumbria.

BEFORE

Before unification into a single realm under kings of Wessex, Anglo-Saxon England comprised a multiplicity of small kingdoms.

THE HEPTARCHY
By the end of the **7th century ≪ 10–11**, the many small tribal units of the **Angles, Saxons,** and **Jutes** had coalesced into seven major kingdoms. These were Wessex, Kent, Sussex, Essex, East Anglia, Mercia, and Northumbria. Kent had been the first to emerge and, owing partly to its close Continental connections, was for a long time the most sophisticated. By the 8th century, the Mercia of **King Offa** (757–796) was the dominant power.

TODAY A COUNTY, ONCE A KINGDOM
Some kingdoms, such as Kent, Essex, and Surrey, have survived as modern-day counties. Others, such as Hwicce (around Gloucester) and Deira (south-east Yorkshire), have disappeared entirely.

Conversion to Christianity after the arrival of St Augustine's mission from Rome in 597 helped this unification process – a united Church welcomed partnership with broad-based secular powers, and enhanced royal authority with religious coronations. The monks who wrote the Anglo-Saxon Chronicle gave the title of "Bretwalda" to seven early Anglo-Saxon kings, implying that they had some sort of overlordship above their peers. The title was never a formal one, and final unification had to wait until the 10th century.

Alfred the Great
King Alfred of Wessex (849–899), reigned from 871 as the self-styled "King of the Anglo-Saxons" and the only English king to be given the epithet "Great". Alfred saved the Anglo-Saxon monarchy in the face of dire adversity. With some justification, he is generally seen as the first king of England. This role arose more by force of circumstance than deliberate policy, because, by the time of his accession, the greater part of England had been overrun by Viking invaders.

Alfred's landmark achievement was beating off the Danish Great Army, obliging its leader Guthrum to convert to Christianity in 879, and dividing England between Anglo-Saxon territory and the Scandinavian-held Danelaw. He strengthened his realm with fortified towns, known as burhs, enabling him to beat off later Viking attacks. A man of peace as well as war, England's first known literate monarch codified the law, encouraged literature, and even translated four Latin works into Old English.

Kings of England
Anglo-Saxon kings ruled as well as reigned, and Wessex was fortunate to be governed by a line of remarkable warrior-kings. Alfred's son Edward the Elder (reigned 899–924) as well as his grandsons, Athelstan, Edmund, and Eadred, expanded their rule north and east, thereby creating the Kingdom of England. While Edward's sister Ethelfleda (who ruled Mercia from 911–918) led

King Alfred's Jewel
Inscribed "Alfred had me wrought", this remarkable treasure is more than 1,100 years old. The enamel figure on gold plate, covered by rock crystal and gold-framed, was probably originally used to tip a ceremonial wand.

the anti-Danish campaign in the Midlands, Edward the Elder took East Anglia and drove north to the River Humber. His son, Athelstan, who reigned from 924–939, then captured the Viking

> **"** This year, **Edgar,** *ruler of the English,* was **consecrated king** by a great assembly. **"**
>
> ANGLO-SAXON CHRONICLE, 973 CE

kingdom of York. By moving into Northumbria, he grew more powerful than any ruler since Roman times.

Edmund "The Magnificent", who reigned from 939–946, and Eadred, who followed Edmund and ruled until 955, tightened the grip on Northumbria further still. After a brief period of uncertainty, the crown passed in 959 to the sixteen-year-old Edgar the Peaceable (c.942–975). His coronation at Bath years later in 973, where he was anointed and received the allegiance of Britain's lesser kings, announced that the Kingdom of England was here to stay. Remarkably, modern British coronations follow the form that St Dunstan devised for Edgar more than a millennium ago.

Ethelred the Unready
Brother succeeding brother is a reminder of the uncertain nature of the Anglo-Saxon royal succession. Close blood relationship was key, but nomination by the predecessor and approval by the nobility were also needed. Therefore, unsurprisingly, a

Viking vessel
The first English Kings lived when Vikings dominated many parts of the British Isles and northwest Europe. These seafarers set out from their homeland of Sweden, Denmark, and Norway, where this ship was buried.

The death of King Harold
The writing above this section of the famous Bayeux Tapestry reads, "King Harold is slain". The image and written sources suggest the last Anglo-Saxon king died when an arrow entered his brain through an eye socket.

king's death often produced instability, sometimes marked by violence. Thus the reign of the ill-named and disliked Edward the Martyr (962–978), a son by Edgar's first wife, crowned in 962, ended when he was slain in Corfe Castle by the supporters of a son by Edgar's second wife. This son was the 12-year-old Ethelred (c.966–1016). Ethelred's name means "noble

counsel" and his soubriquet "Unread" ("no counsel") was a play on words later mistranslated as "Unready". Edward was, in fact, prepared to face the renewed Norse attacks that began

17,900 KG The weight of silver paid by Ethelred to the Danes in 1012 to stop them raiding England.

in 980, but he did not deal with them effectively. He organized a creditable military resistance and used the well-tried tactic (employed by no other than Alfred the Great) of paying the raiders

"Danegeld" to encourage them to leave. However, he failed to unite the country behind him and, by the time of his death, much of England was once more in Danish hands.

England's crown up for grabs
Though he never boasted of being able to control the tide, as the much-told tale relates, Cnut the Dane (c.985–1035), crowned in 1016, proved to be one of England's more able early kings. He married Ethelred's widow, Emma of Normandy, dispersed rivals to his crown, listened to reliable aristocrats, kept on good terms with the Church,

reissued the laws of King Edgar, and extended his rule over both Denmark and Norway – all to no long-term avail. His strangely named sons, Harold Harefoot (1015–40), crowned in 1035, and Harthacnut (c.1018–42), crowned in 1040, both died young, and the crown reverted in 1043 to the Wessex line in the person of Edward the Confessor, son of Queen Emma and Ethelred the Unready.

St Edward (England's only canonized monarch), had spent much of his early life in Normandy, and gained a respect for its people. He may or may not have been particularly holy. Whatever the reason for his sainthood, after a reign marked by tensions with the Godwin Earls of Wessex, Edward died childless. The English crown was up for grabs.

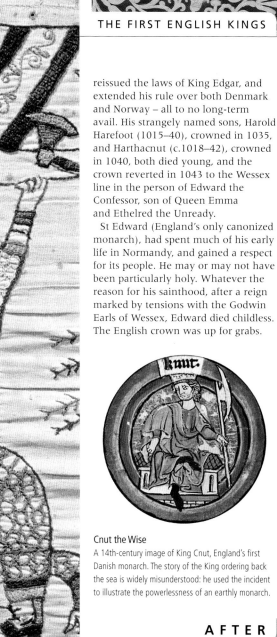

Cnut the Wise
A 14th-century image of King Cnut, England's first Danish monarch. The story of the King ordering back the sea is widely misunderstood: he used the incident to illustrate the powerlessness of an earthly monarch.

AFTER

The Anglo-Saxons left an enduring imprint on England's language, its culture, and its monarchy.

ENGLAND'S ANGLO-SAXON LEGACY
Most obviously, it is to the Germanic invaders that England (Angle-land) owes its very name and, thanks to the ambitions and talents of its kings, the eventual emergence of a single, monarchical state. England's Anglo-Saxon ancestors also left behind the framework of counties and diocese, and the idea of a jury.

A NEW LANGUAGE IS BORN
The core of the modern English language is made up of words that reach back to Anglo-Saxon times. However, the Viking and **Norman conquests 16–17 >>** transformed the grammar within which the words were used. By the **12th century 21 >>**, a new Anglo-Saxon-Norse-Norman language, referred to as Middle English, had emerged, and is a language that modern English speakers can just about understand.

The Bayeux Tapestry

Probably made in Canterbury, England, the Bayeux Tapestry is both a spectacular work of art and a unique historical source. In a series of embroidered coloured pictures, this 11th-century equivalent of a video tells the story of William the Conqueror's invasion of England and victory over King Harold at Hastings.

The events of 1066 changed for ever the history of Britain and its monarchy. Historians can draw on a number of contemporary accounts of that momentous year, but no source can match the tapestry manufactured at the command of William the Conqueror's half-brother, Bishop Odo of Bayeux, to adorn his new cathedral at Bayeux, France.

Woven with dyed wool on linen cloth, the Bayeux Tapestry is a remarkable piece of Romanesque artwork, measuring approximately 70 m (230 ft) long and 50 cm (20 in) tall. Many skilled hands must have worked for several months to create a tapestry of this size. It comprises 58 continuous panels, each headed by Latin text explaining what is depicted. The message is unequivocal: Harold, the last Anglo-Saxon monarch, was a usurper, and God and right were on the side of William, Duke of Normandy, in his attempt to win the crown.

As well as giving the Norman side of the story that culminated with the death of Harold and the defeat of his army on Senlac Hill outside Hastings on 14 October 1066, the tapestry is an invaluable insight into 11th-century life and customs. Its stylized images provide information on subjects such as weaponry, battle tactics, clothing, cooking, and boat-building.

The tapestry's history matches that of its dramatic subject. Having remained virtually unnoticed in Bayeux Cathedral for more than 500 years, the tapestry survived the 16th-century French Wars of Religion and began to attract interest in the early 18th century. French military leader Napoléon Bonaparte displayed it as propaganda when hoping to invade England, but locked it away again when his plan was called off. Strangely, Heinrich Himmler of Germany's Nazi Party coveted the tapestry as a record of "glorious Germanic history", and it was almost taken to Berlin in 1944. It was returned to Bayeux after World War II and is now on display in a special museum.

> " The **English** were in serious **difficulty** after they lost their king… but they still fought on… till the **day drew to a close.** "
>
> **MASTER WACE**, NORMAN POET, FROM *ROMAN DE ROU*

Coronation of Harold II
This panel from the Bayeux Tapestry shows Harold II being offered the sword and sceptre after being crowned the King of England in 1066. The Latin titulus or inscription reads, "Here sits Harold, King of England. Archbishop Stigand."

BEFORE «

Before the Norman Conquest of 1066, most kings spoke Old English, the language of their subjects, and shared their customs and traditions.

IMPOSING FOREIGN MONARCHS
Harold I « **12–13**, the last Anglo-Saxon monarch, came from a Sussex family and was Earl of Wessex before being confirmed as king by the nation's elders. The Norman Conquest changed all this, imposing a foreign monarchy and aristocracy on a subservient people.

A NORTHERN EMPIRE
Foreign rule was not unknown in England. The North Sea Empire of **King Cnut** « **12–13**, had included Denmark, Norway, and part of Sweden.

The **Normans**

The Normans changed the realm of England for ever. William I, William II, and Henry I secured its frontiers, reorganized its government, modernized its church, restructured its language, and remoulded its architecture, enabling the state to survive the turmoil following Henry I's death.

On the death of Edward the Confessor (see pp.12–13), on 5 January 1066, three men claimed the English crown. Harold Godwinson (1022–66), Earl of Wessex, had received Edward's deathbed nomination, a wish confirmed by the Witan, a council of elders. The Duke of Normandy, William the Bastard (1028–87), claimed that in 1051 Edward had promised him the crown, and that during a visit to Normandy Harold had sworn to uphold this claim. The third candidate, citing

> "[The King]… compelled… nobility… that, if he should **die without male** issue, they would… **accept his daughter.**"
>
> WILLIAM OF MALMESBURY, ON HENRY I, 1127

an agreement made almost 30 years earlier, was King Harold III of Norway (1015–66), known as Harold Hadrada (which translates as "hard ruler").

Godwinson was crowned as Harold II on 6 January, but his reign was to last only until October. On 25 September, he travelled north and smashed Hadrada's invasion force at Stamford Bridge, killing its leader. Three days later, news came of Duke William's landing on the south coast. Covering 386km (240 miles) in just 13 days, Harold hurried to face the new danger.

The two armies met on Senlac Hill outside Hastings. William's mounted knights prevailed. Harold was slain; the crown was now William's for the taking. Having burnt and ravaged his way along the coast, he received the submission of London, and entered the city for his coronation on Christmas Day.

William the Conqueror

The seizure of England made William the Conqueror one of the most powerful men in northern Europe. However, power did not bring peace, and he spent much of his reign defending his possessions both in England and France.

Holding down an English population of between one and two million with just 10,000 Frenchmen was no easy task, and he faced revolts in each of the first four years of his reign. His response included the "Harrying of

100,000 The number of people who died of starvation during the Harrying of the North in 1069–70.

the North" – a set of campaigns in the winter of 1069–70 to subjugate the northern regions and eliminate the possibly of revolt in alliance with a

Church and state
This fanciful miniature from the 13th-century Latin chronicle *Flores Historiarum* (*Flowers of History*) depicts Henry I surrounded by churchmen, highlighting the mutual benefit of a good relationship between King and Church.

THE TOWER OF LONDON

Tower of London
This English print shows the Tower from the River Thames, and dates from 1700. The Tower, founded at the end of the 1070s as part of the Norman Conquest, dominated the skyline, daily reminding Londoners of the dire risk of defying the monarch.

Danish army. William paid the Danes to return home, but destroyed the stock and crops of the northern shires to starve the locals into submission. Further, he pursued a strategy of castle building, fierce reprisals, and seizing estates still in Anglo-Saxon hands. By appointing Frenchmen to important positions in church and state, he slowly brought the country under control.

Uneasy at their neighbour's new power, the King of France and Count of Anjou sought to discomfort and unsettle William in Normandy. The Conqueror's ambitious half-brother Odo and thin-skinned eldest son, Robert Curthose (meaning "Short Breeches"), also turned against William, obliging him to spend more time on the continent than in his new kingdom. Possibly realizing the difficulty of ruling both Normandy and England, William bequeathed Normandy to Robert and England to his second son, William Rufus.

William Rufus
William II (1056–1100), who ruled England from 1087 until his death, was named "Rufus" thanks to his red hair or complexion, and was by some accounts a chivalrous warrior-king. He presided over a fashionable court where long hair was in vogue. Such a circumstance, coupled with the fact that he never married and produced no illegitimate children, has led some to believe he was gay. It is equally likely that any scandal attached to his name sprang from the imagination of ecclesiastical chroniclers, for Rufus quarrelled fiercely with Archbishop Anselm of Canterbury. Foremost among the issues that divided them was the question of "lay investiture", the ceremony by which a new abbot or bishop received their office from the King. Anselm challenged this, claiming that the church was superior to any secular power. However, finding little support among his fellow clergy, Anselm went into exile in 1107. When not squabbling with Anselm,

Curthose objected, of course, and the war between the two lasted until Henry I's victory at Tinchebrai (1106) gave him possession of the Duchy of Normandy, and control over his brother. Though Henry I continued to fight off predators in the Duchy, Robert, at least, was in prison, where he spent the last 28 years of his unhappy life.

Possessing more diplomacy than his predecessor, Henry I agreed with Archbishop Anselm that, while the church could hold the theoretical power of investiture, the King would maintain real power. As the church possessed at least one-quarter of all England's wealth, no king could afford to give it total independence.

Henry I proved a sturdy upholder of law and order. His administrative reforms, associated with Bishop Roger of Salisbury, produced the first references to a key financial institution known as the Exchequer.

After the untimely death of Henry I's only legitimate son, Prince William, the succession question clouded the closing years of his reign. Henry I's anxiety proved fully justified when most of the barons refused to honour their oath to accept his daughter Matilda (see box) as sovereign; the ensuing 19 years were scarred by civil war and lawlessness.

Domesday Book
William the Conqueror commissioned a survey in 1085–86 to ascertain the precise extent of his new realm, including the nature and value of every piece of land, and the livestock on it. The results were recorded in the 913-page *Domesday Book*.

Rufus had to deal with his own elder brother, Robert Curthose. Robert felt he had been short-changed when his father gave England to Rufus, and a long series of conflicts between the two brothers ended only when Robert joined a crusader army in 1096; Rufus lent him 10,000 marks for the venture, accepting Normandy as security. In 1100, the King was killed while hunting in the New Forest. An accident, said the court; divine justice, said the church.

Henry I and Matilda
Rufus and Robert's much younger brother, Henry Beauclerc (1068–1135) was the brightest and best educated of the Norman kings. He also had a reputation for ruthless brutality and lasciviousness, fathering at least 20 illegitimate children.

Upon Rufus's mysterious death, he immediately seized the Treasury at Winchester and two days later had himself crowned Henry I. Robert

AFTER »

After the Normans came the far more numerous Plantagenets, who held the throne in a long succession of 14 kings.

ESTABLISHING A NATION
Starting from the northern kingdom that had been secured by their predecessors, the **Plantagenet kings 20–21** » expanded their realm into Ireland, completed the conquest of Wales, came close to adding Scotland to their domains, and challenged for supremacy in France.

AN END TO RULE BY FOREIGNERS
By the time of the reign of **Richard II 21** », the monarchy was fully reintegrated, with both the nation and the court using Middle English. This was the language of the poet Geoffrey Chaucer (1343–1400), known as the Father of English Literature.

EMPRESS 1102–67

QUEEN MATILDA

Not since Queen Boudicca led a British revolt against the Romans in 61 CE had a woman wielded as much power as Matilda. She was wed to the Holy Roman Emperor (making her "Empress"), and then to Geoffrey, Count of Anjou. But most importantly, in 1127 Henry I made his barons swear to support her as his successor.

A medieval monarch was expected to be a warrior, and so the bold move was not appreciated. On Henry's death, Stephen of Blois seized his cousin's crown. The Empress fought robustly for her rights, but never acceded to the throne. In her peaceful later years she exerted considerable influence.

The **Plantagenets**

The Plantagenets occupied the English throne from 1154–1399, longer than any other royal house. Under monarchs of varying ability, the family clung to power through such crises as the signing of the Magna Carta, the Black Death, and long wars with Scotland and in France.

BEFORE

The Plantagenet line can be traced to 821, to a couple named Tertullus and Petronilla, of Rennes, in Brittany.

COUNTS OF ANJOU AND PLANTAGENETS
Ingelger (c.850–899), son of Tertullus and Petronilla, became the first Count of Anjou (where the name "Angevin" stems from). The title passed to Fulk the Red and on to Geoffrey of Anjou (1113–51). His marriage to Matilda, daughter of **Henry I of England ‹‹ 16–17** and his wife of Anglo-Saxon descent, produced a bloodline combining Anjou, Normandy, and Wessex. However, the family did not use the Plantagenet surname for another 200 years.

Coronation of Richard the Lionheart
This 14th-century illustration depicts the coronation of Richard the Lionheart on 3 September 1189 in Westminster Abbey, London. Richard lived much of his 10-year reign away from the country, spending only six months in England, according to some sources.

The Plantagenet monarchy was one of extreme contrasts. The family gave England some of its most able kings: Henry II (1133–89); Edward I (1239–1307); Edward III (1312–77); and the great chivalric hero, Richard the Lionheart (1157–99), but also threw up the infamous John (1167–1216) and the tragically dim-witted Edward II (1284–1327).

The Angevin Empire
As Count of Anjou, the Plantagenet Henry II, son of Empress Matilda (see pp.16–17), was master of the Angevin Empire, which stretched from Hadrian's Wall to the Pyrenees. The lands had been acquired through marriage to Eleanor of Aquitaine (see pp.18–19) in 1152 and succession to the throne of England two years later.

A man of boundless energy, Henry II ruled from 1154–89, spending 20 years expanding his empire by occupying Ireland, driving into Wales, Scotland, and Brittany, and forcing the Count of Toulouse into submission. Meanwhile, at home, he regularized England's Common Law in a network of courts, and strengthened central government.

But it was all too good to last. The King's reputation was damaged when a conflict over the entitlements of the church led to the murder in 1170 of Thomas Becket, Archbishop of Canterbury, in the cathedral itself. The martyred Becket eventually gained sainthood while Henry's reputation plummeted still further. During his final years, he raised excessive taxes, made corrupt appointments, and faced a series of devastating rebellions led by his wife and truculent sons.

Lionheart and Lackland
Richard I, the Lionheart, who reigned from 1189–99, was a legend in his own lifetime. A generous yet fearless warrior who led the successful Third Crusade (1189–92), he also ensured England was well governed during his absence, and managed, more or less, to hang on to his massive Angevin inheritance. In the end, his bravery was his undoing: scorning to wear his chain mail, he was hit by a crossbow bolt during the siege of Châlus; the wound turned gangrenous and, having forgiven the lad who fired the bolt, he died in his mother Eleanor's arms.

Even before he was crowned in 1199, the standing of King John (bitingly known as "Lackland" and

The body of Becket is laid to rest

Christ welcomes Becket into heaven

Murderous knights disturb Becket at prayer

Becket is assassinated while facing an altar in Canterbury Cathedral

French Reliquary Casket, 1180–90
Fragments of what were believed to be Becket's hair, clothing, and bones were contained in this casket, made in Limoges. The scene depicts the assassination of Becket, an event that shocked the Christian world, earned Becket martyrdom, and caused the cathedral to become a pilgrimage site.

"Uneasy lies the head that wears the crown."

WILLIAM SHAKESPEARE, *HENRY IV, PART II*, 1597

"Softsword"), was tarnished by opportunistic rebellions against his ailing father, Henry II, and absent brother, Richard the Lionheart. As king, John fell out with the pope and with the baronage over his capricious behaviour and loss of most of the Angevin Empire. As a result, a year before his death, John was obliged to sign the Magna Carta (Great Charter, see box) that put the monarch unequivocally under the law.

King and parliament

Ascending the throne in 1216 at the age of nine, the naive, peace-loving Henry III (1207–72) was out of his depth throughout his long and troubled reign. Attempts to win back lost French lands came to nothing and, in 1258, he was forced to accept limits on royal authority set out in the Provisions of Oxford. During the Barons' War (1264–68), Henry III's own brother-in-law, Simon de Montfort (see box), virtually took control of the throne, and Henry III held on to his position only thanks to the dashing exploits of Prince Edward, his son and heir.

Crowned in 1274, Edward I sought consent from the newly formed parliament to approve his taxation. He further enhanced parliament's standing by using it to promote statutes to tidy up local government. All monarchs had been expected to govern with the consent of their peers since the 5th century. However, the emergence of the Commons meant that this consent might now stretch to all those

with political and economic influence. Edward I is primarily remembered as a warrior. As well as going on crusade, he fought fierce (and costly) campaigns to hold on to Aquitaine. Nearer home, he subdued Wales, giving its people his eldest son as their prince, and made determined attempts to bring Scotland under the English crown. This left his pitifully inept son, Edward II, crowned in 1308, with a bitter legacy of debt and an unwinnable war with the Scots.

A lack of political competence and reliance on unsuitable male favourites drained any support Edward II might have had. The invasion in 1326 by his wife and her lover, Roger Mortimer, found the King virtually friendless. He was deposed and imprisoned in Berkeley Castle, where he was murdered.

War, plague, and revolt

Edward III, crowned in 1327, restored Plantagenet prestige through military victories. In the early years of the Hundred Years' War (1337–1453), he vanquished the French at Crécy (1346)

Battle of Crécy from Froissart's Chronicle
This illustration from the 15th-century chronicle by Jean Froissart depicts a scene from the Battle of Crécy, fought during the Hundred Years' War. Edward III won a crushing victory over the French on 26 August 1346.

and captured the French king at Poitiers (1356). Abandoning attempts to rule Scotland, he ushered in long years of domestic peace in England. Edward III also made use of Justices of the Peace – unpaid royal servants, such as knights, who, since 1195, had been responsible for maintaining law and order in their own locality. Edward III's encouragement of them strengthened the bond between king and gentry.

Working with parliament, Edward III's government had ridden out the pressing effects of the arrival in 1348 of a seaborne bubonic plague pandemic, known as the Black Death. The disease

3,500,000 Estimated number of English deaths caused by Bubonic Plague (Black Death), 1348–49.

caused a steep and sudden population decline, resulting in labour shortages, price rises, and social unrest.

Edward III's son, Edward, the Black Prince (1330–76), died before his father so Edward III's grandson, Richard II, (1367–1400) was crowned in 1377. Unfortunately, Richard's arrogant behaviour sabotaged his grandfather's achievements. Having bravely outfaced the rebels in the 1381 Peasants' Revolt (see pp.22–23), Richard II developed an over-inflated opinion of the status of monarchy, sharply at odds with the views of his people. He lost control of the government around 1387–88. Richard II's cousin, Henry Bolingbroke (1367–1413), crowned Henry IV in 1399 (see p.24), finally removed Richard II from the throne and had him thrown in prison, where he was murdered the following year.

DECISIVE MOMENT

FIRST PARLIAMENT

First mentioned in the 1230s, parliaments were large gatherings at court to discuss affairs of state and show support for government policy, especially taxation. In 1264, rebel leader Simon de Montfort 6th Earl of Leicester (c.1208–65) called a parliament attended by four knights from each shire. The following year, he invited two prominent citizens from major towns to join the knights of the shire (Commons), alongside barons and senior churchmen (Lords). The assembly possibly met in the Chapter House of Westminster Abbey (left). Soon, such parliamentary gatherings became the practice, giving rise to the claim that de Montfort's assembly marked the birth of modern parliaments.

The **Peasants' Revolt**

Arising out of the labour shortage following the Black Death, the Peasants' Revolt of 1381 tested the mettle of young Richard II. His brave but duplicitous behaviour in the face of grave danger led to the suppression of the revolt.

The widespread mortality brought on by the Black Death, or plague, produced a shortage of labour. Accordingly, the simple law of supply and demand led to wage rises and calls for an end to the unpaid feudal labour required of serfs. A Statute of Labourers (1351) had some success in pegging wages at pre-plague levels, but discontent mounted as fresh outbreaks of the plague reduced the pool of labour still further. Meanwhile, England was engaged in the unsuccessful and badly run Hundred Years' War with France. In order to fund this prolonged battle, Richard II introduced several unfair taxes, including the poll tax of 1380, which was the final straw for the peasants.

Early in the summer of 1381, the people of Kent and Essex, two of England's more prosperous counties, rose in revolt. Lawyers and grasping landlords were slain, and legal documents burned, before the rebel army advanced to London. There, they joined the mob to open prisons and destroy the property of John of Gaunt, the King's uncle, and other unpopular magnates. The 14-year-old Richard II, stuck in the Tower of London with his ministers and a small troop of soldiers, watched in horror.

On 14 June, Richard left the Tower with his bodyguard to talk to the opposition. He heard their demands and issued charters declaring the abolition of serfdom. On hearing this, many of the revolutionaries turned for home. Still, when the Tower's gates were opened to readmit the King, hundreds of rebels poured in. They dragged out and beheaded Lord Chancellor Simon Sudbury, Lord High Treasurer Robert Hales, and a handful of other officials. Richard met the remaining rebels at Smithfield the following day. After their charismatic leader Wat Tyler was killed in a scuffle, his followers dispersed. In the aftermath of the revolt, Richard revoked his concessions and ordered the rebel leaders to be rounded up and hanged.

> **"** … the **time** is come… in which ye may (if ye will) **cast off** the **yoke of bondage,** and recover **liberty."**
>
> **JOHN BALL,** RADICAL ENGLISH PRIEST, IN A SERMON TO THE REVOLTING PEASANTS AT BLACKHEATH, 12 JUNE 1381

Pacifying the rebellious
This section from Jean Froissart's *Chronicles* depicts Richard II meeting the rebels in June 1381 to discuss their demands. The King waits in the boat while two negotiators speak to the crowd. In the background, rebels can be seen capturing the Tower of London.

Lancaster and York

The deposition of Richard II split the Plantagenets into factions, notably the Lancastrians and Yorkists. While their confrontations devastated much of the old aristocracy, thanks in part to the genius of William Shakespeare, they also gave us the monarchy's great hero, Henry V, and its villain, Richard III.

As England's wealth grew and its system of government became more sophisticated, the role of the monarch required an increasingly broad range of skills. He needed to balance the factions of powerful nobles, manage parliament, keep the gentry and merchant classes on his side, oversee the machinery of central government, and lead the country in times of war, even riding into battle. Men like Henry V (1387–1422), and, to a lesser extent, Edward IV (1442–83), handled the job well. For a man of lesser abilities, like the feeble Henry VI (1421–71), it was all too much. Without a strong monarch to restrain them, the ambitious aristocracy descended into an orgy of bloodletting.

Lancaster ascendant

Having seized the throne from Richard II and arranged for his murder, Henry Bolingbroke, Duke of Lancaster, was crowned Henry IV in 1399 (see p.21). He then spent the rest of his troubled reign fighting to hold on to his stolen prize. Rebellions came from the Earl of Huntingdon, Richard II's half-brother, and from the Percy Family of Northumberland, who had helped Henry IV to the crown. Scots and Welsh, keen to take advantage of England's troubles, made ready allies. Further difficulties arose from money squabbles with parliament, and from a radical new sect, known as Lollards, who wanted to reform western Christianity.

Once an admired crusader knight, Henry IV ended his days a sick and exhausted wreck. When he finally died in 1413, his son Henry V was crowned

BEFORE

The division of the houses of York and Lancaster can be traced back to 1386.

A KING DEPOSED, AN HEIR CHEATED
Richard II, son of **Edward III's ‹‹ 20–21** firstborn male, had no children. In 1386, he declared Roger Mortimer, Earl of March and a descendant of Edward III's second son, his heir. Henry Bolingbroke, Duke of Lancaster, and descended from Edward III's third son, deposed Richard II and took the throne as **Henry IV ‹‹ 21**. At this point, the Mortimer side of the family picked up the Duke of York title.

1ST EARL OF WARWICK 1428–71

RICHARD NEVILLE

Nicknamed "Kingmaker" a century after his death, Neville was an astute, wealthy man. In 1455, he sided with the Yorkists to defeat Henry VI. Six years later he helped Edward of York to the throne as Edward IV. In 1469, Neville captured Edward IV, and then let him go. He rebelled once more in 1470 (joining with the Lancastrians), exiling Edward IV and restoring the now insane Henry VI. Neville's power-broking finally ended when Edward IV came back to England and slew him at the Battle of Barnet in 1471.

Contemporary portraits of contrasting kings
These portraits, taken from oil-on-panel paintings, depict Henry V, on the left, and Richard III. Henry V was a much admired monarch, while Richard III, final king of the House of York and the last of the Plantagenets, has few defenders.

king, and proved to be arguably England's most able monarch. A meticulous nationalist, he insisted that official documents were written in English, not French or Latin, and he encouraged the adoration of English saints, such as Thomas of Canterbury (see p.20) and Henry's holy predecessor, Edward the Confessor (see p.13).

In 1414, Henry V dealt swiftly and efficiently with a Lollard rising, and a plot to put Edmund Mortimer on the throne in 1415. He then decided to test his right to the French throne in battle.

Henry's success is the stuff of legend. He trounced a much larger French force at Agincourt, conquered Normandy, and, by the Treaty of Troyes in 1420, was declared heir to the throne of France. Where this would have led, we shall never know; dysentery took his life on 31 August 1422.

Lancaster descendant

Henry's son by Catherine of Valois, daughter of Charles VI of France, was nine months old when he ascended the throne as Henry VI – the youngest age of succession of any English monarch. A few weeks later, he was declared King of France, but until Henry came of age in 1437, his uncle, John, Duke of Bedford, governed his realm as the head of a regency council.

Things went well until 1429, when visionary and military commander Joan of Arc (1412–31) instigated a French fight-back. Matters at home and abroad slipped from bad to worse when the pious, peace-loving, and wholly apolitical Henry VI took the reins of government into his own hands and, by 1453, the kingdom

Battle of Agincourt 1415
This illustration, taken from the 1484 manuscript "Vigils of King Charles VII" by Martial d'Auvergne, shows Henry V outnumbered by, yet victorious over, the French forces at Agincourt during the Hundred Years' War (1337–1453).

was in chaos. A serious rebellion led by Sussexman Jack Cade had been put down only with great bloodshed, and virtually all England's French possessions had been lost. The king, who had taken a hugely unpopular French wife, Margaret of Anjou, failed to control his squabbling lords. To cap it all, at this point Henry VI suffered a mental breakdown (possibly due to schizophrenia). Civil war flared and, in 1461, the 19-year-old Earl of March (1442–83), who, technically, had a better claim to the throne than Henry VI, was crowned Edward IV, while the deposed king was imprisoned in the Tower of London.

never seen again. The slaughter of adult nobility was commonplace in the later 15th century, but the murder of children was not, and Gloucester, crowned Richard III in 1483, faced rebellions. He survived for only two years, then became the last English king to die in battle. The victor of the Battle of Bosworth, Henry Tudor (see pp.28–29), a grandson of Catherine of Valois, supposedly found Richard III's crown in a thorn bush and immediately put it on.

"What **misery**... this region hath **suffered** by the **division** of Lancaster and York."

EDWARD HALL, FROM HIS *CHRONICLE*, 1548

York divided

Edward IV was a tall, pleasure-loving warrior king who, having won his throne on the battlefield, in 1469–71 came close to losing it the same way. He fell out with the overmighty 1st Earl of Warwick (see box), who then dragged Henry VI out of the Tower and put him on the throne again. But the mentally deranged king inspired no one. After further conflict, Henry VI and his only son were murdered in 1471, and Edward IV retook his crown. He governed well and has sometimes

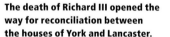

4 The number of kings who were murdered or died a violent death between 1399–1485.

been credited with founding a "new monarchy". But his marriage to a commoner, Elizabeth Woodville, stirred baronial resentment, and his early death brought more bloodshed.

Edward IV's son, the 12-year-old Edward V reigned for 78 days in 1483 but was never crowned. He and his younger brother Richard of York were sent to the Tower by their uncle, Richard of Gloucester (1452–85), and

AFTER

The death of Richard III opened the way for reconciliation between the houses of York and Lancaster.

TUDORS UNITE TWO HOUSES
Henry Tudor 28–29 », Richard III's conqueror and a distant relative of the Lancasters, brought reconciliation. Now crowned as Henry VII, he married Richard III's niece, Elizabeth of York. Thus were the symbolic white rose of York and the red rose of Lancaster brought together to form the red-and-white rose of **The Tudors**.

THE KING IN THE CAR PARK
Richard III's remains were lost for 500 years. In 2013, however, after a dig in a car park once the site of Greyfriars Priory Church, it was confirmed with DNA evidence that the King had been rediscovered. Despite his reputation as a child-murderer, in 2015, thousands of people watched his body carried in procession to Leicester Cathedral to be reburied.

The **Wars** of the **Roses**

Between 1455 and 1487, England was afflicted with chronic instability as supporters of two rival branches of the royal House of Plantagenet fought for power, influence, and the greatest prize of all – the Crown.

At the heart of the conflict lay competition for the throne between descendants of Edward III's second and third sons, who belonged to the house of York (represented by the white rose) and Lancaster (represented by the red rose) respectively. The year 1455 is generally seen as the start of the wars, although violence had broken out before this. The throne was occupied by the Lancastrian, Henry VI, but due to his mental infirmity, Richard Duke of York acted as Lord Protector – the de facto ruler.

The term "war", in fact, inaccurately describes what followed. Over the next 30 years, there were only 60 weeks of campaigning. Other than at Towton, the armies were small and loss of life not particularly heavy. On the other hand, numerous nobles lost their lives, two kings were murdered, and a third died in battle.

The first phase of fighting (1455–1461) saw Henry VI fall into Yorkist hands. Margaret, his queen, raised an army and liberated him, but after the battle at Towton (1461), which was the bloodiest ever on British soil, Henry and Margaret fled to Scotland, leaving Edward IV to be crowned king. Henry was recaptured in 1465 and killed following the Battle of Tewkesbury (1471).

Edward IV's rule brought 12 years of peace. Fighting was rekindled after his death in 1483 when his brother Richard imprisoned and allegedly killed his 12-year-old son and heir, Edward V, and crowned himself Richard III. The coup was so badly received that when Henry Tudor (see pp.25, 28) landed with a small force in Wales, he gained enough support to defeat and kill Richard III in battle. As Henry VII, he defended his crown at the battle of Stoke (1487), which marked the end of the Wars of the Roses. Tudor propagandists later exaggerated the misery of the wars to strengthen loyalty to the new ruling family.

> **"** …what execrable plagues this famous region hath suffered by the **division and dissension** of the renowned houses of **Lancaster and York."**
>
> **EDWARD HALL,** LAWYER AND HISTORIAN, 1548

The Battle of Barnet
This 15th-century painting shows Edward IV (seen wearing a crown) piercing Richard Neville, leader of the Lancastrian army, with his lance at the crucial Battle of Barnet in 1471. This battle, along with the subsequent Battle of Tewkesbury, secured the throne for Edward IV.

The **Tudors**

The Tudors were the first recognizably modern royal dynasty, helping explain their enduring popularity with novelists, playwrights, and film-makers. Artists and writers have also been drawn to the immense personalities of Henry VIII and Elizabeth I, two giants on the tapestry of English monarchy.

Arguably the most colourful of all the royal dynasties, the Tudors steered the country through its transformation from a late medieval state to an early modern one, from 1485–1603. Moreover, the Tudors were fortunate that their period of power coincided with an unprecedented flowering of arts and culture, especially in literature and the theatre, with which they have been associated ever since.

Episcopal flattery
Above the island castle of England, guarded by a dragon, lion, and greyhound (all Tudor symbols) the Bishop of Chichester's couplets praising Henry VIII lie between the roses of Lancaster, York, and Tudor.

« BEFORE

In the 814 years that elapsed from the accession of King Alfred in 871 to the arrival of the first Tudor monarch in 1485, the English throne had only once been occupied by a woman.

DISPUTED ACCESSION
Stephen of Blois « 17 disputed the right of his cousin, **Matilda « 17**, to accede to the throne. Though she fought back, Stephen seized the crown. Under the Tudors, the resistance to a female monarch receded when, for almost half the period of Tudor rule, a woman wore the English crown (**Mary I** and then **Elizabeth I**), setting a strong precedent.

Without a doubt, the England that Elizabeth I handed on to her Scottish successor in 1603 bore little resemblance to the England that her grandfather, Henry Tudor (1457–1509), had seized just 114 years earlier (see p.23).

Father and son
Crowned Henry VII in 1485, Henry Tudor laid the foundations of the renowned regime. It was not an easy task. The Yorkists (see pp.24–25) still hoped to make a come-back based on two pretenders: Lambert Simnel, who claimed to be a son of Edward IV's brother, and Perkin Warbeck, who said he was the younger of the two princes imprisoned in the Tower (see p.25). Simnel was eventually pardoned and permitted to work in the royal kitchens, but Warbeck was executed in 1497.

By encouraging trade and clamping down on overmighty subjects, by 1500, Henry VII's reign was relatively secure. He bolstered his position by the marriages of his daughter, Margaret, to James IV of Scotland (see p.31) and his son, Arthur, to the Spanish princess, Catherine of Aragon.

Few reigns were as dramatic as that of Henry VII's second son, Henry VIII (1491–1547), who became heir to the throne on the early death of Arthur in 1502.

Handsome, intelligent, well-educated, sporty, and musical, he ascended the throne the ideal Renaissance prince. He left it 38 years later a bloated parody of his former self. With papal permission, he married Catherine, Arthur's widow, and while the highly skilled Cardinal Wolsey managed the day-to-day business of government, the young king enjoyed himself with a short war in France, tournaments, hunting, and music- and love-making. However, when Catherine bore a daughter, Mary, but not the longed-for son and heir, Henry revealed

The epitome of majesty
This portrait of Henry VIII, aged 49, was painted at the time of his marriage to Anne of Cleves by Hans Holbein the Younger. The message behind it is unequivocal: cross this man at your peril.

Ruins of Fountains Abbey, North Yorkshire
Ostensibly disillusioned with monastic behaviour, Henry VIII and Thomas Cromwell dissolved the monasteries for fiscal gain. Fountains Abbey was the hub of a thriving Cistercian business enterprise.

Following the successes of the long reign of Elizabeth I, which glowed all the brighter in light of the ensuing turmoil, reservations about having a woman on the throne evaporated.

LONG LIVE THE QUEENS
In the 417 years between Elizabeth I's death and 2020, **four women have worn the crown** (Mary II, Anne, Victoria, and Elizabeth II) for a total of 149 years. The decision – enshrined in the **Succession to the Crown Act** – to give **males and females equal right of succession** from 26 March 2015 means that this statistic is likely to rise.

the ruthlessness that would besmirch his reign. The Pope refused him a divorce, so he employed a lawyer, Thomas Cromwell, to use Parliament to break with Rome and establish the Church of England, headed by the King. As England began its participation in the Protestant Reformation, all opposition was crushed, monasteries were dissolved, and their wealth diverted to the royal coffers.

Anne Boleyn, Henry's next wife, gave birth to another daughter, Elizabeth. Four more wives gave Henry just one son between them when, finally, in 1537, Jane Seymour produced Prince Edward. However, Jane died days later.

son to Lady Jane Grey, a great-niece of Henry VIII, and had her proclaimed queen. The coup was foiled by popular opinion, and Northumberland was executed in 1553, as was Jane in 1554.

"Calais" engraved on her heart
Crowned Mary I in 1553, the Queen alienated many of her subjects with a campaign to restore Roman Catholicism that involved burning 300 Protestants. Her deeply unpopular marriage to a foreign king, Philip II of Spain, was childless. And finally, under her reign England's last possession on continental soil, Calais, was lost in an unnecessary war with France in support of Spain.

Mary, whose statue had stood in every church in the land. How could she ever be replaced? An explicit reply never issued from Elizabeth I, but she shrewdly used her unmarried status and her nickname, the "Virgin Queen".

Elizabeth I's persecution of dissenters was moderate, too, and she executed Roman Catholics for the crime of treason, not for professing their faith.

Ably assisted by councillors, such as Sir William Cecil, Sir Nicholas Bacon, and Sir Francis Walsingham, when possible, she also avoided confrontation with her parliaments and in foreign affairs. An exception to this was when parliament threatened to withhold funds until her marriage was settled (see p.33). She let loose on them her formidable powers of rhetoric and made it clear that the well-being of her realm was her priority, and to marry or not was her private affair.

In the end, though, years of tension with the Roman Catholic powers of

1554 portrait of Queen Mary I
History is rarely kind to losers, and so it was with Mary Tudor, also known as Bloody Mary. Bigoted and devoid of charisma, she lacked the sensibility to realize how bitterly her people hated her austere Catholicism, her Spanish marriage, and – eventually – herself.

> " [King Henry VIII] is much **handsomer** than any sovereign in Christendom … **very fair** and his whole frame **admirably proportioned.** "

A VENETIAN VISITOR TO LONDON, 1519

Further expensive wars with France and Scotland left the realm despoiled, exploited, and, by the time Henry VIII died, riven by religious strife. Edward VI (1537–53) was just 10 years old when his father passed away. Henry VIII had left government in the hands of his son's maternal uncle, the Duke of

12,000 The number of monks, canons, friars, and nuns thrown out of their dwellings when Henry VIII dissolved the monasteries.

Somerset, and a 16-man council. The Duke and Archbishop Thomas Cranmer sought to make the Church of England wholly Protestant, encouraging iconoclasm and sanctioning an English Prayer Book, causing much discontent.

In 1549, Somerset was removed from office by John Dudley. Now Duke of Northumberland, Dudley stabilized government finances and, encouraged by the young king, pressed ahead with the conversion of the country to Protestantism. When Edward VI fell fatally ill, Northumberland married his

As Mary I lay dying of stomach cancer, she declared that the word "Calais" would be found engraved on her heart.

The shift from Catholicism
If religious persecution was the keynote of the reign of Mary I, the reign of her sister, Elizabeth I (see pp.32–33), who ruled from 1558–1603, was characterized by caution. Raised in the Protestant faith, Elizabeth steered the Church of England away from Catholicism towards a moderate Protestantism that blended the new faith with Roman Catholic hallmarks, such as ecclesiastical vestments and bishops. England's relatively swift shift from Roman Catholic to Protestant had left many of her subjects mourning familiar practices and beliefs, above all, the cult of the Virgin

Queen of the seas
This rare English gold coin dating to 1558–1603 bears an image of Elizabeth I and a warship. It was during the reign of the last Tudor monarch that England began to consider itself a major naval power.

Spain and France spilled over into war. The spark was ignited in 1587 when Elizabeth I executed her Roman Catholic cousin, Mary Queen of Scots (1542–87) for continually plotting to overthrow her.

The highlight of the Queen's reign came in 1588, when her navy, aided by stormy weather, prevented invasion by the supposedly invincible Spanish Armada. Thereafter, however, victories were difficult to come by. The Treasury was drained by costly campaigns at sea, in Ireland, and in support of European Protestantism. An economic downturn accompanied by meagre harvests brought about widespread poverty. Together, these factors conspired to bring the reign of "Gloriana", also fondly known as "Good Queen Bess", to an end with a whimper rather than a blaze of glory.

DECISIVE MOMENT

THE CHURCH OF ENGLAND

In 1521, Pope Leo X gave Henry VIII the title *Fidei Defensor* (Defender of the Faith), the initial letters of which can still be seen on British coins. The accolade was in recognition of a book the King had written defending the position of the Roman Catholic Church. In the light of this, Henry's subsequent break with Rome and the establishment of the Church of England with himself as its Supreme Head, was all the more startling.

Indeed, the break with Rome was one of the few truly revolutionary events in English history. Henry VIII's move paved the way for English Protestantism and added considerably to his prestige.

As Supreme Head of the Church of England, a title conferred by the 1535 Act of Supremacy, Henry VIII acquired vast wealth and a quasi-spiritual authority. It was no coincidence that around the same time he was being addressed as "Your Majesty" – the first British monarch to be given this style.

Persecutor persecuted
Antoine Caron's painting records the arrest and execution for treason (1535) of Lord Chancellor Sir Thomas More. A highly respected scholar, More had also been a tireless pursuer of Protestants.

Born 1533 Died 1603

Elizabeth I

"I have the body but of a **weak and feeble woman**, but... the heart... of a king."

ELIZABETH I AT TILBURY, 1588

Queen Elizabeth I was born into a world of danger and intrigue. The birth of a daughter was a disappointment to her father, Henry VIII (see pp.28–29) and, by the time Elizabeth was two and a half years old, her mother, Anne Boleyn, was executed for adultery. Officially bastardized, Elizabeth learned not to draw attention to herself until her legitimacy was restored in 1543.

The next trauma occurred in 1547–49 when Thomas Seymour, three times her age, attempted to seduce her with the connivance of her stepmother, Catherine Parr. If this had any effect on Elizabeth's decision to shun marriage, we shall never know.

Journey from captivity to throne

Elizabeth's position was precarious during the reign of her Roman Catholic half-sister, Mary I (1516–58), and Elizabeth was imprisoned in the Tower of London on suspicion of complicity in plots to overthrow Mary. Nothing was proved, and so she was moved to less harsh custody in Woodstock, Oxfordshire. Happily for Elizabeth, the dying Mary recognized her as heir to the throne and she acceded peacefully in November 1558.

So who was this 25-year-old woman whom the people of London welcomed with unstinting joy as her coronation procession wound its way through the streets to

Westminster Abbey in January 1559? Contemporaries' overriding impression was one of majesty. Elizabeth, a born actor, carried herself like a queen. Stately and regal on all occasions, she could be capricious, waspish even. When annoyed, her comments were made all the sharper when delivered in her high, shrill voice. As she aged, she disguised the ravages of time

Armada Portrait, 1588
This arresting portrayal, attributed to George Gower (1540–96), depicts Elizabeth I after her rout of the Spanish Armada. Surrounded by symbols of imperial majesty, she exudes power and magnificence.

English warships confront the Spanish Armada
The sea was described as "groaning under the weight" of the Spanish fleet, which had been sent to convey troops to attack and invade England in 1588. The Armada's decisive defeat was Elizabeth I's finest hour.

fluent in French, Welsh, and Spanish, as well as Classical Latin and Greek.

and smallpox under a thick layer of ceruse (a poisonous make-up blend of white lead and vinegar), yet the queen was no painted doll. She rode fearlessly and with skill, frightening many with her daring. On the dance floor she was as nimble as she was tireless. Inside her active body lurked an equally active brain. Elizabeth received lessons from expert tutors in grammar, the various branches of mathematics, music, theology, history, philosophy, and literature. She was by all accounts an extremely quick learner and, by the age of 11, was

"Beggar-woman and single"

After the 29-year-old Elizabeth had survived an attack of smallpox, many were certain that she would marry in order to secure the succession. Her reasons for never doing so remain something of a mystery. She observed from her sister's reign how marriage to a foreigner could alienate her subjects; she also knew that marriage to an Englishman would arouse jealousy and disputes. Thus, likely for a number of reasons, she chose to remain single, but this was risky. Had she died before 50, instability would have ensued while a successor was searched for, throwing the realm into turmoil.

In 1559, the queen came closest to marrying when she fell in love with Robert Dudley. When his wife Amy died after falling down stairs, however, tongues wagged that she been murdered to free her husband for Elizabeth. It was clearly impossible, under such circumstances, for a marriage to go ahead, but she remained close friends with Dudley for another 10 years.

Other candidates for Elizabeth's hand were very much political. Among those, she considered, or, pretended to consider, marriage to Philip II of Spain (her sister's widower), King Eric XIV of Sweden, Archduke Charles of Austria, Duke Henry of Anjou, and Francis, his brother. But true to her

words of 1563 – "beggar-woman and single, far rather than queen and married" – she turned them all down. After all, she quipped, she was already married: to the people of England.

Her image as "Gloriana" was tied in with what is now seen as a Golden Age. Elizabeth I was at the heart of this national awakening, taking pride in the achievements of men like the naval commander, Sir Francis Drake (c.1540–96), who circumnavigated the globe in a single expedition. She served as patron as well as inspiration in the literary arts, too. The English language had never before been as richly used as it was in the works of William Shakespeare (1564–1616), Christopher Marlowe (1564–93), and poet Edmund Spenser (1552/53–99), to name a few, who were working at the height of their creative powers.

Though her splendour was fading fast towards the end, she could still stir the hearts of her people. "Though God hath raised me high," she flattered in her final speech to Parliament, "yet this I count the glory of my crown, that I have reigned with your loves." Elizabeth I died a much-loved queen. The high level of public lamentation on her death was unprecedented.

Elizabeth I arrives at Nonsuch Palace, Surrey
Built by Henry VIII, sold by Mary I to the Earl of Arundel, and returned to Elizabeth I in 1590, Nonsuch Palace marks the peak of all Tudor building projects.

WILLIAM SHAKESPEARE

Son of a Roman Catholic Stratford-upon-Avon businessman, William Shakespeare was a member of the Lord Chamberlain's Men, Elizabeth I's favourite theatre company. English theatre flourished under Elizabeth I's patronage, and Shakespeare, considered the greatest writer in the English language, is known to have written at least 38 plays, and 154 sonnets and longer poems. His brilliant comedies, tragedies, and histories explore the universal human experience. His play, *Twelfth Night, or What You Will,* was written specifically to be performed at Elizabeth I's court for the close of the Christmas season, possibly in 1601.

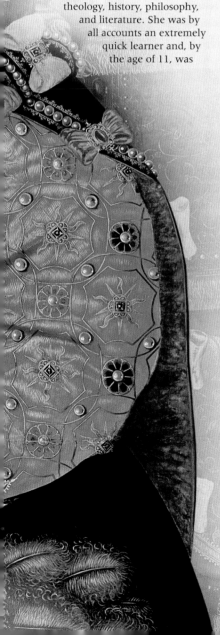

TIMELINE

- **7 September 1533** Anne Boleyn gives birth to the future Elizabeth I in Greenwich Palace; she is recognized as heir to the throne.
- **19 May 1536** Anne Boleyn is executed; Elizabeth is declared illegitimate and loses her right of succession to the throne.
- **June 1543** An act of parliament restores Elizabeth to the line of succession, after her brother Edward VI and sister Mary.
- **28 January 1547** Henry VIII dies; Elizabeth becomes a ward of his widow, Catherine Parr. He is succeeded by his son, Edward VI.

ELIZABETH'S SIGNATURE

- **20 March 1549** Catherine Parr's fourth husband, Thomas Seymour, with whom Elizabeth has been closely associated, is executed for treason.
- **19 July 1553** Elizabeth's Catholic sister Mary accedes to the throne.
- **18 March 1554** Elizabeth is imprisoned in the Tower of London for alleged complicity in a rebellion against Mary led by Sir Thomas Wyatt; she is released on 19 May.
- **25 July 1554** Mary marries Philip II of Spain in Winchester Cathedral; Roman Catholicism is restored as the primary religion in England.
- **17 November 1558** Elizabeth accedes to the throne on the death of Mary; she is crowned in Westminster Abbey on 15 January 1559.
- **8 May 1559** The Act of Supremacy asserts the Queen as head of the Church of England, restoring the Anglican Church.
- **1564** Elizabeth gives the title of Earl of Leicester to her favourite Robert Dudley.
- **9 November 1569** The Catholic Earls of Northumberland and Westmoreland lead the Northern Rebellion against Elizabeth.
- **20 February 1570** The Northern Rebellion is defeated.
- **4 April 1581** Elizabeth knights Francis Drake after he completes a voyage around the world.
- **1585** Anglo–Spanish War begins: Elizabeth supports the Netherlands, in revolt against Spanish rule.
- **July 1588** The Spanish Armada, an attempt by Philip II of Spain to invade England, fails.
- **1590–96** Edmund Spenser's epic poem *The Faerie Queene*, in praise of Elizabeth (or Gloriana in the poem), is published.
- **4 August 1598** William Cecil (later known as Baron Burghley), Elizabeth's chief advisor since the start of her reign, dies.
- **30 November 1601** Elizabeth makes her last address to Parliament.
- **24 March 1603** Elizabeth dies in Richmond Palace, Surrey.

Monarchs of Scotland

That the land between the Shetland Isles and the River Tees became a single state owes less to geography or anthropology than to the dynamism of some ambitious monarchs. Over centuries, a succession of heroes and rogues forged the Scottish nation.

« BEFORE

Though invaded by the Romans on several occasions and subjected to legion garrisons in the south and east, Scotland never became part of the Roman Empire.

MERGING PEOPLES

For much of the early medieval period, it was a land of tribal regions and small realms, so Scotland's emergence as a single kingdom was slow. Among these small realms, it was the **Kingdom of the Dál Riata** ("land of the Scots") that absorbed all the others, including the **native Picts**. A people shrouded in mystery, the Picts slowly merged with the Scots of the Dál Riata, and disappeared from history.

ENIGMATIC ORIGINS

The origin of the Scots (or Scotii) of Dál Riata is unknown. They spoke the same Irish Gaelic as the **Scotii of Ireland**, and shared a cultural heritage. If they moved from Ireland to the Western Isles of Scotland or not is unclear.

King Kenneth mac Alpin, (c.841–859), and his successors gradually extended the realm of the Scots of Dàl Riata until it covered most of present-day eastern Scotland from the River Tweed to the Central Highlands.

The making of a kingdom

The Alpin dynasty ended with Malcolm II (1005–34), who, in 1019, consolidated his southern frontier by defeating Uhtred, Earl of Northumbria. The new ruling house, Dunkeld, began in 1034 with Duncan I (1001–40) and continued in 1040 with Macbeth (c.1005–57). Malcolm III (1034–93), the next king, moved Scotland closer to mainstream Europe through contact with England's Norman conquerors and through his marriage to Margaret, an Anglo-Saxon princess who was later made a saint. Four of St Margaret's sons wore the Scottish crown in succession, but it was her youngest child, David I, born in 1083, and who ruled from 1124–53, who was arguably the most capable of all Scotland's monarchs. David I used Anglo-Norman barons (including two

future Royal Families, the Bruces and the Stewarts) to build up a feudal-style regime. William I (1143–1214), "the Lion", crowned in 1165, continued this process and extended royal authority into Galloway and the far north. Alexander II (1198–1249), who was crowned in 1214, defeated

Great Seal of Alexander II
Rejecting monarchical solidarity, Alexander II sided with the barons who had rebelled against England's King John (see pp. 20–21) and, in 1216, drove his forces as far south as Dover on the Channel coast.

Castle of history now a medieval ruin
The "Honours of Scotland", the oldest crown jewels in the British Isles, were smuggled out of Dunnottar Castle to keep them from the hands of Oliver Cromwell's New Model Army (see pp.40–41).

and three years later received the whole of the Western Isles into his kingdom. Thus, on the death of his son, Alexander III (1241–86), who had been crowned king aged 7, Scotland was a relatively unified and competently governed medieval state.

Sadly, Alexander III's death ushered in a crisis that nearly undid all the nation building. When Alexander III's

The roots of the Stewart dynasty
Robert the Bruce, later Robert I, is shown with his first wife, Isabella of Mar. The dynasty was descended from the marriage of their daughter Marjorie to Walter Stewart, 6th High Steward of Scotland.

heir, his granddaughter, Margaret (1283–90), died en route to Scotland, the disputed succession was referred to Edward I of England (see p.21). Edward I chose John Balliol (c.1248–1314), who reigned as King of Scots from 1292–96. However, Edward I treated Balliol like a feudal subordinate. The Scots rebelled but were soon crushed, and John was deposed and taken south.

During the ensuing 10-year interregnum, Scottish resistance to Edward I's wish to take over Scotland focussed first on William Wallace (whose ancestors had come to Scotland with the Stewarts), and then on Robert the Bruce (1274–1329).

21 The number of Scotland's 43 monarchs who died violent deaths between 841–1603.

Though he had previously sided with the English, in 1306, Bruce declared himself Robert I of Scotland. What happened next is as much legend as history. Edward I died on the way north to teach Bruce a lesson. The incompetent Edward II (see p.21) dithered and his army was soundly defeated by the Scots in 1314 at Bannockburn. Though England recognized Bruce's kingship in 1328, fighting again flared under Scotland's David II (1324–71), who was crowned in 1331, until Edward III (see p.21) was distracted by the Hundred Years' War.

The Stewarts
David II was succeeded by Robert II (1316–90), the son of Bruce's daughter, Marjorie, and Robert, 7th High Steward of Scotland. (The Royal Family still holds this title: Prince Charles is the 29th High Steward.) The reign of Robert II, crowned aged

Trappings of martyrdom
This is the prayer book and rosary used by the Roman Catholic Mary, Queen of Scots during the night before her execution in 1587 for plotting against her Protestant cousin, Elizabeth I.

Hollow spheres made of gold

Crucifix with pearl pendants

Hand-illuminated Book of Hours

54, was marked by rising lawlessness. Under Robert III (1337–1406), crowned in 1390, this escalated. His son, James I (1394–1437), was captured, aged 12, shortly before Robert III's death and was held in prison for 18 years in England. The paternalistic James I, crowned in 1424, angered many with his high taxes and amassing of royal estates, and an angry knight killed him.

In 1437, aged 6, James II (1430–60) was crowned. He survived a turbulent minority, but came of age only to be blown to pieces when one of his own cannon exploded during the siege of Roxburgh Castle.

James III (1451–88), son of James II, was defeated and killed in Sauchieburn, outside Stirling, during a rebellion headed by his own son.

In James IV (1473–1513), crowned in 1488, Scotland finally found a king of international stature. A builder and a naval man, James IV's rich court thronged with artists. Sadly, he could not resist the traditional Scottish pastime of raiding England. In 1513, at Flodden, James IV was slain and his army was annihilated. Noble factions, both Catholic and Protestant – and mutually hostile – competed for control of the monarchy and the administration during the reigns of next three Stewarts: James V (1513–42); Mary (1542–67); and James VI (1567–1625). When adult, James V, restored firm government.

His Catholic daughter, Mary, Queen of Scots, lacked his skills and eventually lost her crown and her head (see p.29). Mary's son, James VI, (see pp.38–39) ruled Scotland with skill until 1603, when he inherited the English crown and moved to London as James I.

James of the Fiery Face
James II's nickname came from a large red birthmark on his face. Though it was said to indicate a fiery personality, the genial king was one of the most popular of the Stewart monarchs.

AFTER »

After the union of the Scottish and English crowns under James VI and I, Scotland's monarch was based in a foreign land. Scottish independence came under increasing threat.

UNION WITH ENGLAND
By the later 17th century, Scottish business was unable to compete with England's commercial might. Eventually, in 1707, the Scottish parliament accepted the **Act of Union 39** », uniting the administrations of the two nations.

DEVOLVING POWER TO SCOTLAND
In the 20th century, a resurgence of Scottish nationalism led to a 1988 Scotland Act. Accepted by a referendum in Scotland, it devolved major powers to **a new Scottish parliament** and central administration.

Mary, Queen of Scots' bed chamber
Holyrood was the setting for one of history's most famous murders. From the 18th century, fascinated tourists began visiting the crime scene – the oak-panelled rooms occupied by Mary, Queen of Scots.

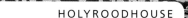

ROYAL RESIDENCE

Holyroodhouse

The Palace of Holyroodhouse in Edinburgh was an important residence even before the union of the crowns in 1603. With previous inhabitants including Mary, Queen of Scots, it has been the scene of many turbulent events in the complex relationship between England and Scotland.

Holyrood was founded as an Augustinian abbey in 1128 by David I, son of St Margaret of Scotland, an Anglo-Saxon princess who fled to Scotland after the Norman conquest. According to legend, it was built on the site where the King had a vision of the Cross – the "Holy Rood" – glowing between the antlers of a stag while out hunting on Holy Cross Day.

Towers and turmoil

When Edinburgh became the capital of Scotland in 1437, successive monarchs found the royal chambers at the abbey far more comfortable than Edinburgh Castle. Keen to impress his new queen, Margaret Tudor, daughter of Henry VII, James IV (1473–1513) had the abbey guesthouse converted into a palace. James also decided to develop the grounds: in 1507 a loch was drained to make space for gardens and sports such as tennis, hawking, and archery.

James V (1512–42) made further improvements, building new lodgings in a huge tower protected by a moat and drawbridge. His fortifications proved a shrewd investment: Holyrood was attacked and burned more than once during conflict with England throughout the 1540s, but the tower survived. It was there that in 1566 James V's daughter – Mary, Queen of Scots (1542–87) – witnessed the brutal murder of David Rizzio, her Italian secretary and rumoured lover. Rizzio was stabbed 56 times by a group led by Mary's husband Lord Darnley, and it is claimed that his bloodstains can still be seen in the Northwest Tower today.

After her enforced abdication and flight to England in 1567, the palace became home to Mary's son, James VI, Scotland's first Protestant king. By the time he acceded to the English throne in 1603, the household had swollen to around 600. However, with the court's move to London, Holyrood faded in importance: Charles I was crowned King of Scotland there in 1633, but from 1646 the palace was entrusted to the care of the Duke of Hamilton (his descendents still hold the post of Keeper). Occupied by Cromwell during the Civil War, the building went up in flames again in 1650; what remained of the palace was used as a barracks.

Holyrood's fortunes revived after the restoration of the monarchy in 1660. Rebuilt in 1679 as an elegant, symmetrical Renaissance palace designed by the architect Sir William Bruce, its turbulant history continued unabated. Charles II never stayed in the building he commissioned, but his brother, James VII and II, had strong connections. In 1686–87 James controversially set up a Jesuit College in the grounds and reintroduced Catholic worship to the abbey – which then became a target for the mob in the Glorious Revolution of 1688. In 1745, Holyroodhouse was again linked to the Jacobite cause (see p.40), when James's grandson, Bonnie Prince Charlie, held court there after seizing Edinburgh in an attempt to restore the Catholic line to the British throne.

Modern traditions

Despite its long association with the Royal Family, it was only in the 1920s that Holyroodhouse formally became its official residence in Scotland. The tradition of Holyrood Week – a summer celebration of Scottish history and culture – is a highlight of the royal year. With the Royal Company of Archers in attendance, the Queen entertains thousands of guests from all walks of Scottish life at garden parties and an investiture ceremony. The palace is open to visitors all year, unless the family is in residence.

Ceremonial displays

The baroque stairs, decorated with tapestries, frescoes, and plasterwork, lead to the State Apartments, where an investiture ceremony is held during Holyrood Week. Each year the week begins with the Lord Provost handing the key to the city of Edinburgh to the Queen.

THE GREAT STAIR

THE 16TH-CENTURY NORTHWEST TOWER

CEREMONY OF THE KEYS, 2014

BEFORE

Before accession to the throne of England, the Stewarts had ruled a relatively small kingdom on the fringes of Europe.

SUDDEN AND UNEXPECTED DEATH
Violence was never far beneath the surface in Scotland, and numerous of **James VI's predecessors ‹‹ 34–35** came to untimely ends.

PINCHED BY PRIEST AND PURSE
A source of vexation for James VI had been his kingdom's austere **Presbyterian Church**, popularly known as the Kirk. Established in 1560, it was run by a General Assembly and had its own courts. James, who thought Presbyterianism incompatible with monarchy, won the right to appoint two bishops, but only with the Kirk's approval. Equally humiliating, Scottish kings were **embarrassingly poor**. Small wonder, then, that James could not believe his luck when, upon the death of **Elizabeth I ‹‹ 28–29, 32–33** into his lap dropped **the crown of England**.

> " The **authority** of a king is the **keystone** which closeth up the arch and order of **government.** "

THOMAS WENTWORTH, ENGLISH STATESMAN, 1628

The **Stuarts**

Having ruled Scotland for 230 years, the Stewarts survived as monarchs of a joint kingdom for another 111 years. During that time, their status was dramatically redefined. By 1714, the divinely appointed "loving father" of the people had become a constitutional monarch.

James I
James VI of Scotland and I of England was arguably the most academic of all Britain's monarchs. His rigorous, brutal, but intellectually stimulating education inspired him to write a number of works, ranging from *Basilikon Doron* (1599) on kingship, to a treatise on witchcraft (entitled *Daemonologie*, 1597), and his celebrated anti-smoking propaganda, *A Counterblaste to Tobacco* (1604).

Not since the Normans (see pp.16–17) had a ruling dynasty made such a dramatic impact. It began when the first Stuart (or Stewart as the Scots prefer; the "u" spelling is a Frenchism) united the crown of Scotland with that of England: James VI became James I (1566–1625) of England because of his descent from Henry VIII's sister, Margaret (see p.28).

Forty years later, the two nations were torn by civil wars (see pp.40–41) that led to the trial and execution of Charles I (see box). An experiment with republicanism collapsed, as did an attempt by Charles II (1630–85) and the Roman Catholic James II (1633–88) to set up a European-style absolute monarchy. The outcome was a "Glorious Revolution", and the constitutional monarchy of the later Stuarts – Mary II (1662–94) and William III (1650–1702), and Anne (1665–1714).

The road to republicanism

James VI and I was an unusual figure, and a fascinating, if unattractive, tangle of contradictions. For a long time, partly thanks to character assassination by aggrieved courtiers, he was thought the "wisest fool in Christendom". Modern historians take a more kindly view. It is true that he rowed with parliament, made a fool of himself over male favourites, and was useless with money. At the same time, he avoided war and gave the world the incomparable Authorized Version of the Bible. He also prevented an orgy of bloodshed between Roman Catholics and Protestants in 1605 after a group of

160,000 Estimated number of Civil War casualties in England and Scotland.

English Catholics were caught plotting to kill him by blowing up the House of Lords in the so-called Gunpowder Plot.

Charles I (1600–49), James VI and I's son, was crowned in 1626. In modern parlance he was a conviction politician. Sadly, he was not a great politician, and his convictions were those of a continental monarch, not a British one.

Two issues divided him from his people: his belief that he had been appointed king by God through the "Divine Right of Kings", and his lack of money and aversion to raising it by conventional means. He made things

DECISIVE MOMENT

THE EXECUTION OF KING CHARLES I

On 30 January 1649, the course of British history – and the history of the monarchy itself – changed forever with the execution in London of Charles I. After attempting to reach a negotiated settlement with a king described as "that man of blood", Oliver Cromwell and other Parliamentary leaders put Charles I on trial for High Treason.

The King rejected the authority of the court, but he was found guilty and executed, ushering in 11 years of republican rule.

Though the monarchy was restored in 1660, the shadow of the execution could not be wiped away. In the final instance, the monarch was subject to the will of the people, not a divinely appointed superhero.

problem for Charles II was his brother and heir, James, Duke of York (1633–1701), a man in his father's mould.

James horrified the political nation by converting to Roman Catholicism, a faith linked in the 17th-century mind with tyranny, gunpowder plots, arbitrary taxation, and every other conceivable wickedness. Crowned James II in 1685, his pursuit of pro-Catholic policies was the stuff of his subjects' worst nightmares. When his second wife, an Italian Catholic, gave birth to a son in 1688, raising the prospect of a line of Roman Catholic monarchs, religious leaders and members of parliament decided to oppose the King.

Constitutional monarchy

James II's two daughters by his first wife, Anne Hyde, were Protestant. It was Mary, the elder sister, to whom the opposition turned. In 1688, they invited her and her Dutch husband, William, back from the Netherlands where they lived, requesting also that they bring invasion forces to depose the King. William and Mary duly arrived and James fled to France. In 1689 his replacements were crowned Mary II and William III in what is known as the "Glorious Revolution". Their reign lasted until 1702.

The pragmatism of that bloodless revolution was enshrined in 1689 in a Bill of Rights establishing Britain's constitutional monarchy. The Crown was certainly not powerless, but royal and governmental expenditure were now separate, and the monarch was compelled to appoint ministers who had the backing of Parliament. This meant that England's commercial interests were now more in tune with those of the government and, as a result, the economy boomed.

Scotland, unable to compete with England's mercantile power, accepted the Act of Union (1707) joining English and Scottish parliaments together to form one Parliament of Great Britain, based in London.

The last Stuart sovereign
Through her close personal friendship with Sarah Churchill, wife of John Churchill, 1st Duke of Marlborough, Queen Anne inadvertently helped launch one of Britain's most celebrated political dynasties.

The Act united England, Scotland, and Wales into Great Britain for the first time.

War with France resumed under Mary II's sister Anne, crowned in 1702. She was fortunate to find, in John Churchill, a military commander of exceptional ability whose victories on the continent were unmatched since Agincourt (see p.25). After nearly a century of turbulence, the surprising Stuart legacy turned out to be one of unprecedented stability and prosperity.

AFTER

Little more than a century after Scotland's James VI had united the Scottish and English crowns, James II's Catholic faith lost the Stuarts almost everything they had gained.

ROVING COURT
Louis XIV allowed the **exiled James II** to set up court in a royal château near Paris. The French government found the Stuarts **politically awkward** and, on Louis XIV's death, Pope Clement XI rescued them and set up James II's son as "James III" in Rome.

FOCUS OF DISCONTENT
Though no longer resident in Great Britain, the Stuarts still had a number of supporters in England, Scotland, and Ireland. Known as **Jacobites 48 »**, from *Jacobus* (Latin for James), they included those opposing the government, fervent Roman Catholics, and sentimental conservatives given to drinking toasts to the "kings over the water".

worse when he tried to impose a prayer book on the Scots that was almost exactly the same as the English prayer book. The Scots rebelled and Charles I launched a military campaign against them that not only failed, but is thought to have led to a wider Civil war (see pp.40–41). The defeated King was put on trial and executed.

The spectre of Catholic absolutism

Britain became a republic for 11 years (1649–60), most of them dominated by the towering figure of Oliver Cromwell (see pp.40–41). Though rejecting the crown, as Lord Protector, he was king in all but name. A successful one, too, who united the British Isles under a single government, earned it respect abroad, governed well, if sternly, and supported "liberty of conscience". On his death, however, there was no one to step into Cromwell's giant shoes,

and in 1660 Charles I's son, Charles II (1630–85) was invited to take up his late father's crown.

Charles II had hankerings for a Roman Catholic, absolutist monarchy but he kept them quiet. Like his father, he was irked by the need to rely on Parliament for money and got round the difficulty by negotiating secret funding from France. However, a bigger

Gunpowder Plot conspirators
The infamous conspirators who planned to blow up James I are depicted here. The discovery of the plot on 5 November 1605 is still celebrated annually in the United Kingdom with fireworks and bonfires.

BEFORE

After the end of the Wars of the Roses in 1487, England stayed clear of civil war for the next century and a half.

QUEEN'S CAUTION MAINTAINS PEACE
The Tudors **‹‹ 28–29** experienced serious **rebellions**, notably the Pilgrimage of Grace (1536–37), Kett's Rebellion (1549), Wyatt's Rebellion (1554), and the Rising of the North (1569–70), but nothing on the scale of the French Wars of Religion (1562–98) or Europe's Thirty Years' War (1618–48). This contrast was largely thanks to effective local government and the cautious religious policy pursued by **Queen Elizabeth I ‹‹ 29** and **‹‹ 32–33**.

11 YEARS' TYRANNY?
Between 1629–40 **Charles I ‹‹ 38–39** ruled without Parliament. This was perfectly legal, so many accepted it. But using the royal prerogative to raise funds (thereby bypassing the need for Parliament), made it tyrannous in the eyes of his enemies. Demanding Ship Money from inland counties, for example, when normally only coastal counties had paid, smacked of continental Catholic **absolutism**.

Battle of Marston Moor, 1644
The Civil War's biggest battle featured both Prince Rupert of the Rhine, the leading Royalist commander, and the "Ironsides" commander, Oliver Cromwell. Owing partly to the Prince's hot-headedness, victory fell to the latter.

Britain's Civil Wars

Between 1639–51, the British Isles were rocked by civil wars. Whether seen as a Great Rebellion, the Wars of the Three Kingdoms, or the first modern revolution, the conflicts altered the course of British history for ever and led to Britain's first and only experience of republican rule.

To understand the causes of the 17th-century civil wars, we need to remember that Charles I (see pp.38–39) was king of three realms: England, Scotland, and Ireland. We must also grasp how deeply people of the time felt about religion, especially about the Catholic–Protestant divide.

Very generally, Catholics considered Protestantism, especially Puritanism, dangerously anarchic as it put ultimate authority in the hands of each man and his Bible; Protestants, on the other hand, regarded Catholicism ("Popery") as the faith of tyrants who mistrusted the people and valued subservience above truth. England's Protestant Church was a compromise, making it a target for both Catholics and Puritans.

Scotland was mostly Presbyterian (a type of Protestantism), while Ireland was mostly Catholic. This powder keg of faiths required the most delicate of handling to stop it exploding. Sadly, for himself and his kingdoms, Charles I seemed incapable of understanding this.

LORD PROTECTOR, MILITARY AND POLITICAL LEADER (1599–1658)

OLIVER CROMWELL

Born into a family of minor gentry in Huntingdon, Cromwell converted to Puritanism in the 1630s. Elected to Parliament, during the Civil War he rose to prominence as an efficient military commander. He was the driving force behind the move to have Charles I executed. His swift conquests of Ireland and Scotland made him by far the most powerful man in the British Isles and, in 1653, he accepted the position of Lord Protector. However, the republican regime collapsed shortly after Cromwell's death.

Scotland's Prayer Book Rebellion
Charles I and Archbishop William Laud of Canterbury favoured reforming the Church of England to place greater emphasis on ceremony, sanctity, and art. This alienated many English subjects, to whom the new policy looked like Catholicism by the back door; after all, Charles I had a Catholic wife. His high-handed behaviour, attempting to rule without Parliament after 1629, and raising money by somewhat questionable means, only increased his opponents' worries.

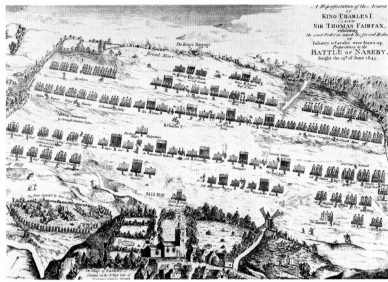

New Model Army triumph

Parliament's reorganized New Model Army, commanded by Sir Thomas Fairfax, put the defeat of the Royalists beyond question when it annihilated Charles' army at the Battle of Naseby, June 1645.

surrender his prerogative power of commander-in-chief. When Charles I's attempted military coup failed, he left London to prepare for war.

The two sides were well matched, though Parliament controlled London and the navy. After 1643, Parliament also had the support of a Scottish Presbyterian army and, from 1644, its forces were reorganized into the best fighting force of its day: the New Model Army. The King had the backing of a number of wealthy aristocrats but, interestingly, several counties refused to take sides, and raised their own soldiers to keep out both King and Parliament.

Parliamentary victory

Charles' best hope was to strike first. After an indecisive battle at Edgehill, he tried to enter London but was turned back. The King's nephew, Prince Rupert, an experienced commander,

In 1637, when the King and Laud tried to impose an Anglican-style Prayer Book on Scotland, the Scots rejected it with violence and drew up a National Covenant to defend Presbyterianism. They obliged Charles I to find £850 a day to keep the Scottish army from descending into England. Raising a sum of that size, as the Scots knew, meant summoning Parliament.

Breakdown leads to impasse

Parliament passed a number of measures to curb royal power. These culminated in a Grand Remonstrance

(1641), which listed all the opposition's grievances. At this point came news of the slaughter of thousands of Irish Protestants, victims of an uprising against the strict rule of Charles I's minister, Thomas Wentworth. An army had to be sent to Ireland, but who would command it? The Parliamentarians dared not give the King an army lest he use it against them; the King refused to

Cartwheels for ease of manoeuvrability

Cheap and lethal

Lightweight and easy to construct, falconets were the Civil Wars' most popular cannon. They fired a 1lb (0.45kg) shot approximately the same size and weight as a falcon, hence their name.

achieved a number of successes in 1643. However, in 1644, he suffered a serious defeat at Marston Moor, in Yorkshire, where Oliver Cromwell's East Anglian "Ironsides" made a significant contribution to the Parliamentary victory.

In 1645, the New Model Army swamped the royalist forces at Naseby, and the royalists in Scotland were also defeated. Charles surrendered to the Scots, who handed him over to Parliament. As peace talks dragged on, the Parliamentarians divided between Presbyterians, allied to the Scots, and the more radical Independents of the

Though there were no more civil wars after those of the middle of the 17th century, there were more major battles fought on British soil.

WARS IN BRITAIN AND IRELAND
In 1685, a Protestant invasion by the Duke of Monmouth (1649–85), an illegitimate son of **Charles II 42 »**, was crushed at Sedgemoor. After his flight from England, **James II « 38–39** was overcome in Ireland at the Battle of the Boyne in 1690. In 1715 and 1745, supporters of the **exiled Stuarts** were quelled only after bloody battles and, in 1746, the army of Bonnie Prince Charlie (1720–88) was famously destroyed at **Culloden 48 »**. More recently, Ireland was torn by fighting between the Irish and the British (1919–21), and then experienced a full-scale civil war, 1922–23.

New Model Army. The former wanted a national church along the lines of the Scottish Kirk; the latter believed each congregation should remain independent of any national church. Charles ineptly tried to play off one side against the other, but his slipperiness alienated both.

The bloody end

After the New Model Army crushed a royalist uprising of English and Scots, known as the Second Civil War (1648), Cromwell and other army leaders lost patience. A specially convened court found Charles I guilty of treason. On 30 January 1649, he was beheaded on a platform erected outside his father's Banqueting House in Whitehall.

The execution of the King did not bring the Civil War to an instant end. First, there was the question of Ireland. Crossing there in 1649, Cromwell slaughtered the people of Drogheda and Wexford to warn others against resistance. After this, the country was systematically brought back under English rule. Charles I's son, now Charles II (see pp.42–43), landed in Scotland. The Scots were irked at not having been consulted over the fate of Charles I, but their anger counted for nothing when their forces were destroyed by Cromwell at Dunbar (1650) and Worcester (1651), finally bringing the Civil Wars to a close.

> " … the **smallest He** that is in this kingdom **hath a right** as the **greatest He**."

THOMAS RAINBOROUGH, IN DEBATES HELD BY THE PARLIAMENTARY ARMY, 1647

The Restoration

The restoration of Charles II in 1660 marked the return of a crowned head of state. Parliament was now a fixture, and the settlement was an important step towards constitutional monarchy.

When Oliver Cromwell's son Richard was unwilling to continue his father's Protectorship (see pp.40–41), General George Monck arranged for the Long Parliament (elected in 1640) to dissolve itself and opened negotiations with Charles II, then in the Netherlands. Guided by Edward Hyde, the future Earl of Clarendon, Charles issued the Declaration of Breda offering a general pardon, a free parliament, and "liberty to tender consciences". On these terms, the King was welcomed home.

The Act of Indemnity and Oblivion forgave the past behaviour of all except those who had signed Charles I's death warrant and a handful of others. The Restoration Parliament voted Charles II £1.2 million per year with which to run his court – an amount that would prove inadequate. All laws issued after 1641 were scrapped, and confiscated land returned. However, land sales made during the interregnum (period between monarchs) to help the King remained valid.

While the Parliament had been in power, Puritanism had dominated – the excesses of the royals had been condemned and an austere lifestyle encouraged. However, the majority of the society was Anglican and held different views. The restoration of an Anglican monarch brought with it new laws that limited the rights of non-Anglicans. Puritans were labelled "Dissenters" and anti-Puritan sentiment spread throughout society. Theatres were reopened after an 18-year hiatus tforced by the former government, and women appeared on stage for the first time. To the delight of the rakish King, the new wave of Restoration comedies reached levels of bawdiness previously not allowed.

Restoration euphoria was too good to last. The settlement had left many former Royalists and Parliamentarians feeling aggrieved, and Charles was soon squabbling with his parliaments over money, his secret dealings with France, and the probable succession of his Catholic brother, James, Duke of York.

> "The **joy** was… so universal that **His Majesty** said… he **doubted** it had been **his own fault** he had been **absent…**"
>
> **EDWARD HYDE,** EARL OF CLARENDON, IN HIS *HISTORY OF THE REBELLION AND CIVIL WARS IN ENGLAND*

Charles II in royal regalia
This portrait was painted in a formal style to emphasize the continuity of the royal line. It depicts Charles II wearing St Edward's Crown and carrying the new orb and sceptre commissioned after the earlier regalia was destroyed during the interregnum.

ROYAL RESIDENCE

Windsor Castle

The oldest inhabited castle in the world, Windsor has been the British monarchy's family home for just under 1,000 years. Some of the most resonant rituals and myths of royalty were created here. It is reputedly the Queen's favourite residence, and the symbolic heart of the monarchy.

According to legend Windsor Castle was built on the site of an old Celtic camp where King Arthur once lived. History tells a different, though scarcely less incredible story. The castle dates back to the first precarious years of the Norman monarchy, a time when the King was in a constant power struggle with the barons, his command only as secure as his last victory.

Medieval fortress

Windsor was founded by William the Conqueror in 1070, four years after the Battle of Hastings, and was one of a ring of nine fortresses built to protect London from local Saxons. The site selected for the castle, above a bend in the River Thames near the village of Windlesora, was on the edge of Saxon territory. William appropriated the forest around it as a royal reserve and hunting ground to supply the castle with wood, deer, boar, and river fish.

The first fortress was a wooden motte and bailey, with three wards arranged around a central mound. In the 12th century, William's grandson, Henry II (1133–89), replaced the wooden palisade surrounding the fortress with a stone wall interspersed with square towers. He also built a stone keep on the irregular mound at the core of the castle – the now famous Round Tower.

These new fortifications were soon put to the test in 1214 during the insurrection of barons protesting at the ruthless taxation and limitless powers of King John (1167–1216). The following year a conference was held at Windsor, which culminated in the King being forced to agree to the restricted powers set out in the Magna Carta (see p.21). The document was sealed at Runnymede meadow, 5 km (3 miles) along the Thames from Windsor.

Romantic traditions

It was in the next century, during the reign of Edward III (1312–77), that Windsor Castle began to emerge as the evocative symbol of ancient tradition, monarchy, and chivalry that it is today. Between 1350 and 1377 Edward spent £50,000 renovating the castle – the largest amount spent by any English medieval monarch on a single building, which may make Windsor England's most expensive secular building project of the Middle Ages. Partly financed by ransoms paid on prisoners taken at Edward's victories in France at the battles of Crécy, Calais, and Poitiers, Windsor Castle was transformed from a medieval fortress into a lavish Gothic palace, with a (literal) king's ransom spent on extravagant furnishings.

Many enduring royal rituals were also established at this time. Edward III revived the cult of King Arthur, and in 1344 created his own Round Table at Windsor. Traces of the structure – the centrepiece of a festival where 300 knights gathered to joust, feast, dance, and watch the re-enactment of scenes from the stories of King Arthur – were discovered by archaeologists in 2006. Inspired by Arthur, Edward created his own inner circle of knights, the Order of the Garter, and was instrumental in establishing St George, who was in fact a Greek Christian from Palestine, as the patron saint of England. Windsor's chapel is dedicated to St George, and images of the knightly saint destroying the dragon abound.

Lavish hospitality remained a feature of life at Windsor in the 15th century, despite the castle's relatively small size. In 1416 Henry V instructed the Dean and Chapter of Windsor to prepare their "logyns and mansions" to receive the multitude accompanying the Holy Roman Emperor Sigismund, who hoped to broker a peace between England and France by moderating the King's ambitions. Liberally entertained by Henry in London and in Windsor, Sigismund ended up installed as a knight in the Order of the Garter, and signed the Treaty of Canterbury, which supported English claims to France. »

THE LONG WALK

WINDSOR GREAT PARK

Windsor Castle from the air
Aerial view shows the Round Tower on the original motte and the bailey below it, with neo-Gothic towers and battlements added by George IV to create a more imposing edifice.

ST GEORGE'S CHAPEL

THE DEAN'S CLOISTER FOUNTAIN

Impressive surroundings
The castle is surrounded by Windsor Great Park – 2,000 hectares (5,000 acres) of parkland, including a deer park and some ancient oaks as old as the castle itself. Lined with London plane trees and horse chestnuts, the Long Walk cuts straight through the landscape for over 4 km (2½ miles), and provides a magnificent and unforgettable approach to the castle. It was originally laid out by Charles II and planted with 1,652 elm trees; the carriage way was added by Queen Anne. Inside the castle walls, the red and gold uniforms of the Yeomen of the Guard, the oldest British military corps still in existence (here on the steps of St George's Chapel), are a familiar sight – as is the recurring motif of St George slaying the Dragon.

>> The Tudors made only minor additions and modifications to the castle, choosing instead to limit the size of their retinues at ever more extravagant Garter feasts. However, pressure on space increased under Elizabeth I, who used the castle to entertain diplomats, and became a source of friction in the early 17th century – when James I came to hunt at Windsor, his English and Scottish attendants would squabble over rooms.

"It is the **most romantique castle** that is in the world."

SAMUEL PEPYS, DIARIST, 26 FEBRUARY 1666

Charles I commissioned Inigo Jones to make improvements to the 14th-century apartments, but his plans were interrupted by the outbreak of Civil War. Instead the castle was commandeered by Oliver Cromwell for use as his headquarters and as a prison for captured royalist officers. Charles himself was held at Windsor for the last three weeks of his reign; after his execution his body was returned there by night, and buried without ceremony in a vault beneath St George's Chapel.

Restoration

Determined to make Windsor a symbol of the restored monarchy, in 1668 Charles II appointed the architect Hugh May to supervise modernization. The Royal Apartments were the last word in Baroque extravagance: the opulent tapestries and textiles were so costly they were only exposed when the King and Queen were in residence to prevent the colours fading. They remained virtually unchanged until George III decided it was time to give them a fashionable neoclassical restyle.

George IV, on the other hand, was aware of the symbolic power of the castle, and focused on enhancing the Gothic character of the exterior. He increased the height of the Round Tower and had medieval-looking towers and battlements built. Inside, he created a 168m (551ft) gallery – the Grand Corridor – and changed the interior décor to French Empire. By the time the King took up residence at the end of 1828, his improvements to the Castle had cost nearly £300,000.

Fortunately his successors felt there was little left to do, although Queen Victoria added a new private chapel, designed by Edward Blore, at the eastern end of St George's Hall. It was here, on 20 November 1992, that fire broke out, and damaged or destroyed almost 20 per cent of the castle area.

The long process of repair and restoration began immediately, with a Restoration Committee chaired by The Duke of Edinburgh. The areas that had been worst hit, such as St George's Hall, were redesigned in a contemporary Gothic style, while others, such as the Grand Reception Room and State Dining Room, were restored to the condition in which George IV had left them. Within five years the restoration was complete, and the castle open to the public.

Interior features

Two of George IV's drawing rooms were painstakingly restored after the 1992 fire. St George's Chapel (below) – one of England's finest Gothic churches, with magnificent fan vaults and heraldic standards belonging to the Queen, Prince of Wales, and the 24 Knights of the Garter – was untouched by the blaze.

GREEN DRAWING ROOM

CRIMSON DRAWING ROOM

FAN-VAULTED CEILING IN ST GEORGE'S CHAPEL

St George's Hall
Badly damaged in the 1992 fire, the castle's main
reception room was rebuilt in a contemporary
Gothic style. State banquets are held here with
room to seat up to 160 guests.

The **Hanoverians**

In 1714, determined never again to have a Catholic monarch, the British offered the crown to a German prince from Hanover who was distantly related to James VI and I. Though power ultimately rested in Parliament, the Hanoverians still wielded significant political influence.

BEFORE

At the beginning of the 11th century, in the time of Edward the Confessor, a belief grew up that a touch from royalty could cure scrofula, an unsightly skin disease, popularly known as the King's Evil.

THE KING'S EVIL

Such was the demand for the healing powers of the anointed sovereign that ceremonies were held where a monarch laid a healing finger on hundreds of afflicted subjects. Gold coins, known as touchpieces, were handed out to those who received the royal remedy. In time, just touching a coin that had itself been in contact with a monarch was thought to be curative. By the 18th century, the belief was dying out, and **Queen Anne ≪ 38–39** was the last monarch to touch for the King's Evil.

The Battle of Culloden
In 1745, Charles Edward Stuart (or, Bonnie Prince Charlie) led the last Jacobite attempt to regain the throne. Landing in Scotland, he reached Derby before retreating to Scotland where, in 1746, his army was destroyed at Culloden.

William III and Mary II (see pp.38–39) were childless. Mary's sister, Queen Anne (crowned in 1702) had 16, all of whom predeceased her. To bypass the exiled Catholic Stuarts (see p.39), Parliament passed an Act of Settlement in 1701 stipulating that the sovereign must be Anglican; parliamentary consent was required for wars in defence of non-British territories; only British natives might hold office or receive grants of crown lands. Thus on Anne's death in 1714, the crown passed to George, Elector of Hanover, great-grandson of James VI and I (see pp.38–39). As Anne's closest living Protestant relative, his German birth was weighed up and deliberately overlooked.

With Parliament choosing the sovereign, belief in the Divine Right of Kings ended. The Hanoverians had been enthroned for purely pragmatic reasons and were expected not to thwart Parliament. However, their theoretical powers were considerable, and they influenced events through their right to choose the first minister. More significantly, in an age when many parliamentary seats were in the pockets of wealthy landlords, their political patronage could be crucial.

Kings and electors

The negatives of George I (1660–1727) are easy to list. He spoke little English, was more attached to his native Hanover than to Britain, publicly fell out with his son, and kept his wife under house arrest back in Germany on charges of adultery. He took his job of King seriously, however, attending cabinet meetings, refusing to be rattled by anti-Hanoverian xenophobia, and welcoming religious toleration. Above all, he did not try to push his authority too far, thereby establishing his family's status as acceptable heads of state.

More opinionated than his father, George II (1683–1760), reigned from 1727 and kept up the Hanoverian tradition of falling out with his son and heir, Frederick, Prince of Wales (d.1751). He also followed his father's example of relying on an oligarchy of

The German King
Crowned King in 1714 at the age of 54, George I was always more interested in the affairs of his native Hanover than those of his adopted country.

> " It is the **pride of kings** which throws mankind into **confusion.**"
> TOM PAINE, *COMMON SENSE*, 1776

government ministers. Most prominent of these was Robert Walpole, generally recognized as Britain's first Prime Minister (in office 1721–42). George II took a close personal interest in two major European conflicts: the War of Austrian Succession (1740–48) and the Seven Years' War (1756–63). He was the last British king to lead men into battle (Dettingen, 1742), though he was criticized for doing so under the colours of Hanover, not Britain.

Family man and invalid
It is important to distinguish between George III (1738–1820) the family man and invalid, and the king who reigned from 1760. In the former role he attracts much sympathy; in the latter he was painfully out of his depth and lacked the wit to realize it, often with disastrous consequences.

George III treated his 15 children by his wife, Charlotte of Mecklenburg, much as he did his ministers: he sought goodness and obedience, and tried to direct them in the paths of virtue. This led to frequent confrontations with his dissolute eldest son, George (1762–1830), whom the King did not understand. Nor did he really understand much else that was going on around him – calls for reform of parliament and greater religious toleration, for instance, and the grievances of the American colonists who broke away from Britain in their War of Independence (1775–83).

The King suffered from porphyria, a kidney disorder with distressing symptoms that appeared as madness. He suffered breakdowns in 1765 and 1788 and, from 1811 onwards, he was permanently incapacitated. Ironically, at a time when he was playing no part in affairs of state, he was at his most popular, thanks to Britain's successful wars against Napoleon (1803–14).

Pavilion of controversy
The merits of Brighton's flamboyant Royal Pavilion, designed in the Indo-Islamic style and started in 1787 as a seaside bolthole for the Prince of Wales, have always divided opinion.

Prince Regent in retrospect
Sir Thomas Lawrence's portrait of George IV as Prince Regent was painted two years after he ascended the throne. His regency (the time in 1811–20 when he acted as sovereign) resulted from his father's incapacity.

Hanoverian swansong
George IV, better known as the Prince Regent, a role he had enjoyed since 1811, reigned as King from 1820–30. Crowned at the age of 57, he was obese (nicknamed the "Prince of Whales"), sick, vain, extravagant, and lazy. He brought the monarchy to a new low.

Those seeking to defend him point to his patronage of the arts (a quality rarely seen in the modern British monarchy) and hold up London's

£240,000 The total cost of the coronation of George IV, which was held in 1821.

Regent Street and the Royal Pavilion, Brighton, as examples of his precious architectural legacy. More valuable was his visit to Scotland in 1822, the first by a reigning British sovereign since Charles II (see pp.42–43), in 1650. George IV's visit played an important part in strengthening the bond between Scotland and England.

On George IV's death in 1830, the crown passed to his brother, William IV (1765–1837), who was aged 64. Bluff and eccentric, he was known as "Sailor Bill" because he had served in the Royal Navy. In 1832, he reluctantly submitted to the will of the people and supported the passing of a bill to reform the electoral system, yet two years later he became the last monarch to appoint a Prime Minister (Lord Melbourne, in office 1834 and 1835–41) without Parliament's full support.

Like his brother George IV, William IV lived as husband and wife with a woman to whom he was not married and with whom he had many children. But the two legitimate daughters born to his wife, Queen Adelaide, both died young. As a result, William IV's crown passed to his 18-year-old niece, Victoria (see pp.50–61 and 66–67).

AFTER

By the end of the Hanoverian era in 1901, any remaining mystique in the public's eye surrounding the monarchy had evaporated.

BAD EXAMPLE OF ROYALTY
Generations of family friction, eccentricity, and vulgar irresponsibility had left the Royal Family resembling other aristocratic dynasties whose fortunes had come through **accident of birth** rather than effort or talent. Many would have believed the touch of the drug-addicted Prince Regent more likely to spread disease than cure it.

STEP BY STEP
Though the monarchy was in urgent need of a make-over by the time of **Victoria's accession 54–55 »**, the path to popularity was not straightforward. For the first 20 years of her reign, Victoria, and to a greater extent her husband, **Prince Albert**, set new standards of sobriety and duty, and the monarchy's reputation rose. It then nosedived when the Queen withdrew from public life in 1861 after the **sudden death of Albert 60–61 »**. It had recovered by the end of her reign, and has largely retained public approval ever since.

Born 1819 Died 1901

Queen Victoria

"I am very **young**… but I am sure… few have more… **real desire** to do what is **fit** and **right** than I have…"

QUEEN VICTORIA, IN HER DIARY, 20 JUNE, 1837

By the end of her long life, Victoria had become Britain's longest-reigning monarch. She was the only child of the Duke of Kent, the fourth son of George III, and his German wife, Princess Victoria of Saxe-Coburg-Saalfeld. Thanks to Victoria's longevity and Britain's industrial, naval, and financial predominance globally throughout the 19th century, her name came to be applied to an entire era. Today, the adjective "Victorian" has contradictory implications. Positively, it is associated with diligence, self-reliance, thrift, and honesty: in a 1982 television interview, British Prime Minister Margaret Thatcher said, "Victorian values were the values when our country became great." Negatively, the term is equated with prudishness, narrow-mindedness, hypocrisy, and rigid inflexibility.

The Victorian paradox

Victoria was a fascinating bundle of contradictions, as was the age in which she lived. She welcomed the use of chloroform in childbirth but rejected electric light. She used the railway extensively, but was terrified of high speeds and would never travel at more than 65kph (40mph). On other occasions, for instance, during the numerous attempts to assassinate her, she showed remarkable bravery.

In her personal life (see p.54) Victoria could be either warm and sympathetic or cold and distant. She took a close interest in all appointments to her several

Royal photo portrait, 1897
Victoria, Queen of the United Kingdom of Great Britain and Ireland from 1837, Empress of India from 1876, seen in the year of her Diamond Jubilee, marking 60 years on the throne.

Young Victoria
German court painter Franz Xaver Winterhalter (1805–73) first visited England in 1842 and painted the young Victoria's portrait. She had been queen for five years at this point, and married for two.

Gold bracelet
Presented to Victoria by Marie-Amélie, Queen of the French, in May 1852, the portraits depict Prince Albert and the four eldest of Queen Victoria's children. The sixth frame holds plaited hair.

households, yet, when her librarian tried to introduce his daughter to her on a royal visit to the library, she snubbed him with a curt, "I came to see the library." Though Victoria liked children, she hated being pregnant, detested breastfeeding, and had little time for babies. To her older sons and daughters she was often an infuriating mother who rarely practised what she preached.

Victoria referred to Albert, Prince Consort and her key advisor, as her "angel". But even Albert dared not approach her when she was in one of her notoriously furious tempers, and was on occasion reduced to passing her notes under her door. Albert, in ill health, travelled to visit his son who was in the grip of a scandal concerning an actress. Anxious and exhausted, Albert died of typhoid fever in 1861. Victoria blamed her eldest son, for her husband's early death, writing that thereafter, "I never can or shall look at him without a shudder."

Sometimes Victoria could be brusque and energetic, and at other times sentimental. After Albert's demise, Victoria had her husband's rooms in all of the royal palaces and castles maintained as they always had been, with towels and linen changed daily, and hot water for washing and shaving brought in each morning.

Personal politics

As in her personal life, it is hard to find consistency in Victoria's political life. She respected hard work and was herself diligent. Then, after Albert's death, she shut herself away from public life, and on numerous occasions threatened to abdicate or take herself off to Australia. When in London or

Ear trumpet
Victoria suffered some hearing impairment in later life and was given this silver-engraved ear trumpet in 1880.

Matriarch of Europe
Victoria surrounded by family. Her grandson, Kaiser Wilhelm II, sits at the bottom left while Tsar Nicholas II of Russia and his wife Alexandra (Victoria's grand-daughter) stand behind the Kaiser. Albert, Prince of Wales, Victoria's eldest son, stands behind the Tsar.

Windsor, she hankered after the peace of Balmoral, the castle in the Scottish Highlands she and Albert had built together; once there, she missed life down south.

By today's standards, Victoria's interference in politics would have been wholly unacceptable. However, in her day, such interventions fell just within the bounds of what was permissable. The "three rights of the crown" – "to be consulted, to encourage, and to warn" – as espoused by English journalist and essayist Walter Bagehot (1826–77) were only just emerging at that time.

While believing she was above politics, Victoria fought to separate personal feelings from her official role. Being closely related to several European royal families put her in an uncomfortable position because, while the British government wanted to pursue foreign policies that increased Britain's power abroad, Victoria feared that such policies would undermine and humiliate the royal families elsewhere, leaving them vulnerable to being overthrown.

Public affection finally restored

Towards the end of her reign, when the greatly expanded franchise (the right to vote) was drawing the country slowly towards democracy, Victoria's political influence waned. This was clearly illustrated in her relations with William Gladstone (1809–98), a British liberal politician who was the greatest political figure of his generation. She did not favour him, yet she reluctantly appointed him prime minister on four separate occasions. Nevertheless, she never once allowed the aged Gladstone to take a seat in her presence, and

31 The number of living grandchildren Victoria had at the time of her death.

37 The number of living great-grandchildren Victoria had at the time of her death.

complained, "He speaks to me as if I were a public meeting." What she seems to have resented most about the Liberal leader was his ability to carry the masses with him. As the "People's William", he posed a threat to the "People's Victoria".

Over time, the queen's popularity grew, and the celebrations for her Jubilees of 1887 and 1897 were genuinely enthusiastic. When Victoria died in January 1901, she was the respected figurehead of a massive empire that was home to one person in four of the world's population. With Albert's help, she had restored the prestige of the British crown, set standards of behaviour that would serve as a template for her successors, and (as much by luck and judgement) found a role for constitutional monarchy in an age of democracy.

TIMELINE

- **24 May 1819** Alexandrina Victoria is born at Kensington Palace, London.
- **26 June 1830** William IV assumes the throne. With no legitimate children to succeed him, his niece Victoria becomes heiress presumptive.
- **1830** The Regency Act says that Victoria may not become queen until she is 18.
- **24 May 1837** Victoria turns 18 and becomes eligible to assume the throne should her uncle die.
- **20 June 1837** Victoria becomes Queen of the United Kingdom of Great Britain and Ireland when William IV dies of heart failure.
- **28 June 1838** Coronation ceremony at Westminster Abbey, London.
- **10 February 1840** Victoria marries her cousin Prince Albert of Saxe-Coburg-Gotha in the Chapel Royal at St James's Palace, London.
- **6 May 1840** Britain issues the world's first postage stamp, costing one penny, which bears the image of Queen Victoria.
- **10 June 1840** Edward Oxford fires two bullets into the coach carrying the pregnant Victoria. It is the first of seven attempts on her life.
- **21 November 1840** Victoria's first child, Princess Victoria Adelaide Mary Louisa, is born. Victoria and Albert will have a further eight children.
- **1 May 1851** Victoria opens the Great Exhibition in Hyde Park, London, which showcases international culture and industry.
- **7 April 1853** Chloroform is administered to Victoria in childbirth, lending credibility to its use as an anaesthetic during labour.
- **17 November 1855** Explorer David Livingstone names the Victoria Falls on Africa's River Zambezi after the Queen.
- **1856** Balmoral Castle is completed.
- **26 June 1857** Victoria Cross awarded for the first time; 62 soldiers and sailors receive it.
- **14 December 1861** Devastated by the death of Albert, Victoria sinks into depression and withdraws from public life.
- **1870** The republican movement has strong support on account of the unsociable behaviour of the "Widow of Windsor".
- **1 May 1876** Prime Minister Benjamin Disraeli proclaims Victoria "Empress of India".
- **1887** Golden Jubilee marks 50th year of Victoria's reign. The celebrations help draw her back into public life.
- **23 September 1896** Victoria's reign surpasses that of George III's as the longest in British history.
- **1897** Diamond Jubilee is marked by six days of celebrations in London and elsewhere, ending with a Review of the Fleet at Spithead.
- **22 January 1901** Victoria dies of a cerebral haemorrhage at Osborne House, Isle of Wight, bringing to an end a reign of nearly 64 years.

VICTORIA CROSS

The archetypal Victorian family
Victoria and Albert pose for a photograph with their nine children in March 1861. The stiff poses are partly explained by the need to remain motionless while a photograph was being taken.

BEFORE ❮❮

From 1714, the kings of Great Britain were also Electors of Hanover, which gave them the right, with eight others, to elect the Holy Roman Emperor.

CLOSE TIES WITH EUROPE

Elector of **Hanover ❮❮ 48–49**, is a largely honorary title but, as long as the British king held this title, it tied Britain closely to European, especially German, politics. This tie also drew Britain into a continental land war during Napoleonic times (1799–1815). At the end of the conflict, Hanover became a kingdom, a development that gave three British monarchs, **George III**, **George IV**, and **William IV ❮❮ 48–49**, a double crown.

LONG LIVE THE KING!

The monarchy, in the period before Victoria ascended the throne, had been largely secure due, in part, to the steadiness of the prevailing political system, and the longevity of the kings. From 1714–1837, there were only five monarchs, one of whom, **George III, reigned for 60 years.**

Queen Victoria's coronation service
This painting by Charles Robert Leslie (1794–1859) shows the Queen towards the end of the service, kneeling to receive the Sacrament. She wears no jewels and the Crown has not yet been placed on her head.

Victoria becomes Queen

A botched coronation and a row over her ladies in waiting did not augur well for the reign of the strong-willed young Queen Victoria. But marriage to her handsome, earnest-minded first cousin, Prince Albert of Saxe-Coburg-Gotha, gave her longed-for stability and domestic joy.

Victoria's father died when she was eight months old, and the fair-haired, blue-eyed princess spent most of her childhood in the seclusion of London's Kensington Palace. Her over-protective, ambitious mother, aided by Sir John Conroy, Victoria's mother's (possible) lover and personal adviser, brought up Victoria according to a meticulous, complex set of rules, which they named the "Kensington System" after the palace. The system was designed to make the princess an easily manipulated cypher.

Under the system, her every action was observed and recorded, and the young Victoria was even kept away from other children. Supported by her devoted governess Louise Lehzen, Victoria resisted strongly and, on the death of George IV (see p.49) in 1830, Victoria became heiress presumptive, prompting her renowned remark, "I will be good." Seven years later she acceded to the throne when her uncle William IV (see p.49) died without legitimate offspring. Until then, Victoria was made to sleep in her mother's room. However, on moving into Buckingham Palace – the first sovereign to take up residence there – she demanded a bedroom of her own. She also used her new-found authority to banish the hated Conroy from the royal household.

Coronation beaker, 1838
This fine silver goblet was commissioned as a souvenir to mark the coronation of Queen Victoria. It has two applied plaques. One (left) shows the portrait bust of the Queen and the other a scene from the Coronation.

Coronation

The public immediately took to the 18-year-old Victoria. Her youth, purity, and piety were a refreshing contrast to the unseemly antics of her Hanoverian predecessors (see pp.48–49).

Nevertheless, she soon discovered the kind of tribulations a sovereign must contend with, as her Uncle Leopold

Victoria's First Meeting with the Privy Council
Just hours after learning of William IV's death, Victoria held her first meeting with her councillors in the Red Saloon, Kensington Palace, at 11 am on 20 June 1837. Aged 18, she wrote that she was "not at all nervous".

(1790–1865) and later first King of the Belgians, warned her. Difficulties arose over her coronation. In the House of Commons, the traditionalist Tory party were accused of using the ceremony as propaganda to promote the monarchy, while Radicals said

the £79,000 bill for the coronation, twice that of William IV's in 1831 (see pp.49), was wasteful and Britain would be better as a republic.

Complaints or no complaints, on 28 June 1838 the ceremony went ahead. It began with the longest procession the streets of London had seen since the return of Charles II in 1660 (see pp.41–43). Cheered by a crowd estimated to number around 400,000 ("millions of my loyal subjects… assembled in every spot,"

> "His… **excessive** love and **affection** gave me feelings of **heavenly love** and **happiness.**"
>
> QUEEN VICTORIA, IN HER DIARY, 10 FEBRUARY 1840

gushed Victoria later) the youthful queen rode in the ornate Gold State Coach to Westminster Abbey.

At this point things began to go wrong. There had been no rehearsal, and no one was quite sure where to go or when. The music of a massive orchestra and choir was out of time because the choirmaster was forced to conduct from his seat at the organ.

The entire chaotic ceremony, which involved the queen in two changes of formal attire, lasted a sleep-inducing five hours. The tedium was relieved only when an 82-year-old peer, appropriately named Lord Rolle, tripped and rolled down the chancel steps. When he had recovered, Victoria won the hearts of those present by getting up and coming down the steps to meet him so he didn't have to attempt the ascent again.

Early Difficulties

Victoria ultimately found happiness in her marriage. She first met her future husband, her cousin Prince Albert of Saxe-Coburg-Gotha (1819–61), in 1836. She was powerfully struck by his looks and serious yet sympathetic personality. They met again in 1839, and five days later, on 15 October, Victoria proposed to him, and he accepted. It was a love match bonded by a strong physical attraction that enabled the couple to weather even the roughest emotional storms.

The wedding took place in the Chapel Royal at St James's Palace, London, on 10 February 1840. As they had done for the coronation, excited crowds lined the streets to see the Queen travel

136 The weight in kilos (300 lb) of the cake baked for the wedding of Victoria and Albert. More than 1,000 guests each tasted a morsel.

from Buckingham Palace to the chapel. Also, as at the coronation, the music was poor. But no one seemed to mind and, after an enormous wedding breakfast in Buckingham Palace, the couple left for a honeymoon in Windsor Castle.

Victoria was soon pregnant. A daughter, Victoria (1840–1901), was born the same year on 21 November. A further eight children followed: Albert Edward, Prince of Wales (1841–1910); Alice (1843–78); Alfred (1844–1900); Helena (1846–1923); Louise (1848–1939); Arthur (1850–1942), Leopold (1853–84); and Beatrice (1857–1944). Victoria's old governess and confidante Louise Lehzen ran the busy household until, after a heated quarrel in 1842 between Victoria and Albert, who detested Lehzen, she was pensioned off.

Despite such squalls, the relationship between the royal couple deepened

AFTER ≫

Under ancient German law codes, as Queen Victoria acceded to the throne, Britain's 123-year connection with Hanover ended. In the future, wars loomed.

LINKS WITH GERMANY LOOSEN
The Germanic kingdom's Semi-Salic law, dating back to the 6th century, **forbade female accession** to the throne as long as a male alternative existed. Accordingly, in 1837, Victoria's uncle, **Ernest Augustus**, the eldest surviving son of George III, took the crown of Hanover and left Britain to his niece.

FIRST STEP TOWARDS WORLD WAR I
With the British monarch no longer **ruler of Hanover**, a close link with Germany was gone. This may be seen as the first step in a chain of events that led to Britain and Germany going to war. In 1914, German troops **advanced through Belgium**. Britain held that this infringed Belgium's neutrality, and **declared war** on Germany 79–81 ≫.

and Albert was soon his wife's wise advisor as well as her lover. When Victoria's pregnancies grew visible and prevented her appearing in public ceremonies, it was Albert who assumed her duties. As their family expanded, the monarchy became more of a shared partnership between them. A part of Victoria always resented this sharing of power, but she usually welcomed it and even permitted Albert to dictate her political letters.

Queen Victoria in the crown jewels
After her coronation, Victoria is depicted in the regalia and vestments of a British monarch. The imperial state crown she wears is set with such gems as St Edward's sapphire (front), which dates back to 1042.

Palazzo style
The gardens were also designed by Prince Albert and provide the perfect the setting for his Italian Renaissance villa with wide terraces that open out to glorious views of the sea.

ROYAL RESIDENCE

Osborne

Designed by Prince Albert in the style of an Italian Renaissance villa, the house at Osborne on the Isle of Wight, with its splendid views over the Solent, was intended to provide the Royal Family with a luxurious seaside retreat, well away from the pressures of court life.

Queen Victoria and Prince Albert bought the Osborne Estate on the Isle of Wight in 1845. Owned by Lady Isabella Blachford, the estate was recommended to them by the Prime Minister, Sir Robert Peel. Victoria, who had fond memories of childhood holidays on an adjoining estate, declared "it is impossible to imagine a prettier spot." Albert was equally charmed by the site: it reminded him of the Bay of Naples which he had visited in 1838. The existing house, however, was too small for the royal couple, their growing family, and entourage, so work began immediately on a new building.

Ideal home

Inspired by his memories of Italy, Prince Albert worked closely with the property developer Thomas Cubitt to create an informal family home. The first part, the three-storey Pavilion accommodating the private rooms of Queen Victoria and Prince Albert and the royal nurseries for their children, was completed in 1846. The Household Wing, providing rooms for members of the royal household, was finished in 1848. At this point the original house was demolished and replaced with the Main Wing, linked to the Household Wing by the Grand Corridor. The finished building was dominated by two Belvedere towers, with huge plate glass windows looking over the grounds to the sea.

Victoria and Albert gradually created their ideal world, building a model farm, estate cottages, lodges and dormitories, and a sea wall along the coast. The estate had terraced Italian gardens, and a private beach, where the children and their mother all learned to swim.

Hidden in the woods is a wooden chalet, the Swiss Cottage, where the royal children were taught household skills. The Princesses learned to bake and would occasionally serve tea to their parents and guests. They kept household accounts, which Albert inspected. The older boys, Bertie and Alfred, helped to lay the foundations. An entry in Queen Victoria's journal describes how Prince Alfred "worked as hard and steadily as a regular labourer" – and was paid by Albert at the same rate. Each child had their own garden plot where they cultivated fruit, vegetables, and flowers. Despite the miniature tools and monogrammed wheelbarrows, this was no mere game. The under-gardener assessed all the produce, and Albert paid the market price to the child who had grown it.

In the main house, the Queen received a panoply of distinguished guests: prime ministers Robert Peel, Benjamin Disraeli, and William Gladstone; inventor Alexander Graham Bell, who demonstrated the telephone at Osborne; and members of European royalty, including Emperor Napoleon III and Kaiser Wilhelm II.

After Albert's death, Victoria took refuge at Osborne, and eventually it became her preferred residence. In 1885 she agreed to the marriage of her youngest child, Beatrice, on condition she continued to live at Osborne. A new wing was built, with apartments for the Princess and her family, and an opulent reception room was added, encrusted with Mughal-inspired stucco-work, known as the Durbar Room.

Queen Victoria died in her bedroom at Osborne on 22 January 1901. Her children did not share her love for the house, and Edward VII presented it to the nation. After stints as a Naval College and convalescent home, the house is now run by English Heritage and is open throughout the year.

Informal seaside retreat

Private rooms like the nursery were all furnished with comfort in mind, but the Durbar Wing had a more impressive space for formal entertaining. Despite the privacy of the estate, Victoria was wheeled to the sea in her bathing machine when she wanted a swim.

QUEEN VICTORIA'S BATHING MACHINE

NURSERY BEDROOM

PEACOCK OVERMANTLE IN THE DURBAR ROOM

The **Great Exhibition**

Organized by the Royal Society for the Encouragement of Arts, Manufactures and Commerce (RSA) and strongly backed by Prince Albert, the Great Exhibition of the Works of Industry of all Nations, in Hyde Park, London, attracted 6.2 million visitors. It successfully promoted Britain's position as the world's leading industrial nation.

The proposal to hold an international exhibition in London to show off British ingenuity and promote harmony between nations came from Henry Cole, a civil servant and member of the Society of Arts, and was backed by Victoria's far-sighted husband, Prince Albert. The idea was not a new one. France had held an Industrial Exposition in Paris in 1844, and the concept had been copied in Madrid (1845), Brussels (1847), and Lisbon (1849). This put pressure on Britain, the undisputed leader of global finance and manufacturing, to organize something bigger and better than anything attempted before.

A royal commission looked into the matter and Lord Russell's Liberal government gave the project its backing. The committee charged with bringing the project to fruition by 1 May 1851 was chaired by the civil engineer William Cubitt. Alongside him sat Prince Albert, the celebrated railway engineers Isambard Kingdom Brunel and Robert Stephenson, and the architect Charles Barry. They struggled to find a suitable building plan until the well-known gardener, Joseph Paxton, came up with a design for an enormous greenhouse using cast plate glass, cast iron, and laminated wood. In just nine months the Crystal Palace, the world's largest glass structure, was built in Hyde Park, London, on time and on budget.

The 100,000 exhibits packed into the 10 hectares (25 acres) of floor space included the Koh-i-noor – then the world's largest diamond – a voting machine, a Colt revolver, and the first ever public conveniences. The Great Exhibition was an outstanding success, attracting an average daily attendance of 42,000 visitors and making a profit of £186,000 – money used to set up several institutions, including the Museum of Manufacturing (later known as the Victoria and Albert Museum) in Kensington. The queen visited the site several times during its construction and almost daily once the Great Exhibition was open.

> " Its **grandeur** does not consist in *one* thing, but in the **unique assemblage of** *all* **things.**"
>
> **CHARLOTTE BRONTË,** WRITER, IN A LETTER TO A FRIEND

The Crystal Palace
The Great Exhibition – housed in the spectacular Crystal Palace – showcased Britain as the "workshop of the world". It displayed an extraordinary array of innovative goods and machinery from Britain and its empire, as well as from other nations.

Victoria after Albert

The sudden death of Albert in 1861 left the 42-year-old Queen totally devastated. The years of semi-seclusion that followed undid much of the good work she and her husband had accomplished to raise the prestige of the monarchy, and fed a surge of angry republicanism.

Marriage to Victoria was never easy, and there was always something of a power struggle between her and Albert. She bowed to the inevitable, nevertheless, especially during her pregnancies, and allowed him, as her Private Secretary, to deal with official business.

Albert was better educated than Victoria, his mind clearer and sharper, so his contributions were much appreciated. As well as handling correspondence, he met with ministers and urged "sympathy and interest for that class of our community who have most of the toil and fewest of the enjoyments of this world".

A royal partnership

With Albert to lean on, Victoria rode out the dangers of pregnancy and childbirth. She also survived several assassination attempts. When Europe

BEFORE

As Victoria had been raised fatherless, it has been suggested that she could only function effectively when there was a certain type of man in her life.

CRAVING FOR A FATHER FIGURE

Before her marriage, Lord Melbourne (1779–1848), who was Prime Minister when Victoria ascended the throne, fulfilled the fatherly mentor role. Between 1840–61, Prince Albert was the only male company she needed, combining the roles of lover, father, and companion. The loss of this complex, multi-layered relationship was, arguably, a blow from which she never fully recovered.

exploded into revolution in 1848, he reassured her; and he soothed her when she was dubbed the "Famine Queen" when the Irish were starving in the Great Famine of 1845–52. Her gift of £2,000 towards famine relief, though just 0.5% of her £385,000 annual income from the civil list, was still the largest single donation.

In the 1840s, Albert supported his wife's wish for closer relations with France. Their efforts led to a meeting with King Louis Philippe in 1843, the first such encounter since the time of Henry VIII (see pp.28–29).

In the next decade, as well as working on the 1851 Great Exhibition in London and the reform of Cambridge University, of which he was Chancellor, Albert assisted with the Crimean War against Russia. He also arranged for

£600,000 The amount left to Queen Victoria in Albert's will.

their eldest daughter, Victoria (Vicky), to marry Prince Frederick William (Fritz) of Prussia in 1858, when Vicky was 17. The next year she gave birth to a son: the future Kaiser Wilhelm II.

A dreadful year

1861 was the unhappiest year of Victoria's life. The year started badly with Albert not keeping well. When the Queen's mother died in March and Victoria reacted with hysterical grief, rumours spread widely that she had gone mad, like her grandfather George III (see pp.48–49).

Worse was to come as Albert's health deteriorated. Then, on 12 November, news arrived that shocked them to the core: Albert Edward, the Prince of Wales (see pp.72–73), had been having an affair with an Irish actress. Despite his strict schooling (or perhaps because of it), Bertie was developing into a Hanoverian-style playboy. Victoria was mortified; Albert became more ill, and by December was clearly dying. He passed away, surrounded by his wife and five of their children, on Saturday, 14 December 1861. The contemporary diagnosis was typhoid fever; a more likely diagnosis is cancer, Crohn's disease, or kidney failure.

Mourning

Victoria reacted to Albert's death with fits of frenzied weeping and going about as if in a dream. She always

Queen with her husband, Albert, 1854
The pose, though extremely formal, manages to suggest the couple's complex relationship: Victoria, admiration tinged with a hint of irritation, looks up at her tall, upright, and slightly preoccupied husband.

wore black henceforward and, though she did smile on occasion, she was continually reminding others of her loss. She avoided appearing in public, preferring self-imposed seclusion at Windsor, Osborne House, or Balmoral. Before long the public were declaring that the "Widow of Windsor" was neglecting the duties for which she was paid from the public purse.

At Balmoral, Victoria met John Brown, a handsome estate worker some seven years her junior. The couple developed a close friendship and understanding: she was buried with a lock of his hair, and wrote when he died, "Perhaps never... was there... so warm and loving a friendship between the sovereign and servant."

Royal target
The first attempt on Victoria's life was made by Edward Oxford on 10 June 1840. The would-be assassin fired two pistols at close range before being apprehended. He was later declared insane.

MONARCHY RECOVERS

Though Victoria's recovery from illness produced a wave of affection towards her in the autumn of 1871, it was the Prince of Wales's brush with death later in the year that decidedly swung public opinion back in the Royal Family's favour. Victoria's abject misery over her son had been picked up and telegraphed around the Empire, provoking widespread sympathy; joy at his recovery was similarly wide-ranging. The episode carried the tide of popular feeling back towards the monarchy, and dealt a major blow to British republicanism.

A gold cross tops a 54m (176ft) tall memorial

Exterior mosaics manufactured in Murano, Venice

> ## "God's will be done! A heavenly peace has descended… it cannot be possible… Oh! God! Oh! God!"
>
> QUEEN VICTORIA, ON THE LOSS OF ALBERT, 16 DECEMBER 1861

Some say the couple were lovers – Victoria's daughters certainly joked that they were, and their mother was mocked in print as "Mrs Brown".

We will probably never know the truth about the relationship, but rumour and innuendo dragged the Queen's reputation still lower. By 1870, a significant wave of republicanism was sweeping the country. The *National Reformer*, a popular Radical newspaper, proudly declared itself "Atheist, Republican, Malthusian", and its editor, Charles Bradlaugh, drew large crowds to his speeches criticizing the monarchy. In 1870, a popular rally in Trafalgar Square called for Victoria's removal.

Micro-managing matriarch

Stubbornly refusing to bow to public opinion, the Queen instead channelled her energies into controlling her family. Her means were duplicitous, picking up stories from informers and playing off one child against another. Her favourite, possibly because he resembled Albert and did what he was told, was her third son, Prince Arthur. His elder brother, Bertie carried on where he had begun in the year of his father's death, chasing women and enjoying himself. Victoria kept him at arm's length, never trusting him with government papers.

Her daughters, including royal wives, she tried to keep on an even tighter rein. She insisted that the doctor who attended Alexandra, the Danish princess whom Bertie married in 1863,

Albert Memorial, London

Funded by public subscription, this neo-Gothic monument was opened in 1872. The golden statue of the robed Albert was placed within it three years later.

send her full and intimate reports of her daughter-in-law's condition. Vicky she labelled a "cow" for breastfeeding, contrary to her mother's wishes. Victoria hoped her youngest daughter, Beatrice (nicknamed "Baby") would remain single. When Beatrice became engaged to Prince Henry of Battenberg, however, Victoria refused to speak to her for seven months.

Bertie's brush with death

Had the hostile mood of 1870 persisted, Victoria's reign might well have ended in ignominy. But, just as illness had started her decline, so it played an important part in turning things round.

Towards the end of 1871, she fell seriously ill with a badly infected abscess in her armpit. When she recovered, with the help of a new antiseptic spray invented by British surgeon, Joseph Lister, the public responded with warmth. A month later, in October, Bertie caught typhoid fever while staying with Lady Londesborough, near Scarborough. The outbreak, probably emanating from the poor state of the Lady's drains, had killed the Conservative politician Lord Chesterfield, and the Prince himself was now in mortal danger. Victoria was in despair: her son was at his lowest on the exact anniversary of Albert's death 10 years earlier. The press published detailed reports on Bertie's progress and, in Britain and overseas, public rejoicing at the Prince's recovery was widespread and genuine. It carried over into the enthusiastic reception afforded Bertie and his mother when they attended a thanksgiving service at St Paul's Cathedral the

The Queen and her gillie, c.1863
For 150 years, the precise nature of the relationship between Victoria and John Brown, her gillie (a hunting and fishing guide) at Balmoral, has been the subject of speculation.

next February. In May 1872, Bertie's brother organized a special Thanksgiving Day concert in the Crystal Palace, and commissioned the renowned composer Arthur Sullivan to write a "Festival Te Deum" for it. The work gained a triumphant reception, especially as it was dedicated to the Queen herself, and confirmed that the monarchy's crisis had passed.

AFTER

From 1861 onwards, Victoria found male companionship in a number of very different types of men.

POLITICAL ADVISOR
Prime Minister Benjamin Disraeli (1804–81) was a flattering companion: "Everyone likes flattery," he confessed, "and when you come to royalty you should lay it on with a trowel."

EMOTIONAL ATTACHMENTS
John Brown was Victoria's emotional stay, and perhaps even her lover. After his death in 1883, another male friend came to court. Hafiz Mohammed Abdul Karim (affectionately referred to as "the Munshi", meaning clerk or teacher) was the son of a Muslim hospital assistant in India. Having crossed to Britain to work in Buckingham Palace during the **1887 Golden Jubilee year 66–67 »**, he remained a close companion to Victoria for the remaining 15 years of her life.

Statue of Albert, seated ceremonially, wearing the robes of the Garter

Allegorical sculptures representing the Industrial Arts at four corners

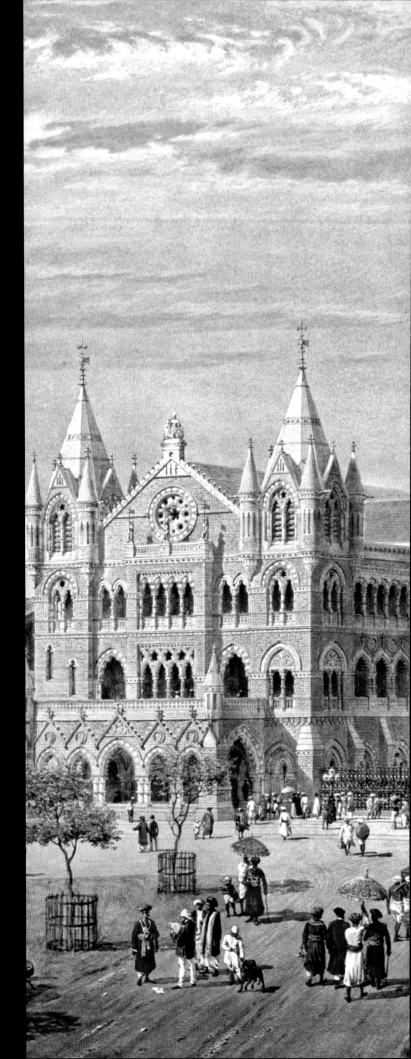

Empress of India

Victoria was delighted when the Royal Titles Act of 1876 gave official recognition to her status as an empress: she was now on a par with the German and Russian royal families. Nevertheless, in some circles the new nomenclature was seen as a somewhat vulgar European import.

Though India was regarded as the "jewel in the British Crown", until 1857 London governed it only indirectly. Day to day administration was shared between the East India Company and Indian princes. The arrangement fell apart during the extremely violent rebellion of 1857, also known as the Indian Mutiny, India's First War of Independence, and the Great Rebellion. The following year, the Government of India Act placed administration in the hands of the British government – the British monarch became India's Head of State.

By the time the Prince of Wales (later to become Edward VII) made his eight-month tour of India, beginning in October 1875, the subcontinent had settled down and the royal visit was a great success. This was in no small part due to his open-minded nature and refusal to accept the racism that many members of the Raj – the British government in India – practised. Back home, the Conservative Prime Minister Benjamin Disraeli, the Queen's favourite, took advantage of the visit to introduce a Royal Titles Bill in 1876. He even persuaded Victoria to open Parliament in person for the first time since Prince Albert's death. The new law gave official sanction to her use of the title Empress of India, a move that would, Disraeli hoped, strengthen the bond between Britain and India. On 1 January 1877, Lord Lytton, Viceroy of India, marked the occasion with the Delhi Durbar, a spectacular celebration in the Indian capital.

Victoria had long been annoyed that the heads of the Russian and German royal families had sported a title she did not possess, and she warmly welcomed the elevation. She took to signing herself "V.R. & I.", *Victoria Regina et Imperatrix* (Victoria Queen and Empress).

> ## "I am an empress and in common conversation am sometimes called Empress of India."
>
> **QUEEN VICTORIA** TO SIR HENRY PONSONBY

Victoria Terminus
Now known as Chhatrapati Shivaji Terminus, this massive railway station in Mumbai (formerly Bombay), India, was completed just in time to commemorate Victoria's Golden Jubilee in 1887. A monument to colonial rule, the edifice was built using locally procured materials, but fashioned in European style.

:

« BEFORE

BEFORE

The attitude of George III towards his American colonies, and their successful rebellion (1775–83) against him, taught Britain a valuable lesson.

AMERICAN WAR OF INDEPENDENCE
British North America had been subject to **English law** until the 18th century, but laws passed after 1763 to raise revenue for Britain united the American colonies in **acts of rebellion**. In reprisal, Britain passed yet more laws. The colonists rejected their legality, and political leaders wrote a **Declaration of Independence** in 1776. In the ensuing war, which ended in 1783, Britain lost its colony and the **United States of America was born**.

ASSET FOR THE MOTHER COUNTRY
From this time onwards the men and women living in the **colonies**, especially those of European descent, were treated with greater respect than before. Even so, the colonies were still regarded as primarily existing for the **benefit of the mother country**, as providers of food and raw materials, as captive markets for British goods, and places where **surplus population** could go, and to which undesirables might be sent.

From **Empire** to **Commonwealth**

Victoria was figurehead of the largest, most diverse empire the world had ever seen. Efforts to bring its component nations closer together led to the creation of the Imperial Federation League and Colonial Conferences, from which today's Commonwealth of Nations emerged.

The huge British Empire headed by Queen Victoria (see pp.50–51) was an unusual entity – if it was an entity at all. Britain's global lands had been accumulated over a long time in a wide variety of ways. Some had been conquered, some purchased, some simply occupied, and others gained through negotiation (not always scrupulous) with previous owners.

Broadly speaking, the colonies were of two types. There were those like India and Kenya where the indigenous people made up the bulk of the population, and those like Australia and Canada where European settlers had swiftly overwhelmed the small indigenous populations. British territories in the Caribbean, such

as Trinidad and Jamaica, were different again. Here the indigenous peoples had been all but replaced by immigrants from Europe, West Africa (as slaves), and, latterly, Asia.

During the 19th century, the monarchy became the focal point for the swelling empire. In 1875–76, Queen Victoria's son, the Prince of Wales (see pp.72–73), made a highly successful tour of the

Safeguarding the empire
One way Britain protected its far-flung Empire was to increase the size of its Royal Navy. HMS *Dreadnought*, commissioned in 1906, became a tangible symbol of Britain's invincibility on the open seas.

subcontinent. During his visit, he showed Indians of every degree that they were the equals of his subjects at home. The tour also laid the ground for his mother to assume the title Empress of India in 1876 (see pp.62–63).

Empire under threat
There had always been many who felt uneasy about Britain's acquisition of an overseas empire. The rebellion of the American colonists in 1775–83 (see p.49), for instance, had attracted a number of

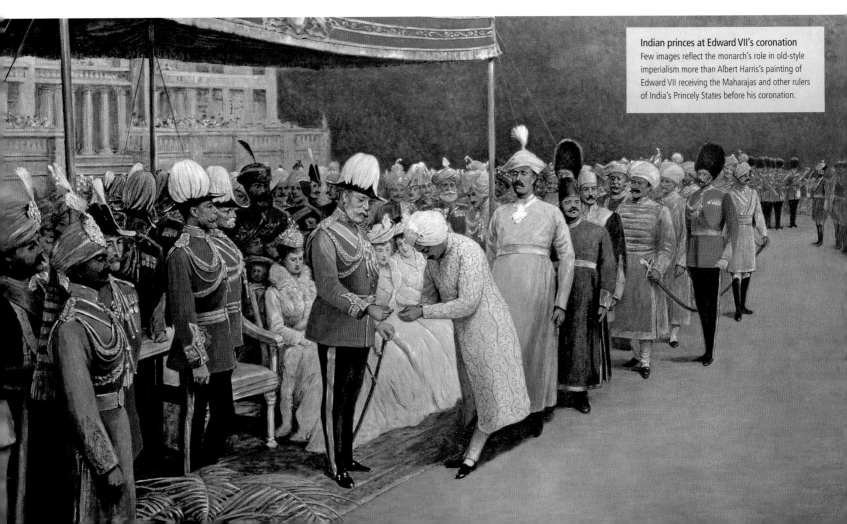

Indian princes at Edward VII's coronation
Few images reflect the monarch's role in old-style imperialism more than Albert Harris's painting of Edward VII receiving the Maharajas and other rulers of India's Princely States before his coronation.

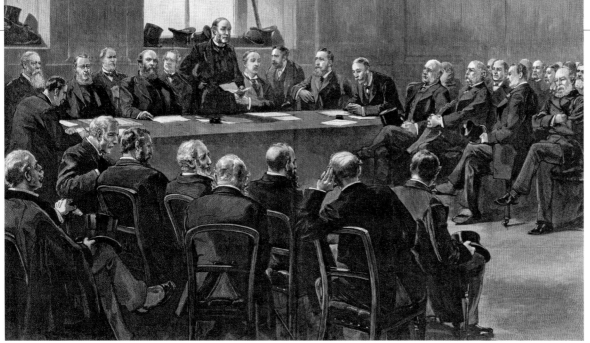

The Colonial and Imperial Conferences were early indications of a change in attitude towards the colonies.

EMPIRE TO COMMONWEALTH
The word "commonwealth", widely used in the 16th century, had been revived in the 19th century as an alternative to "empire". By 1917, the South African leader Jan Smuts was talking of the "British Commonwealth of Nations". In 1949 the word "British" was axed and the modern Commonwealth of Nations, a voluntary association of 53 states, was born. **King George VI 94–95 »** gladly acted as its figurehead, a role granted to his daughter, **Elizabeth II 134–135 »** on her accession.

"**Africa** is still **lying ready** for us. It is **our duty** to **take** it."

CECIL JOHN RHODES, BRITISH IMPERIALIST, IN HIS *CONFESSION OF FAITH*, 2 JUNE 1877

British supporters. Moreover, as the mother country edged towards a more representative form of government, rights were extended to the colonies of settlement. New Zealand became a self-governing member of the British Empire in 1852. Three years later, New South Wales established parliamentary rule over domestic matters, followed by Victoria, Tasmania and in 1856, South Australia. Queensland joined them in 1859, and Western Australia in 1890. Canada became the self-governing Dominion of Canada in 1867, and South Africa's Cape Colony started electing its own government in 1872.

"Scramble" for colonies
The mood of imperialism that swept through Europe in the 1880s led to a "scramble" for colonies in Africa, and heightened tension between the major powers. Britain's scattered empire was increasingly vulnerable. One response to the threat was to build up the Royal Navy. In 1889, Britain planned for 10 new battleships, 38 cruisers, and numerous smaller vessels in order that its navy would be larger than the fleets of any two other powers combined. A second response was to unite the peoples of the empire in an Imperial Federation League, or IFL. This was launched in 1884, and drew inspiration from the federal structure of the US and the way in which the Dominion of Canada had been organized. Supporters of the move were mainly Conservatives, though well-known Liberals such as the education reformer EM Forster also joined. Its

ultimate aim was to unite all Britain's colonies into a type of super-state under an imperial parliament. The plan was to start with Britain and the colonies of settlement, then expand into a kind of Anglo United Nations as other colonies joined. New technology, it was hoped, would overcome issues of geographical separation. IFL supporters argued that the alternative was imperial disintegration and decline.

The living symbol
This Empire Day postcard of 1907, designed for sending from the "mother country" to some corner of the empire, illustrates the monarch's key role in binding together Britain's far-flung colonies and dominions.

Meeting of equals
From the 1887 Colonial Conference onwards, British ministers learned to negotiate and not to simply issue orders when meeting with the elected leaders of the dominions: all were subjects under the same monarch.

However, the proposal ignored the vast cultural differences between the peoples of the empire, the colonies' burgeoning nationalism, and Britain's unwillingness to be influenced, let alone dictated to, by colonials. Nevertheless, the proposal planted a seed that, as a very different type of plant, grew into one of the most inspiring institutions of the modern world: the Commonwealth of Nations, headed by Queen Elizabeth II.

First Colonial Conference
Called by the IFL and chaired by Prime Minister Lord Salisbury, the first Colonial Conference met in 1887 when representatives from all parts of the Empire were gathered in London for Victoria's Golden Jubilee (see pp.66–67). Over 100 delegates, including several prime ministers, attended, although India was not represented. The agenda mainly concerned defence. In return for a British pledge not to withdraw its naval presence unilaterally from the Pacific, Australia offered to pay £126,000 annually towards the maintenance of the Royal Navy's fleet in their part of the world. A trans-Pacific telegraph cable was proposed, and it was agreed that the Queen's official title should now read, "Queen of the United Kingdom of Great Britain, Ireland, and the Colonies, and all Dependencies thereof, and Empress of India."

Emergence of the Commonwealth
Further Colonial Conferences were held in 1894, 1897, and 1902. Between then and World War II, seven more meetings

or, Imperial Conferences, were held at irregular intervals. By 1936, this type of meeting was called a "Commonwealth of Nations", giving the dominions equal status to Britain within it.

The Colonial and Imperial Conferences were early indications of a British change in attitude towards the colonies. But while areas largely peopled by those of European descent had been granted self-government, other areas did not enjoy such new rights, and remained subjects of the Empire just as before.

In all cases, Britain had retained control over defence and foreign affairs, though its dealings with Australia and New Zealand in 1887 indicated that even in this field Britain's dominant position

£126,000 The amount of money **Australia offered to pay towards its own defence at the 1887 Colonial Conference.**

was open to negotiation – another small but crucial step nearer a new relationship. Over the next 75 years, the concept of an interdependent partnership between free and independent peoples developed into the Commonwealth of Nations.

Australia's coat of arms
Though granted by George V in 1912, the design symbolizes the independent Commonwealth of Australia rather than the country's monarchy. Of the six state badges, only two feature a crown.

65

Victoria's Golden Jubilee memorabilia
This impressive array of tickets, invitations, and souvenir programmes illustrates how the celebrations captured the public imagination, sweeping away any republican sentiment lingering from the previous decade.

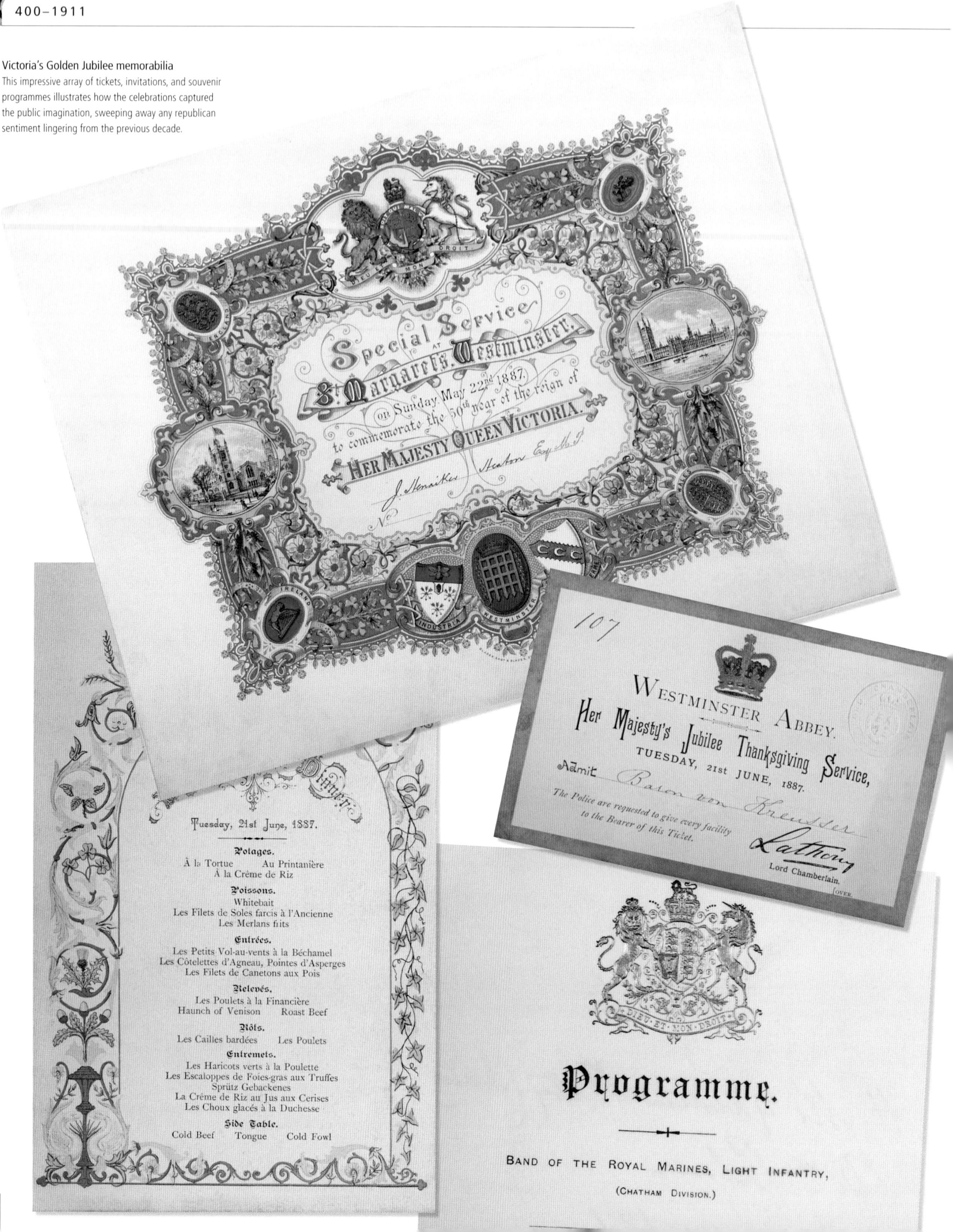

DIEU ET MON DROIT
SCOTLAND
ENGLAND
Special Service
AT
St. Margaret's Westminster.
on Sunday May 22nd 1887,
to commemorate the 50th year of the reign of
HER MAJESTY QUEEN VICTORIA.
J. Henniker Heaton Esq M.P.
No.
WALES
IRELAND
INDUSTRIA
WESTMINSTER
107
Westminster Abbey.
Her Majesty's Jubilee Thanksgiving Service,
TUESDAY, 21st JUNE, 1887.
Admit Baron von Kreusser
The Police are requested to give every facility to the Bearer of this Ticket.
Lathom
Lord Chamberlain.
[OVER.
Dinner.
Tuesday, 21st June, 1887.
Potages.
À la Tortue Au Printanière
À la Crême de Riz
Poissons.
Whitebait
Les Filets de Soles farcis à l'Ancienne
Les Merlans frits
Entrées.
Les Petits Vol-au-vents à la Béchamel
Les Côtelettes d'Agneau, Pointes d'Asperges
Les Filets de Canetons aux Pois
Relevés.
Les Poulets à la Financière
Haunch of Venison Roast Beef
Rôts.
Les Cailles bardées Les Poulets
Entremets.
Les Haricots verts à la Poulette
Les Escaloppes de Foies-gras aux Truffes
Sprütz Gebackenes
La Crême de Riz au Jus aux Cerises
Les Choux glacés à la Duchesse
Side Table.
Cold Beef Tongue Cold Fowl
DIEU ET MON DROIT
Programme.
BAND OF THE ROYAL MARINES, LIGHT INFANTRY,
(CHATHAM DIVISION.)

Victoria's Jubilees

Though never fond of pomp, Victoria went along with the jubilee festivities of 1887 and 1897, and was a gracious host to the European royalty who came to honour her. Both occasions were hugely popular triumphs of careful organization, setting a precedent for future events.

Queen Victoria's Golden Jubilee was as much a national event as a monarchical one. Great Britain was a wealthy and powerful nation, with the largest empire ever seen. When Queen Victoria reached the 50th year of her reign, the country revelled in its successes.

At first, the Queen was irritated by the thought of all the "hustle and bustle" involved in a jubilee. She was also aware that not that many years

before, the monarchy – and Victoria in particular – had been deeply unpopular; even in 1887, crowds booed her when she visited London's East End. Eventually, she came to see that a jubilee might not be such a bad idea, and so the party was launched.

Invitations went out to Queen Victoria's extended family and to heads of state in every continent. Jubilee souvenirs were manufactured by the thousand. Worldwide, museums, bridges, streets, and even burial grounds were named or renamed in honour of the Queen and Empress.

The two days of official jubilee pageantry began on 20 June. The first day saw a massive state luncheon. The next day, Victoria was driven in an open landau to Westminster Abbey for a service of thanksgiving. She returned to Buckingham Palace for another luncheon, after which she waved to the cheering crowds from the palace balcony. A dinner took place that evening with representatives of every crowned head in Europe. Fireworks followed as bonfires flickered from hilltops across the land.

Given the success of the Golden Jubilee, there could be no doubt but that the 60th year of Victoria's reign would be celebrated similarly. After all,

by 1897, she had reigned the longest of any monarch in British history. But the mood in the country had changed.

By now, the Queen herself was old and frail, tension with Germany and serious difficulties in Ireland and South Africa darkened the international situation, and doubts were growing about the morality of maintaining a subservient empire. To combat this, Colonial Secretary Joseph, with the Queen's approval, gave the 1897 jubilee a distinctly imperial twist.

Celebrations for the Diamond Jubilee took place on 22 June. London was festooned with Union Jacks and the flags of other nations, and hawkers plied their souvenirs as hundreds of thousands took advantage of the national holiday to throng the streets along which the 17-carriage royal procession passed. Dressed in her customary black, the Queen was deeply moved as the crowds cheered and broke into spontaneous outbursts of "God Save the Queen".

Ticket to view the Royal Procession, June 1897
Reserved seats were sold from which to watch the royal procession pass by. Victoria herself accepted only reluctantly the need for such "continental" fanfare.

The days that followed were filled with further parades, inspections, unveilings, addresses, and receptions. Victoria soldiered on through them, not always in the best of humour, but aware that it was her duty to attend. In response to countless expressions of affection and gratitude, including 1,310 congratulatory telegrams from all around the world, Victoria wrote a thank-you letter to the people of Great Britain and sent a telegram to the Empire. "From my heart", it read, "I thank my beloved people. May God bless them".

Her old foe William Gladstone (see p.51) had hoped she would use her Diamond Jubilee to announce her abdication. Evidently, he had underestimated his adversary.

> ## "No one… has met with such an **ovation** as was given to **me.**"
>
> QUEEN VICTORIA, IN HER DIARY, 20 JUNE, 1897

« **BEFORE**

Celebrations marking the fiftieth anniversary of previous monarchs had been decidedly low-key.

GOLDEN JUBILEE PRECEDENTS
The 50th anniversaries of both **Henry III « 21** and **Edward III « 21** had passed quietly. There was more enthusiasm in 1809, however, when a nation at war marked the Golden Jubilee of **George III « 48–49** with country-wide festivities. Owing to the King's illness, the Royal Family took part only by accompanying him to a private church service in Windsor, followed by a fireworks display.

Victoria at St Paul's Cathedral, 22 June 1897
Frailty left the Queen unable to climb the steps into the cathedral, so a short service of thanksgiving was held outside, which she watched from her open coach. The crowds' cheers in support of the Queen were deafening.

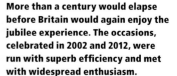

AFTER »

More than a century would elapse before Britain would again enjoy the jubilee experience. The occasions, celebrated in 2002 and 2012, were run with superb efficiency and met with widespread enthusiasm.

LEARNING FROM THE PAST
Britain's unparalleled experience in organizing displays of monarchical grandeur ensured that **Queen Elizabeth II's Golden Jubilee 260–61 »** and **Diamond Jubilee 282–83 »** celebrations were better arranged and choreographed, and probably even more popular, than those of her illustrious forebears.

The **Crown Jewels**

The symbolic regalia worn by the monarch for the coronation and other state ceremonies, these have been kept in the Tower of London since the early 14th century, after a series of thefts from their first home in Westminster Abbey.

1 The Armills of Queen Elizabeth II Created for the 1953 Coronation, these 22-carat gold bracelets were the gift of several Commonwealth nations. 2 Coronation spoon and Ampulla Holy oil is poured through the beak of the gold, eagle-shaped ampulla into the silver-gilt spoon to anoint the new monarch. The spoon was probably first used in 1199 at the Coronation service of King John. 3 St Edward's Crown Created for the coronation of Charles II in 1661 (along with the Sceptre with the Cross and the Sovereign's Orb, right), this replaced the medieval crown the Parliamentarians had melted down in 1649, and is used at the moment of coronation. Traditionally, the jewels adorning the crown were hired and returned but in 1911 it was permanently set with semi-precious stones, and now weighs 2.23kg (5lb). 4 Queen Victoria's small diamond crown This 10 cm- (4 in-) diameter diamond-encrusted crown was created at the Queen's own expense after the death of her husband, Prince Albert, and was designed to sit on top of the mourning veil she wore for the rest of her life. It was designed to be lightweight and comfortable. 5 The Sceptre with the Cross This was redesigned in 1910 to house the Cullinan I Diamond. 6 The Sovereign's Orb Representing Christ's dominion over the world, the orb is placed in the monarch's right hand during the coronation service to symbolize his or her role as Defender of the Faith.

Jewelled *cross-patté* (footed cross)

Spherical gold *Monde*

3 ST EDWARD'S CROWN

Arch encrusted with jewels

Crown is set with 440 gemstones

Solid gold frame

Ermine cap border

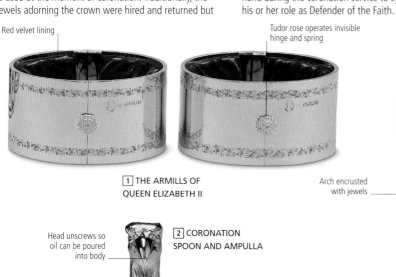

Red velvet lining

Tudor rose operates invisible hinge and spring

1 THE ARMILLS OF QUEEN ELIZABETH II

Head unscrews so oil can be poured into body

2 CORONATION SPOON AND AMPULLA

Base (and wings) added in 1661 for the coronation of Charles II

Freshwater pearl

4 QUEEN VICTORIA'S
SMALL DIAMOND CROWN

5 THE SCEPTRE
WITH THE CROSS

Removable openwork
silver-frame arches make
crown more versatile

Crown is set with
1,187 brilliant- and
rose-cut diamonds in
open-backed mounts

Velvet cap

Step-cut
emerald

Faceted
amethyst
Monde

Sturdy enamelled
setting holds 530-carat
(106g/3.74oz) diamond

Emerald sits at centre of
cross encrusted with
rose-cut diamonds and
decorated with pearls

Octagonal step-cut
amethyst *Monde*

6 THE SOVEREIGN'S ORB

Drop-shaped
Cullinan I diamond

Enamelled
collar covers a
joint between
sections of rod

Hollow gold sphere
mounted with emeralds,
rubies, sapphires, and
diamonds set between
single rows of pearls

End of an Era

By the time Victoria's 64-year reign came to an end, the majority of her millions of subjects worldwide had known no other monarch. Her passing was not just an important moment for the British crown; it marked the end of an era.

Contemporaries were convinced that the coincidence in 1901 of Victoria's death and the close of a century was deeply significant. For the journalist RD Blumenfeld, "perhaps the most glorious era in English history" had ended. Writing a short time afterwards, HG Wells preferred to look forwards: "the supreme dramatic phase in the story of England is about to come". Both men agreed on one thing, however: life would never be the same again.

The Diamond Jubilee was followed by three hard years. Victoria, painfully lame, was plagued by cataracts, and subject to memory lapses. Her affection for the Munshi (see p.61) unsettled palace life, and the death of her son-in-law, Emperor Friedrich II of Germany, troubled her. Nevertheless, she kept in touch with public affairs, inspecting troops from a wheelchair, and celebrating the victory at Omdurman in the Sudan. Accounts of this battle, however, suggested it was a one-sided massacre and nothing to celebrate. When a war against the Boers of South Africa was going badly, she remained obstinately optimistic and sent the soldiers chocolate. She kept her diary until her last days, and still bombarded politicians, soldiers, and naval officers with streams of letters.

The end finally came at Osborne House on the Isle of Wight. The family, including Kaiser Wilhelm, had gathered beforehand, and her son, the future Edward VII, was at her bedside. She had made the arrangements for her own funeral. Wrapped in her wedding veil, her body was taken to Windsor Castle. Here it was laid inside a half-ton coffin (actually there were three, one inside the other like Russian dolls) and carried on a gun carriage through the streets of the town for a service in St George's Chapel on 2 February. After lying in state for two days, the coffin was taken to Frogmore Mausoleum in Windsor Great Park where Victoria was laid to rest beside her dear Albert.

For several days, the nation was gripped by a sense of profound shock as the reality of Victoria's passing sank in. In the words of Elizabeth Longford, "One phrase was on many lips – God help us".

"Today seems very curious – pubs shut… Streets seem deserted."

LONDONER JC DIX, WRITING IN A LETTER TO HIS BROTHER, 2 FEBRUARY 1901

History in the making
Silent crowds line the streets of Windsor as Queen Victoria's funeral cortège passes by on 2 February 1901. Owing to a last-minute technical hitch, the gun-carriage bearing the coffin was hauled by a team of sailors rather than horses of the Royal Artillery.

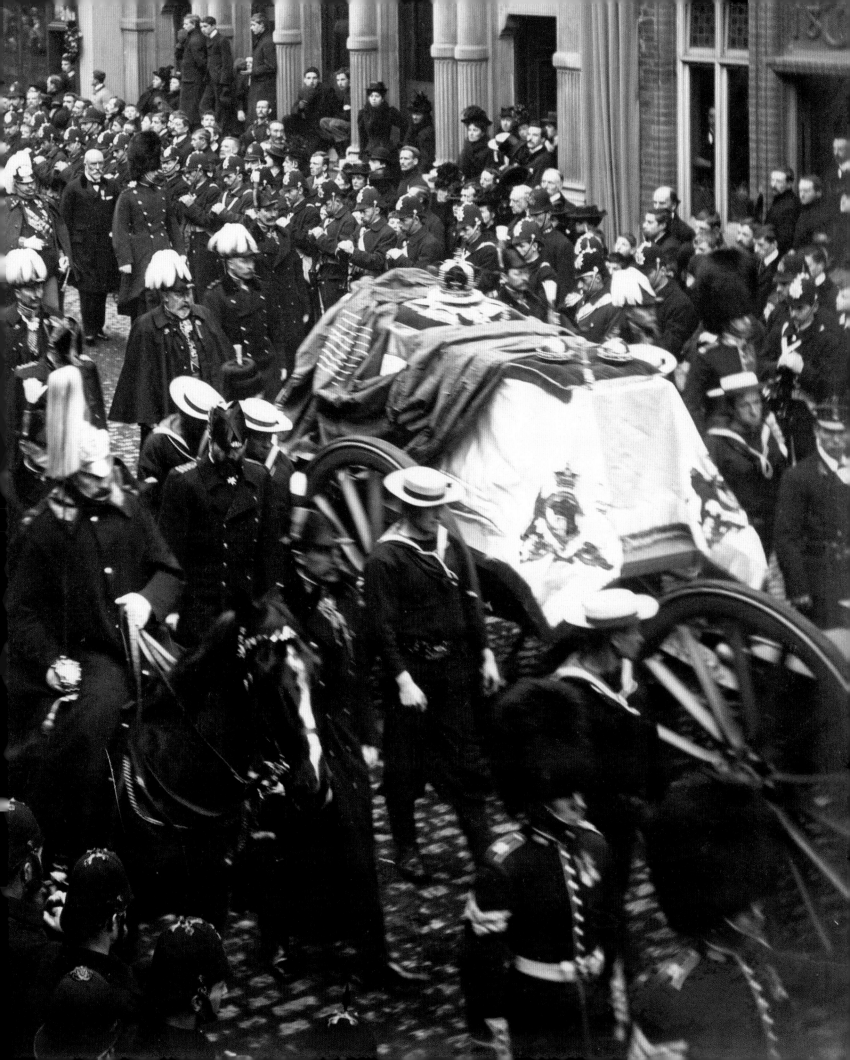

Born 1841 Died 1910

Edward VII

> "King Edward is the **first...** to be **attended** in his coronation by... **statesmen** from our self-governing colonies."
>
> *THE TIMES*, 1902

His Imperial Majesty King Edward VII
Though Edward VII's parents had forbidden him from joining the army, English painter and illustrator, Sir Luke Fildes, considered a military pose and uniform appropriate for the coronation portrait of the head of the world's most powerful empire.

Albert Edward was the second child and first son of Queen Victoria and Prince Albert (see pp.60–61). As a boy, he was subjected to a rigorous education designed by his father to make him the ideal modern constitutional monarch. It was not a success. Bertie was no scholar, and his failings in the classroom added to a sense of inadequacy engendered by his mother's dislike of small children.

After fruitless months at the universities of Edinburgh and Oxford, and excluded from a career in the army by his parents, the heir apparent developed a new style of royal visit. In his role as Prince of Wales, he toured overseas and attended important opening ceremonies at home. Three royal tours stand out.

Prince Albert Edward
Edward Albert, Prince of Wales, and Princess Alexandra (1844–1925) are seen here with their first child, Prince Albert Victor (1864–92). The boy led a troubled life and died before both his parents.

The first, a four-month trip round the United States and Canada, persuaded New Yorkers to say prayers for the British Royal Family for the first time since 1774. The 1875–76 visit to India prepared the ground for his mother's acceptance of the title Empress of India. His 1903 trip to Paris, made as King, helped promote good relations between Britain and its oldest enemy.

Playboy Prince
The Prince's easy, non-judgemental manner won him many friends, though not all of them had gained his parents' approval. In 1863, at the age of 21, he married Princess Alexandra of Denmark. The relationship remained amicable and, even when Edward was involved with someone else, Alexandra chose not to protest. Queen Victoria, however, was less understanding. Where her husband Albert's life had been all science, politics, welfare, and earnest causes, her son's was all cigars, wine, shooting,

> "I thought **everyone must know** that a short jacket is… worn with a silk hat at a **private** view in the morning."
>
> EDWARD VII TO HIS PRIVATE SECRETARY

horse-racing, and feasting; he was even named in court cases involving divorce and betting. Style mattered to him, too. It was Edward VII who started the fashion of leaving the bottom button of a waistcoat undone. His less frivolous side led him to patronize the arts, including founding the Royal College of Music.

Delayed coronation
Albert Edward was 59 when he acceded to the throne as Edward VII. He was a highly popular figurehead and, to ensure every detail of his coronation was in place, the ceremony was postponed until 26 June 1902, more than a year after his accession. On 24 June, however, the King underwent emergency surgery for acute appendicitis, and the coronation was delayed until 9 August. Alexandra was crowned Queen immediately after the King. Despite the fact that some foreign delegations had returned home, it was a great success and set the tone for future coronations.

Uncle of Europe
Edward had never shown much interest in politics and Victoria had fed this apathy by denying him access to state papers until the 1890s. As King, Edward VII continued much as before. His most valuable role was as an unofficial ambassador for peace abroad. Related to the Royal Families of Belgium, Bulgaria, Denmark, Spain Germany, Greece, Portugal, Norway, Romania, Russia, and Sweden, he used his position as "Uncle of Europe" to foster good relations. At home, the generous-hearted King favoured alleviating the lot of the poor and

The coronation that never was
These tickets were issued for the coronation in Westminster Abbey of Edward VII and Queen Alexandra, first planned for 26 June 1902, and for the procession two days later. Both were cancelled due to the King's illness, and the coronation rearranged for 9 August.

disadvantaged, but disliked radicalism. For example, he disapproved of giving women the vote in parliamentary elections, and was opposed to Irish Home Rule. His most active political participation was to promote the modernization of the armed forces.

At the very end of his life he was forced into the centre of the political arena. In 1909, to pay for old age pensions and further battleship building, the Liberal firebrand chancellor Lloyd George proposed a 2 per cent tax on those earning more than £5,000 a year. Defying parliamentary convention, the Conservative-dominated House of Lords rejected the proposal. This was a constitutional matter, so Edward had to be involved. He urged moderation, advising the Lords to accept a bill from the popularly elected House of Commons. The Conservatives refused and forced a general election. The new House of Commons then planned a law curbing the Lords' power of veto. As the peers would never accept such a move, to get it through the House of Lords the King had to be prepared to appoint enough Liberal peers to outvote the Conservatives. Throughout the whole process, Edward VII sought compromise. In the end, he did not have to make the "disgusting" decision to create new peers. On 6 May 1910, he suffered a number of heart attacks and died. People mourned the first sovereign for centuries to have truly won their hearts. It is fitting testament to this affection that the years between Victoria's death and World War One are commonly referred to as "Edwardian".

Royal hunter
King Edward VII, here posing with a shotgun, was a devotee of the hunt. Like many of his royal predecessors, his quarry included women as well as wild animals.

TIMELINE

- **9 November 1841** Queen Victoria gives birth to her first son, the Prince of Wales, in Buckingham Palace, London.

- **25 January 1842** Given his father's name, the boy is christened as Albert Edward at St George's Chapel, Windsor Castle.

- **1860** Albert Edward becomes the first heir to the British throne ever to visit North America.

- **1861** The Prince of Wales's affair with actress Nellie Clifden brings Prince Albert to Cambridge to remonstrate with his son; Victoria later blames the Prince's behaviour for bringing on her husband's fatal illness.

- **1862** The Prince of Wales undertakes a popular tour of the Middle East.

- **1863** Marries Princess Alexandra of Denmark.

- **1870** The Prince of Wales is called as a witness in a high-profile divorce case.

- **1871** National rejoicing at the recovery of the Prince of Wales from typhoid helps the Royal Family regain some lost popularity.

CORONATION STATIONERY, 1902

- **1883** Demonstrating an interest in the arts, the Prince of Wales opens the Royal College of Music.

- **14 January 1892** Death from influenza of the Prince of Wales' elder son, the controversial Prince Albert Victor, who some have claimed was Jack the Ripper. Aged almost 50, the Prince of Wales is finally permitted to see Cabinet Papers.

- **22 January 1901** Death of Queen Victoria and accession of Albert Edward, Prince of Wales, who chooses the title Edward VII.

- **9 August 1902** After the King is successfully operated on for appendicitis, his coronation finally takes place in Westminster Abbey; Queen Alexandra is crowned alongside him.

- **1903** Edward VII makes a formal visit to Paris, where he is warmly welcomed.

- **1908** Controversially, the King summons the new Prime Minister, HH Asquith, all the way to Biarritz to have his post officially sanctioned. Edward VII undertakes an impressive state visit to Russia on behalf of Britain, helping ease tension between the two imperial powers.

- **1909–10** Edward VII urges compromise on the House of Commons, which is divided over the House of Lords' powers of legislative veto.

- **6 May 1910** Edward VII dies of heart failure.

2

THE HOUSE OF WINDSOR

1911–1947

THE HOUSE OF WINDSOR
1911–1947

1911		1918		1923	

22 JUNE 1911
George V is crowned.

4 AUGUST 1914
Britain declares war on Germany.

»George V Coronation cup

DECEMBER 1914
Queen's Work for Women Fund created by Queen Mary to supply clothing for the army. George V visits British Field HQ on Western Front for the first time. German navy raids Scarborough, Hartlepool, and Whitby, killing 137 and injuring 592.

7 MAY 1915
Sinking of the *Lusitania* kills 1,198 civilians.

≫ Graves of soldiers, many of whom died in the Battle of the Somme, in Ovillers Military Cemetery, Picardie, northern France

31 MAY 1915
German Zeppelins bomb London.

9 JANUARY 1916
Last British troops evacuated from Gallipoli, Turkey, as the Ottoman Empire triumphs.

2 MARCH 1917
George V's cousin, Tsar Nicholas II, abdicates.

17 JULY 1917
George V issues proclamation changing name of British royal house from German-sounding Saxe-Coburg-Gotha to Windsor.

FEBRUARY 1918
The King gives Royal Assent to the Representation of the People Act giving women of property over 30 the vote.

17 JULY 1918
Tsar Nicholas II and his family murdered by Bolshevik revolutionaries, sending shock waves through the Royal Families of Europe.

MAY 1916
Britain's wheat supply is depleted. The King entreats families to reduce bread consumption. The Women's Land Army is established to increase agricultural productivity.

1 JULY–18 NOVEMBER 1916
Battle of the Somme. More than one million soldiers die.

11 NOVEMBER 1918
Germany signs Armistice agreement with Britain. A letter from George V is reproduced and distributed to all returning prisoners of war – the first ever mass communication from a reigning monarch.

11 NOVEMBER 1920
King George V unveils the Cenotaph war memorial in Whitehall, London. The body of the Unknown Warrior – an unidentified British soldier who died in World War I – is buried at Westminster Abbey.

21 NOVEMBER 1920
The Irish Republican Army (IRA) kills 14 British undercover agents in Dublin. In retaliation the Auxiliary Division of the Royal Irish Constabulary open fire on a crowd at a Gaelic Athletic Association Football match in Croke Park, killing 13 spectators and 1 player and wounding 60.

JUNE 1921
Unemployment reaches 2.2 million.

11 NOVEMBER 1921
First Poppy Day – memorial day for soldiers who died in World War I – held.

≪ Poppy commemorating World War 1

1922
Following World War I, British Empire is at its greatest ever extent, ruling over one-quarter of the world's population.

DECEMBER 1922
Irish Free State is formed with George V as its monarch. Northern Ireland parliament votes to remain part of United Kingdom.

26 APRIL 1923
Albert, Duke of York, marries Elizabeth Bowes-Lyon at Westminster Abbey.

≫ Marriage of The Duke and Duchess of York

23 APRIL 1924
George V makes first ever royal radio broadcast, opening the British Empire Exhibition in a purpose-built stadium at Wembley.

16 JANUARY 1926
BBC radio play about a workers' uprising in London causes panic.

21 APRIL 1926
Birth of future Queen Elizabeth II.

3 MAY 1926
General strike sweeps the nation, provoking fears of revolution.

13 MAY 1927
George V changes his title to King of the United Kingdom of Great Britain and Northern Ireland, acknowledging that the Irish Free State is no longer part of the kingdom.

1929
The BBC makes the first experimental TV transmission.

DECEMBER 1930
Unemployment increases to 2.5 million.

WEDDING GROUP.
THEIR HIGHNESSES – THE DUCHESS OF YORK. THE DUKE OF YORK. H.M. THE KING.
THE EARL OF STRATHMORE. H.M. THE QUEEN.

The ancient certainties of Victorian and Edwardian life, when Britain was the centre of a vast empire, and the divisions of class went largely unquestioned, were crumbling. The beginning of the modern era, these crucial decades were years of world war and revolution. They witnessed the collapse of the British Empire, the fall of many European monarchies, the rise of fascism and communism in Europe, and at home, the growth of socialism and the women's movement. If the British monarchy was to survive, it was essential to adapt to the new realities and to mould a constitutional monarchy fit for a more egalitarian nation.

1931

1938

1943

»

1931
Edward, the eldest son of George V, organizes the National Relief Fund for Britain's many unemployed.

24 AUGUST 1931
The Great Depression brings about a national crisis. On advice of George V, an all-party government is formed.

10 DECEMBER 1935
English physicist James Chadwick wins Nobel Prize for discovery of the neutron.

20 JANUARY 1936
King George V dies. Edward, Prince of Wales, succeeds as King Edward VIII.

❯ Portrait of Edward VIII

9 JULY 1938
Gas masks issued to all British civilians.

29 SEPTEMBER 1938
Prime Minister Neville Chamberlain and Hitler sign the Munich Agreement, allowing Germany to annex parts of Czechoslovakia, which it calls the Sudetenland.

JANUARY 1940
Britain calls up two million 19- to 27-year-olds for military service. Food rationing introduced.

» Ration pack supplied to British soldiers on active service

MARCH–APRIL 1945
Last enemy action on British soil as a V-1 flying bomb strikes Datchworth, Hertfordshire. On 15 April British troops liberate the Bergen-Belsen concentration camp.

SPECIAL RATION TYPE C
27 P/21
CONTENTS
BOILED SWEETS
FRUIT BAR
SWEET BISCUITS
OATMEAL MUNCH
CHEWING GUM
J.B.B. LTD. PKD.

11 DECEMBER 1931
Statute of Westminster is the first step in the transformation of the Empire into the Commonwealth.

OCTOBER 1932
Oswald Mosley founds British Fascist Party. Hunger March arrives in London from Scotland. Several violent clashes with police.

27 APRIL 1939
National Conscription introduced – all men aged 21 and over have to undergo six months' military training.

4 JUNE 1940
Dunkirk evacuation ends. Churchill makes his "We shall fight on the beaches" speech.

JULY--OCTOBER 1940
The Battle of Britain, a German air campaign against Britain, begins. Germany launches the London Blitz – 57 consecutive nights of bomb raids.

MAY–SEPTEMBER 1943
Dambuster raids and Allied invasions of Sicily and mainland Italy boost morale.

8 MAY 1945
Churchill makes a victory speech and appears on the balcony of Buckingham Palace with the Royal Family. Street parties are held throughout the country to celebrate what was being referred to as Victory in Europe (VE) Day.

25 DECEMBER 1932
George V delivers the first Royal Christmas Day message on BBC radio.

9 FEBRUARY 1933
Oxford Union debating society passes a motion stating "This house will in no circumstances fight for its king and country."

JUNE 1939
George VI and Queen Elizabeth visit the US and Canada – whose support will be vital if there is war.

NOVEMBER–DECEMBER 1940
Blitz continues in industrial cities including Coventry, Birmingham. Manchester, and Liverpool, with hundreds of casualties.

1941
As the war spreads into the Middle East and Asia, the National Service Act is passed.

12 AUGUST 1933
Churchill makes first public speech on dangers of German re-armament.

21 JANUARY 1934
Around 10,000 attend Mosley's British Union of Fascists rally in Birmingham.

7 MARCH 1936
Germany re-occupies Rhineland, a demilitarized zone as per the treaty of Versailles.

OCTOBER 1936
Battle of Cable Street between British Union of Fascists and anti-fascist demonstrators. 207 unemployed miners march from Jarrow to London.

LATE AUGUST/EARLY SEPTEMBER 1939
Children are evacuated from cities throughout Britain; army and navy are mobilized; blackout is imposed across the country. Britain declares war on Germany on 3 September.

❯ King George VI and US President Franklin Roosevelt

26 JANUARY 1942
First US troops destined to fight in Europe arrive in Belfast.

25 FEBRUARY 1942
15-year-old Princess Elizabeth registers for war service.

NOVEMBER 1942
Major Allied victory at 2nd Battle of Alamein, followed by Allied victory at Tobruk.

❯ Elizabeth II aiding the war effort

11 JULY 1934
A total of 41 squadrons added to RAF as part of new air defence programme.

6 MAY 1935
An ailing King George V celebrates his Silver Jubilee.

10 DECEMBER 1936
Edward VIII abdicates. Prince Albert becomes King George VI.

12 MAY 1937
George VI crowned.

NOVEMBER
Salisbury Plain and South Hams of Devon evacuated as preparations are made for the Normandy Landings.

6 JUNE
On D-Day, 155,000 Allied troops land on the beaches of Normandy.

29 MAY 1946
Princess Elizabeth and Philip Mountbatten are photographed together for the first time.

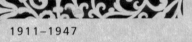

Born 1865 Died 1936

George V

"You can't shake hands with a clenched fist."

GEORGE V, ON PEACEFUL NEGOTIATIONS DURING WORLD WAR I

Inheriting the throne from his flamboyant, crowd-pleasing father Edward VII in 1910, King George V inevitably appeared uncharismatic by comparison. He was a dutiful character of simple tastes, behaving and dressing like an average English landowner. His favourite pursuits were hunting, sailing, and stamp-collecting. The responsibilities of his public role weighed upon him, and he far preferred a quiet private life. Yet this seemingly dull king proved the ideal monarch to lead his country through troubled times.

Career in the navy

As the second son of the Prince of Wales, George was not born to rule. He was trained for a career as a naval officer, while his elder brother Albert Victor was groomed as the future king. Prince George performed his naval functions competently, rising in rank on merit, and enjoyed the life at sea. This tranquil, relatively normal existence ended abruptly at his brother's untimely death in 1892.

Future king

Aged 26, George inherited his brother's role as the future king and also his brother's betrothed, Mary of Teck, known as "May". Despite the unfortunate circumstances leading

Strong ties
The young prince George is photographed with his mother Queen Alexandra. Edward VII and Alexandra were warm, loving parents, and George formed an especially close bond with his mother.

to their union, a solid love and respect developed between the couple after the wedding, if not before it. George was to be a faithful and devoted husband who depended heavily on his wife's support.

Family life

It was typical of George's modest tastes that he chose York Cottage in the grounds of the Sandringham Estate as a family home. The royal couple had six children – David (1894), Albert (1895), Mary (1897), Henry (1900), George (1902), and John (1905), who was an epileptic and kept separate from the rest of the family, dying aged 13. As a father George was a strict disciplinarian and emotionally reserved. It has often been said that his sons were damaged by the fear he inspired. It is more likely, however, that they were hurt by their parents'

King George V
The King poses for an official portrait in his coronation robes. At heart, a man of simple tastes, George V submitted dutifully to the "fancy dress" required for royal ceremonial occasions.

frequent absences because, after the accession of Edward VII in 1901, the royal couple were required to leave their children for six months at a time to make official visits to distant parts of the empire, including Australia and India. The children were raised by hired hands.

Accession to the throne

The death of Edward VII in May 1910 was a personal blow to George. "I have lost," he wrote in his diary, "the best of friends and the best of fathers." He took the throne in a period of acute political crisis, with a Liberal government in conflict with the Conservative-dominated House of Lords, suffragettes campaigning for votes for women, Irish nationalists pressing for Home Rule, and trade unionists threatening mass strikes. Fortunately Edward had taken care to educate his son in the business of monarchy and provide him with sensible advisors. George V performed his functions as a constitutional monarch with serious dedication. Although a conservative in politics as well as on moral issues, he scrupulously avoided partisan involvement in political issues, while attempting to exercise influence in favour of compromise and the peaceful resolution of disputes.

> "Try living on **their wages** before you **judge** them."
>
> GEORGE V, 1926

World War I

George V's role in World War I and its aftermath (see pp.80–81) won him widespread respect and affection among the British people, but the fall from power of his relatives Tsar Nicholas II in Russia and Kaiser Wilhelm II in Germany were a sharp

Family portrait
Photographed at Balmoral in 1906, George stands next to Mary, with baby John in her arms. The other children are, left to right, Princess Mary and the princes Harry, George, David (later Edward VIII), and Albert (George VI).

reminder of the potential for popular disaffection. The monarchy would have to work to maintain its position as a focus for loyalty in the United Kingdom and the empire. Although much of the effort to popularize royalty devolved upon his eldest son, the charismatic Prince of Wales (see Edward VIII, pp.90–91), George V accepted the need to make contact with his people, most strikingly in the use of the new medium of radio (see pp.88–89). In 1924 he had the formal task of inviting newly elected Ramsay Macdonald to form Britain's first Labour government, an event regarded by many people at the time as heralding a social revolution. The King took a more relaxed view of Labour's rise to power. "They have different ideas to ours as

they are all socialists," he told his mother, "but they ought to be given a chance and ought to be treated fairly".

Illness and death

From the mid-1920s the King's health went into serious decline. Suffering from lung disease, he almost died in the autumn of 1928 and the following year underwent two major operations. His grandchildren, including the future Elizabeth II, were a great comfort to him in his declining years. He showed them greater warmth than he had his own children. He disapproved of his eldest son, the Prince of Wales, much preferring his more dutiful second son. There is no doubt George V was out of step with his times. He was a narrow-minded conservative, disapproving of most innovative social customs, from divorce and cocktails to women smoking. But it was his respectability and simple decency that made him so well liked by his people. After his death in January 1936, more than 800,000 people filed past his body lying in state at Westminster Hall.

Imperial monarch

A souvenir postcard celebrating George V's coronation emphasizes the King's role as a focus for the loyalty of the far-flung British Empire and the different nations of the United Kingdom.

TIMELINE

- **3 June 1865** Born at Marlborough House, London, second son of Edward, the Prince of Wales, and Alexandra.

- **January 1892** Becomes his father's heir after his elder brother dies; is made the Duke of York.

- **6 July 1893** Marries Mary of Teck at St James's Palace, London.

- **November 1901** Becomes the Prince of Wales when his father accedes to the throne.

- **6 May 1910** Accedes to the throne on his father's death.

- **1911** Crowned in Westminster Abbey, London (22 June); formally presented as the Emperor of India at a Durbar in Delhi (12 December).

- **July 1914** Hosts an all-party conference in an attempt to resolve deadlock over Ireland's future.

- **4 August 1914** Britain enters World War I.

- **October 1915** Injured by a fall from his horse while visiting British troops in France.

- **March 1917** Rejects asylum to Tsar Nicholas II after the Tsar abdicates the Russian throne.

- **17 July 1917** Changes the name of the royal house from Saxe-Coburg-Gotha to Windsor.

- **11 November 1918** Armistice ends the fighting in World War I.

- **11 November 1920** Unveils the Cenotaph in Whitehall as a remembrance of the war dead.

- **22 June 1921** Opens the first parliament of Northern Ireland at Stormont, Belfast.

- **23 April 1924** At the opening of the British Empire Exhibition at Wembley, becomes the first monarch to speak on radio.

- **May 1926** During Britain's General Strike, urges the government to adopt a conciliatory approach to strikers.

- **1928** Falls seriously ill because of lung disease, convalescent through to 1930.

THE CONVALESCENT KING WITH THE QUEEN

- **25 December 1932** Makes the first royal Christmas radio broadcast to the nation.

- **6 May 1935** After 25 years on the throne, his Silver Jubilee is celebrated with festivities.

- **20 January 1936** Dies at Sandringham; interred at St George's Chapel, Windsor Castle (28 January).

With so many of Queen Victoria's descendants on European thrones, great power relationships were a family affair for the British monarchy.

EUROPE DIVIDED
By 1907, Europe was divided between the alliances of France, Russia, and Britain on one side, and Germany and Austria on the other. The British royals had cousins on both sides. Kaiser Wilhelm II was Victoria's grandson and Tsar Nicholas II was married to Victoria's granddaughter. The Royal Family disliked its German cousin, but maintained relations.

KING GEORGE V WITH KAISER WILHELM II

When Britain declared war on Germany, entering World War I on 4 August 1914, King George V and other members of the Royal Family had to appear on the balcony of Buckingham Palace to acknowledge cheering crowds. Like the majority of his subjects, however, King George was more horrified than enthused at the onset of war. His most immediate concern, expressed that evening in his diary, was for the safety of Prince Albert (the future George VI), who was serving as an officer in the Royal Navy.

Role of the Royals
Over the following four years the war expanded into a conflict of awesome dimensions, costing a million British and Commonwealth lives and requiring the mobilization of the entire resources of society. The role of a constitutional monarch in this "total war" had to be invented, as there was no precedent to follow. George V played no part in determining war strategy and had only a limited influence on senior appointments – in 1915 he supported moves to replace General Sir John French by General Douglas Haig as commander of British armies in France, but this was exceptional. Instead, the Royal Family focused on its ability to affect morale and inspire social solidarity.

George V was tireless in his duties. He made official visits to the Western Front in France, talking with generals, inspecting troops, awarding medals – he conferred 50,000 decorations with his own hands – and witnessing some of the devastation of trench warfare. Meeting the gravely wounded was the

Viewing the battlefield
George V surveys the devastation wreaked by the British victory at Messines in 1917. The Royal Family was fully aware of the harsh realities of the warfare in the trenches.

The Royals in Wartime

In 1914, four years after George V's accession, Britain was plunged into the most deadly conflict in its history. Throughout World War I, the Royal Family fulfilled its role as a focus for national unity and patriotism. Other European monarchies collapsed under the strain of war, but George V emerged more secure than ever in his people's affections.

Inspecting the troops
King George V meets British troops on a visit to the Western Front in France during World War I. The king travelled to the front five times in the course of the conflict.

"It is a **terrible catastrophe,** but it is **not our fault.**"

GEORGE V, ON DECLARATION OF WAR, 4 AUGUST 1914

most painful royal duty – the king visited more than 300 hospitals in the course of the war. On one of his trips to the Western Front, in October 1915, he was injured by a fall from his horse, fracturing his pelvis, becoming himself a minor war casualty. He never fully recovered – the injury pained him for the rest of his life. When German Zeppelin airships and Gotha aeroplanes bombed London, King George and Queen Mary toured bomb-damaged areas. Recognizing the democratic nature of a conflict that involved the nation, they were careful to include factory districts and the working-class East End of London in their excursions.

The Royal Family could not, of course, in any real sense share the sufferings and deprivations of the British people at war, but symbolic gestures had impressive impact. In April 1915, when the government was pressing for potentially highly unpopular

limits on alcohol consumption, intended to increase the efficiency of industrial workers, George V himself "took the pledge", renouncing alcohol for the duration of the war. Few British workers followed his example, but it undoubtedly lessened the resentment brought about by anti-drink laws.

Three of the royal children were old enough to participate in the war effort. The Prince of Wales (the future Edward VIII) served in the British Army as a staff officer, although he was barred from entering combat. Prince Albert did see action, taking part in the battle of Jutland in 1916 as a sub-lieutenant on board HMS *Collingwood*. Princess Mary, only 17 years old when the war began, promoted women's involvement in war work such as nursing in military hospitals and the "Land Girls" farm labor. She herself trained to become a nurse in the last year of the war.

Family ties

The Royal Family participated fully in the rabid anti-German sentiment generated by the war. The king wrote in his diary: "I shall never submit to those brutal Germans and I am sure the British nation is of the same opinion." Still, at a time when dogs known as German shepherds were being hastily renamed Alsatians and owners walking dachshunds were stoned in the street, the Royal Family was saddled with the embarrassingly Germanic name Saxe-Coburg-Gotha. Voices were occasionally heard insinuating that the royals were not truly British. Such comments incensed the King, who remarked: "I may be uninspiring, but I'll be damned if I'm alien." In July 1917, to settle the issue, he proclaimed a new dynastic name, adopting the unimpeachably English "Windsor."

In truth, only the most aggressive anti-royalists could imagine George V

Royal nurse

The young Princess Mary served as a part-time nurse in a London hospital in 1918. Gift boxes paid for by a fund bearing her name were distributed to all British soldiers and sailors at Christmas 1914.

PRINCESS MARY GIFT BOX

and his family being complicit with Kaiser Wilhelm. In spring 1917, however, George's kinship with Tsar Nicholas II presented a more pressing problem. Forced to abdicate by a popular uprising at the start of the Russian Revolution, the Tsar sought to take his family into exile in Britain. The British government saw no objection, but George V and his advisors did. Knowing that a section of the British people viewed the Tsar as a tyrant and had welcomed his overthrow, they did not want the monarchy to risk unpopularity by being associated with him. The Tsar was thus denied refuge in Britain. When, the following year, he and his family were murdered by Bolshevik revolutionaries, George V felt both grief and guilt. Yet the judgment was surely correct that the association of the Royal Family with the Tsar might have alienated a part of the British working class.

At the Armistice in November 1918, the King found himself hailed by

Call to arms

A poster calls for volunteers to join the British army. Every one of the 8 million British and imperial troops who fought in the war served officially in the name of the king.

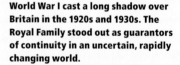

cheering crowds, as he had been at the outbreak of war. His straightforward sense of duty and dogged courage had earned him widespread respect and admiration. Britain's wartime prime minister, David Lloyd George, later wrote: "One outstanding reason for the high level of loyalty and patriotic effort which the people of this country maintained was the attitude and conduct of King George."

AFTER

World War I cast a long shadow over Britain in the 1920s and 1930s. The Royal Family stood out as guarantors of continuity in an uncertain, rapidly changing world.

REMEMBRANCE CEREMONIES

After the war there was a strongly felt need for regular remembrance of those who had sacrificed their lives. George V played a prominent role in the early remembrance ceremonies, laying the first wreath at the Cenotaph in November 1920.

MONARCHY AND NATIONHOOD

Participation in the war gave Commonwealth countries an increased sense of identity and nationhood. The monarchy became vital as a symbolic link between Britain and effectively independent Canada, Australia, and New Zealand.

Parliamentary procession
King George V and Queen Mary, seated in the Gold State Coach, are at the heart of this solemn, courtly procession on its way to the State Opening of Parliament in 1924.

ROYAL RESIDENCE

Buckingham Palace

The official London residence of the British monarch since 1837, Buckingham Palace is also a working palace, where Queen Elizabeth carries out her ceremonial and official duties. It is the principal venue for state occasions and forms the backdrop to many national celebrations.

Buckingham Palace evolved out of the much smaller Buckingham House, built by the Duke of Buckingham in the early 18th century. A grand town house, which George III later bought for his wife, Queen Charlotte, it became known as the Queen's House, and 14 of George III's 15 children were born there.

Architect John Nash was responsible for modernizing and enlarging Buckingham House into a palace in the 1820s for George IV. The King wished to remodel London as a neoclassical city and he needed a palace that would reflect Britain's standing in the world. With Greek revival colonnades and pedimented porticoes enclosing a grand forecourt, and a magnificent, Roman-style triumphal arch for processions, his design was regarded as an architectural masterpiece. But Nash had vastly exceeded his budget and, after the King's death in 1830, he was dismissed for overspending.

Edward Blore was appointed as Nash's replacement. There was a lot of unfinished work for him to do, including the fitting-out of the state apartments to Nash's designs. The new King, William IV, showed no interest in moving into the palace. In 1837 his successor, Queen Victoria, became the first monarch to use Buckingham Palace as her official residence in 1837.

The palace was certainly a theatrical setting for royal receptions, but the reality of living there turned out to be rather less luxurious. There were no bathrooms, so the Queen had to bathe in a portable bathtub, and the chimneys smoked so much that lighting fires was discouraged and the palace was freezing cold. The insufficient ventilation caused unpleasant odours, and when gas lamps were installed, there was serious concern about possible explosions. There were reports as well that the

staff, taking advantage of the teenage Queen, were lazy and that the palace was filthy and neglected.

In February 1845, Blore was instructed to prepare plans for a new wing, in part to provide space for Victoria's growing family. This wing meant that the triumphal arch had to be moved to its present site near Speaker's Corner, where it became known as Marble Arch. But the most significant element of Blore's design was the central balcony on the new main façade, incorporated at Prince Albert's suggestion, and used for the first time in 1851 for the inauguration of the Great Exhibition. »

Marking the Queen's birthday

Trooping the Colour takes place on Horse Guards Parade, where the Queen inspects her troops. The procession begins and ends at Buckingham Palace. The ceremony also marks the sovereign's official birthday, a tradition that goes back to 1748.

CONCLUSION OF TROOPING THE COLOUR AT BUCKINGHAM PALACE

Theatrical entrance
The state apartments are reached via the Grand
Staircase – a theatrical design by Nash, with its
gilded-bronze balustrade, illuminated by natural
light through an engraved and etched glass dome.

>> In Victoria's time the palace was a place of great entertainment. Famous contemporary musicians performed there, including Felix Mendelssohn and Johann Strauss II. There were extravagant costume balls, as well as more formal receptions and banquets.

When Queen Victoria was widowed in 1861 and withdrew from public life, she left Buckingham Palace, preferring

"The **wind moaned** in the chimneys like a thousand ghosts."

MARION CRAWFORD, GOVERNESS, ON HER FIRST NIGHT IN BUCKINGHAM PALACE

the relative intimacy of her other residences. The palace was seldom used, and, in response to the lack of royal interest, a note was found pinned to the railings in 1864, saying: "These commanding premises to be let or sold, in consequence of the late occupant's declining business."

After Victoria's death, Buckingham Palace became a hub for the glamorous set that circled around Edward VII and Queen Alexandra. Debutante balls and lavish parties were held in opulent rooms redecorated in fashionable belle époque cream and gold. Under George V, the emphasis returned to official entertaining, though he did arrange a series of command performances of jazz musicians, including Louis Armstrong in 1932, while Queen Mary oversaw the restoration and extension of the royal collection of art.

Pollution, meanwhile, had decayed the original soft French stone of the façade, and, in 1913, it was replaced with white Portland stone.

Despite all these improvement works, this was no fairy-tale palace, and in 1936, when George VI and Queen Elizabeth took up residence, they discovered a gloomy, dilapidated place with awkwardly placed electrical fittings, endless corridors, and chilly rooms infested with mice.

Under the present Queen, the palace has been restored and the emphasis is firmly on its role as official residence and reception venue. Around 50,000 people visit the palace each year as guests at banquets, lunches, dinners, receptions, and garden parties.

Following the crisis provoked by the annus horribilis of 1992, Buckingham Palace has been at the forefront of initiatives to make the royal family seem more approachable. In 1993 the state rooms were opened to the public for the first time (initially to finance the restoration of Windsor Castle) and the palace has continued to open every summer. To date, more than six million people have visited.

Open to the public
Some tours of the palace include the White Drawing Room, the royal art collection, and the ballroom, with the table laid as if for a state banquet.

WHITE DRAWING ROOM

PICTURE GALLERY

THE BALLROOM

Pomp and ceremony
Designed by Nash, the Throne Room is perhaps the
most majestic and dramatic of all the state rooms
in Buckingham Palace. It is used for coronation and
wedding photos, and to receive formal addresses.

The First King's Speech

George V became the first British monarch to make a studio broadcast when he addressed the people of his empire live on radio on Christmas Day 1932. The speech was heard by 20 million listeners in countries as distant as Canada, India, and Australia. Originally planned as a one-off event, the royal Christmas message became a tradition that is maintained today.

The British people first heard their King's voice on radio on 23 April 1924, when the fledgling British Broadcasting Company – then a private concern – transmitted the speech made by George V at the opening of the Empire Exhibition at Wembley Stadium. Since few people had wirelesses, the speeches were broadcast through loudspeakers in public places such as parks and department stores. In general though, George V was suspicious of radio, as of all other innovations, and was disinclined to involve himself in the new medium.

In 1932, the director-general of the now state-owned British Broadcasting Corporation (BBC), John Reith, needed a gimmick to launch the company's ambitious new Empire Service. He approached George V with a proposal for a Christmas broadcast and overcame the King's reluctance by giving him a guided tour of the BBC studios in London. The King was to speak from his home at Sandringham, an arrangement that required only the smallest possible disturbance of his routine. The text for the broadcast was written by ageing novelist and poet Rudyard Kipling, the "bard of empire".

On Christmas Day, people across the world heard a firm, gentle voice begin: "I speak now from my home and from my heart to you all; to men and women so cut off by the snows, the desert, or the sea, that only voices out of the air can reach them." People did indeed find it magical that the King's voice could be heard in their living room. Focusing largely on the technological achievement of radio, the brief speech was judged an impressive success. Such was the popular enthusiasm that George V agreed to broadcast every year, with his last Christmas message transmitted in 1935, less than a month before his death.

> **"To all – to each – I wish a Happy Christmas. God Bless You!"**
>
> **GEORGE V,** ROYAL CHRISTMAS MESSAGE, 1932

George V on air
King George V gave his first radio message from an office at Sandringham that had been transformed for the occasion into a temporary studio. In this photograph, George V delivers his 1933 Christmas Day message from the same makeshift studio.

Born 1894 Died 1972

Edward VIII

"I... do **hereby declare** my **irrevocable determination** to **renounce** the **throne**..."

EDWARD VIII, IN HIS *INSTRUMENT OF ABDICATION*, 10 DECEMBER 1936

Young Edward
As a young man, the future Edward VIII was a stylish figure who charmed the people of Britain and the empire. However, his personality was not well suited to the formal responsibilities of kingship.

First son of the Duke of York, the future George V, Edward was christened Edward Albert Christian George Andrew Patrick David – Edward after his deceased uncle; Albert after Queen Victoria's long-mourned spouse; and George, Andrew, David, and Patrick after the four patron saints of England, Scotland, Wales, and Ireland, respectively. Within the family, he was always known as David.

Edward had a strict upbringing; he commented on it later: "The laws of behaviour as revealed to a small boy tended to be ruled by a vast preponderance of 'don'ts'". His relationship with his father was neither close nor comfortable. Following the family tradition, Edward entered naval college, but George V's accession to the throne in 1910 truncated his eldest son's naval career, as it was considered unsuitable for the Prince of Wales.

Edward showed early signs of rebellion against his assigned role in life shortly after his father's coronation

in 1911. As a gesture designed to encourage Welsh loyalty to the crown, it was decided that Edward be formally invested as Prince of Wales at Caernarvon Castle. Since no such investiture had occurred for 600 years, a ceremony was invented with copious fanciful historical detail. The teenage Prince was required to wear a costume so ridiculous that, on the eve of the event, he declared he would refuse to take part. After a fierce row with his father, the Prince relented and the ceremony went ahead without a hitch. However, the fuss was indicative of the Prince's potential discomfort with the kind of royal duties that George V unquestioningly accepted.

Edward served as an army officer in World War I. He was denied an active role by order of Lord Kitchener, the secretary of state for war, who held that although the Prince's death would be an acceptable loss, his capture by the enemy might prove a severe embarrassment. Despite reduction to a passive role, however, Edward's service as an aide-de-camp on the staff of the commander in chief in France and later as a staff officer in the Mediterranean zone was sufficient to support a claim to have "done his bit" for the war effort.

Popular prince

After the shock of the war, with its heavy death toll, there was an urgent need to promote the Royal Family as a focus for loyalty. Young, suave, and charming, Edward was put to work touring the empire. He was received

Prince of Wales
Edward was 17 years old at the time of his investiture as Prince of Wales in 1911. The Prince was forced to wear a fanciful pseudo-historical costume, which caused him great embarrassment.

with particular warmth in Britain's dominions, where he was seen as a refreshing change from the old-fashioned George V. At the British Empire Exhibition, held at Wembley in 1924, the Canadian pavilion exhibited a life-size statue of Edward made of refrigerated butter. The prince was equally well-received by the British working class. He made well-publicized visits to industrial areas and promoted clubs for the unemployed, showing a comfortable and relaxed manner in the company of ordinary working men.

Unsuitable king

While Edward brought a welcome change to the image of British royalty in public, in private he behaved in a manner that appalled his father and worried the political elite. He mixed with the raffish, fashionable society of the 1920s and adopted its customs – drinking cocktails, dancing to jazz, and engaging in casual adultery. His affairs with married women, notably Freda Dudley Ward, Lady Furness, and finally, Wallis Simpson, were considered incompatible with the Royal Family's role as exemplars of the traditional moral order. A servile press kept the

Nazi visit
The Duke of Windsor inspects soldiers during his visit to Nazi Germany in 1937. The former king's close relations with the Nazi regime were a source of considerable disquiet for the British government.

social issues. He was critical of the government's complacent acceptance of high levels of unemployment in the 1930s, although his sympathies lay not with the socialists but with politician Oswald Mosley's Fascist

> ## "After I am **dead,** the boy will ruin himself in **12 months.**"
> GEORGE V, SPEAKING OF HIS SON EDWARD TO PRIME MINISTER STANLEY BALDWIN

British people in ignorance of these liaisons, but in private, George V disapproved of his eldest son's manners and morals, openly preferring his second son, Albert.

The Prince of Wales must have already harboured doubts about the desirability of becoming king. When his father's illness obliged him to take over many of the King's functions in the late 1920s, he found the tasks tedious and performed them unreliably. He chafed at the restrictions placed upon his expression of views on political and

movement. Conservative politicians feared that, once on the throne, he might breach the rules of constitutional monarchy and intervene in politics to their detriment.

None of these issues were known to the British people, who embraced their new monarch with enthusiasm at his accession in January 1936. The abdication crisis (see pp.92–93), precipitated by Edward's strong determination to marry Wallis Simpson, brought about a sudden and sharp disillusionment. The

abdication was in part a coup by the political establishment to remove a ruler they distrusted, but also an escape route for a king who had no enthusiasm for the rituals and responsibilities of his role. The politicians of the "king's party" who tried to keep Edward on the throne found that the monarch himself was a lukewarm supporter of their cause. Finally, on 10 December 1936, Edward signed an instrument of abdication, becoming the only British king ever to renounce the throne voluntarily.

Life in exile

Created Duke of Windsor, Edward married Simpson and settled in France. Although he received a title and financial support, the Duke was effectively cut off from his family, who took a dim view of his behaviour. The itch to intervene in public affairs led to an ill-judged visit by the Windsors to Nazi Germany in 1937, including a meeting with Hitler. After Britain and Germany went to war in 1939 the Duke was given employment with the British army in France, but rumours spread that the Windsors were engaged in traitorous contacts with the enemy.

After the fall of France, Prime Minister Winston Churchill, once one of Edward's keenest supporters, dispatched the Duke to the Bahamas – an exile lightly disguised by appointment to governorship of the islands. After the war, the Windsors returned to France, settling into the lifestyle of celebrity socialites. Over time, there was some defrosting of relations with the Royal Family and, at his death, Edward's body was brought back to England for interment in the Royal Burial Ground, Frogmore, at Windsor.

DUCHESS OF WINDSOR (1896–1986)

WALLIS SIMPSON

Born Bessie Wallis Warfield, Wallis Simpson grew up in Baltimore, Maryland, US. In the course of her first two marriages, to US Navy pilot Earl Spencer and American shipping executive Ernest Simpson, she became a socialite mixing in a decadent international set. After her marriage to Edward, she became Duchess of Windsor but was not allowed to be known as "Her Royal Highness". When she died in 1986 at her home in France, she was buried alongside Edward at the Royal Burial Ground.

TIMELINE

23 June 1894 Born at the White Lodge, Richmond, Surrey.

1907–09 Attends Osborne Naval College and the Royal Naval College at Dartmouth.

6 May 1910 Edward's father accedes to the throne as George V.

13 July 1911 Invested as Prince of Wales at Caernarvon Castle.

1912–14 Attends Magdalene College, Oxford, where he excels at sport but does not take a degree.

1914–18 Joins the Grenadier Guards and serves as a staff officer with the British army in France during World War I.

1916 Awarded the Military Cross for his role in World War I.

1919 Makes official visit to Canada and the US.

1920–21 Visits Australia, New Zealand, and India.

1924 Presides over the British Empire Exhibition.

1928–30 Performs many of the functions of a king during his father's illness and convalescence.

January 1931 Meets Wallis Simpson for the first time.

1934 Becomes involved with Wallis Simpson.

20 January 1936 Accedes to the throne on the death of George V.

August–September 1936 Holidays with Wallis Simpson in the Mediterranean.

27 October 1936 Wallis Simpson begins divorce proceedings against her second husband, Ernest Simpson.

16 November 1936 The King informs Stanley Baldwin that he intends to marry Simpson, precipitating the abdication crisis.

10 December 1936 Abdicates, renouncing the throne for himself and his descendants, and moves to France.

3 June 1937 Marries Wallis Simpson at the Chateau de Condé, near Tours, France.

October 1937 The Windsors make a visit to Nazi Germany, meeting Adolf Hitler.

September 1939 Outbreak of World War II; Edward is made a general and attached to the British military command in France.

June 1940 Flees France as it is overrun by German troops, and ends up in Portugal.

August 1940–March 1945 Sent by Winston Churchill to the Bahamas, where he serves as Governor.

1945 Returns to live in France, where he stays for the rest of his life.

28 May 1972 Dies at his home in Paris.

KING EDWARD VIII POSTAGE STAMP FROM 1936

Edward VIII's Abdication

The abdication crisis of 1936 is often seen as the romantic tragedy of a king who renounced the throne for love. But it was also a political plot in which a troublesome monarch was overthrown because he was considered unsuitable to reign.

Until December 1936, most of the British public had no idea that their monarchy was in crisis. Reports of Edward VIII's liaison with twice-divorced American socialite Wallis Simpson had appeared in foreign newspapers and magazines but were kept out of the British press. Instead, news focused on preparations for Edward's coronation, due to take place the following year. Britain's Conservative Prime Minister Stanley

BEFORE

When Edward VIII became king at age 41 on 20 January 1936, he seemed destined for a lengthy reign.

A PROMISING FUTURE
Edward was already well known to the British people and the empire through his prominent role as **Prince of Wales «90–91**. A more charismatic figure than his father, he had been sent on **tours of the Commonwealth** in the 1920s to encourage loyalty to the crown. He had also made well-publicized visits to **Depression-hit industrial areas of Britain** to show royal concern for the hardships of the working class. Since 1934, however, Edward had been involved with a married American woman, Wallis Simpson – a relationship that would cost him the crown.

Baldwin had, from the outset, serious doubts about the new king. Edward's father George V had ruled as an impeccable constitutional monarch, avoiding any public expression of opinion on political matters. He had also established the moral rectitude of the Royal Family as an example to the nation. Baldwin correctly surmised that Edward was unlikely either to keep out of politics – he was known to sympathize with politician Oswald Moseley's British Union of Fascists – or set a suitable moral example. Baldwin's concern for Edward's liaison with Simpson was shared by other figures of the establishment, including the head of the Church of England, Cosmo Lang.

Breaking point
In October, Baldwin confronted the King with cuttings from the foreign press reporting his summer holiday with Simpson in the Mediterranean. It was made clear to the King that the matter could not be kept under wraps indefinitely. Meanwhile, Simpson won

325 DAYS The duration of Edward VIII's reign.

a divorce ruling against her husband in a court in Ipswich, Suffolk, opening the way for a possible marriage to Edward. The drama came to a critical point at a meeting between the King and the Prime Minister on 16 November.

Edward informed Baldwin that he intended to marry Simpson. Baldwin replied that having an American divorcee as queen would be unacceptable to the British people, the Commonwealth, and the Church of England. Edward said that, if this were the case, he would abdicate rather than renounce the marriage.

Two days later, visiting the Welsh valleys, an area of high unemployment,

Performing a king's duties
Surrounded by heralds, Edward prepares for the State Opening of Parliament at the House of Lords on 3 November 1936. This would be the first and last time that he would carry out this ceremony.

the King commented in the presence of journalists that "something must be done" to find these people work. Widely reported in the press, this remark drew a favourable response as an expression of the King's concern for his people. Baldwin and his colleagues, however, interpreted it as a criticism of the government's economic policy and thus a wholly inappropriate intervention for a constitutional monarch.

As far as the British people were concerned, the abdication crisis began on 3 December. The decision to go public was triggered by an outspoken attack on the King's morals by Alfred Blunt, the Bishop of Bradford. Suddenly the situation was blazoned in newspaper headlines and on billboards across the country. By the time this occurred, the issue had narrowed to a simple choice. Edward would not withdraw from his plan to marry, while Baldwin and the British establishment were determined there should never be a Queen Wallis. Still, it was suggested that the idea might be acceptable if the marriage was morganatic, that is, Simpson would not enjoy the title and privileges of a queen. However, this proposal gained little support in Parliament and was opposed by Commonwealth leaders in Canada and Australia. Baldwin therefore felt justified in rejecting the idea.

Stepping down
A diverse collection of politicians attempted to organize a last-ditch defence of the King. Edward's backers included Moseley's Fascists, press baron Max Aitken, and a small group of Conservative Members of Parliament led by future prime minister Winston Churchill. Although there was widespread sympathy for the King, Edward's supporters were unable to find adequate backing for a revolt

Official menu
This is the menu for the official dinner at Buckingham Palace after the State Opening of Parliament in November 1936. A week before this function took place, Wallis Simpson had filed for divorce, precipitating the abdication crisis.

against the government's stand. The King himself was stubborn in his commitment to Simpson and showed no desire to retain the throne. If anything, his brother, the Duke of York was more distressed at the prospect of gaining the crown than Edward was at losing it. Placed under intolerable pressure, Simpson offered to withdraw from her relationship with the King, but it made no difference. On 10 December, Edward signed his abdication.

The following evening Edward, now the Duke of Windsor, made a moving, dignified radio broadcast from Windsor Castle, beginning: "At long last I am able to say a few words of my own". He declared his allegiance to his successor George VI and explained his inability to carry a king's "burden of responsibility". That night, Edward boarded a Royal Navy warship at Portsmouth and sailed for France and Wallis Simpson.

Edward's first radio broadcast
Edward VIII makes his first radio broadcast as king in March 1936. The next time he would address the nation and empire on radio would be in December to announce his abdication.

Wedding day
The Duke and Duchess of Windsor pose for photographs on their wedding day in June 1937 outside the Chateau de Condé in France. The Duke's family was not present at the ceremony.

"I have found it **impossible** to... discharge **my duties as king**... without the **help and support** of **the woman I love."**

EDWARD VIII, FROM HIS ABDICATION SPEECH, DECEMBER 1936

AFTER ≫

George VI was crowned king on 12 May 1937 at the coronation that had been intended for Edward VIII. Meanwhile, Edward became a politically unsettling exile.

ROYAL EMBARRASSMENT
On 3 June 1937, **Edward married Simpson in France** and the couple settled there. The following October, they **visited Nazi Germany**, meeting Adolf Hitler. This became a serious embarrassment once Britain went to war with Germany in 1939.

THE WINDSORS VISIT BRITAIN IN 1967

RENEWING TIES
Edward returned to France after a five-year stint as **Governor the Bahamas,** and the couple settled into the lives of minor international celebrities. Their contacts with the Royal Family were distant – the Duke **attended George VI's funeral** in 1952, but not Elizabeth II's coronation the following year. From around 1965, the Windsors began to visit Britain at will and attended a number of royal occasions, including the centenary of Queen Mary's birth in 1967. The Queen visited the couple for the first time in France in 1972, shortly before the Duke's death.

Crown stickers
These windscreen stickers were used on royal cars during the 1930s. The black and white stickers were used for ordinary cars from the Royal Mews.

Coronation invite
Invitations to George VI's coronation were issued by the Earl Marshal – 16th Duke of Norfolk Bernard Fitzalan-Howard. As chair of the coronations Executive Committee, he extended invitations to everyone from members of the Royal Family to trade union representatives.

After the coronation ceremony
On 12 May 1937, after his coronation ceremony at Westminster Abbey, King George VI and his family appeared on the balcony of Buckingham Palace to greet the crowd below. From left to right are: Queen Elizabeth, Princess Elizabeth, Queen Mary, Princess Margaret, and George VI.

The Unexpected King

The abdication had dealt a huge blow to the credibility of the monarchy. Throughout Europe, royal families had recently been toppled from their thrones, and at home, the familiar established order was questioned by many.

BEFORE

Edward VIII's abdication brought into question the relevance of the monarchy as the embodiment of responsibility and virtue.

AN UNCERTAIN FUTURE
Edward VIII's abdication << 92–93 divided the nation, with traditionalists shocked at the dereliction of duty, and radicals declaring that the King should do whatever he wanted – largely because he was irrelevant. Consequently, when George VI inherited the throne, its future seemed uncertain.

RELUCTANT RULER
While Prince Albert and his family duly fulfilled their royal duties, they lived out of the spotlight. **Hampered by crushing shyness and a debilitating stammer**, Albert found public speaking a torment. After a particularly harrowing performance at Wembley in 1925, he began speech therapy.

George V had long harboured grave reservations about his first son Edward's ability to be king. The King had more faith in his second son Prince Albert and his granddaughter, Elizabeth's, abilities as potential monarchs. Despite this, the King had done nothing to prepare Albert for any kingly duties. Albert, who had always been overshadowed by his extrovert older brother Edward, was forced to step into his shoes after the abdication crisis (see pp.92–93). His coronation as George VI was held on the same day that had earlier been set aside to crown Edward. The *Illustrated London News* had already commissioned paintings of the event, and had to ask the artist to substitute Edward's face with George's.

Troubled times
This was an inauspicious time to be appointed king. Not only had the abdication dealt a huge blow to the credibility of the monarchy in England, but the familiar, established order was in question throughout Europe and the British Empire. In India and Ireland, there were cries for home rule and republicanism. Meanwhile, dictators were taking over Europe – Joseph Stalin was in power in the Soviet Union; Adolf Hitler had marched into the Rhineland; Francisco Franco had staged an uprising leading to civil war in Spain, and fascist Italy and Germany had forged an alliance. At home, unemployment was high, and rising tensions between the left and right wings had already led to civil unrest.

In this context, Edward – a playboy king who admired Hitler and cared more for his private life than his country – seemed not only to threaten the existence of the monarchy, but the very survival of democratic Europe.

An unlikely candidate
George VI, a shy and serious man with little self-confidence and a crippling speech impediment, seemed an unlikely candidate to reverse the fortunes of the monarchy and country. However, his

"Dickie, this is absolutely terrible. I **never wanted this** to happen; I'm quite **unprepared** for it… I've **never** even **seen** a **State Paper**."
GEORGE VI, TO LORD MOUNTBATTEN UPON HEARING OF HIS ACCESSION

modesty, determination, unshakable diligence, combined with an iron sense of duty enabled him to become a respected figurehead, who saved the reputation of the monarchy and earned the respect of both politicians and people.

Before the abdication, Prince Albert and his family lived a relatively quiet life, in between attending to various royal duties. Hampered by his stammer, Albert rarely spoke in public. According to royal biographer, Dermot Morrah, there were even moves among "some men of authority" to settle the crown instead on Albert's younger brother, the more charismatic Prince George, who had the added advantage of having already produced a male heir.

Albert and Elizabeth were deeply opposed to the abdication. They were furious with Edward and suspicious of Wallis Simpson. Both were reluctant to accede to the throne, but their sense of duty won over. George VI applied himself to his new role with tenacity, reading official papers, educating himself in constitutional matters, and working closely with his prime ministers. Inevitably, his inexperience and naivety showed at times, especially under the pressures leading up to World War II. Desperate to avoid another war, he backed Prime Minister Neville Chamberlain's policy of appeasing Hitler so fervently that many members of Parliament felt he was compromising his constitutional role of political impartiality.

Significant visit

Perhaps the most significant action of George VI, as Europe prepared for war, was the visit he made to the US in June 1939. Both President Franklin D Roosevelt and the King were keenly aware of the importance of the visit. Roosevelt believed that war was imminent, and that "Great Britain would be our first line of defence." He stated that he would convince his country to drop its policy of isolationism. George knew that American help would be essential if the Allies were to win the war. After an informal picnic, the King and Roosevelt talked late into the night, with George taking meticulous notes, which he sent back to the British government. Among these notes he wrote: "If London was bombed, USA would come in." By the following September, Britain was at war with Germany.

With the US president
George VI and US President Franklin Roosevelt travel from Union Station to the White House. This was one of the many meetings that helped foster the diplomatic relations necessary for the Allied Powers to weather and win World War II.

George VI went on to essay his kingly responsibilities with considerable success. On the personal front, his relationship with his elder brother was strained.

BENEFICIAL ALLIANCE
George VI's successful diplomacy in the US had significant returns. After Britain declared war on Germany, US President Roosevelt extended support by **repealing the arms embargo** so that arms could be sold to France and Britain. He then passed the **Lend Lease Act** permitting lending, leasing, selling, or bartering of arms, ammunition, and food to "any country whose defense the President deems vital to the defense of the US." America formally joined the conflict in December 1941.

Back home, George VI stayed in constant consultation with British Prime Minister **Neville**

Chamberlain 102–103 », and his successor Winston Churchill, throughout the war.

FALLING OUT
Continued acrimony between George VI and his elder brother fuelled the latter's fascination with Hitler, whom he met in 1937.

GEORGE VI WITH BRITISH PRIME MINISTER NEVILLE CHAMBERLAIN

Born **1895** Died 1952

George VI

"I pray to God… that nothing will come between Bertie and Lilibet and the throne."

GEORGE V, ON HIS DEATHBED, 1936

Full dress uniform
George VI is pictured here
in full dress coat in the rank
of Admiral of the Fleet. He also
wears a collar and badges of
the order of the Thistle, and
stars of the orders of the
Garter and the Thistle.

P rince Albert, or Bertie as he was fondly referred to – the second son of the Duke and Duchess of York (later crowned King George V and Queen Mary) – was a shy, unassuming boy. He grew up in the shadow of his glamorous elder brother Edward. Albert was born in 1895 on the inauspicious day of the anniversary of the death of Queen Victoria's beloved husband Prince Albert – 14 December (see pp.60–61). This reportedly caused the Queen some distress. The news, two days later, that her new great-grandson was to be called Albert "that dear name which

is a byword for all that is great and good…" appeared to have offered her some solace.

The Duke of York and his family lived in York Cottage, a glum mock-Tudor villa on the Sandringham Estate. The future king, George V, was a severe father – a typical Victorian patriarch – and while his first son, Edward, thrived on rebellion against authority, Albert's self-confidence shrivelled in the face of the constant cycle of reprimand and disapproval considered normal by parents of the era. As in most aristocratic – and many middle class – families of the time, the York children had very little contact with their parents. They lived in a separate part of the house with a battalion of nannies, nursemaids, and tutors, and were expected to stay there, except, according to the

Time with the Queen
Albert (seated on a cushion) is pictured here with his siblings – Mary (on the chair), Edward (standing), and Henry, as a baby – all gathered around their great-grandmother, Queen Victoria.

Countess of Airlie, when invited to their mother's boudoir after tea, or for "a less pleasurable interview with their father in his sitting room." The Countess, a close confidante of Albert's mother, the Duchess of York, was a frequent visitor to the house, "I never saw the children run along the corridors," she wrote, "they always walked sedately, generally shepherded by nurses or tutors." By contrast, their grandparents, Edward VII and Queen Alexandra, were effusive, fun, and relaxed – although considered far too indulgent by George and Mary – and they provided the children with some respite from the harsh regime of home.

Unpleasant childhood
Sandwiched between his charismatic golden-haired elder brother David, and his father's favourite (and only daughter) Mary, Albert seems at times to have been neglected – emotionally by his parents and physically by a nanny, who gave him so little to eat that he developed an intestinal condition that remained with him for the rest of his life. There are also reports of uncontrollable fits of rage at his older brother, most probably provoked by merciless teasing and taunting.

Sensitive, self-effacing, and insecure, Albert was forced to wear an iron leg brace to correct knock-knees, and it was made very clear to him that his natural left-handedness was a defect. The message to the child was clear: he was not good enough. Around the age of 7 or 8 – the same time that he was being forced to write with his right hand – he developed a debilitating stammer.

Beating the hardships
Sent away to Naval College at the age of 14, Albert was small, timid, and had no experience of the world

Engagement
The future King George VI loved Elizabeth Bowes-Lyon deeply and became engaged to her in London on 18 January 1923. They married later in April in Westminster Abbey.

beyond the sheltered life at home at Sandringham. At first he was taunted and bullied: "It never did me any good to be a prince, I can tell you, and many was the time I wished I hadn't been. It was a pretty tough place." However, he soon began to make friends, winning people over with his lack of pretension and his sense of humour. He also showed a physical grit and determination that made him excel at sport.

Academically, Albert struggled, coming 68th in a class of 68 at his end-of-term exams. At his next school, the Naval College at Dartmouth, he was immediately assigned a young lieutenant as tutor and finally began to apply himself. At the end of term his hard work was rewarded with a special gift from the lieutenant – a set of fake silver spoons, made of an amalgam that melted in a cup of tea. Bertie tried the trick at Sandringham, and it worked perfectly – although apparently his father George V was not amused.

times before she agreed to marry him. When she finally gave her consent, Albert sent his parents a telegram. The wording had been pre-arranged, and simply read, "All right. Bertie".

Marriage
The wedding was held on 26 April 1923 in Westminster Abbey. The newly formed British Broadcasting Company (BBC) requested permission to record and broadcast the event on radio, but the Abbey Chapter vetoed the idea. After the wedding – and a long trip to Africa – the couple settled down into a house on Piccadilly, where they lived when their daughters Elizabeth and Margaret Rose were born. They lived the kind of life typical of the aristocracy of the time – comfortable and privileged, sheltered and old-fashioned, but by no means extravagant.

The abdication of Edward VIII was the end of life as the Yorks had known it. They left their family home on Piccadilly for Buckingham Palace, and the comfort of minor renown and routine royal duties for the pressures of office and worldwide fame. On 12 May 1937, the date initially intended for Edward VIII's coronation, Albert was crowned as King George VI.

"I'm only a **naval officer, it's the only thing I know.**"

PRINCE ALBERT, SOON TO BECOME GEORGE VI, TO LORD MOUNTBATTEN, 1936

The determination Albert had eventually demonstrated at school was soon to pay off in other ways. He fell in love with the young Elizabeth Bowes-Lyon, but felt quite out of his league. At ease socially, and with an engaging enthusiasm for life, she was one of the most popular girls of her day. "He's always talking about her," his mother remarked to Lady Airlie, "She seems a charming girl, but I don't know her very well." Having been assured by Lady Airlie, Mary of Teck (now Queen Mary) too became convinced that Elizabeth was the only woman who could make Albert happy. Elizabeth was cautious, however, and in the end, Albert had to ask her three

George Cross
King George VI created the British civilian and military medal, the George Cross, in 1940 for "acts of the greatest heroism or of the most conspicuous courage in circumstances of extreme danger."

People's king
At first glance, a man less suited to be king would be hard to imagine. He was sensible and agreeable but not quite the stuff of great monarchs. But George VI reigned at an extraordinary time, and it may have been his essential modesty and diffidence – combined with his grit and determination – that made him a monarch capable of guiding Britain through a period of war. He knew how to listen, and understood that he had a lot to learn. The people warmed to their unassuming king, moved by his speech difficulties and appreciating his evident humanity and dedication to duty. When it came to the day he had to inform the nation that it was at war via live radio broadcast (see pp.102–03), his words carried a human touch, uncommon in royal speeches of the time. He gave the impression there was no them and us, but simply "we".

(see pp.102–03)

TIMELINE

- **14 December 1895** Born in York House on the Sandringham Estate, second son of Prince George, Duke of York, and Mary of Teck.
- **22 January 1901** Death of Queen Victoria, who is succeeded by her son, King Edward VII. Prince Albert becomes third-in-line to the throne.
- **1909** Attends Royal Naval College at Osborne House (see pp.56–57) on the Isle of Wight.
- **22 June 1911** Albert's parents, George and Mary of Teck, are crowned King and Queen.
- **1913–1916** Joins the Royal Navy and serves in World War I. Ill health forces him to retire from active service after the battle.
- **1918** Transfers to the recently established Royal Air Force and becomes the first member of the Royal Family to have a pilot's licence.
- **1920** Leaves Cambridge University and begins to take on more royal duties. Visits to coal mines, factories, and railyards earn him the nickname "Industrial Prince". He meets Elizabeth Bowes-Lyon for the first time.
- **26 April 1923** Marries Elizabeth Bowes-Lyon.
- **21 April 1926** Elizabeth Alexandra Mary, the future Queen Elizabeth II, is born.
- **11 December 1936** Abdication of Edward VIII; Albert becomes King. The Irish Free State removes all mention of the monarch from the Irish Constitution.
- **12 May 1937** Coronation of George VI on the day previously intended for Edward VIII's coronation.

STAMP PRINTED, BUT NOT ISSUED, TO COMMEMORATE EDWARD VIII'S CORONATION

- **June 1939** Visits the US with Queen Elizabeth.
- **3 September 1939** George VI announces over the radio that Britain is at war with Germany.
- **13 September 1940** Buckingham Palace is bombed when the King and Queen are in residence.
- **1940–44** The King has weekly meetings with Prime Minister Winston Churchill. He visits troops overseas, and gives support to those suffering at home.
- **8 May 1945** Victory in Europe Day is celebrated. The Royal Family cheers the crowd standing outside Buckingham Palace from the balcony.
- **1947** Partition of India and creation of Pakistan. George is no longer Emperor of India, but becomes King of India and Pakistan.
- **1950** India becomes a republic within the Commonwealth. George is no longer King of India, but Head of the Commonwealth.
- **September 1951** George VI has his left lung removed after the discovery of a malignant tumour.
- **6 February 1952** Dies in bed of a coronary thrombosis at the age of 56.

Elizabeth and Margaret's Childhood

In April 1926, Britain was in crisis as a bitter miners' dispute threatened to erupt into a nationwide strike. Against this tumultuous backdrop, the news of the birth of Elizabeth – then, third in line to the throne – provided a welcome distraction.

On 21 April 1926, after a long and difficult labour, Elizabeth Bowes-Lyon – wife of Prince Albert – was about to be given a Caesarean section at the London house of her parents, the Earl and Countess of Strathmore. Elizabeth Alexandra Mary was born at 2:20 am. Shortly after the announcement of the birth was made, an excited crowd gathered outside the house to watch the arrival of telegrams, gifts, and visitors.

Four days later, the miners' dispute culminated in a state of emergency being declared in the country. On 3 May, a general strike was called. Industries and key services were frozen, and workers took to the streets. The strike lasted six days, yet public interest in the new infant persisted as crowds would gather outside the Strathmores' house for a glimpse of the royal infant. On 29 May, Elizabeth was christened at Buckingham Palace.

Popular baby

In January 1927, Elizabeth's father and mother left for a six-month-long royal visit to Australia. The baby was left in London in the care of nurses, nannies, and grandparents – normal practice among the upper classes of the time. But in the Australian press, fascination with the new baby was considerable, and "Betty", as she was dubbed, became the most famous baby in the world. Chocolates, china sets, hospital wards, and even an area in Antarctica were named after Elizabeth. She also appeared on a stamp in Newfoundland. Once her love of horses became known, Madame Tussaud's wax museum created a model of her on a pony.

Women's magazines speculated at length on Elizabeth's character. They reported that, at 21 months, she had stood on a table at a party at Sandringham, hurling crackers at the guests. Other reports stated that visitors to the family house at Piccadilly were likely to be bombarded with teddy bears flung down the stairwell. But as per popular press, the little scamp was also a golden-curled angel whose smile had greater power over her grandfather, King George V (see pp.78–79), than anyone else in the kingdom. The Archbishop of Canterbury reported arriving at the palace to find the King

Princess's pets
Elizabeth poses with two corgis – her favourite breed of dog – at her home in Piccadilly, London, in July 1936. Elizabeth's first corgi, Dookie, was a gift from George VI in 1933 (see pp.108–109).

« **BEFORE**

World War I plunged Britain into an economic crisis, with crippling national debt and high unemployment.

GOOD NEWS AT A DARK TIME
What began as a miners' dispute on the issue of poor wages and working hours was threatening to snowball into a general strike. Fearing social **anarchy and revolution,** the government mobilized soldiers and civilians to maintain order. Despite the crisis, **public interest** in the birth of a royal baby – the third in line to the throne – was huge. This was perhaps because it symbolized tradition and continuity at a time of great instability.

Wooden doll's house
This Tudor style doll's house was created in 1932 by Florence Palmer of Etchinghill for an exhibition. Elizabeth Bowes-Lyon acquired it for her daughters to play with.

pretending to be a horse, "shuffling on hands and knees along the floor while the little Princess led him by the beard".

Model siblings

In 1930, with the birth of Princess Margaret, the close-knit York family was complete. Elizabeth and her sister Margaret led a sheltered childhood. Occasional public appearances were much photographed and filmed by the press, with the princesses presented as role models for the nation's children. Mothers would attempt to copy for their daughters whatever the princesses were wearing.

Queen in waiting

The only true glimpse of young Elizabeth that has been made public is an essay she wrote on 12 May 1937, the day after her father's coronation. It reads: "At the end the service got rather boring as it was all prayers. Grannie [Queen Mary] and I were looking to see how many more pages to the end, and we turned one more and then I pointed to the word at the bottom of the page and it said 'Finis'. We both smiled at each other and turned back to the service." Elizabeth was already 11 when she wrote this. For the past five months, she had known that unless her parents had a son, she too would be monarch one day.

AFTER »

After the abdication of Edward VIII, Elizabeth's father became king and she became next in line to the throne. Three years later, as Hitler threatened to conquer Europe, Britain declared war on Germany.

QUEEN IN THE MAKING
George VI had been completely unprepared for the **duties of monarchy** when he came to the throne, and was determined that Elizabeth be better equipped. He guided her through the complexities of royal duties and procedure as best he could, enlisting the help of experts, where necessary **106–107 »**. Monarchies were toppling across Europe, and the abdication had left the British public with little faith in the Royal Family. George VI believed that it was essential for Elizabeth to have an **unshakable sense of duty** if the British monarchy were to survive. During World War II Elizabeth followed the example of her parents, and took her first steps towards becoming a **figurehead for the nation 106–107 »**.

> " [Princess Elizabeth] is a **character.** She has an **air of authority** and **reflectiveness** astonishing in an infant."
>
> WINSTON CHURCHILL, DESCRIBING 2-YEAR-OLD ELIZABETH II, 1929

Coronation day
Princess Elizabeth stands with her mother on the balcony of Buckingham Palace on the day her parents were crowned King and Queen. The princess wore a long dress, train, and coronet for the ceremony.

The **Royal Family** in **World War II**

When Britain and France declared war on Germany on 3 September 1939, George VI was still establishing his role as king. Following the example set by his father in World War I, he focused on the role of Royal Family to boost morale, and inspire social cohesion and national spirit.

I n many ways the epitome of the reserved, dutiful family man, King George VI became an unlikely symbol of national resistance. For ordinary working- and middle-class British people, this serious, modest man who was happiest when at home with his wife and children, came to represent the values that Britain was fighting for. While a more glamorous, dashing king may have served only to emphasize the gulf between rich and poor, this hesitant man, ill at ease in the spotlight, was widely seen to have inspired a sense of common humanity.

school education made compulsory up to the age of 14. Newspaper circulation was on the increase, and – even more significant – almost every home in the country had a radio, and every town a cinema. World War II was the first war in which politicians and the King could communicate directly with the populations, not only of Britain, but of the Commonwealth and even with what remained of the Empire.

On the day war was declared – 3 September 1939 – George VI not only had to deliver the most important speech of his life, but had to do so live on radio. Anticipation was high,

that had been bombed, especially in the East End. The Palace was also hit many times by German bombs. On 13 September 1940, it suffered a direct hit when the King and Queen were in the Palace. Few workers were injured

King's speech
In the official photograph of the event, King George looks calm and regal in his naval uniform, sitting at his desk in front of a microphone. Actually, he delivered the speech standing in shirt sleeves at a lectern in a small room with the window open.

" I'm glad we've been bombed. It makes me feel I can look the East End in the face."

QUEEN ELIZABETH, AFTER THE BOMBING OF BUCKINGHAM PALACE

Society had changed since World War I. Britain had had its first Labour government, Ireland had declared itself an independent republic, women had won the vote and were increasingly going out to work, and society was more educated than ever before with

and throughout the country, streets emptied as the nation gathered around their radio sets. The stakes could not have been higher, and the King knew it. He delivered the speech(see p.97), and the only person present in the room was his speech therapist Lionel Logue. Lionel advised the King to forget about the audience and simply speak to him. The technique worked. For all his sobriety, George was the first people's king.

Bombing of Buckingham Palace
Throughout the war, King George and Queen Elizabeth ignored advice to move out of London to the safety of Windsor Castle. They mostly remained at Buckingham Palace, making regular visits to give support to communities,

(see p.97)

Resilient in wartime
Queen Elizabeth and King George VI inspect the destruction at Buckingham Palace, following the German air raid during the Blitz, on 10 September 1940. They were not present in the Palace when it was bombed that day.

« BEFORE

George VI was still finding his feet as king after unexpectedly inheriting the throne following the abdication of his brother, Edward VIII.

CHANGING ORDER
World and social order was in a state of transition and crisis with the **collapse of many monarchies and fascist experiments in Europe.** The **British Empire** was in **decline,** while the **US was on the rise.**

and the chapel was destroyed. On the same day, the King and the Queen visited West Ham in the East End. She later said, "I felt as if I was walking in a dead city... all the houses evacuated, and yet through the broken windows one saw all the poor little possessions... just as they were left."

The fact that the Royal Family had suffered too only endeared them more to the population. Like most people in Britain, George and Elizabeth lost relatives in the war. In 1942 the King's younger brother, Prince George, Duke of Kent, was killed.

Support to the war-torn nation

Weekly newsreels regularly included footage of the Royal Family – visiting bombsites, munitions factories, hospitals, soup kitchens, troops –

among the footage of war devastation. This footage was designed to raise people's morale. There were films too of George VI's several visits to troops on active service in France at the beginning of the war in 1939, and in North Africa in 1943, following the victory of El Alamein – a city in Egypt where Britain fought the Axis forces twice in World War II. In June 1944, ten days after D-Day, he visited his army on the Normandy beaches, and later that year visited the troops in Italy and the Low Countries. Although not involved in strategy, he met Prime Minister Winston Churchill in private every Tuesday throughout the war, building up a relationship of mutual trust and respect – one of the closest relationships ever to exist between a prime minister and monarch.

JOIN THE ATS

Wartime campaign
British women who wanted to work for the army during World War II joined the Auxiliary Territorial Service (ATS). It had 200,000 members by the end of 1943. Princess Elizabeth served as a driver and a mechanic in the ATS.

AFTER

George VI became a highly respected monarch, but the stress of office had grave consequences for his health.

NEW WORLD ORGANIZATIONS
The beginnings of a new post-war world order with the **formation of the United Nations (UN)** in 1945 and the **North Atlantic Treaty Organization (NATO)** in 1949. At home, legislation, including various acts setting up the welfare state, came into force, aiming at a healthier, better educated, and more socially equal Britain.

KING'S DECLINING HEALTH
King George VI always had a **delicate constitution**, and the **stress of office** – in particular, leading the nation during World War II – **severely affected** his fragile health. A heavy smoker, he was eventually **diagnosed with lung cancer.** The King suffered a **coronary thrombosis,** a fatal blood clot to the heart, **132 ≫** and died in his sleep in 1952 at the age of 56.

All members of the Royal Family – including the children – were expected to set an example to the nation by contributing to the war effort. Princess Elizabeth not only made her first radio broadcast to the country's children at the age of 14 (see p.106), but sewed items for troops and raised funds with a Christmas pantomime. She joined the Auxiliary Territorial Service (ATS) later.

In recognition of the demands that modern warfare inflicted on ordinary people, the King decided to create medals to honour men and women – military and civilian – who had performed acts of outstanding courage. In 1942 the George Cross was awarded to the people of Malta in recognition of the bravery they displayed during the long siege by the Germans.

9 The number of times Buckingham Palace was directly bombed by German planes during World War II.

Victory day

It is perhaps an indication of the relationship that had grown through the war years between the Royal Family and the British public, that on 8 May 1945 , on the night of Victory in Europe (VE) Day, after appearing on the balcony of Buckingham Palace to cheering crowds, the King agreed to his daughters' rather unexpected request. "We asked my parents if we could go out and see for ourselves", Elizabeth later revealed. Princess Elizabeth, 19, and her 14-year-old sister, Princess Margaret, with caps pulled down low over their eyes, mingled anonymously with the crowds. Describing it afterwards, Elizabeth said, "We walked through the streets, a line of unknown people linking arms and walking down Whitehall, swept along on a tide of happiness and relief... I think it was one of the most memorable nights of my life."

Working in the ATS
Princess Elizabeth learns to change a car wheel as a subaltern in the Auxiliary Territorial Service (ATS) in 1945. By the end of the war she was promoted to Junior Commander.

Elizabeth's Teenage Years

Although Elizabeth and Margaret were raised in a privileged and sheltered environment, their lives were turned upside down at a very young age by two major events – the abdication of Edward VIII and the outbreak of World War II.

After the abdication crisis (see pp.92–93) of 1936, Elizabeth's father became king and the family moved from their Piccadilly town house to Buckingham Palace. The Piccadilly house was hardly modest – it had 25 bedrooms and a staff of 16 – but it was a thriving and much-loved family home, typical of the kind of London base maintained by wealthier members of the aristocracy. Marion Crawford (see pp.98–99),

« BEFORE

There was every reason to assume that Edward VIII would continue to be king and produce heirs of his own. It seemed very unlikely that Elizabeth would ever accede to the throne.

A PRIVILEGED PRINCESS
Elizabeth and Margaret led the kind of **sheltered, undemanding lives** considered appropriate for aristocratic girls – lives in which the greatest achievement was to some day marry well. Education was not taken very seriously – both girls were **home schooled**, with dancing and riding as well as maths and English on the curriculum. Lessons were often interrupted when the Princesses' mother thought of something more fun to do.

governess to Elizabeth and Margaret for 16 years, remains the main source for information on the Princesses' lives at the time.

A new home
According to Crawford, there was nothing lovable about Buckingham Palace. It was bleak, vast, cold, and infested with rodents: "You may think a royal palace is the last word in up-to-date luxury but nothing could be further from the truth. Living at Buckingham Palace was rather like camping in a museum – one that's dropping to bits… that first night, the wind moaned in the chimneys like 1,000 ghosts. The palace had only recently had electricity installed… My bedroom light, for instance, could only be turned on and off by a switch two yards outside in the passage… Food had to come the better part of half-a-mile from the kitchens at the Buckingham Palace Road end to the dining room at the Constitution Hill end. We also needed the vermin man, who fought an endless battle against the mice with cardboard traps that had a lump of aniseed in the middle and treacle all around."

If Crawford's account is to be trusted, it was she who worried about the Princesses being too isolated, and suggested that they join the Girl Guides. The 1st Buckingham Palace Guide Company met for the first time on 9 June 1937. It comprised 20 members, all of whom were daughters of the aristocracy or members of the royal household and Palace staff. A Brownie pack – a Guiding group for girls aged 7 to 10 years old – was started for Margaret with 14 members.

Preparing to be Queen
George VI was determined that Elizabeth be better prepared for the duties of monarchy than he

Girl Guides
Dressed in Girl Guide uniforms, Elizabeth and Margaret prepare to release a carrier pigeon with a message to Chief Guide Lady Olave Baden-Powell on the occasion of her late husband's birthday in 1943.

had been. He encouraged her to sit with him as he studied state papers (see p.130), and engaged Henry Marten, Vice-Provost of Eton College, to give her an intensive course of lessons in constitutional history, the role of monarchy, and parliamentary procedure. Meanwhile, Margaret's education was less rigorous and regimented.

Thanks to their parents' royal visits to Australia, New Zealand, Canada, and the US, the Princesses had the opportunity – rare at the time – to learn about foreign countries and cultures from people who had actually travelled. In 1939, on a tour of the US, Elizabeth's mother wrote to her describing a now famous picnic at President Franklin D Roosevelt's home in New York State: "We all sat at little tables under the trees round the house, and had all our food on one plate – a little salmon, some turkey, some ham, lettuce, beans & HOT DOGS too!"

Occasionally, the girls accompanied their parents on royal visits. In July 1939, 13-year-old Elizabeth with her parents and sister, visited the Royal Naval College at Dartmouth. Prince Philip of Greece (see pp.124–25), a boisterous 18-year-old cadet, was given the task of looking after the girls. In her account of the meeting, Crawford said "He [Philip] played games with them [Elizabeth and Margaret], jumped over tennis nets, wolfed down plates of food and generally romped, ending by

Wartime broadcast
In 1940, Elizabeth made her first radio broadcast to the nation's children, many of whom had been evacuated. At the end, Margaret joined in too.

rowing his boat until the King had to Royal Yacht until the King had to bellow to him to go back." Elizabeth was apparently charmed.

War breaks out
A few months later, when war broke out, the King and Queen remained in London, while the girls were removed to Windsor Castle. It was a gloomy, eerie place – windows had been blacked out, paintings removed for safety, chandeliers suspended three inches above the ground so they wouldn't shatter in the case of a bomb, and furniture shrouded in dust sheets. The King kept pigs at one of the estate farms, and the girls tended an allotment – a plot of land for growing vegetables or flowers – and kept rabbits. Bathtubs at both Windsor and Buckingham Palace had a black line painted on them to ensure that no one bathed in more than 13 cm (5 in) of water. During air raids, shelter was taken in one of the castle dungeons, where beetles scuttled across the floor. However, the Princesses had the rare luxury of a bathroom in their air raid shelter. On one occasion, the librarian took the girls down to the vaults and

"**Thousands of you...** have had to leave your homes… My sister Margaret Rose and I **feel so much for you** as we know… what it means to be **away from those we love** most of all."

ELIZABETH II, FROM HER FIRST RADIO BROADCAST TO THE NATION'S CHILDREN, 1940

AFTER »

Prepared by her father, George VI, for her eventual role of monarch, Elizabeth grew up to be a rather serious young woman.

A DEDICATED QUEEN
Elizabeth was made deeply aware of the implications and **duties of monarchy** by her experience of World War II. In a **radio speech** broadcast throughout the Commonwealth from South Africa on her 21st birthday, she made a **solemn dedication:** "I declare before you that my whole life, whether it be long or short, shall be devoted to your service and the service of our great Imperial Commonwealth, to which we all belong. But I shall not have the strength to carry out this resolution unless you will join in it with me."

ELIZABETH AND PHILIP
After their 1939 meeting, Elizabeth and Philip would be thrown together on several other occasions **114–15 »**, sowing the seeds for their **marriage 120–21, 266–67 »**.

showed them the Crown Jewels (see pp.68–69), hidden in battered leather hatboxes stuffed with newspaper.

The girls continued their work as Girl Guides at Windsor during the war, and, like girls throughout the country, knitted and made brooches to be sold for the war effort. In 1940, they began to put on yearly pantomimes to raise money to support the troops. The King saw the Princesses' efforts and quipped "At least if I am dethroned the girls will be able to earn their living." In October 1940, Princess Elizabeth, with Margaret by her side, made her first public speech –

a live radio broadcast to the nation's children, many of whom had been ordered to be evacuated.

Of the two children, Margaret was more funny, capricious, and naughty, and tended to attract all the attention. Elizabeth, on the other hand, was shy, serious, and socially ill at ease. She said of her sister: "It's so much easier when Margaret's there – everyone laughs at what Margaret says."

Forays outside Windsor were rare, though the girls did sometimes accompany their parents on public engagements. At age 15, Elizabeth joined the Auxiliary Territorial Service (ATS) as a volunteer, and learned to drive a lorry and maintain an engine. Guiding continued to give the Princesses an occasional taste of normality. In 1944, the two were filmed

at camp, washing up, giggling in dugouts, and singing songs with the rest of the company, watched by their mother. The nation read with glee reports of the Queen drinking tea from a stained, chipped mug presented to her by Margaret.

On her 18th birthday in 1944, George VI appointed Elizabeth a Counsellor of State, making her responsible for performing his official duties at times when he was abroad or absent due to illness. This was no mere ceremonial task; shortly afterwards, when the King was away in Italy, it was Elizabeth's duty as Counsellor to sign a reprieve for a murderer. The Princess had so far been sheltered from the less savoury aspects of life, and was unprepared for the task and seemingly disturbed by it. "What makes people do such terrible things?", she asked, "One ought to know! There must be some way to help them. I have so much to learn about people."

First official engagement
A special parade was organized at Windsor Castle to celebrate Elizabeth's 16th birthday – her first official engagement. The Princess, newly appointed as colonel-in-chief of the Grenadier Guards, inspected the regiment.

Family Pets

The Royal Family's love of canines has a long history, with pet dogs, ranging from pugs to King Charles spaniels appearing in royal portraits from the 17th century onwards. Since the reign of Queen Victoria, royal dogs have had their own graveyard at Sandringham.

Elizabeth II is renowned for her love of corgis: the Crown coin that commemorated her Golden Jubilee shows her with a corgi. In 2012, three of her dogs, Monty, Holly, and Willow, featured in the opening ceremony for the Olympic Games.

The Queen's love of corgis began as a child. In 1933, her father bought one as a family pet. Although officially named Rozavel Golden Eagle, the household servants began calling him Dookie, a cutesy nickname version of "Duke". Since then Elizabeth has bred 30 corgis, most of them descended from her 18th birthday present, a corgi named Susan, who accompanied the Queen and Prince Philip on their honeymoon in 1947. Although corgis remain her favourites, Elizabeth has also had labradors, a golden retriever, a cocker spaniel, a shih tzu and has bred several dorgis, a corgi-dachshund cross.

The Royal Family's love of animals is not limited to dogs. Elizabeth is a skilled horsewoman and world-class race horse owner. At times, the Royal Family has been given rather unusual animals as presents. During World War II, Earl Mountbatten (see pp.192–93) turned up with a chameleon for Elizabeth and Margaret; in 1956, Soviet leader Nikita Khrushchev gave a brown Syrian bear to six-year old Princess Anne; while in 1961, on a state visit to the Gambia, Elizabeth and Philip were presented with a baby crocodile – a gift for one-year-old Prince Andrew. The Queen's private secretary kept the baby crocodile in his bath until it could be donated to London Zoo.

The Queen's children and grandchildren have inherited her love of animals. They own dogs of various breeds and work as patrons for a wide range of animal charities.

> "The **Queen** carries a **magnet** when having clothes fitted… to **comb the room** for any **stray pins and needles** so the **dogs** don't hurt their **paws.**"
>
> **A ROYAL DRESSMAKER**, IN BRIAN HOEY'S *PETS BY ROYAL APPOINTMENT*

The Queen and her dogs
This picture of Elizabeth II was taken by photographer Lisa Sheridan in the gardens of Balmoral Castle in 1952. Sheridan became the Royal Family's most trusted photographer after a commission to photograph the royal corgis for a book on dogs in the early 1930s.

Born **1900** Died 2002

Queen Elizabeth, the Queen Mother

"[Elizabeth is] the **most dangerous woman** in **Europe.**"

ADOLF HITLER, ON ELIZABETH'S ABILITY TO BOOST BRITISH MORALE DURING THE WAR

The first "commoner" to marry into the Royal Family, Elizabeth Bowes-Lyon was born into one of the most important aristocratic families in Scotland. Her marriage to Prince Albert was considered a step towards political modernization as princes had thus far only married into other royal families. She had an idyllic childhood complete with everything from woodland dens, to candlelit balls. Elizabeth was largely educated at home, with emphasis on preparation for a good marriage.

Growing up

World War I began when Elizabeth was only 14. The family castle, Glamis, was turned into a military hospital,

Early life
Known as Buffy at home, Elizabeth was the ninth of 10 children. She spent most of her early childhood at her parents' country home, St Paul's Waldenbury in Hertfordshire, north of London.

Portrait of a queen
In this official portrait from 1954, Elizabeth wears a satin frock embroidered with gold and silver thread and crystal beads. Her jewellery and tiara are made of diamonds.

and Elizabeth and her sister Rose helped nurse the wounded men. Four of their brothers joined the army; one was captured and imprisoned, while another was killed. Nonetheless, frivolity was resumed with gusto after the war. Elizabeth was one of the London set's "It girls" – charismatic, lively, and outgoing, but blessed with the good sense to do nothing that could earn her the dreaded reputation of being "fast".

New challenges

It was Elizabeth's zest for life and easy informality that Prince Albert, the Duke of York, loved. These qualities were not, however, appreciated by the senior royals. When Elizabeth gave an interview about her engagement and referred to her fiancé as Bertie, George V, her future father-in-law, was furious. Once they were married, Elizabeth worked behind the scenes to help Albert overcome his stutter and build up his self-confidence. Determined that life for their children should have none of the bleak formality of Albert's Victorian upbringing, she created a warm family home.

Elizabeth was not shy of making her feelings known. Invited to dinner at Balmoral by Edward VIII, she found herself being welcomed by the new King's lover, twice-divorced American socialite Wallis Simpson.

Elizabeth walked straight past her, saying "I came to dine with the King", and seated herself at Edward's right hand. A few months later, Edward abdicated (see pp.92–93) and Albert was crowned King George VI and Elizabeth became Queen. For them, the challenge was not simply that of having inherited the monarchy, but having done so as World War II approached. In an effort to avoid another war, Elizabeth committed the only overtly political act of her life. When Prime Minister Neville Chamberlain returned from having convinced Hitler to sign a treaty for peace, she invited him onto the palace balcony, a clear breach of protocol, as Parliament had not yet voted on the treaty.

When war did break out, Elizabeth's role was to give moral support. On her first visits to London's East End bombsites, dressed in flimsy pastels,

Setting a precedent
Elizabeth and the Duke of York were wed at Westminster Abbey on 26 April 1923. The eight bridesmaids were: (left to right) Mary Cambridge, Diamond Hardinge, Mary Thynn, Elizabeth Elphinstone, May Cambridge, Katharine Hamilton, Betty Cator, and Cecilia Bowes-Lyon.

high heels, and ropes of jewels, she was jeered at and pelted with rubbish. Elizabeth soon realized her folly, and dressed more modestly.

After the war, palace life went back to normal. But the King's health was failing, and in 1952, he died. Elizabeth blamed Simpson for his

Birth of Elizabeth
The Duchess of York had her first child – Elizabeth Alexandra Mary, known to the family as Lilibet – by Caesarean section at 2.40 am on 21 April 1926. Her second child, Margaret Rose, was born four years later.

became completely impossible." The Queen Mother responded, "Then I think I should be thankful you're not responsible for me."

What Prince Charles referred to as Elizabeth's "effervescent enthusiasm for life" also manifested itself in an extravagant love for the finer things

> "The curious thing is that **we are not afraid.** I feel that **God** has enabled us to face the situation **calmly.**"
>
> QUEEN ELIZABETH, IN A LETTER TO ARCHBISHOP OF CANTERBURY COSMO LANG TWO DAYS AFTER EDWARD VIII'S ABDICATION, 12 DECEMBER 1936

Coronation gowns
For her coronation, Elizabeth wore a silk gown, with pure gold thread embroidery in a rose-and-thistle pattern. Her daughters wore white silk gowns with cream lace.

death, believing that if her husband had not been forced to be King he would not have died so young.

Later years
Queen Elizabeth, the Queen Mother, following her daughter's accession, retained her self-possession. In 1968, when student demonstrators hurled toilet rolls at her, Elizabeth stopped and picked them up, as though someone had misplaced them. "Was this yours?", she said, turning to a student, "Oh, could you take it?" The students fell silent.

Elizabeth could handle politicians equally well. On one occasion, she asked former Foreign Secretary Lord Carrington why the Tories had replaced Prime Minister Margaret Thatcher. He replied "Well, frankly Ma'am, towards the end she

in life – at one point resulting in a £4 million overdraft. But the Queen Mother still had fans from all walks of life. Never pretentious, she remained adamantly and unapologetically herself until her very last days.

Birthday celebrations
The Queen Mother waves to the public on her 90th birthday in August 1990. Celebrations began earlier, on 27 June, with a parade at Horse Guards Parade.

(see pp.92–93)

TIMELINE

- **4 August 1900** Born to Claude Bowes-Lyon and his wife, Cecilia Cavendish-Bentinck.
- **4 August 1914** Turns 14; Britain declares war on Germany.
- **27 September 1915** Elder brother, Fergus, is killed in action at the Battle of Loos.
- **28 April 1917** Elder brother Michael, also serving in the army, is reported missing in action.
- **May 1917** The family learns that Michael has been captured after being wounded. He remains in a prisoner of war camp for the rest of the war.
- **1921** Turns down Prince Albert's first proposal of marriage.
- **22 February 1922** Serves as bridesmaid at the wedding of Princess Mary, daughter of King George V and Queen Mary.
- **1922** Refuses Prince Albert's second proposal of marriage.
- **13 January 1923** Accepts Albert's third proposal.
- **26 April 1923** Marries Prince Albert and becomes Duchess of York.
- **1925** Organizes speech therapy for Albert with Australian Lionel Logue.
- **21 April 1926** Gives birth to Elizabeth Alexandra Mary, the future Queen Elizabeth II.
- **6 January 1927** Embarks on a six-month-long world tour with Prince Albert.
- **21 August 1930** Gives birth to Margaret Rose.
- **11 December 1936** Becomes Queen Elizabeth as Albert accedes the throne on Edward VIII's abdication.
- **12 May 1937** Is crowned Queen Elizabeth in coronation ceremony at Westminster Abbey; Albert becomes King George VI.
- **30 September 1938** Prime Minister Neville Chamberlain appears on the balcony of Buckingham Palace at the Queen's invitation, following his visit to Hitler seeking appeasement.
- **17 May 1939** Visits Canada with George VI, who is the first reigning monarch to visit the nation.
- **26 April 1948** Celebrates 25th wedding anniversary with George VI.
- **6 February 1952** George VI dies; Elizabeth II becomes Queen.
- **April 1975** Visits Iran, where the people are bemused by her habit of speaking to everyone regardless of status or importance.
- **8 May 1995** Opens the 50th anniversary Victory in Europe celebrations.
- **4 August 2000** Turns 100.
- **9 February 2002** Death of Princess Margaret.
- **30 March 2002** Dies in her sleep at the Royal Lodge, Windsor Great Park.

QUEEN MOTHER'S 80TH BIRTHDAY COIN

The **First Tour** in **Africa**

The British Empire was disintegrating. With India on the cusp of independence, attention fell on South Africa, with its prodigious sources of gold and diamonds. South Africa had backed Britain during the war, but Anti-British Afrikaners were on the ascendant, among them pro-Nazi racists.

The royal tour began with King George VI, Queen Elizabeth, and Princesses Elizabeth and Margaret boarding HMS *Vanguard*. News reels of the voyage include the princesses enthusiastically playing deck games with the sailors, arguably the most relaxed images of the Princess to have been made public. But once on land, the fun stopped.

They were welcomed by a crowd of more than 250,000 white South Africans on their arrival in Cape Town on 17 February. Colourfully staged encounters with tribal kings followed, including an occasion on which the royal entourage was greeted by hundreds of Basuto tribesmen thundering through the dust on horseback. Commemorative stamps were issued and Princess Elizabeth received gifts of diamonds for her 21st birthday. But despite this elaborate show of South Africa as a model colony, the Royal Family was aware that the reality was very different.

Members of South Africa's Indian community in Natal boycotted the royal tour in protest of the Ghetto Act, designed to curtail Indian ownership of property in white areas. The Afrikaner press was also hostile. Detesting the overt signs of racial separation, and appalled by the authorities opposing him decorating black South Africans for war service, George VI found speech-making increasingly difficult. He referred to the officious Afrikaner police as Gestapo.

The Royal Family left for the UK on 24 April. Within a year, South Africa had passed apartheid legislation. The impact of her disturbing visit endured, as Elizabeth would go on to show her support for anti-apartheid activist Nelson Mandela on several occasions. She went so far as to signal her distance from Margaret Thatcher when the British Prime Minister referred to Mandela as a terrorist.

> **"**In view of the **disabilities imposed** upon… **coloured** peoples, it would be improper… to share the rejoicings of the white of South Africa.**"**
>
> **MAHATMA GANDHI,** ENDORSING THE BOYCOTT OF THE ROYAL TOUR

Into Africa
On 22 March 1947, the Royal Family visited the Natal National Park in South Africa. In addition to national parks, the Royal Family also took time to visit game reserves and the Victoria Falls. However, throughout the tour, they were keenly aware of the racial tensions plaguing the country.

« **BEFORE**

The first two decades of the 20th century saw many of Europe's monarchs toppled by war and revolution. Centuries of dynastic marriage had created a intricately interrelated web of royalty.

ROYAL MARRIAGES

In 1863 Queen Victoria arranged the marriage of her eldest son, the future Edward VII to Alexandra, eldest daughter of King Christian IX of Denmark. By the outbreak of World War I, the grandchildren of either Victoria or Christian occupied the thrones of the UK, Russia, Germany, Greece, Spain, Denmark, Norway, and Romania – **closely related monarchs** found themselves **on opposite sides.**

MATCHMAKER

Prince Philip's uncle, **Louis Mountbatten**, had done much to **engineer the match** between Elizabeth and Philip, to the extent that Philip wrote to him saying "Please, I beg of you not too much advice in an affair of the heart, or I shall be forced to do the wooing by proxy." Mountbatten had hoped for his name to be immortalized in the surnames of the would-be Queen's descendants.

> " His **wardrobe** was **scantier** than that of many a **bank clerk**... he had **only one civilian suit** and his **socks** were **full of darns.**"
>
> JOHN DEAN, PHILIP'S VALET

Elizabeth as a bridesmaid
In October 1946, as speculation mounted about their relationship, Princess Elizabeth was bridesmaid and Prince Philip an usher at the wedding of Lord Mountbatten's daughter Patricia to Lord Brabourne.

Elizabeth and Philip

They seemed an unlikely couple – the shy, dutiful, and serious Princess Elizabeth and the exuberant, outspoken, and penniless exiled Prince Philip of Greece. Although third cousins, their childhoods could not have been more different.

At the age of 13, Elizabeth visited the Royal Naval College at Dartmouth with her parents and sister (see p.106). While there, she met her royal cousin, 18-year-old Prince Philip of Greece. The next time they met was when Philip came to watch the Princesses' performance in the annual Christmas pantomime (see p.107) at Windsor. Shortly afterwards a photograph of the Prince appeared on Elizabeth's mantelpiece, and when her governess, Marion Crawford, warned that she was risking gossip, she changed it for one of Philip with a bushy beard. "There you are, Crawfie, I defy anyone to recognize him in this. He's completely incognito." Following the pantomime, they started writing regularly to one another, as Philip joined the Royal Navy as a cadet.

Apt match

The son of Prince Andrew of Greece and Princess Alice of Battenberg, Philip moved from place to place, after his family was exiled from Greece in 1922. Later, with Nazism on the rise, he left Germany for Scotland and became one of the first pupils to attend Gordonstoun school (see p.124, p.162). Philip seems to have taken delight in giving his address as "no fixed abode" in the visitors' books of the grand town mansions and country estates to which he was invited, often showing up only with what he was wearing – plus a razor.

Outspoken, self-reliant, and unrestrained, with a cheery sense of humour and uncrushable zest for life, Philip was no average young aristocrat. The general opinion was that he was "rather unpolished", rude, and overbearing. However, for Elizabeth, who was accustomed all her life to fawning and flattery, Philip's forthrightness and unconventionality came as a breath of fresh air.

War hero

In July 1943, during World War II, his ship, HMS *Wallace* took part in the Allied landings in Sicily. Off the coast of southeast Sicily, at the dead of night, the ship came under repeated bombardment. Prone and unprotected, the ship seemed doomed, until Philip came up with a plan to throw overboard a wooden raft with smoke floats to create the illusion of debris ablaze on the water. The German plane was fooled into attacking

At work
Prince Philip undertakes the role of an instructor at the Petty Officers' Training Center at Corsham, Wiltshire between 1946 and 1947. He became engaged to Princess Elizabeth while working here.

"Elizabeth **began** to **take more trouble** with her **appearance** and to play the tune 'People Will Say We're In Love', from *Oklahoma*."

MARION CRAWFORD, ELIZABETH'S GOVERNESS

the decoy while the *Wallace* sailed to safety. This extraordinary initiative by Prince Philip helped save many lives.

Beginning of a long liaison
Back in London after the war, Philip and his black MG sports car became regular visitors to Buckingham Palace. The first occasion he seems to have invited himself, as he wrote to Elizabeth afterwards apologising for his "monumental cheek". "Yet however contrite I feel," he wrote, "there is always a small voice that keeps saying 'nothing ventured, nothing gained' – well I did venture and I gained a wonderful time." According to Crawford, Philip did most of his courtship in the old nursery, at tea time, with Margaret in attendance. She wrote, "Just as there was nothing polished about Philip, who often wandered about in his shirtsleeves, so there was nothing fancy about these meals: just fish and some sort of sweet, washed down with orangeade. After dinner, it would be high-jinks in the corridors as the three of them played ball (a good many lightbulbs suffered) and raced about like a bunch of high-spirited children."

Philip and Elizabeth did, however, occasionally go out together, but despite taking care always to be seen in company with other friends, speculation in the press became fevered. Visiting a factory aged 19, Elizabeth was hugely embarrassed when the crowd began asking "Where's Philip?" Shortly afterwards, Philip was invited to Balmoral, where he seems to have shocked other guests by brashly going shooting with a borrowed gun, wearing flannel

trousers instead of plus fours. A footman revealed to the press that his "solitary naval valise" contained no spare shoes, pyjamas, or slippers and that his only walking shoes had to be taken to the local cobbler to be repaired. It is believed that it was at Balmoral in 1946 that Philip proposed to Elizabeth and she accepted. Initially the King and Queen seemed to share the common misgivings about Philip. But as they got to know him, they grew to appreciate his direct manner, joshing humour, and love of the countryside. On one occasion Philip, wearing a borrowed kilt, curtseyed to the King, allegedly because the kilt was so short that it was the only way of maintaining modesty. Philip was fun, an extrovert, a good foil to Elizabeth's seriousness.

In early October 1946, at the wedding of Lord Mountbatten's daughter Patricia to Lord Brabourne at Romsey Abbey, the two got together again. Philip was an usher, and he

escorted the Royal Family from their car. The media caught Philip and Elizabeth looking at each other affectionately as she moved to remove her fur coat. With no official announcement of an engagement, the speculation in the media increased.

As a prelude to the impending engagement, Philip's uncle, Lord Mountbatten, had long campaigned for Philip to be naturalized. Mountbatten secured the agreement of Home Secretary and Prime Minister to Philip's naturalization in 1946. He was then known as Lieutenant Philip Mountbatten. Ironically, it turned out that the procedure had been unnecessary – a law of 1705 stated that descendents of Sophia of Hanover (mother of George I) were British.

Separated for a while
In early 1947, it was decreed that Elizabeth and her sister would accompany their parents on a trip to South Africa on what was to be a four-month royal tour (see pp.112–13). She would be 21 when she returned. The couple wrote to each other throughout their separation and Elizabeth put Philip's photograph on her dressing table during the trip. Elizabeth

returned, pale and thin, and so relieved to get back, that she danced a jig on the deck as the ship, HMS *Vanguard*, steamed into Portsmouth harbour.

On 10 July 1947, the long-awaited engagement of Princess Elizabeth and Philip Mountbatten was announced coinciding with a garden party being celebrated at Buckingham Palace.

Engagement announcement
Elizabeth and Philip stroll on the terrace at Buckingham Palace after the announcement of their engagement in July 1947. The engagement ring is a diamond solitaire set in platinum with five smaller diamonds on each side.

AFTER

With the announcement of Princess Elizabeth and Prince Philip's engagement, public interest in the future Queen's consort abounded.

CONSPIRACY THEORY
As a descendent of the Greek-Danish royal dynasty, with his four sisters married to German aristocrats, it was inevitable that after **World War II,** conspiracy theories about the **pro-German** (and even pro-Nazi) sympathies of Philip would arise.

Family portrait
The portrait of the Royal Family following the announcement of the engagement of Elizabeth to Philip Mountbatten features (from left to right): Elizabeth, Philip, Queen Elizabeth (later the Queen Mother), King George VI, and Margaret.

3
ELIZABETH II
1947–1960

« St Edward's Crown, used during the
coronation of a new sovereign

ELIZABETH II
1947–1960

1947	1948		1950	1951	1952

21 APRIL
Elizabeth celebrates her 21st birthday with a Commonwealth broadcast.

10 JULY
Buckingham Palace announces the engagement of Princess Elizabeth to Prince Philip of Greece.

˅ Announcement of the engagement

30 JANUARY 1948
Assassination of Mahatma Gandhi.

6 SEPTEMBER 1948
Peter Townsend accompanies Princess Margaret to the coronation of Queen Juliana of the Netherlands.

30 APRIL 1948
Silver wedding anniversary of George VI and Elizabeth.

29 JULY 1948
London Olympics, which come to be known as the Austerity Games, commence.

14 NOVEMBER 1948
Birth of Prince Charles.

JUNE
Korean War begins; over 100,000 British soldiers serve with the multinational United Nations (UN) forces until 1953.

« Prince Charles's christening

MARCH
The Duke of Windsor publishes his memoirs: *A King's Story.*

3 MAY
George VI opens the Festival of Britain – a showcase for British enterprise and ingenuity.

7 JULY
The Duke of Edinburgh leaves the Royal Navy to focus on his duties as consort.

31 JANUARY
Elizabeth and Philip are waved off on tour of Africa by George VI.

6 FEBRUARY
George VI dies in his sleep at Sandringham, but Elizabeth is in Kenya and does not learn for several hours that she is now Queen.

16 FEBRUARY
Funeral of George VI, with coffin borne through London, then placed in a crypt at Windsor.

˅ George's grieving widow and daughters

15 AUGUST
The King loses the title of Emperor of India, following July's India Independence Act; Pakistan becomes a separate nation.

20 NOVEMBER
Elizabeth marries Philip at Westminster Abbey.

12 MARCH 1949
George VI undergoes an operation.

28 APRIL 1949
Foundation of the modern Commonwealth with the London Declaration.

JULY 1949
Elizabeth and Philip move into Clarence House, which has been extensively refurbished.

NOVEMBER 1949
Elizabeth and Philip move to Malta where Philip is stationed with the Royal Navy.

15 AUGUST
Princess Anne is born.

NOVEMBER
Marion Crawford publishes *The Little Princesses.*

« Princess Elizabeth's wedding procession

26 OCTOBER
Winston Churchill becomes British Prime Minister for the third time.

4 NOVEMBER
Elizabeth attends State opening of Parliament, her first major state function.

25 DECEMBER
Stone of Scone, a block of red sandstone placed under the coronation chair in Westminster Abbey since 1296 and associated with Scottish nationhood, is stolen. It is recovered four months later.

SEPTEMBER
George VI has a lung removed due to cancer.

» En route to State Opening of Parliament, 1952

The post-war years brought joy, tumult, and glory to the life of Elizabeth, as she celebrated marriage and motherhood, mourned the death of her father and grandmother, and dedicated herself to a life of service amidst the pomp and circumstance of her coronation. In the years that followed she would travel the world, inspiring excitement and devotion from Fiji to Fife. She oversaw a period of transition for Britain's international status, all the while managing to balance the needs of her family with the demands of monarchy. Meanwhile, Elizabeth's sister Margaret wrestled with her own agonizing dilemma in choosing between love and duty.

1953

NOVEMBER
Elizabeth and Philip embark on a tour of the Commonwealth.

» Tea caddy commemorating Elizabeth's visit to Australia

24 MARCH
Death of dowager Queen Mary, aged 85.

29 MAY
Conquest of Everest by Edmund Hilary and Tenzing Norgay.

« Elizabeth II's Coronation Day

2 JUNE
Coronation of Queen Elizabeth II at Westminster Abbey.

1954

12 JANUARY
Queen Elizabeth opens the New Zealand parliament.

15 APRIL
Queen Elizabeth and Philip return from Commonwealth tour.

6 MAY
English athlete Roger Bannister breaks the four-minute mile record.

4 JULY
End of rationing in UK after over a decade of privation.

1955

17 FEBRUARY
UK announces it has the H-bomb.

5 APRIL
Sir Anthony Eden becomes PM after Churchill resigns due to ill health.

14 AUGUST
Annigoni portrait of the Queen draws massive crowds to the Royal Academy.

18 SEPTEMBER
UK annexes Rockall, a tiny speck of rock in the Atlantic Ocean, in order to preempt Soviet expansion in the region.

31 OCTOBER
Margaret announces that she will not marry Peter Townsend.

IS SHE SAD?

SEVEN HOURS APART —THEN DINNER WITH PETER...

« Margaret's doomed romance in the news

1956

24 MARCH 1956
The Queen Mother's horse, Devon Loch, stumbles within feet of the finishing post in the Grand National.

23 APRIL 1956
Nikita Khrushchev, Soviet leader, visits the Queen at Windsor.

OCTOBER 1956
Anglo-French forces, which had attacked Egypt after it nationalized the Suez Canal, are forced to withdraw under international pressure. The debacle signals the end of Britain's imperial pretensions.

31 DECEMBER 1956
Prince Philip launches the Duke of Edinburgh Awards.

10 JANUARY 1957
Harold Macmillan becomes Prime Minister after Anthony Eden's resignation causes constitutional crisis.

6 MARCH 1957
Gold Coast becomes first African colony to gain independence as Ghana.

OCTOBER 1957
Queen tours North America and meets President Eisenhower.

⌃ First televised Christmas message

25 DECEMBER 1957
Queen Elizabeth delivers the first televised Christmas message.

1958

3 JULY 1958
End of presenting debutantes at court; the last deb curtsies to the Queen at Holyrood, following the final Buckingham Palace ball in March.

26 JULY 1958
Commonwealth Games begin at Cardiff, Wales; Charles is named Prince of Wales.

APRIL 1959
Queen Mother and Princess Margaret visit Pope John XXIII at the Vatican.

JUNE–AUGUST 1959
Queen and Prince Philip undertake the longest royal visit ever to Canada, partly to open the St Lawrence Seaway.

»

BEFORE «

In 1947, two years after the end of the war, and in the wake of the harshest winter in living memory, Britain was held fast in the grip of austerity, with rationing getting worse rather than improving.

Most goods were rationed, with coupons needed to buy clothing, sweets, sugar, petrol, meat, cheese, butter, lard, margarine, tea, and soap. Petrol was restricted by law to use for "essential motoring" and holidaying abroad was banned. Prime Minister Clement Attlee admitted, "I cannot say when we will emerge into easier times."

IN KEEPING WITH THE TIMES
In October 1947, **new restrictions came into force.** The weekly rationing of meat was reduced to a single shilling's worth, potatoes were restricted, and the clothing ration was cut. While 32 coupons had been available earlier, the allowance for the next five months was just 20 coupons. Against this backdrop, the **relatively opulent event**

CLOTHING RATION BOOK

planned for the Royal Wedding aroused **fierce resentment**. "Any banqueting and display of wealth at your daughter's wedding," the Camden Town branch of the Amalgamated Society Of Woodworkers warned the King, "will be an insult to the British people at the present time. You would be well advised to order a very quiet wedding in keeping with the times."

On the way to the abbey
The wedding procession advances towards Westminster Abbey. Travelling in the Irish State Coach at the head of the procession is Elizabeth, accompanied by her father dressed in his uniform as Admiral of the Fleet.

The **Wedding** of **Elizabeth** and **Philip**

Amidst the grey austerity of post-war Britain the wedding of Princess Elizabeth to Philip Mountbatten offered a flash of colour and gaiety, triggering a national and global outpouring of celebration... and fascination.

The engagement (see pp 114–15) of Princess Elizabeth to Philip Mountbatten was announced in July 1947, with the wedding planned for November. Despite a strong school of thought that the wedding should be low-key, keeping in mind the dismal state of national finances, the opposing faction won out. The royal wedding would be celebrated with royal pomp and circumstance, providing, Churchill declared, "a flash of colour on the hard road we have to travel." But the King would bear the bulk of the cost, paying for it from the income from the Crown Estates.

High society
One minor obstacle was the groom's lack of estate; Philip had abandoned his Greek and Danish royal titles on becoming a naturalized British citizen. On the eve of the ceremony King George VI bestowed upon him the honorific "His Royal Highness" and awarded him the Order of the Garter. On the wedding morning, he was created Duke of Edinburgh, Earl of Merioneth, and Baron Greenwich. The King remarked, "It is a great deal to give a man all at once, but I know Philip understands his responsibilities."

Wedding guests – an array of surviving royalty from around the world – stayed at Claridge's, including the Queen of Spain, the King of Romania, the King and Queen of Denmark, and the Kings of Norway and Iraq. Philip Mountbatten had not one but two stag parties the night before the wedding, while the King hosted a dance at the palace for visiting royalty, which saw the Duke of Devonshire assaulted by an Indian rajah and the King himself lead a raucous conga line through the state apartments.

Like any cottager in the Dales
On 20 November, the princess emerged clothed in a beautiful ivory satin dress by Norman Hartnell. Like other brides, Elizabeth had been awarded extra clothing coupons to help her prepare, but unlike the others, she was able to rely on extravagant gifts from family and other sources. Her tiara was a gift from her grandmother. Her wedding ring was crafted from a piece of gold sent from Wales. "There is enough for two rings", she told Philip, "We can save a piece for Margaret."

Some 2,000 guests waited to greet her at Westminster Abbey. Conspicuous by their absence were Philip's sisters, tainted by Nazi connections, and the Duke and Duchess of Windsor, who were not invited (see pp.92–93). The service was intended to be as simple and unaffected as that of "any cottager who might be married in some small country church in the Dales this afternoon," gushed the Archbishop of Canterbury. A huge audience listened in on radio, and although highlights were televised, television set ownership across the country was minuscule at that time. Huge crowds surged down the Mall to call for the newlyweds, and especially the King, to come out and greet them.

Kept warm by a corgi
At the wedding breakfast for 150 close friends, the cake, made by McVities and Price, was 2.74 m (9 ft) high in four tiers and weighed 227 kg (500 lbs). The princess changed into another Hartnell dress – a pale blue number described as "love in a mist" – and the couple were driven to Waterloo Station in an open

> **10,000** The number of pearls imported from the US for Elizabeth's wedding dress.

The grand cake
The decorations on the wedding cake included the coats of arms of both families, monograms of bride and groom, and regimental and naval badges.

carriage. Elizabeth kept warm with a hot water bottle underneath a rug on her lap and her favourite corgi, Susan, alongside her. From there, Philip and Elizabeth went by train to Winchester, to spend the first night of their honeymoon at Broadlands, the country home of Philip's uncle Lord Mountbatten.

After their honeymoon, their first home would be Windlesham Moor, in Surrey, while they waited for Clarence House to be refurbished (see pp.122–23). This grand but now rather dilapidated house was near to Buckingham Palace, allowing the King to keep his daughter close. At Windlesham Moor they sorted through the eclectic array of about 3,000 gifts they had received, which included 500 cans of pineapple from Queensland, a piece of lace made from yarn Gandhi had spun himself, and a rabbit tea cosy, two pieces of soggy toast, and a rock from Mt Snowdon sent by an elderly Welshman.

"It is a far more **moving thing** to **give your daughter away** than to be married yourself.**"**

KING GEORGE VI, TO THE ARCHBISHOP OF YORK, 20 NOVEMBER 1947

The newlyweds
Elizabeth and Philip are seen here posing for a photograph after the wedding. The princess's ivory duchess satin dress is embroidered with garlands of lily heads and white York roses with orange blossoms and ears of corn.

AFTER »

The marriage of Elizabeth and Philip has withstood the constant scrutiny and pressures of royal obligations. But for some time after the wedding, the focus shifted to Princess Margaret.

SPOTLIGHT ON MARGARET
With Elizabeth now married, public and media attention soon began to focus on Margaret. On 21 August 1948, she celebrated her 18th birthday with an **official "coming out" onto the social scene.** For some time now the spotlight would be on the **beautiful and glamorous young princess and her prospects for marriage.**

ENDURING PARTNERSHIP
After their wedding, Philip, in a letter to his mother-in-law, stated that Elizabeth "is the only thing in this world which is absolutely real to me". Elizabeth and Philip would go on to celebrate their **silver anniversary** and, later, their **golden anniversary.** In 2007, they completed 60 years together, making the Queen the first British monarch to celebrate a **diamond wedding anniversary 266–67 ».** They celebrated their **platinum – 70th – wedding anniversary** in 2017.

SILVER ANNIVERSARY STAMP, 1972

In the library
Despite a refurbishment before Prince Charles took up residence, on his insistence many of the contents in the house are arranged as they were in Queen Elizabeth's time, including her books in the library.

ROYAL RESIDENCE

Clarence House

This elegant Georgian residence is attached to St James's Palace and shares its gardens. For more than 50 years it was the much-loved London home of the Queen Mother. It is now the official London residence of the Prince of Wales and Duchess of Cornwall.

In the late Georgian period, London had become one of the most influential cities in the world. It was, however, smelly, crowded, and disorganized. Determined to create a city whose architecture reflected its growing importance on the world stage, the Prince Regent, later George IV, hired three architects whose remit was to transform London. The most inspired of these was John Nash, who created iconic buildings such as Buckingham Palace and Marble Arch, and changed the face of the city for ever with grand ceremonial boulevards such as the Mall and Regent Street.

One of the buildings he created along the Mall was Clarence House, built for the Duke of Clarence, who became King William IV on the death of his brother in 1830. A white stucco Classical mansion on three storeys, it was a far more restrained and intimate building than Buckingham Palace. William was a man who shunned pretension and formality, and on his accession to the throne he decided to remain in Clarence House instead of moving to Buckingham Palace – simply adding a passage to connect it with the state apartments of St James's Palace for ease of access.

Clarence House later became the home of Queen Victoria's mother, the Duchess of Kent, who added a conservatory, created a new private entrance from The Mall (the original entrance was from a public road), and replaced the house's sombre crimson damasks with the pale painted wallpapers then in vogue. When the Duchess died, Queen Victoria's second son, Prince Alfred, Duke of Edinburgh, took up residence. After his marriage in 1874 to the Grand Duchess Marie Alexandrovna of Russia, the House was lavishly renovated, receiving a fourth storey and an opulent Orthodox chapel (which no longer exists).

Headquarters of the British Red Cross and Order of St John of Jerusalem during World War Two, Clarence House was again refurbished in the late 1940s to make it a family home for Princess Elizabeth, the Duke of Edinburgh, and the one-year-old Charles. They moved to Buckingham Palace after Elizabeth succeeded to the throne in 1952.

The Queen Mother

In the latter half of the 20th century, Clarence House became synonymous with Queen Elizabeth, the Queen Mother, who lived there for over 50 years. She was an enthusiastic hostess of luncheons, evening receptions, and afternoon teas; and a keen collector and patron of the arts. The house is still decorated with important objects and works of art.

Restoration

After the death of the Queen Mother in 2002, the house became the official residence of Prince Charles and his sons. It underwent essential renovation and redecoration, though great pains were taken by Prince Charles to use sustainable materials and to preserve the style and atmosphere created by his grandmother. Charles's main innovation was the formal, organic garden, which he designed himself in memory of the Queen Mother. It incorporates an ancient pear tree and a black mulberry reputed to have been planted in the time of James I.

Use today

Every year the Prince and the Duchess receive thousands of official guests from this country and overseas, and bring together people from all walks of life through seminars and receptions. On the initiative of Prince Charles, the house and its garden are open to the public for one month every summer.

House and home

Clarence House is said to have the atmosphere of a family home, despite its offices for staff and guards outside. The Garden Room, which leads out to the garden, was created by knocking two rooms together to provide a large entertaining space for Queen Elizabeth.

THE GARDEN ROOM'S 1945 PORTRAIT OF ELIZABETH

SUNDIAL IN THE FORMAL GARDEN

GUARD OUTSIDE CLARENCE HOUSE

Born 1921

The **Duke** of Edinburgh

"The **Queen** has the **quality** of tolerance in **abundance.**"

PRINCE PHILIP, 1997

Born in a villa named Mon Repos on the island of Corfu in Greece, Philip was the product of the tangled 19th-century heritage of European royalty. His family was of German-Danish background, but by a quirk of dynastic fate, he was born a Prince of Greece as well as Denmark. Philip's full dynastic name at this point was Schleswig-Holstein-Sonderberg-Glucksburg.

Around the start of the 20th century, monarchies were being widely discarded by nationalist, republican, communist, and fascist movements. When Philip was just 18 months old, his father, Prince Andrew of Greece, and his mother, Princess Alice of Battenberg, were exiled to Paris and relieved of their titles as a result of a coup. This made Philip, in the words of his official biographer, "nameless, stateless, and penniless" despite his noble birth.

Aged 7, Philip was sent to Surrey, England, to live with his maternal relatives, whose name he later

adopted; in the wake of anti-German sentiments during World War I, Philip's grandfather Prince Louis Battenberg anglicized his name to Mountbatten on request of King George V, and in 1946, Philip followed suit. Meanwhile, back in 1933, just as Adolf Hitler came to power, Philip was sent to school at a castle in Germany. Although some members of his family – including his sisters – supported the Nazis, Philip had a distinctly antipathetic reaction to their ideology. Along with his inspirational headmaster, Kurt Hahn, he was chased out of Germany and relocated to Gordonstoun School in Scotland, where he excelled.

In the navy

As World War II loomed, Philip followed in the footsteps of his illustrious Mountbatten relatives by joining the Royal Navy via cadetship at the Royal Naval College, Dartmouth. In 1939, when George VI and Queen Elizabeth toured the college, Philip was asked to escort Princess Elizabeth, then only 13 years old, and her sister Margaret. Philip was Elizabeth's third cousin, since, like most European royalty, he could trace his descent back to Queen Victoria.

The Philip Movement

Philip is the object of veneration in one of the world's strangest religions, the Philip Movement, which emerged in the 1960s on the island of Tanna in the South Pacific. Worshippers regard the prince as a divine being and treasure the signed photos he has sent them.

In uniform
Philip, seen here wearing his naval uniform, had a fairly distinguished naval career. In 1942, at 21 years old, he became one of the youngest first lieutenants in the Royal Navy.

Graduating top of his class in 1940, he embarked on a glittering though ultimately short-lived naval career. After marrying Elizabeth, Philip went on to take command of a ship of his own, but was forced to give up his career when the princess became Queen in 1952. Philip bitterly regretted his retirement from the service – "I'd much rather have stayed in the Navy, frankly," he said in 1992.

By royal appointment

The course of Philip's life changed forever when he struck up a romance with young Elizabeth, whose soft demeanour concealed a core of steel. At the time of the courtship, the young naval

officer had a raffish reputation and a fast sports car to match, and there was both public and royal opposition to the pairing. However, Elizabeth's will would not be denied, and Philip soon became His Royal Highness The Duke of Edinburgh, Earl of Merioneth, and Baron Greenwich. Today he is the longest serving consort in British royal history, as well as the oldest ever male member of the British Royal Family.

Social blunders

Alongside his many years of faithful service as consort, Philip has also pursued passions of his own. He became a skilful carriage driver, helping to formulate the rules of the sport. He has also long nurtured an interest in wildlife – both hunting and conserving it. This contradiction was illustrated in 1961, when in the same year that he was made president of the new World Wide Fund for Nature (WWF), he sparked controversy by shooting a tiger in India. Controversy has, in fact, become one of Philip's trademarks, particularly his propensity for gaffes, or social blunders.

Four-in-hand
Philip, along with his groom and navigator, drives through a water obstacle at the Lowther Driving Trials in Cumbria in 2005.

On an official visit to Papua New Guinea in 1988, he asked a British student who had trekked across the country, "You managed not to get eaten then?", while after the Royal Variety Performance in 1969 he famously asked singer Tom Jones, "What do you gargle with – pebbles?", later adding, "It is very difficult to see how it is possible to become immensely valuable by singing what I think are the most hideous songs." Philip is not, however, lacking in self-awareness: "Dontopedalogy is the science of opening your mouth and putting your foot in it," he once told the General Dental Council, "a science which I have practised for a good many years."

Philip's monogram
Popular with European royalty since the Victorian era, monograms are used to identify and decorate a person's items. Philip's monogram graces everything from letterheads to handkerchiefs.

Encouraging the youth

One of Philip's most enduring contributions to public life has been his scheme for young people – the Duke of Edinburgh's (DofE) Award. The award grew out of the Prince's formative experiences with Kurt Hahn at Gordonstoun School. Hahn had initiated an awards scheme at the school to encourage young people to set and surpass their own targets for physical achievement, in line with his philosophy that while physical education is paramount, competition can be counterproductive. After the war, Hahn was keen to extend his scheme across Britain, and Philip helped him achieve his vision.

Philip said, "I could see that some such 'achievement-based' programme, without requiring membership, might be a valuable tool for… the development of young people… to respond to Hahn's four major concerns about the development of young people… the decline of compassion, the decline of skills, the decline of physical fitness, and the decline of initiative." The scheme was launched in 1956, with Bronze, Silver, and Gold Awards. To earn them, boys needed to achieve targets in fields as diverse as physical fitness, volunteering, and expeditions. Two years later, a DofE scheme was introduced for girls. Philip described the development of the programme: "I put together a group of women, and asked them to devise a similar programme, which they thought would be appropriate for girls in the same age groups." The Awards soon went international, operating in 22 countries by 1966. Today, over 2 million Awards have been achieved in the UK alone, and over 7 million young people from 132 countries have taken part in the scheme since 1956.

PHILIP ADDRESSES WWF'S SECOND INTERNATIONAL CONGRESS IN 1970

> **"Prince Philip… has been a constant strength and guide."**
>
> QUEEN ELIZABETH, DIAMOND JUBILEE ADDRESS, MARCH 2012

« BEFORE

Public excitement about the imminent arrival of a royal baby reached fever pitch in the days before Princess Elizabeth's first child was due.

A BUZZ IN THE AIR

Crowds of **well-wishers congregated** in front of Buckingham Palace as the delivery day grew near. They were so noisy and excited that Elizabeth's family became genuinely concerned that the clamour would **disturb the Princess**. Her parents suggested that she move to a quieter room overlooking the gardens on the other side of the palace, but she refused. Elizabeth insisted, "I want my baby to be born in my own room, amongst the things I know."

33 The number of generations in the line of descent from William the Conqueror to Prince Charles.

Proud parents
Princess Elizabeth and the Duke of Edinburgh smile for the camera with Prince Charles after his christening in the Music Room at Buckingham Palace on 15 December 1948.

The **Births** of Charles and **Anne**

Within a year of their marriage, Princess Elizabeth and the Duke of Edinburgh were celebrating the birth of their first son. In the years that followed, the couple went on to have another three children.

In the spring of 1948, Elizabeth and her husband Philip made a triumphal visit to Paris, greeted by cheering crowds and prompting French newspapers to declare that it was like the Norman Conquest (see pp.16–17) in reverse, with the English winning over the French this time. Discerning observers noted that, despite her enthusiasm for Parisian horse racing, nightclubs, and shops, the young Princess looked tired and needed frequent rests.

Later that year, Buckingham Palace confirmed what was widely suspected: Elizabeth was expecting a child. The announcement was made on Derby Day, on 4 June, when the famous flat horse race takes place at Epsom Downs Racecourse in Surrey. The Princess duly appeared at the racecourse, and greeted the crowds with good cheer. Correspondence flooded in from all over the world, with an avalanche of cards, gifts, and pregnancy advice. The pram that had borne Elizabeth and her sister Margaret as infants was retrieved from storage and decorated in gender-neutral yellow, so that, said Elizabeth, "No one can guess whether we want a boy or a girl."

The custom is only a custom

While Elizabeth was nearing full term, her father's health was declining, along with his grasp of state matters, and his temper became more volatile. Both privately and publicly, the young Princess was moving centre stage as her parents were pushed to the margins. It was clear that Elizabeth would soon be queen, and the public appetite for news of her and her new family was insatiable.

Meanwhile, ministers and courtiers wrestled with a thorny issue: the venerable tradition of ministers attending the birth of a royal heir. This custom stemmed from medieval anxieties about the succession and the provenance of royal babies. It had served as a safeguard against plots to smuggle into the royal birthing chamber babies who were not the legitimate offspring of the monarch, or more precisely, against the risk that others might cast aspersions on the legitimacy of royal heirs. Clearly, this rationale was now antiquated, along with the custom itself. Victoria had modernized it somewhat in the 19th century, by insisting that her ministers wait outside in the

corridor rather than actually being present at her bedside while she was in labour. James Chuter Ede, the Home Secretary, ruled that there was no constitutional imperative for him to attend the birth, writing, "The custom is only a custom… there is no legal requirement for its continuance." But the traditionalist King, along with the Queen, felt strongly that the Home Secretary should attend the birth. The issue came to a head in early November, when the Canadian High Commissioner mentioned to Sir Alan Lascelles, the top courtier in the Palace, that he was expecting to attend the birth alongside the Home Secretary and other representatives of the Dominions. Lascelles realized that, constitutionally speaking, if one of them were to be present, all the others would also be entitled to attend, so "there would be no less than seven ministers sitting in the passage". This was enough to convince the King that what he now admitted was an "archaic custom" was obsolete. Lascelles was relieved, and he later wrote that he

delivered by Sir William Gilliatt, the royal gynaecologist, with the help of forceps. Elizabeth was unconscious throughout the labour. As was customary at the time, she was given a powerful anaesthetic to induce what was known as "twilight sleep", and which caused amnesia for the labour itself. Here Elizabeth was following royal tradition, as her great-great-grandmother Victoria had pioneered the use of anaesthesia in childbirth in the 19th century.

Philip had been playing squash while waiting for the news. He arrived, accompanied by the cheers of the

AFTER »

After becoming Queen, Elizabeth would go on to have two more children – becoming the first reigning monarch to have a baby since the birth of Victoria's youngest daughter Princess Beatrice.

MORE ROYAL BIRTHS

On 19 February 1960, Elizabeth gave **birth to Andrew Albert Christian Edward** at Buckingham Palace. She wrote to a friend: "The baby is adorable, and is very good, and putting on weight well. Both the older children are completely riveted by him, and all in all, he's going to be terribly spoilt by all of us, I'm sure!" Four years later, on 10 March 1964, the Queen gave **birth to Edward Antony Richard Louis,** also at Buckingham Palace.

" Prince **Charles,** as he is to be named, is an **obedient sitter.** "

CECIL BEATON, PHOTOGRAPHER, DECEMBER 1948

"had long thought that the practice… was out-of-date and ridiculous." The Princess's labour would be a private affair.

Breach of trust

Just before the baby was due, Elizabeth made a visit to Marion Crawford, her former nanny who had just retired from royal service after 17 years. In 1948, Crawford left the royal household to set up home with her husband. At this time, she and the Princess were still very close, with Elizabeth confiding in her that she did not fear childbirth: "After all, it's what we're made for." Unfortunately, relations between Crawford and the Royal Family were soon to turn sour. In a bid to improve her finances, the former nanny collaborated with journalists on a series of articles for the American press that included what today seem like harmless reminiscences. To the secretive royals, however, this was a traitorous breach of trust. The problem was compounded when, in 1950, Crawford's memoirs of her time as royal nanny were issued as a book titled *The Little Princesses*. All contact with the former nanny was immediately severed and the breach was never healed.

Royal births

All this lay in the future, when, at 9.14 pm on 14 November 1948, a baby boy weighing 3.34 kg (7 lb 6 oz) was

crowd on the Mall, to meet his new son, who was to be named Charles Philip Arthur George. The choice of the name Charles was somewhat controversial, given the ill-starred fate of a previous English monarch of that name (see pp.38–39), but Elizabeth and Philip liked the sound of it. When Charles does come to the throne, he may not necessarily take the title Charles III, as he could choose to reign under a different name, in similar fashion to his grandfather and great-uncle.

Charles's arrival sparked a tidal wave of correspondence from well-wishers, and prompted the Princess to announce that food parcels would be sent to every child in the country born on the same day. The baby Prince was christened in December the same year. Not long after this, mother and son had to endure two months of forced

separation because of measles, and less than 18 months later, Elizabeth and Philip celebrated the arrival of their second child – a girl.

Born at 11.50 am on 15 August 1950, the new baby weighed exactly 2.7 kg (6 lb). She was named Anne and was given middle names reflecting her immediate heritage: Elizabeth after her maternal grandmother, the Queen; Alice after her paternal grandmother, Alice of Battenberg; and Louise after a great-aunt. The Duke of Edinburgh toasted her arrival with champagne, and after registering her names with the Westminster registrar, was presented with his daughter's identity card, ration book, and a bottle of cod-liver oil. Shortly after Anne's birth, her mother wrote "The baby is quite unlike her brother, so it will be interesting to see whom she will take after when she is older."

Blessing the new Princess
Princess Elizabeth cradles Princess Anne while Queen Elizabeth holds Prince Charles on the Princess's christening day in October 1950. The ceremony was conducted by the Archbishop of York, Cyril Forster Garbett.

Grounded childhood

Charles and Anne pose in coats on the Prince's fourth birthday. The little Prince and Princess can be seen in this attire in many other photos from the time. Their mother insisted on being frugal with clothes at a time of continued rationing.

Their happiest time
For a few months, Elizabeth was able to live a carefree life as a naval officer's wife in Malta. The Duke of Edinburgh's valet recalled: "They were so relaxed and free. I think it was their happiest time."

Born 1926

Elizabeth II, the Early Years

"I declare... that my **whole life,** whether it be long or short, shall be **devoted to your service.**"

ELIZABETH II, IN HER SPEECH ON HER 21ST BIRTHDAY, 1947

Learning to be queen
King George VI prepares his elder daughter Elizabeth for the role of queen. Here he is going through some state papers with her in a study at Windsor Castle in 1942.

To get a clear picture of the early years of Elizabeth II's reign, it is important to know that she was never intended to rule. Her childhood was sheltered and insular, and she had regular contact with her parents. Elizabeth and her sister Margaret lived in a little world of their own. In her 1950 book, *The Little Princesses*, Marion Crawford – "Crawfie", the governess who stewarded the education and early years of the lives of Elizabeth and Margaret, recalled that their nanny, Clara Wright (known as Alah) "had entire charge in those days of the children's out-of-school lives – their health, their baths, their clothes – while I had them from 9 to 5. (Alah) had to help her an under-nurse and a nursemaid".

In childhood Elizabeth was third in line to the throne, but since it was not her father but her uncle David who would inherit the crown as Edward VIII, few could have suspected that she would ever sit on it. Yet in late 1936 came the abdication of Edward VIII (see pp.92–93). "The shock of those terrible December days was literally stunning", recalled Queen Elizabeth, the Queen Mother. Her daughter was now destined to become queen. The new King George VI was very different in character from his flighty and self-indulgent brother, David. George VI and his wife would go on to instil their values in their daughter. The influence of her parents has been evident throughout her reign in her approach to the role of monarch, forming her overriding characteristics: an exceptional sense of public service married to traditional values.

Good works

Before Elizabeth took the throne would come the drama and challenges of World War II, with her own war service and an increasing public profile. In May 1944, Elizabeth gave

Equestrian love
Elizabeth II is really fond of horses. In this photograph, she and the Queen Mother are admiring the greatest flat racehorse Sea Bird II winning the prestigious Epsom Derby in June 1965.

a public address, to promote the Queen Elizabeth Hospital for Children in Hackney, east London, a charitable institution named after her mother. There she pledged her support for voluntary traditions at a time when the fashion was for ever-increasing state intervention in welfare. Thus she launched what has become a central feature of the royal project up to the present day: the role of "good works". Currently, the Crown's patronage list extends to more than 3,000 organizations – the Queen alone has 800. According to British historian David Cannadine: "charitable activity has become the place where the royal culture of hierarchical condescension, and the popular culture of social aspiration, have successfully merged."

Devoted to service

Another early clue to the type of queen Elizabeth would be, came in her 21st birthday broadcast to the Empire (see p.107), made in 1947. Recalling the dedication of her ancestors, she told the people she, too, would be devoted to their service. Duty has become perhaps the overarching principle of Elizabeth II's reign, but this in turn has led to some difficulties in balancing priorities, because alongside being the monarch of several nations and head of the Commonwealth, the Queen has also been a devoted wife, mother, daughter, and sister.

The two sides of Elizabeth have not always been easily reconciled. For instance, during her epic

Sticking with tradition
With a passion for stamps running in the Royal Family, Elizabeth here is going through her collections in 1946. Her father George VI kept his stamps in blue binders, while her collection is kept in green books.

Commonwealth tour of 1953–54, she was away from her young children Charles and Anne for more than six months. This was followed in 1956 by a three-month period in which her husband Philip was absent putting the new yacht *HMY Britannia* through its sea trials, a separation that excited much speculation about their marriage. Moreover, when it came to her sister Margaret, and the agonising choice she faced over marrying Group Captain Peter Townsend (see pp.154–55), the steeliest side of the young Queen's personality came to the fore. She bluntly refused to support Margaret in choosing love over duty.

A perfect balance

Yet against these examples of a harsh devotion to duty, can be set the overwhelming evidence of her devotion to family. The Queen's Christmas message of 1956 (see

"We should **remember** that in spite of all the scientific advances and **great** improvements in our **material welfare,** the family remains as the **focal point** of our **existence.**"

QUEEN ELIZABETH, CHRISTMAS MESSAGE, 1965

pp.156–57), for instance, included these touching words in respect of her husband's long absence: "You will understand me, therefore, when I tell you that of all the voices we have heard this afternoon none has given my children and myself greater joy than that of my husband". While they were still alive, Elizabeth would make sure to telephone her mother and sister every day.

There is a kind of conflict central to the persona of the Queen between her public face and her private demeanour. In public, she is widely perceived as reserved and aloof, but many accounts of her in private paint a picture of a woman with a robust sense of humour.

The Queen prefers to focus on her work. At 7 pm every weekday evening of the year, except Christmas and Easter Day, she receives a red despatch box of state papers to go through, which she needs to read and sign where necessary.

Racing mostly
The Queen has long had an abiding love of horses and horse racing. She runs a racing stable of her own and has had many classic winners. This love dates back to her teenage

years and was evidently a strong feature of her early reign; when asked what he and the Queen talked about at their weekly Tuesday meetings, Winston Churchill replied: "Racing mostly."

Private person
The Queen places a lot of value on her privacy, despite being the most famous and possibly most photographed woman in the world. This official photograph was released in January 1956 before her Nigeria tour.

TIMELINE

- **21 April 1926** Born in London, the first child of the Duke and Duchess of York, is named Elizabeth Alexandra Mary.
- **1939** First meets Philip Mountbatten.
- **1936** Death of King George V; Edward, Prince of Wales becomes King Edward VIII; after a tumultuous year of controversy over his politics and personal life, Edward VIII chooses to abdicate. Elizabeth's father becomes King George VI on 12 December.
- **1944** Becomes a Counsellor of State after turning 18, and, following an act of Parliament the previous year, can now become ruler without a regent.
- **1945** Joins Auxiliary Transport Service (ATS) as subaltern and learns to drive and service trucks.
- **20 November 1947** Marries Philip, who is made Duke of Edinburgh.
- **14 November 1948** Birth of Charles, Elizabeth and Philip's first child.
- **15 August 1950** Birth of Elizabeth's only daughter Anne.
- **1952** Death of George VI. Elizabeth II lays to rest her father on 15 February and opens Parliament for the first time on 4 November.

ROYAL COAT OF ARMS OF THE UK

- **2 June 1953** Is crowned Queen; later that year she and her husband embark on a six-month tour of the Commonwealth.
- **January 1957** Becomes embroiled in a constitutional crisis over the leadership of the Conservative party – when Prime Minister Anthony Eden had to resign due to the Suez Crisis. Elizabeth was advised to choose Harold Macmillan rather than R A Butler.
- **19 February 1960** Birth of her second son, Andrew.
- **10 March 1964** Birth of her third son, Edward.
- **May 1970** Inaugurates a new tradition of royal walkabouts on a visit to New Zealand.
- **6 February 1977** Celebrates her Silver Jubilee. Celebrations happened throughout the year.
- **27 August 1979** Assassination of Louis Mountbatten by the Irish Republican Army (IRA); the Royal Family is devastated.
- **November 1979** The Queen is embarrassed by revelations that the keeper of her pictures, Anthony Blunt, was a Russian spy.

Return of the Queen
The new Queen steps down from a 24-hour flight from Kenya, arriving at London Airport at dusk on 7 February 1952. Prime Minister Churchill and other statesmen were waiting to meet her.

Elizabeth becomes Queen

Elizabeth's hopes of a few years of low-profile family life were shattered when the unexpected death of her father propelled her to the throne at the age of just 25 years.

◀◀ BEFORE

King George VI had long been in declining health. His heavy smoking habit lay at the root of a host of serious illnesses.

FAILING HEALTH
The King suffered from severe artherosclerosis, was afflicted with cancer, and had to undergo a number of operations – one to relieve nerve pressure that was causing great pain, and in the autumn of 1951, when his lung cancer had progressed too far, an operation to

42 The number of reigning sovereigns of England since William the Conqueror.

remove a lung. The King himself was not told the lung was cancerous; instead he believed it was removed because of a bronchial blockage.

One consequence of the King's ill health was that the Palace could not countenance foreign tours for the monarch; instead Princess Elizabeth and her husband would deputize for him. In October 1951 they visited Canada and the US, returning in time to spend Christmas with the King at Sandringham. The presence of his daughter prompted the King to rally and he was able to go shooting and enjoy the festivities. Elizabeth had no cause to think twice about agreeing to undertake a mammoth six-month tour of the Commonwealth, starting in February 1952, leaving Prince Charles and his baby sister Anne in the care of their grandparents. The tour would officially begin in Ceylon (now Sri Lanka), but would be prefaced with a romantic stopover in Kenya, where

Elizabeth was delighted to accept an invitation to stay at the unique Treetops safari lodge near the Sagana Lodge – a house that had been given to the royal couple as a wedding present by the Kenyan government. The morning after a family trip to see the musical *South Pacific* at the Drury Lane Theatre, the King waved Elizabeth and Philip goodbye from the tarmac of London Airport. The Princess would never see her father again.

Back at Sandringham, the King seemed in good spirits. On 5 February he went out shooting, wearing a specially designed electrically heated waistcoat, and was able to bag nine hares. That evening he was "in tremendous form and looking so well and happy", the Queen later recalled. The King went to bed at 10.30 pm,

Access all areas
Tickets for admission were issued to the funeral of George VI, which was held at St George's Chapel at Windsor Castle, after a procession had borne the coffin through the streets of London to Paddington Station.

and a watchman saw him adjusting his window around midnight, but when his servant James Macdonald took in a cup of tea to wake him at 7.30 am the next morning, the King

Funeral train
The Royal Train carried the King's body from Norfolk to London. His coffin was taken by gun carriage to lie in state at Westminster Hall, where 300,000 people paid their respects. The train later went to Paddington, and then Windsor for George VI's funeral.

was dead. "There were jolly jokes and he went to bed early because he was convalescing", reflected Princess Margaret, "Then he wasn't there any more". He had died of a heart attack early on the morning on 6 February.

Despite the clear warning signs no one had actually planned what to do in the event of the King's death. Macdonald told the King's wife, and the gamekeepers carried the King's body to the local church, but it was over an hour before a courtier was sent to Downing Street to break the bad news to the recently re-installed Prime Minister, Winston Churchill, a friend of the King. "Bad news?!," cried Churchill, flinging aside state

something similar: "[Elizabeth] had climbed up that ladder as Princess; she was going to have to climb down again as Queen."

Royal aides got wind of the news of the King's death from reporters staying nearby, and furtively tuned into the BBC world service to verify the rumours. They learned that Elizabeth had been Queen for at least five hours, much of which she and Philip had spent fishing. Royal equerry Mike Parker broke the news to Prince Philip, who responded as if the world had collapsed on him. He saw immediately that the idyll of their life together had come to an end. Philip in turn told Elizabeth, who took

sovereign of England, at the age of 25 she was the youngest monarch to accede to the throne since 1837, when Victoria acceded aged just 18. Elizabeth's full title depends on which realm is involved, but in the UK she would henceforth be styled as Her Majesty Elizabeth the Second, by the Grace of God, of the United Kingdom of Great Britain and Northern Ireland, and of Her other Realms and Territories Queen, Head of the Commonwealth, Defender of the Faith; in Latin: Elizabeth II, *Dei Gratia Britanniarum Regnorumque Suorum Ceterorum Regina, Consortionis Populorum Princeps, Fidei Defensor*. In addition she holds numerous other titles and honours. Examples include: Duke of Normandy and Lord of Mann; Member

> # 539 MILLION The number of subjects and citizens on Elizabeth II's accession.

First Class of the Most Esteemed Royal Family Order of Brunei; Grand Commander of the Order of the Niger; and Honorary Companion of Honour with Collar of the National Order of Merit of Malta.

Meeting with the accession council at St James's Palace, Elizabeth told them, "I pray that God will help me to discharge worthily the heavy task that has been laid upon me so early in my

WHAT'S IN A NAME?
On 9 April 1952, Queen Elizabeth II signed an order declaring that "she and her children shall be styled and known as the **House of Windsor**". This was in accordance with the strident views of her grandmother, Queen Mary, who had asserted that her husband had founded the House of Windsor for all time. Philip protested bitterly, lamenting, "I am the only man in the country not allowed to give his name to his children." Queen Mary, the first queen ever to see her grandchild accede to the throne, passed away on 24 March 1953 at the age of 85.

life". On 11 February, the Royal Train from Wolferton, Norfolk, arrived at King's Cross bearing the body of George VI, and was met by members of the Royal Family. After lying in state at Westminster Hall, the coffin was moved to St George's Chapel, Windsor, where the King's funeral took place on 15 February. The lord chamberlain snapped his staff of office in two and tossed it into the grave. Choosing henceforth to be known as Queen Elizabeth, the Queen Mother, the King's wife thanked the world for their sympathies: "I want you to know how your concern for me has upheld me in my sorrow. I commend to you our dear daughter. Give her your loyalty and devotion: in the great and lonely station to which she has been called she will need your protection and your love."

> # "A fair and youthful figure, Princess, wife and mother, is **heir to** our **traditions** and **glories...** to all our **united strength** and **loyalty.**"
>
> WINSTON CHURCHILL, HOUSE OF COMMONS, 11 FEBRUARY 1952

papers, "The worst! How unimportant these matters seem." His private secretary later found Churchill weeping, and protesting in relation to the new Queen that he did not know her and she was only a child.

No sign of tears
The child in question was at one of the most remote places in the world, in terms of communication. She had spent a delightful night filming elephants at the water hole that lay below the branches of the great fig tree in which Treetops sat. But, as the visitors' book records, "For the first time in the history of the world, a young girl climbed into the tree a Princess and climbed down the next day a Queen." This has become a well-worn cliché, and it is unclear who coined the phrase. The new Queen's lady-in-waiting, Pamela Mountbatten, wrote

the news, he said, "Bravely, like a queen." An aide later found her in her room, "seated at her desk, very upright, high colour, no sign of tears." Asked under what name she would rule, she replied without hesitation, "My own name, Elizabeth, of course – what else?" Philip lay on the sofa with a newspaper over his face.

On 7 February, Queen Elizabeth II arrived back in the UK. The 43rd reigning

Grieving family
The Queen Mother, Elizabeth, and Margaret – wife and daughters of George VI – in mourning dress, are on their way to attend the King's funeral. Queen Mary was too ill to attend the actual ceremony.

« BEFORE

Three days before the Queen's first State Opening, the government was finalizing her speech. Traditionally, the speech was written on goat skin vellum with ink that took three days to dry. Once written, it could not easily be changed. Today sending the speech to the Palace for approval is still known as "going goat".

GUNPOWDER SEARCH
On the morning of the Queen's first State Opening, the **Yeoman of the Guard,** the Queen's personal bodyguard, performed a **ceremonial sweep** of the cellars of the palace – a nod to the **Gunpowder Plot of 1605 « 38–39.**

The Queen in Parliament and Politics

One of the first of Elizabeth II's duties as Queen was to attend the State Opening of Parliament. Loaded with pomp and pageantry, this event perfectly encapsulates the nature of the British constitution and the monarch's vital but precarious part in it.

The Queen is head of state of Britain and several other realms, and her role at the top of a constitutional monarchy is at the same time fundamentally symbolic, of vital importance, and extremely delicate. Simply by being at the top of the constitutional "pyramid" she helps to guarantee the rights and liberties of all her subjects, yet it is essential that she is scrupulously apolitical and visibly remains above

> ## "It is Her Majesty's pleasure that they [the Commons] attend her immediately in this house."

GENTLEMAN USHER OF THE BLACK ROD TO PARLIAMENT, 4 NOVEMBER 1952

the political fray. In formal terms, she has the right to be consulted, to encourage, and to warn her ministers via regular audiences with the Prime Minister. Her duties include assenting to the passage of laws through Parliament, and consenting to the debate of bills that affect the Crown. She also has the responsibility for

proroguing or dissolving Parliament, and receives weekly briefings on parliamentary matters.

The Crown in Parliament
By far the Queen's best known and most visible role is to attend the annual State Opening of Parliament ceremony, the ritual that marks the start of a new parliamentary session. The Queen opens Parliament in person, and addresses both Houses with the Queen's Speech – a speech that lays out the legislative programme of her government over the forthcoming session. Neither House can proceed to public business until the Queen's Speech has been read. The ceremony articulates the delicate but time-hardened nature of the British constitution, and the Palace itself describes this as "the most colourful event of the parliamentary year [and] also the most important, because it brings together the three elements of the legislature [the House of Commons, the House of Lords, and the Queen]. The ceremony therefore represents the Crown in Parliament".

The theatre begins before Her Majesty even leaves Buckingham Palace, where one of the government's chief whips (a Member of Parliament who serves, for these purposes, in the archaic office of Vice-Chamberlain of the Household) is offered by Parliament as a symbolic "hostage", to guarantee safe return of the sovereign. This ritual is a holdover from days when there was a genuine edge of jeopardy to relationships between the monarch and Parliament,

with memories still fresh of the regicide of 1649. Charles I was executed by Parliament after tensions over the constitutional relationship between King and legislature boiled over into Civil War (see pp.40–41). At modern state openings, the Vice-Chamberlain is delivered to Buckingham Palace and waits there until the monarch returns.

The royal regalia
While this goes on, the royal regalia are taken from Buckingham Palace to the Palace of Westminster, to await the Queen's arrival. Among them are the Imperial State Crown, which the Queen wears during the opening ceremony, the Cap of Maintenance, which was originally the lining for a crown – given as a gift from the Pope – and the Sword of State, originally made for Charles II, which symbolizes justice and mercy. The crown is taken to the Robing Room to await the Queen.

The Queen and the Duke of Edinburgh, escorted by the Household Cavalry, make the journey between the palaces by State Coach. They are greeted with a fanfare by the State Trumpeters, and the Royal Standard is raised above the Palace of Westminster to signal that the Queen is in residence. The Queen the Imperial State Crown and the Robe of State. She then moves on to the House of Lords via a staircase guarded by the "staircase party", a special detachment of the Household Cavalry, who are the only troops allowed to draw swords in the Houses of Parliament.

White wand and Black Rod
When the Queen reaches the House of Lords she says "My Lords pray be seated", triggering a sequence of events in which the Lord Great Chamberlain raises his wand of office, a signal to the Gentleman Usher of the Black Rod (commonly known as Black Rod). He serves as the Queen's messenger in Parliament, and it is his job to summon the Commons. This is followed by a showpiece moment, in which Black Rod walks to the door of the House of Commons, which is ceremonially shut in his face, to symbolize that the House

of Commons is independent of the Crown. Black Rod knocks three times on the door before the command "Open the door" is given, and he is admitted

The Imperial State Crown
Originally made for Elizabeth II's father, this crown is worn on state occasions such as the State Opening of Parliament. It has three very large stones, and is set with 2,868 diamonds.

Sapphire, linking cross and fleur-de-lis

Ermine band

En route
Queen Elizabeth II, en route to her first State Opening of Parliament, is wearing the George IV State Diadem. She will change this on arriving at Westminster for the Imperial State Crown.

First time on film

The 1958 opening marked the first time in history that the sovereign was photographed reading the speech from the throne in the House of Lords. It was also the first time the ceremony was televised.

to deliver the Queen's summons: "Mr Speaker: the Queen commands this honourable house to attend Her Majesty immediately in the House of Peers." The Speaker and Black Rod then lead the MPs from the Commons to the Lords to hear the Queen's Speech.

A fixed point

The Queen's first State Opening came on 4 November 1952. It was her first major state event, attracting large crowds to watch as she arrived at Westminster. Wearing a specially made parliamentary robe of crimson velvet, decorated with gold lace and lined with ermine, she started her first Queen's Speech with a

Cabochon red spinel, known as the "Black Prince's Ruby"

Cushion-shaped Cullinan II diamond

tribute to her late father. In 2019, she attended her 64th and 65th openings – a remarkable record, which has seen her miss just two: in 1959 and 1963 when pregnant with Andrew and Edward, respectively. During her reign she has held weekly briefings with 14 prime ministers, outlasted 13 US presidents and all the general secretaries of the Communist Party of the Soviet Union, witnessed white smoke coming from the Vatican six times, and seen the building and tearing down of the Berlin Wall. It is often said that one of the great values of her role as constitutional monarch is that she offers a fixed point, stable in a world of constant change.

Although the Queen is kept thoroughly informed about government business and politics, it is important that she does not get involved in making political decisions. When it looks like she has or might, constitutional crisis threatens. Perhaps her greatest constitutional crisis came in January 1957 when Prime Minister Eden resigned in the wake of the Suez crisis (see pp.118–19) and the Queen had to exercise her royal prerogative, choosing between two candidates for his replacement. Informal soundings were taken by peers and the Queen was advised by Churchill; she chose Harold Macmillan over R A Butler, to the surprise of many. A similar situation arose again in

1963, when the Queen was once again advised to pass over Butler, this time in favour of Alec Douglas-Home. In more recent times, the Queen has maintained a careful silence on major constitutional issues such as Brexit and Scottish independence, although this has done little to hinder widespread media speculation about her preferences.

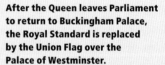

AFTER

After the Queen leaves Parliament to return to Buckingham Palace, the Royal Standard is replaced by the Union Flag over the Palace of Westminster.

THE OUTLAWRIES BILL

The parliamentary session **begins,** but instead of immediately moving to debate the Queen's Speech, both MPs and Lords introduce in their respective chambers what is known as the **Outlawries Bill,** a symbol of the autonomy of both houses from the monarch. **Purely ceremonial,** the bill is not taken forward and members are then able to debate the Queen's Speech and agree an "Address in Reply to Her Majesty's Gracious Speech."

Prime Minister's briefing

The Queen meets with her Prime Minister once a week. Here she is photographed meeting with Tony Blair in 2002. Her favourite prime minister was probably Winston Churchill — she even went to Downing Street for his farewell dinner.

1 ASCOT LANDAU

2 1902 STATE LANDAU

3 GLASS COACH

Three gilded cherubs, representing England, Scotland, and Ireland, support the Imperial Crown

One of four tritons, one on each corner, representing Britain's imperial power

All carvings by English sculptor Joseph Wilton (1722–1803)

4 GOLD STATE COACH

Panels by Italian painter Giovanni Cipriani (1727–85)

Brace, covered with Morocco leather, bears weight of coach

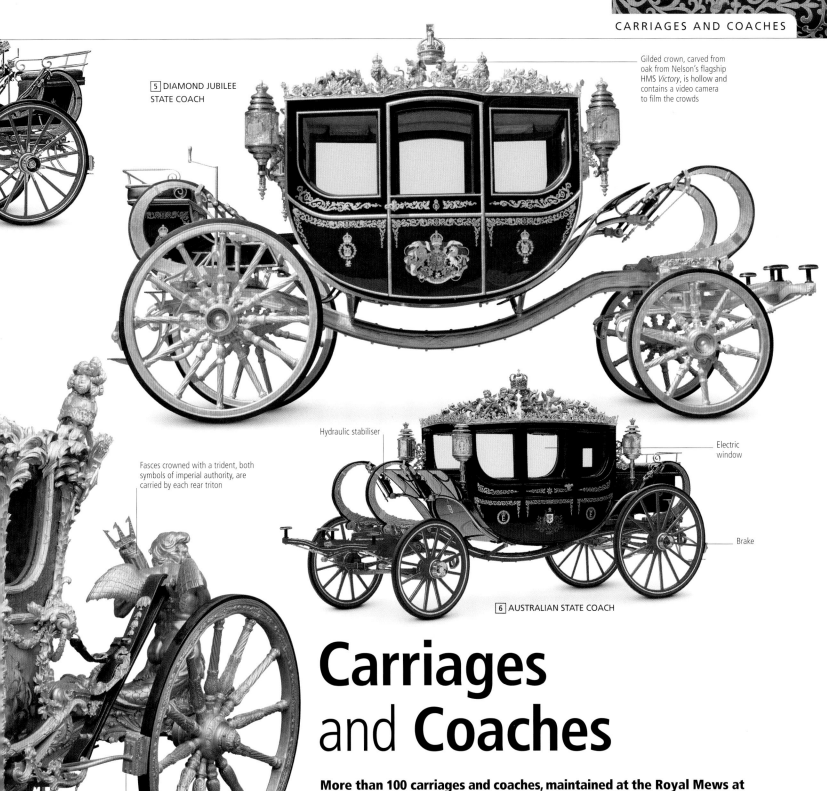

5 DIAMOND JUBILEE STATE COACH

Gilded crown, carved from oak from Nelson's flagship HMS *Victory*, is hollow and contains a video camera to film the crowds

Fasces crowned with a trident, both symbols of imperial authority, are carried by each rear triton

Hydraulic stabiliser

Electric window

Brake

6 AUSTRALIAN STATE COACH

Gilded brake

Ornately carved wheel

Carriages and Coaches

More than 100 carriages and coaches, maintained at the Royal Mews at Buckingham Palace, provide horse-drawn road transport for the Royal Family. They are used for weddings, coronations, and other royal and state occasions.

1 **Ascot Landaus** These light carriages – driven by a postilion mounted on one of the drawing horses – are used each year at the Royal Ascot race meeting. At the wedding of the Duke and Duchess of Cambridge, the bridesmaids travelled by Ascot Landau. 2 **1902 State Landau** This was built for the coronation of Edward VII in 1902. Since it is open-topped, passengers are clearly visible, making it a popular choice for Royal Weddings. 3 **Glass Coach** One of the principal state carriages of the British Monarch, it was built in 1881 and purchased by the Crown for the coronation of George V in 1911. 4 **Gold State Coach** Built in 1762, it has been used at the coronation of every British

monarch since George IV. Weighing four tonnes and pulled by eight horses, it is the most elaborate and unwieldy of all Royal coaches. Queen Victoria complained of the "distressing oscillation" of its ride. 5 **Diamond Jubilee State Coach** This was a private project originally conceived by Australian W J Frecklington to celebrate the Queen's 80th birthday. It incorporates historic fragments, including wood from Sir Isaac Newton's apple tree and Henry VIII's warship *Mary Rose*. It entered service in 2014. 6 **Australian State Coach** Designed by Frecklington in 1988 for the Australian Bicentennial, this enclosed coach incorporates contemporary comforts, such as heating and hydraulic stabilisers.

Rain on the parade
Representing one of the new Queen's realms, the Royal Canadian Mounted Police participate in the Coronation Day parade on 2 June 1953. Vast crowds turned out despite the gloomy weather.

« BEFORE

The coronation dress would reflect the realms and dominions of the Crown and Commonwealth, but the real heavyweight piece of the Queen's ensemble would be the purple Robe of Estate.

FIT FOR A QUEEN

For the coronation the Queen asked Norman Hartnell to make a **white satin dress** similar to her wedding gown. His design incorporated delicate embroidery of the symbols of the different countries of the United Kingdom. The Queen, mindful of her wider estate, asked him to include symbols of the Commonwealth: Canadian maple and New Zealand fern, jute, cotton, and wheat for Pakistan. Meanwhile, heroic labour – 3,500 hours in total – was undertaken by a team of 12 seamstresses from the Royal School of Needlework, stitching over 6.5 m (21 ft) of purple silk velvet to make the Robe of Estate, which was edged in ermine and embroidered with gold.

FROM THE ROOF OF THE WORLD

Just as these efforts were about to bear fruit, a different kind of heroism was played out on the other side of the world. On the morning of the coronation, news began to filter through of a great feat: **Tenzing Norgay and Edmund Hillary had reached the summit of Everest.** "Collectively and acting in unity the men of the Empire can conquer everything", observed the *Evening Standard*, reflecting on the symbolism of the ascent.

Ticket to the main event
Lady Godfrey-Faussett was one of the ticket-holders to the abbey itself. The guests included prime ministers and heads of state from the Commonwealth and foreign royalty, both reigning and non-reigning.

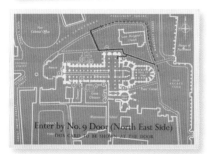

Arrival at the abbey
The Queen entered the abbey through a purpose-built, temporary annex, her train supported by six maids of honour under the instruction of the Mistress of Robes, the Duchess of Devonshire.

The Coronation

Although the weather was in contrast to the glory of the occasion, nothing could dampen the fervour of the crowds lining the processional route nor the enthusiasm of a global audience granted access to an event that combined tradition, reverent solemnity, and genuine joy.

By 1953 Britain was beginning to emerge from the grip of postwar austerity, and the coronation of a new queen offered a bridge between past and future. The ancient and solemn traditions of the coronation ceremony promised to combine with the excitement and glamour offered by the youthful monarch, a glorious alchemy to usher in the start of a new Elizabethan age. The application of technology would bring the pomp and circumstance of the event to a vast audience with an immediacy incomprehensible to previous generations, thanks to the eventual decision to televise the coronation.

Sweet celebration

On the day of the coronation, street parties would be held across the land and civic bodies such as schools and churches would mark the occasion. Churchill's enthusiasm for the coronation was boundless and he incited his government to plan a lavish national party on unprecedented scale (the cost of the coronation would eventually come in at around £2 million), horrifying civil servants by decreeing that everyone should receive an extra pound of sugar in their ration. Sweet rationing would end the day before the coronation, on Churchill's orders. Perhaps partly in recognition of his enthusiasm for the event, Churchill was made Knight of the Order of the Garter the day before.

> # "The coronation was like a **phoenix-time.**"

PRINCESS MARGARET

On 1 January 1953, Westminster Abbey was closed for preparations for the coronation. Overseeing the details of the ceremony was the Earl Marshal, the Duke of Norfolk (by ancient tradition the premier nobleman in the land). His wife stood in for the Queen during two major dress rehearsals, watched by Elizabeth, who conducted her own rehearsals in the palace. The major controversy arose over whether or not the coronation should be televised. While Prince Philip, Chairman of the Coronation Commission, may well have been in

favour of it, Churchill, the Archbishop of Canterbury, and others were opposed. But the televising of Elizabeth and Philip's wedding had set a precedent and public clamour was too great to be ignored, so it was agreed that only the most solemn parts of the coronation – the communion and the anointing – would not be filmed. Over the objections of ministers, it was agreed that the ceremony would be broadcast live on radio and television around the world and interpreted in 44 different languages.

The crowning moment
The coronation ceremony began interspersed with the gleeful chorus of the assembled masses: "God save Queen Elizabeth Long live Queen Elizabeth! May the Queen live forever!"

Into the abbey

At 11 am the Queen arrived at the abbey in the Gold State Coach, accompanied by the Duke of Edinburgh in his uniform as Admiral of the Fleet. She was wearing the George IV State Diadem. St Edward's Crown, which would be used for the coronation itself, had preceded her into the abbey. At 11.15 am. a great procession of dignitaries, foreign and domestic, clergy, and peers entered the abbey through the Great West Door, followed by the Queen with her maids of honour and the Mistress of the Robes. Once she had reached the altar, the Queen was seated in the Chair of Estate while the coronation props were assembled. She curtsied to each corner of the congregation. Now the ceremony could begin (see pp.142–43). After the coronation, a procession of 16,000 people made their way back along the 8 km (5 mile) route to Buckingham Palace, taking two hours. Already, film from the cameras inside the Abbey was winging its way to Canada where it would begin to be broadcast within four hours of the end of the ceremony.

On the day of the coronation, 2 June, a quarter of the world's population took the day off in celebration. Despite persistent drizzle, crowds had camped out overnight along the route of the procession to secure the best views. Carriages, most of them closed, brought dignitaries to the abbey to join the 8,000 guests, including the peers of the realm decked out in their ceremonial dress. After the ceremony, to the delight of the crowd, Queen Salote Tupou III of Tonga would defy the weather and leave the top of her carriage down, wielding a large parasol.

The cultural impact of the coronation was immediate and enduring. The event helped change the way the British consumed their media and their chicken, and triggered an avalanche of memorabilia.

MARKING THE OCCASION

Immediately after the coronation, the Queen hosted a luncheon featuring a dish concocted especially to mark the occasion. This Rosemary Hume and Constance Spry recipe – initially called *poulet reine Elizabeth* – came to be known as Coronation Chicken. In addition to chicken, the dish incorporated curry powder and other spices to reflect the **culinary heritage of the Commonwealth.** Other cultural outpourings included a vast range of **celebratory memorabilia,** from porcelain sets to toy coronation coaches.

BROADCASTING TO THE WORLD

After lunch, the Queen appeared on the balcony at Buckingham Palace, still wearing the Imperial State Crown, while RAF aircraft performed a flypast. That evening she made a **radio broadcast:** "Throughout this memorable day I have been uplifted and sustained by the knowledge that your thoughts and prayers were with me. I have been aware all the time that my peoples, spread far and wide throughout every continent and ocean in the world, were united to support me in the task to which I have now been dedicated with such solemnity." She continued, "Therefore I am sure that this, my Coronation, is not the symbol of a power and a splendour that are gone but a declaration of our hopes for the future, and for the years I may, by God's Grace and Mercy, be given to reign and serve you as your Queen."

TELEVISION REVOLUTION

The televising of the coronation helped accelerate the existing boom in television ownership. One notable casualty was a **3-D film of the coronation** created by Pathé News, for which there was little appetite at cinemas.

CORONATION SOUVENIR CONFECTIONERY TIN

The Coronation Ceremony

In a moving ceremony, replete with ancient traditions, Elizabeth offered solemn oaths, was anointed with holy oil, and received the crown of her ancestors. The service was laden with the physical and metaphorical weight of royal emblems.

As the coronation ceremony moved to its climax, Elizabeth, having arrived at the altar, was seated on the Chair of Estate, or the Coronation Chair. She read the coronation oath and took Holy Communion. The most significant part of the ceremony was the anointment. Hidden behind a silk canopy, the Queen was daubed with blessed holy oil, containing oil of orange, rose, musk, cinnamon, and ambergris – a rare material created in the digestive system of sperm whales. Traditionally, this oil was drawn from a supply dating back to previous sovereigns, but preparations for the 1953 coronation revealed that the last phial had been destroyed in bombing raids on London during World War II. Unfortunately, the pharmacy that made the oil had gone out of business, and it looked as though the recipe might have been lost. But the Coronation Commission was able to locate perhaps the last man from the pharmacy, an elderly person who had kept few ounces of the oil as memento, and he mixed up a batch.

After the anointment, the Queen was dressed in the imperial vestments and handed the trappings and regalia of state. She put on a cloth-of-gold robe, called the *Supertunica,* over the *Colobium Sindonis,* a loose linen tunic. She was then presented with the golden spurs, symbolic of chivalry, and a jewelled sword. These were followed by the armills (gold bracelets), representing sincerity and wisdom. Elizabeth then put on the cloth-of-gold Imperial Mantle robe and received the Sovereign's Orb and the two sceptres: the Sceptre with the Cross, symbolizing temporal power under God, and the Sceptre with the Dove, representing equity and mercy. Finally, she was crowned with the solid gold St Edward's Crown, although for the regalia portrait shown here, it was swapped for the Imperial State Crown.

> **"**I here present unto you, **Queen Elizabeth,** your **undoubted Queen."**
>
> **GEOFFREY FISHER,** ARCHBISHOP OF CANTERBURY, DURING ELIZABETH II'S CORONATION, 2 JUNE 1953

Iconic picture
This famous coronation portrait by photographer Cecil Beaton was shot inside Buckingham Palace after the Queen had returned from her coronation service. A painted backdrop of Henry VII's Lady Chapel in Westminster Abbey was used to create atmosphere.

Coronation Dress

Contemporary fashion and ancient tradition came together at Elizabeth's coronation, with dresses created by fashion designer Norman Hartnell, and robes and regalia by Ede & Ravenscroft, royal tailors since 1689.

1 The Duke of Edinburgh's coronet Created by Ede & Ravenscroft, the coronet consists of a silver gilt circlet with alternating crosses and fleur de lys, and a cap of ermine-fringed crimson velvet, with a gold tassel in the centre. 2 The Duke of Edinburgh's uniform with coronation robe An Ede & Ravenscroft creation, the robe was worn over the full dress uniform of an Admiral of the Fleet, including the star, collar, and badge of the Order of the Garter. 3 Princess Margaret's dress and robe Designed by Norman Hartnell, Princess Margaret's dress is distinctive, yet reflects the white and gold scheme worn by the royal ladies. 4 The Halo Tiara Commissioned from Cartier in 1936 by King George VI, the tiara was given to Elizabeth on her 18th birthday. Princess Margaret wore it to the Coronation. 5 St Edward's Crown This crown of gold is studded with sapphires, tourmalines, amethysts, topazes, and citrines, and weighs 2.23kg (4¼lb). 6 Queen Elizabeth II's coronation dress and robe Designed by Hartnell, the dress has national and Commonwealth floral emblems embroidered on it in gold, silver, and pastel-coloured silks.

Fleur de lys

1 THE DUKE OF EDINBURGH'S CORONET

Tiara studded with 739 brilliant and 149 baton diamonds

4 THE HALO TIARA

Collar of the Order of the Garter

Enamelled blue garter with a red rose alternates with a double gold knot

2 THE DUKE OF EDINBURGH'S UNIFORM WITH CORONATION ROBE

Openwork design of *broderie anglaise*

Marguerites and roses, embroidered in silver thread, in reference to the Princess's name, Margaret Rose

Robe of purple velvet, trimmed with ermine

3 PRINCESS MARGARET'S DRESS AND ROBE

Robe embroidered with wheat ears and olive branches, representing peace and prosperity

FULL VIEW OF QUEEN ELIZABETH II'S CORONATION ROBE

5 ST EDWARD'S CROWN

The neckline – with the inverted "V" of the short sleeves, each tier, and the edge of the skirt – all had a border of alternating lines of gold bugle beads, diamantes, and pearls

6 QUEEN ELIZABETH II'S CORONATION DRESS AND ROBE

White satin skirt constructed with a backing of reinforced cream taffeta to support the heavy embroidery

Red silk-velvet robe trimmed with ermine

Ermine-trimmed robe of English purple silk-velvet; over 6.5 m (21 ft) long, with six hidden handles to make it easier for the maids of honour to carry

NORWICH GATES, 1952

ST MARY MAGDALENE CHURCH

ANMER HALL

SHOOTING PARTY, c.1902–10

ROYAL RESIDENCE

Sandringham

The house at Sandringham stands on an 8,000 hectares (20,000 acre) estate in an area of natural beauty near the coast of Norfolk. It was bought by Queen Victoria in 1862 as a wedding present for the Prince of Wales, later Edward VII, and his future bride, Princess Alexandra.

Although the Sandringham Estate included a substantial Georgian mansion, it was too small for Albert Edward and Alexandra, and they had it demolished. It was replaced in 1870 with a multiple-gable, red-brick, Jacobean-style country house.

The facilities were cutting-edge for the time, and included gas-lighting, flushing lavatories, and a shower, There were large reception rooms for formal and family occasions, but the everyday living quarters were modest by comparison. Plenty of space was even provided for the family menagerie of dogs, cats, and horses.

Sandringham suited Princess Alexandra and her five children very well, which compensated in part for the long absences and infidelities of her husband. Geographically, it lies in a fascinating part of England. It was once part of Doggerland, the land bridge that linked Great Britain and Scandinavia before the last Ice Age. Its similarities to Princess Alexandra's native Denmark are therefore no coincidence, and it is perhaps why she felt at home here.

In 1886 Edward established the Royal Stud at Sandringham, and he soon became one of the most influential breeders in the country, producing two legendary racehorses: Persimmon, which won the famous English races the St Leger and the Derby in 1896, and Diamond Jubilee, which won the 1900 Triple Crown. The Prince ploughed his prize money into the estate, creating a vast walled kitchen garden. This has been recently revived to produce vegetables for the Sandringham Visitor Centre restaurant.

Both Albert and Alexandra were passionate about hunting on the Sandringham Estate, so much so that in 1901, Albert, now crowned Edward VII ordered all the clocks to be set half an hour ahead of GMT (Greenwich Mean Time), to increase the amount of daylight at the end of the day in winter for hunting. The tradition of "Sandringham Time" continued until 1936.

In 1932, under George V, a new Sandringham tradition was born: he made the first live radio broadcast to the Empire from the house on Christmas Day. Queen Elizabeth continued the tradition 20 years later, but made history again in 1957 when she invited the nation into the Library at Sandringham in the first live televised Christmas Day broadcast.

Private times

For Elizabeth, Sandringham holds particular significance. Her father, George VI, was born on the estate and he also died there. He grew up in one of the estate houses, York Cottage, where his happiest times were spent with his grandparents. It was he who planted Sandringham's first apple orchards – the estate is now famous for its apple juices. He also turned a bomb crater on the estate, created during the first German Zeppelin raid in January 1915, into a duck pond.

Since her father's death, it has been the Queen's custom to spend the anniversary privately with her family on the estate.

Public viewings

Sandringham was first opened to the public in 1977. Between April and October, when the Royal Family is not in residence, several of the reception rooms on the ground floor are made accessible.

The decoration of the rooms and their furnishings have changed little from the time of Queen Alexandra and Queen Mary, wife of George V. Lavish gifts from members of the Russian and European royal families, who were frequent guests of the royals at Sandringham, are on display, including a Dresden porcelain chandelier and mirror frame from Kaiser Wilhelm I of Germany. »

Sandringham House
Dating from 1870, the country house built for Albert, the Prince of Wales, and Princess Alexandra was described by their friend Charles Carrington as "the most comfortable house in England".

DAIMLER MAIL PHAETON CAR

LADY AMHERST'S PHEASANT

Snapshots from the estate
Owned by the Royal Family for over 150 years, Sandringham has been a much-loved home to four British monarchs – and with the move of Prince William and his young family to Anmer Hall, a new generation is set to enjoy life on the estate. The Queen particularly likes to spend Christmas at Sandringham, and traditionally joins the celebration at the church of St Mary Magdalene, within easy reach of the house. The spectacular wrought and cast-iron Norwich Gates designed by Thomas Jekyll were a wedding gift to the future Edward VII from the County of Norfolk and City of Norwich. Edward (here seated at the wheel of the car) was very attached to the estate, and indulged his love of country pursuits by hosting regular shooting parties. Today visitors can inspect vintage royal vehicles at the Sandringham Museum, and stroll through the grounds, which are home to over 100 species of birds, including colourful pheasants.

>> The walls of these rooms are hung with family portraits by the leading court painters of the time. An important collection of oriental arms and armour is housed at Sandringham, brought back from the Far East and India in 1876, the year of the Prince of Wales's tour (see pp.72–73) and a special exhibition of them in the Ballroom is changed every year

vintage cars, the highlight being the Daimler Phaeton bought by Edward VII. He was the first British monarch to own a car – but it is not known whether he could drive.

Sandringham is run by the Royal Family as a modern estate. When the Queen acceded to the throne in 1952, Prince Philip was made responsible for its running, and it is only recently

"Dear old Sandringham, **the place I love better** than anywhere in the world."

KING GEORGE V

The estate museum, in the former coach houses and stable block, holds an extraordinarily diverse collection. George V used the museum to gather together all his big game trophies from his other royal residences. There are

that the day-to-day management has begun to be handed over to Prince Charles. Most of the crops are still farmed conventionally, but there is a gradual move over to organic farming. Practices are designed to encourage as

many species of wildlife as possible. With the Prince's eye always on conservation, more than 5,000 trees and several miles of hedges are planted each year, and 10 wetland areas have been created.

The estate features 80 hectares (198 acres) of orchards and soft fruits – including the blackcurrants that Sandringham grows for the drinks brand Ribena. A recent innovation beside the orchards is an experimental organic black truffle plantation. The ground conditions at Sandringham are thought to be ideal for oak and hazel trees infected with truffle spores, while it is hoped that staff at the Sandringham kennels will be able train truffle-hunting dogs.

Sandringham Country Park was first opened to the public in 1968. An area of woodland and open heath, it has been enlarged to cover 240 hectares (600 acres) and comes with two waymarked nature trails.

After Prince William announced his role with East Anglia's Air Ambulance in 2014, he and the Duchess of Cambridge decided to make Anmer Hall on the Sandringham Estate their family home. The Georgian mansion was a wedding present, and a house William knows well from his childhood, when it was leased to his father's friend Hugh van Cutsem. They moved in after some refurbishment and additions, including a conservatory designed by architect Charles Morris, who also did work at Highgrove.

Vintage views of Sandringham

Photographs taken in the 1880s show grand rooms at Sandringham, such as the Saloon and the Dining Room, were crammed with memorabilia from royal trips abroad as well as gifts from foreign dignitaries. Many of the interiors are lit by natural light streaming through bay windows: Queen Mary's desk, covered with family photographs, occupied a bright alcove.

THE DINING ROOM, 1880

THE SALOON, 1882

QUEEN'S MARY'S DESK

Frills and flounces

The Principal Drawing Room was photographed for *Country Life* in the early 1900s. Ornate plasterwork on the ceilings, walls, and doors, and the painted panels, can still be seen by visitors today.

An Anglican abroad
A goodwill ambassador to the Anglican world outside England, the Queen greets James Horstead, the Archbishop of West Africa, at a cathedral in Nigeria, in 1956.

The **Queen** as **Head** of the **Church**

The Queen has always taken her public role as head of the Church of England very seriously. In private she has nurtured an undemonstrative but abiding faith, as well as a commitment to ensure freedom of worship for all.

Among the Queen's many titles is that of "Defender of the Faith and Supreme Governor of the Church of England," a role that is set out in the Preface to one of the foundational documents of the Church of England, where the monarch is described as "being by God's Ordinance, according to Our just Title, Defender of the Faith and... Supreme Governor of the Church of England." The Queen also has a role in the Church of Scotland. Although she is simply an ordinary member and not supreme governor, she is required by the Treaty of Union of 1707

7 **The number of Archbishops of Canterbury during Queen Elizabeth II's reign.**

to preserve the Church of Scotland. Her role is central to the status of both these churches as "established churches", which means that they are regulated by British law.

A significant portion of the Queen's coronation oath was given over to asserting this role. Among other things, the Queen swore "to maintain in the United Kingdom the Protestant Reformed Religion established by law... preserve inviolably the settlement of the Church of England... and government thereof, as by law established in England" to the utmost of her power. To the Queen these are not merely words, but a spiritual charge that she took to her heart. "The sense of spiritual exaltation that radiated from her was almost tangible to those of us who stood near her in the abbey," recalled Dermot Morrah, Arundel Herald Extraordinary, one of the principal organizers of the Coronation in 1953.

The Queen appoints and invests bishops (on the advice of the prime minister and Church Commission), and bishops and parish priests take an oath of allegiance to the Queen and need royal authority to resign. Much as with Parliament, the Queen opens the Synod (the governing assembly of the Church of England), and her assent is required for it to pass measures and canon legislature.

Defending the faith

On a more personal level, the Queen has a deep and abiding faith. Every Sunday, wherever she is, she attends church, including the private royal chapel in Windsor Great Park, St Mary Magdalene at Sandringham, and Crathie Kirk at Balmoral. One commentator remarks that "Her every decision is informed by her faith." For instance, her former Domestic Chaplain Robin Woods, who describes the Queen as "a praying and

Frequent visitor
The Queen meets Pope Francis at the Vatican in 2014. Francis is the fifth pontiff she has met at the Holy City, starting with Pope Pius XII in 1951, a year before her accession to the throne.

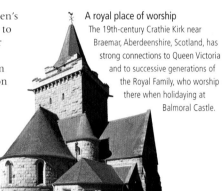

A royal place of worship
The 19th-century Crathie Kirk near Braemar, Aberdeenshire, Scotland, has strong connections to Queen Victoria and to successive generations of the Royal Family, who worship there when holidaying at Balmoral Castle.

believing woman," relates a story about the introduction of a new version of the Church of England prayer book in 1966. Before she signed off on the new version, Elizabeth called Woods, saying, "I don't think

I should sign something which will change the liturgy until at least we've prayed it through."

In a 2012 address at Lambeth Palace, the Queen gave an impassioned defence of the role and value of the Church of England: "The concept of our established Church is occasionally misunderstood and, I believe, commonly under-appreciated... It certainly provides an identity and spiritual dimension for its own many adherents. But also, gently and assuredly, the Church of England has created an environment for other faith communities and indeed people of no faith to live freely."

> " **...woven** into the **fabric** of this **country** the **Church** has helped to build a **better society.** "

THE QUEEN'S LAMBETH PALACE ADDRESS, 2012

Travel and State Visits

Elizabeth II is probably one of the most recognizable women on the planet – partly because she has visited most of it. The Queen's constant tours enable her to connect personally with millions of people.

The Queen has travelled more widely than any other monarch. Her extraordinary history of official overseas visits dates back to 1947, when she was still a princess. That year, Elizabeth accompanied her parents on a tour of Rhodesia (now Zimbabwe) and South Africa, where she celebrated her 21st birthday in Cape Town, with a memorable radio broadcast to the Commonwealth

(see pp.106–107). In 1951, the princess and her husband Philip were sent on a five-week-long coast-to-coast tour of Canada in place of the ailing George VI. However, it was only after Elizabeth's accession (see pp.132–33) and coronation (see pp.140–43) that her truly epic travel itinerary began.

First Commonwealth tour

One of Elizabeth's first duties as newly crowned queen was to undertake a gruelling tour of the Commonwealth that had originally been planned for her father. She took off with Philip in 1953, leaving behind their two young children for a period of seven months. Her goal, she said to the people of the Commonwealth in a Christmas Day message broadcast from New Zealand, was "to show that the crown is not merely an abstract symbol of our unity, but a personal and living bond between you and me."

The highlight of the tour was the 1954 royal visit to Australia, which produced some extraordinary scenes. In

Commemorative tea caddy
The Queen's 1954 visit to Australia caused nationwide excitement. This octagonal tin of tea, with illustrations of Elizabeth and Philip on opposite sides, was specially produced to commemorate the visit.

At sea
Captain Alan McNicoll shows Elizabeth around his ship, HMAS *Australia*, during her 1954 tour of Australia. This ship was part of the escort for the Royal Yacht carrying the Queen during the Australian leg of her coronation world tour.

« BEFORE

The prelude to the Queen's epic 1953–54 tour of the Commonwealth was her coronation tour of the British Isles, including visits to Scotland and Northern Ireland.

FIRST VISIT TO NORTHERN IRELAND
In July 1953, **Elizabeth visited Northern Ireland for the first time.** Accompanied by Philip, she travelled by train through the Ulster countryside and along the north coast. A public holiday was declared, and cheering crowds thronged to see the Queen. Conspicuous in the royal entourage was equerry **Peter Townsend,** brought along to put some distance between him and **Margaret 154–55 ».**

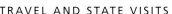

Ballarat, in rural Victoria, more than 150,000 people lined the streets to get a glimpse of the Queen. "We shared in an elevating experience from which we should all emerge better citizens and better Britishers," gushed the *Ballarat Courier* – a local newspaper. At Melbourne Cricket Ground (one of the world's biggest sports stadiums), more than 100,000 children turned out to greet Elizabeth. Excitement turned to hysteria in other parts of the country: 2,000 people fainted while waiting to see the Queen outside Sydney's town hall, and women and children were trampled underfoot as a crowd surged to see the monarch in Lismore, northern New South Wales. It was estimated that some 10 million Australians – about 70 per cent of the population – saw the Queen in person during the visit.

Coming home

Elizabeth's tour of the Commonwealth was scheduled to come to an end in May 1954. The Royal Yacht *Britannia*, built in 1953 by the prestigious Clyde shipyards of John Brown & Co. at a cost of more than £2 million, was enlisted to bring the royal couple home. The yacht would carry Prince Charles and Princess Anne to the Mediterranean, where they would join their parents before sailing back to Britain. The family was reunited on 1 May, when Elizabeth and Philip boarded the yacht at Tobruk, Libya.

On 15 May, the Royal Family received a rapturous welcome as they sailed up the River Thames. Prime Minister Winston Churchill was also on the yacht, having boarded the previous day at Yarmouth, on the Isle of Wight. The twin arms of Tower Bridge were opened to their fullest extent to let the yacht through, and a huge banner bearing the words "Welcome Home" ran across the top of the bridge. A 41-gun salute thundered out from the Tower of London. After bringing the Queen's first Commonwealth tour to a successful conclusion, *Britannia* went on to cover more than a million miles in over 44 years of royal service.

Far and wide

The Queen's Commonwealth tour of 1953–54 was her longest. Since then, she has continued to tour extensively, travelling around 160,000 km (99,419 miles) per year for much of her reign, and making at least one state visit a year. The rest of the Royal Family shares some of the burden with her. In her 1958 Christmas broadcast, after listing out the Royal Family's

The Queen in Africa
Elizabeth is escorted to a dais under a large sunshade to view a parade at Kumasi Sports Stadium during a state visit to Ghana in November 1961. The Queen also visited Sierra Leone and Gambia the same year.

comprehensive travel plans for the year ahead, the Queen famously quipped, "Between us, we are going to many parts of the world. We have no plans for space travel – at the moment."

Historic firsts

During her reign, Elizabeth has visited more than 100 nations, and achieved many historic firsts. In 1986, she became the first reigning British monarch to visit China, and also made first state visits to Russia in October 1994, Brunei and Malaysia in 1998, and South Korea in 1999. In 1995, the Queen finally went back to South Africa for the first time since 1947, after the end of apartheid.

In 2011, Elizabeth became the first British monarch to visit the Republic of Ireland (see pp.270–71), making the first visit to southern parts of the island since the 1911 tour by her grandfather George V. At a state dinner held in her honour, the Queen reflected on the historic import of the occasion, talking of "the peace and understanding we now have between our two nations

> **70,196** The total distance in kilometres (43,617 miles) covered by Elizabeth II during her 1953–54 tour of the Commonwealth.

and between the communities within those two nations; a living testament to how much in common we have."

A royal ambassador

For much of her reign, the Queen has attended up to 10 official engagements a day when on tour, working up to 14 hours a day. It is perhaps not surprising, given the volume of arrangements and security involved, that tours take up to two years to organize. In recent times, the Queen has stepped back from state visits, ceding this responsibility to younger generations.

Elizabeth is of remarkable value as an ambassador for Britain. A visit from the Queen helps the country exert influence, spread its culture and values, and advance its economic objectives. For instance, *Reader's Digest* magazine described the Queen's 1953–54 Commonwealth tour as "possibly the most ambitious and certainly the most successful piece of public relations ever attempted." A visit from the Queen carries unique prestige, due in part to the relative scarcity of ruling royal families since World War II. Lord Chalfont, who frequently served as the Queen's Minister in Attendance on state visits, noted: "The British monarchy occupies a unique band in the spectrum of international diplomacy… [the Queen] has for most people overseas that indefinable quality sometimes described [as] 'glamour'."

AFTER »

Accompanied by the Duke of Edinburgh, Elizabeth continues to undertake one or two official visits abroad each year.

ON BEHALF OF THE QUEEN
In recent times, the Queen has increasingly been **represented abroad by her family** – her son, Prince Charles, and her grandchildren and their wives **294–95 »**. Age is no barrier to service: Prince George made his first visit abroad – a three-week tour of Australia and New Zealand **294–95 »** at only 8 months old.

Her Majesty's Yacht
The Royal Yacht *Britannia* is seen docked alongside the Victoria and Alfred Waterfront during Elizabeth's 1995 historic visit to South Africa after the abolishment of apartheid, or racial segregation. The yacht was decommissioned two years later.

Lovers on parade

A photo of young Princess Margaret, inspecting the troops at a ship launch in 1947, captures royal equerry Peter Townsend in the background. This was at the start of their relationship.

Margaret's Doomed Romance

The young Queen Elizabeth's fledgling rule soon faced a test that pitted changing social mores against the traditional conservatism of the monarchy, as Princess Margaret considered marrying a divorcee, Group Captain Peter Townsend.

On her 18th birthday Princess Margaret enjoyed a glittering coming out. Her private life would now be the talk of the gossip columns, as commentators speculated over the identity of the most likely suitor for perhaps the most eligible woman in the world. The general view was that Margaret ran with a "fast" set: dashing young playboy aristocrats. But in truth she merely dallied with them, for her heart had long been set on an older, more serious figure: Group

Keeping her distance
Princess Margaret's visit to the West Indies in February 1955 was widely seen as an attempt to put some distance between herself and Peter Townsend. It did not work.

Captain Peter Townsend, a war hero whose daring exploits as a pilot during the Battle of Britain were legendary.

Out in the open

The outside world first became aware of the relationship between princess and equerry in 1953. On the day of Elizabeth's coronation (see pp.140–43), Margaret was seen picking a bit of fluff off Townsend's uniform, a gesture that spoke volumes. Their relationship immediately became a media circus, with sensational coverage that disturbed the Palace greatly. After Edward VIII's abdication crisis (see pp.90–91), the thought of another royal getting involved with a divorcee was unacceptable. Various steps were taken to separate the couple. In July 1953 Margaret was sent to accompany the Queen Mother on a tour of Southern Rhodesia (now part of Zimbabwe), while it had been arranged that Townsend would take a new job as the British Air Attache in Brussels. When Margaret learned that he would have left the UK by the time she returned, she collapsed. The Palace, including the Queen herself, were against the match, but when she reached the age of 25 Margaret would be able to marry without permission from the monarch.

£6,000 The annual income that Margaret would have to forego if she married Townsend.

Opposition to the marriage

As Margaret approached her 25th birthday, tension mounted. On 14 October, the Palace issued a statement that no announcement concerning Princess Margaret's personal future was at present contemplated. Various constitutional and religious issues seemed to block any prospect of a union. Meanwhile Prime Minister Anthony Eden had told the Queen that any marriage between the two would not receive parliamentary sanction and that if it took place, a bill would be set out to deprive Princess Margaret of her rights of succession, her title, and her Civil List entitlement.

Hounded by the press

As speculation about their marriage mounted to fever pitch, Margaret and Townsend found themselves at the centre of a media circus. Here the press wait for them to leave a dinner party in late October 1955.

For the love of Peter
Headlines from the *Daily Mirror*, dated 19 October 1955, give a flavour of the pervasive media coverage of Margaret's relationship.

The final decision

Margaret was faced with a stark choice: renounce the marriage, or renounce her royal life. At the end of October, she made her decision and informed the Archbishop of Canterbury, Dr Geoffrey Fisher. On 31 October, after a meeting with Townsend, she issued her statement: "I would like it to be known that I have decided not to marry Group Captain Peter Townsend." It was signed "Margaret" but had been written by Peter Townsend.

> **"We** were both exhausted... we felt mute and **numbed** at the **centre** of this **maelstrom."**
>
> PETER TOWNSEND

155

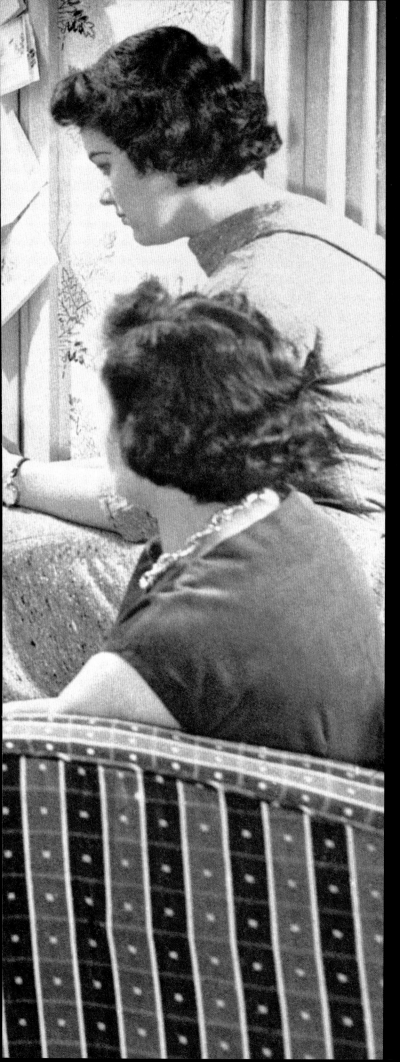

The First Televised Christmas Message

The Christmas broadcast had served to provide a powerful connection between the monarch and the people since the 1930s. In 1957, Elizabeth II was keen to use the latest technology to connect even more directly with the public.

On Christmas Day 1932, George V inaugurated one of the most deeply embedded of British yuletide customs – the royal Christmas message (see pp.88–89). The message was delivered via radio to millions of listeners. Elizabeth II continued this tradition, bringing to it her own love of television. She was a great fan of the new medium: after returning from her 1954 tour of the Commonwealth, she delayed appearing on the balcony of Buckingham Palace until she had finished watching English actress and singer Gracie Fields in the BBC's *Welcome Home Ball*. By 1960, there were 50 TV sets in the Palace.

The year 1957 would mark the 25th anniversary of the first Christmas broadcast on radio. Richard Webber, the BBC's head of outside broadcasting, recalled: "In television, we were keen to do everything that radio had done, so we asked the Palace if the Queen would consider reading the message live on television. She was a young monarch keen to enter into the spirit of the new era, and approved of the idea." The broadcast would be made live from the Long Library at Sandringham.

Elizabeth went from a single run-through into a live broadcast, in which she read from the teleprompter. She was filmed throughout by a single camera, which panned in during the speech. Towards the end of the broadcast, she was to quote some lines from English writer and preacher John Bunyan's *Pilgrim's Progress* and pick up a book as a prop. The Queen was the only one to notice that it was the wrong book, a detail that would not have been apparent to viewers, but she made sure that the correct volume was fetched from the library.

> **"**I should seem a rather **remote figure** to many of you… But now at least for a few minutes **I welcome you** into the **peace** of my own **home."**
>
> **ELIZABETH II,** ROYAL CHRISTMAS MESSAGE, 1957

Gathering round to watch
Millions of viewers watched Elizabeth II's 1957 Christmas message. She struck a chord with her audience by saying: "My own family often gather round to watch television as they are this moment, and that is how I imagine you now."

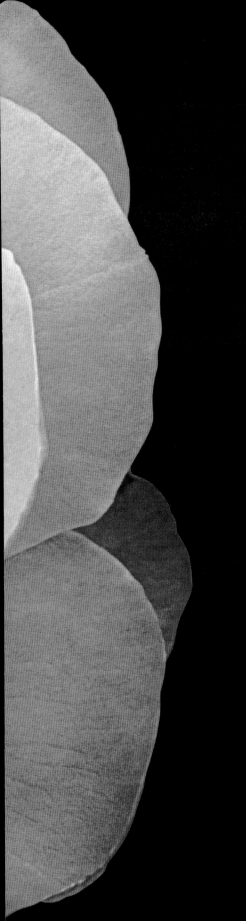

4

QUEEN AND MOTHER
1960–1980

« Hybrid tea rose named "Silver Jubilee" in
honour of Elizabeth II's 25 years on the throne

QUEEN AND MOTHER
1960–1980

1960	1962	1964	1966	1968

3 FEBRUARY 1960
British Prime Minister Harold Macmillan makes his "winds of change" speech to the South African parliament, heralding the decolonization of Africa.

10 MARCH 1964
Elizabeth II gives birth to her third son, Edward.

FEBRUARY
Prince Charles starts his two-term attendance at Geelong Grammar School in Australia.

22 DECEMBER 1966
Rhodesia leaves the Commonwealth, having illegally declared independence the year before.

20 APRIL 1968
Enoch Powell delivers his "rivers of blood" speech, warning of the dangers of increased immigration.

27 SEPTEMBER 1968
US musical *Hair* opens in London following repeal of theatre censorship the previous day.

19 FEBRUARY 1960
Elizabeth II gives birth to her second son, Andrew.

27 MARCH 1966
Football World Cup trophy, which was stolen in London, is found by a dog; England win World Cup at Wembley on 30 July 1966.

≪ The Queen with Prince Andrew and the baby Prince Edward

28 MAY 1967
Aviator and sailor Francis Chichester completes solo round-the-world sailing voyage.

21 JUNE 1969
Royal Family documentary airs on BBC, followed by a second transmission on ITV a week later.

6 MAY 1960
Princess Margaret marries Antony Armstrong-Jones, later created Earl of Snowdon.

21 OCTOBER 1960
The Queen launches the UK's first nuclear submarine.

11 MAY 1962
13-year-old Prince Charles starts at Gordonstoun School in Scotland.

6 AUGUST 1962
Jamaica becomes independent.

JUNE 1963
Government minister John Profumo resigns after involvement in sex scandal.

15 OCTOBER 1964
The Labour party comes to power under Harold Wilson.

24 JANUARY 1965
Churchill dies, state funeral follows six days later.

JUNE 1965
Queen presents Member of the Order of the British Empire (MBE) to each of the Beatles.

21 OCTOBER 1966
Aberfan disaster in Wales; massive mudslide kills 116 children and 28 adults as it buries a school.

2 JULY 1967
The Queen and Prince Philip visit Ottawa for the Canadian centennial.

⌃ An investiture chair

1960
Elizabeth allows her portrait to be used on bank notes for the first time.

OCTOBER 1963
When Prime Minister Harold MacMillan steps down due to ill health, the lack of a replacement sparks a constitutional crisis. The Queen is advised to appoint Alec Douglas-Home.

≪ £1 note; design first issued in 1960

4 JULY 1967
England and Wales decriminalize male homosexuality.

1 JULY 1969
Investiture of Charles as Prince of Wales at Caernarfon Castle.

20 SEPTEMBER 1967
The Queen attends the launching ceremony of the ocean liner *Queen Elizabeth II (QE2)*.

AUGUST 1969
Northern Ireland riots mark climax of year of escalation of sectarian and nationalist conflict known as the Troubles.

31 MAY 1961
South Africa leaves the Commonwealth after other nations reject its apartheid policy and white South Africans vote for a republic.

25 NOVEMBER 1963
The Duke of Edinburgh represents the Queen at the funeral of assassinated US president John F Kennedy.

≪ Launch of the *QE2*

Two decades of upheaval and transition at home and abroad brought an era of rapid change to which the Royal Family managed to adapt, even as it expanded, with the Queen, Princess Margaret, and Princess Anne all having children. The Queen would face multiple challenges, including the widespread decolonization of former overseas territories, changing social mores at home, and the breakdown of her sister's marriage. The public would get their first intimate look at royal life, while national joy over the Silver Jubilee celebrations would soon be overshadowed by private tragedy as a terrorist atrocity struck close to the heart of the royals.

1970

19 JUNE 1970
Ted Heath becomes Prime Minister after shock victory for Conservatives.

JULY 1970
Following visits to Fiji, Tonga, New Zealand, and Australia, Queen Elizabeth tours Canada; the following month Charles and Anne are guests of President Nixon in Washington.

JANUARY 1971
First Commonwealth Heads of Government meeting takes place in Singapore.

1971
Anne wins the European Eventing Championship, and later BBC Sports Personality of the Year.

15 FEBRUARY 1971
Decimalization in UK and Ireland, with introduction of new money.

1972

5 JUNE 1972
Funeral of the Queen's uncle, Duke of Windsor, formerly Edward VIII.

20 NOVEMBER 1972
The Queen and Prince Philip celebrate their silver wedding anniversary.

1 JANUARY 1973
The UK joins the European Economic Community (EEC).

14 NOVEMBER 1973
Princess Anne marries Captain Mark Phillips.

1974

JANUARY 1974
Miners' strike forces Prime Minister Heath to introduce three-day week and leads to collapse of government and general election; this in turn results in hung parliament and fresh elections, returning Harold Wilson to power.

SILVER WEDDING 3P

≪ Stamp commemorating the Queen and the Duke of Edinburgh's silver wedding anniversary

20 MARCH 1974
Attempt to kidnap Princess Anne is foiled.

11 NOVEMBER 1975
Governor-General of Australia sparks a constitutional crisis when he sacks the Australian prime minister.

≪ The wedding of Princess Anne to Captain Mark Phillips

1976

21 JANUARY 1976
Concorde begins transatlantic flights.

≫ Coin commemorating the Queen's Silver Jubilee

JANUARY–JUNE 1976
Cod War between the UK and Iceland erupts due to differences over fishing rights.

19 MARCH 1976
Princess Margaret and her husband, the Earl of Snowdon, separate.

SUMMER 1976
A heatwave brings longest drought and hottest summer on record for the UK.

31 DECEMBER 1976
The Prince's Trust – Prince Charles's charity for young people – is officially launched.

ELIZABETH·II·DG·REG·FD 1977

6 JUNE 1977
The Queen's Silver Jubilee reaches a climax. The extended celebrations include home and foreign tours, Armada beacon chain, Thanksgiving Service at St Paul's Cathedral, nationwide street parties, Thames river procession, and Jubilee walkway.

15 JUNE 1977
Gleneagles Agreement marks the start of sporting boycott of South Africa.

15 NOVEMBER 1977
Princess Anne gives birth to Peter, her first child and the Queen's first grandchild.

1978

1978–1979
Widespread strikes by public-sector unions, together with the coldest winter in 16 years makes what the papers call "the Winter of Discontent".

25 JULY 1978
World's first test-tube baby, Louise Brown, is born in Oldham, Greater Manchester.

MAY 1979
Margaret Thatcher becomes Prime Minister.

27 AUGUST 1979
The IRA assassinates Earl Mountbatten along with three others.

≪ Mountbatten's funeral procession

21 NOVEMBER 1979
Sir Anthony Blunt, the Queen's art advisor, is named as a Soviet spy and the fourth man in the Cambridge spy ring.

The **Childhood** of the **Princes** and **Princess**

The Queen's four children are not at all like each other, despite their similar upbringing. Part of this is probably due to their very different experiences in childhood, as well as the considerable age gap between them.

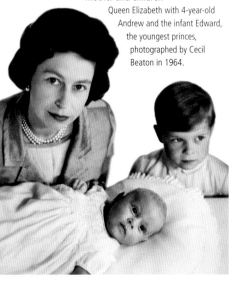

Mother and children
Queen Elizabeth with 4-year-old Andrew and the infant Edward, the youngest princes, photographed by Cecil Beaton in 1964.

« **BEFORE**

Prince Charles's earliest years were rather lonely and he missed out on a close maternal relationship, as he saw his parents very little.

SOLITARY BIRTHDAY
Before Elizabeth acceded to the throne, she was already **leaving her children behind to go on long overseas tours.** When Philip was briefly posted to Malta in 1949, Elizabeth, unencumbered by little Charles, had enjoyed a **carefree few months** there as an officer's wife. Charles celebrated his third birthday with a tea party at Buckingham Palace and a pram ride around Green Park, while his parents were **away on a tour of Canada.**

GREETING WITH A HANDSHAKE
After Elizabeth came to the throne, she threw herself into the role, and five months after the coronation embarked on a tour that saw her **separated from her children for almost six months.** When the children and Elizabeth were reunited in Tobruk, in Libya, as the royal couple made their way back to Britain at the end of the tour, she **greeted Charles by shaking his hand.**

F ew families of the postwar era have had to contend with anything like the level of scrutiny, fascination, adoration, and criticism that apply to the British Royal Family. These unique pressures and influences have shaped the four children of Queen Elizabeth II in different ways.

During the childhoods of Charles and Anne, their mother had only recently become Queen, a role that she embraced wholeheartedly. She dedicated herself to service, the Commonwealth, touring, and the daily business of monarchy, while at the same time deferring to her husband in matters of parenting. By the time Andrew and Edward came along in 1960 and 1964, the Queen was older, wiser, more assertive, and, according to various biographers and royal journalists, determined to provide a warmer and more maternal environment. This, along with significant innate differences in the siblings in temperament and intellect, and the wide gap in age, meant that Charles would have a very different experience from his younger brothers, and turn out to be a very different person from them.

Conflicting views on childhood
The early years of Charles and, to a lesser extent, Anne were characterized by a degree of emotional distance from their parents. It is worth noting, however, that Princess Anne vehemently disagrees with Charles's rather bleak assessment of his mother's lack of affection. "I'm not going to speak for anyone else," Anne told one interviewer, "but I simply don't believe there is any evidence whatsoever to suggest that she wasn't caring. It just beggars belief. We as children may have not been too demanding, in the sense that we understood what the limitations were in time and the responsibilities placed on her as monarch... but I don't believe that any of us, for a second, thought she didn't care for us in exactly

the same way as any other mother did. I just think it's extraordinary that anybody could construe that that might not be true."

Charles's education
Charles's father, Philip, was determined that the little prince should not be spoiled, but toughened up. Part of this would be achieved by his education, and he was sent to a series of suitable institutions. His first school was Hill House, where a 1957 report described him as, "A good, average schoolboy." Later that year he became a boarder at Cheam School, Headley, Hampshire. His parents were keen that he be treated like any other schoolboy, but the truth of his unique status would

> " We would like our **son** and **daughter** to **grow up as normally** as possible so that they will be able to **serve you** and the **Commonwealth** faithfully."
>
> ELIZABETH II, CHRISTMAS BROADCAST, 1958

slip out occasionally, such as the time when, wanting to write home, he enquired, "I know my mother is the Queen, but how do I put that on the envelope?"

In 1958, in a surprise move, the Queen announced that she was making her son the Prince of Wales:

Royal plaything
This miniature version of an Aston Martin DB5, famous from the James Bond movies, was presented to Prince Andrew in 1966 by the car company. It had rotating licence plates and a functional smoke screen.

"This [has been] a memorable year for the principality... I have decided to mark it further by an act which will, I hope, give as much pleasure to all Welshmen as it does to me. I intend to create my son Charles Prince of Wales today."

Philip had absolutely no doubt that the proper destination for his son when he turned 13 would be Gordonstoun, the experimental school that had done so much to shape his own character. The children at

Gordonstoun endured a tough routine of cold showers and cross-country runs, intended to build character. Charles described the prospect as "pretty gruesome", and, reportedly, he was deeply unhappy during his time there, despite being made head boy. His stay at Gordonstoun was marked by one headline-grabbing incident when he got in trouble for ordering a cherry brandy at the age of 14, at a hotel in Stornoway. While Charles was in Scotland, back at Buckingham Palace his future was being mapped out, with a 1965 summit to plan

Bondi beach bum
Prince Charles, during his 1966 sojourn in Australia, smiles broadly as he is fitted with the distinctive bathing cap of the Sydney Surf Club, worn by lifeguards on Bondi Beach in Sydney. In this ceremony, he was made an honorary member of the club.

his higher education and career – a summit to which he was not invited. Soon Prince Charles had become the first heir to the throne to sit public examinations, winning a place at Trinity College, Cambridge.

Private Tutoring

Meanwhile, Anne's early childhood took place out of the public eye, with private tutoring. Mindful of the difficulties facing a young princess in terms of meeting other children, her aunt, Princess Margaret, prompted the formation of a new Buckingham Palace Brownie Pack – a unit of Girl Guides – with little Anne as a founder member. In 1963 Anne went to Benenden School, Kent, to board, and soon fell in love with the world of horse trials and eventing (see pp.186–87), winning her first trials in 1969.

Andrew and Edward

Prince Charles was big brother to two little princes, who would follow him to Gordonstoun. Andrew was educated by a governess up to the age of 8, keeping him close to home – a notable departure from the course followed with Charles – and then went to Heatherdown Preparatory School in Ascot before Gordonstoun. Edward was born in 1964, and for the first time, Prince Philip was present at the birth. Edward was a quiet child who loved listening to Swedish music group ABBA and Irish radio and TV personality Terry Wogan. While Andrew went straight into the navy, Edward was awarded a place at Jesus College, Cambridge, despite poor exam results, which sparked accusations of special treatment. After university he joined the Royal Marines as a university cadet but found the training too arduous and dropped out.

Princess Anne
A portrait of Princess Anne on her 19th birthday, by photographer Norman Parkinson, who also photographed her on her 21st birthday, her engagement, and her wedding.

In their childhood, Charles was a loving older brother to Anne, whose tomboy spirit and no-nonsense pluck he admired, but to Andrew and Edward he was a more remote figure, more like an uncle. Today the relationship between the royal siblings has somewhat cooled. According to a former aide, quoted by the London *Daily Telegraph*, in later life, "There was very little contact between them actually, save at family gatherings and events. Communication used to be dealt with by households – private secretaries. They were very un-close, leading independent lives."

AFTER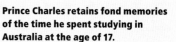

Prince Charles retains fond memories of the time he spent studying in Australia at the age of 17.

DOWN UNDER
From February to July 1966, **he spent two terms at Timbertop,** a remote campus of Geelong Church of England Grammar School in Melbourne, Australia. Despite the fact that Timbertop, too, was tough, it was **an experience the Prince enjoyed very much,** in contrast to his **miserable time at Gordonstoun.**

SHREDDED SHEEP
On one field trip to New Guinea, after seeing examples of the folk art of the Papuan people, the Prince expressed concern about **pre-industrial societies losing their traditional ways of life.** This experience gave him an introduction to the study of anthropology, which may have helped to foster some of his later concerns and pursuits. Charles also **tried his hand at sheepshearing,** but admitted to the press, "I made rather a mess of it and left a somewhat shredded sheep."

Big brother, little brother
Prince Charles entertains his little brother Edward, in a scene from the 1969 behind-the-scenes documentary film *Royal Family* (see pp.172–73). Edward is just 5 years old, while his big brother is nearly 21.

Against the Wall
During an 11-day tour of West Germany in 1965, the Queen and Prince Philip visited the Berlin Wall at Potsdamer Platz. Vast crowds turned out to see them.

Born 1948

The Prince of Wales

> ## "I only **take on** the most **difficult challenges...** to **raise aspirations...**"
>
> CHARLES, PRINCE OF WALES

Prince Charles's full title is His Royal Highness Prince Charles Philip Arthur George, Prince of Wales, KG, KT, GCB, OM, AK, QSO, PC, ADC, Earl of Chester, Duke of Cornwall, Duke of Rothesay, Earl of Carrick, Baron of Renfrew, Lord of the Isles, and Prince and Great Steward of Scotland. This may sound as if he is a bastion of tradition and an archetype of conservatism, and in many ways he is, but he also represents a new breed of royal. Charles is a royal in the classic tradition of engagement and service, but with a distinctive and modern twist. An academic and thoughtful man, he was the first heir to the throne to be sent to school, the first to take public exams, one of the few to go to university rather than straight into the military, and the first to get a degree.

Father and sons
Prince Charles is seen here with his young sons Princes William and Harry at their Kensington home in 1985. As adults, the three are said to be very close and share several common interests.

Conservative radical

Charles's abiding concerns for the conservation of traditions and the environment became apparent early in his life. As a teenager attending school in Australia, he wrote an essay about the threat to traditional societies in New Guinea, while as an undergraduate at Cambridge, he proposed a telling motion to the Union debating society in 1970: "This house believes that technological advance threatens the individuality of man and is becoming his master". Expressing concern about the march of

technology, he confessed to be "in a slightly difficult position", as a result of his status. He still straddles uneasily the line between personal opinion and official impartiality.

Formative influences

Charles was close to his great-uncle Louis Mountbatten, and the pair had affectionate nicknames for one another: "honorary grandfather" and "honorary grandson". Charles had never got a chance to know his real grandfathers – King George VI died when Charles was 4 years old, and Prince Andrew of Greece and Denmark

Man of contradictions

In character, the Prince of Wales is humorous, self-deprecating, intelligent, and passionately engaged with a lot of issues, but also deeply insecure. He is pictured here looking very relaxed during a visit to Pakistan in 2006.

Red Crow
Prince Charles smokes a peace pipe – a ceremonial pipe – during a royal tour of Canada in 1977. During the visit, he was given the name "Red Crow", an Indian Chief of the Kainai tribe.

passed away four years before Charles was born. He also had a difficult relationship with his father.

Mountbatten would later attempt to matchmake his granddaughter, Amanda Knatchbull, into the Royal Family and he vigorously promoted the match to Charles. But the young Prince had little

marvellous… Fortunately I landed… I had visions of myself going round and round until eventually the fuel ran out."

As a father, Charles sought to bring up his children very differently from how he was brought up. He had a strong desire not to create the sense of distance and loneliness he experienced as a child.

Hobby horses
Although a military career was not for Charles, he did take to farming, particularly appropriate for one of Britain's largest landowners. As Duke

> "He has spent an awful lot of his life **searching for a role,** but I think he does now **feel fulfilled** pursuing his **various interests.**"
>
> PENNY JUNOR, ROYAL BIOGRAPHER

interest in being tied down, and would continue to be one of the world's most eligible bachelors into his 30s.

At his father's insistence, Charles pursued a career in every branch of the military, arguably enjoying the Royal Air Force the most. In January 1969, Charles made his first solo flight, and later recalled, "… it was absolutely

of Cornwall, he owns massive estates (see pp.256–57). He pursues organic farming and started the multimillion-pound Duchy Originals brand to market his own produce. Organic farming methodology is just one of many hobby horses for which the Prince is famous.

He is also promotes alternative medicine, especially homeopathy.

He famously admitted to talking to his plants to help them grow. He holds strong views on architecture, outspokenly criticizing buildings he finds distasteful – when he labelled a proposed National Gallery extension "a monstrous carbuncle on the face of a much-loved and elegant friend", the extension was scrapped. He is developing a village at Poundbury in Dorset with buildings that follow his architectural principles. He has long been concerned about climate change, and as the climate emergency worsens, Charles has become increasingly vocal. He gave an opening address to world leaders at 2020's virtual Climate Week.

Forging a new style of monarchy
With advancing years, the Queen has increasingly looked to Charles to serve as a sort of co-monarch. He has moved centre stage in guiding royal strategy,

Prince's Foundation
Charles speaks at the annual conference of the Prince's Foundation for the Built Environment – now known as the Prince's Foundation for Building Community – in 2010. Charles established the charity in 1986.

pursuing a "slimming" agenda that sees the Royal Family pared down to a core of his parents and his own direct family, moving his siblings and their offspring to the margins. Charles himself promises to be a new style of monarch, outspoken and an activist, but this has raised serious political and constitutional issues. These came to a head in the 2015 court battle over the release of the "black spider" memos, the letters in the Prince's distinctive spidery handwriting that he regularly fires off to government ministers to argue policy or push an agenda. "In defining his role as heir apparent," says Catherine Mayer, his biographer, "the Prince has signalled a redefinition of the monarchy. Some courtiers – and the sovereign herself – fear that neither the crown nor its subjects will tolerate the shock of the new."

TIMELINE

TIMELINE

- **14 November 1948** Born Charles Philip Arthur George at Buckingham Palace to Princess Elizabeth and the Duke of Edinburgh.
- **14 November 1951** Celebrates his third birthday without his parents, who are in Canada on a royal tour.
- **6 February 1952** King George VI dies; Charles becomes Duke of Cornwall, Duke of Rothesay, Earl of Carrick and Baron of Renfrew, Lord of the Isles, and Prince and Great Steward of Scotland.
- **2 June 1953** Attends coronation of his mother.
- **7 November 1956** Starts school at Hill House in central London.
- **26 July 1958** Charles is created Prince of Wales.

PRINCE OF WALES COAT OF ARMS

- **1 May 1962** Starts school at Gordonstoun in Scotland.
- **17 June 1963** Causes media storm by ordering cherry brandy at a hotel in Stornoway, Scotland.
- **February–July 1966** Spends two terms at Timbertop, a remote annexe of Geelong Church of England Grammar School in Australia.
- **8 October 1967** Starts studying archaeology and physical and social anthropology at Trinity College, Cambridge.
- **1 July 1969** Charles is invested as Prince of Wales at Caernarfon Castle.
- **23 June 1970** Becomes first heir to the throne to gain a university degree.
- **29 July 1981** Marries Lady Diana Spencer.
- **21 June 1982** Birth of Prince William.
- **15 September 1984** Birth of Prince Harry.
- **9 December 1992** Separates from Diana.
- **28 August 1996** Divorces Diana.
- **31 August 1997** Diana dies in a car crash.
- **November 1998** Charles's press secretary provokes a furore after an interview in which he suggests that the Prince would like the Queen to abdicate in his favour.
- **9 April 2005** Marries Camilla Parker Bowles.
- **20 September 2013** Passes the age of 64 years, 10 months, and 5 days to become the likely holder of the record for oldest person to be crowned in British history, when he eventually succeeds the Queen, surpassing William IV who became king in 1830. Charles is also the longest serving heir apparent.
- **22 January 2020** Prince Charles addresses the Davos Conference of world leaders, warning of the "approaching catastrophe" – climate change.

DUCHESS OF CORNWALL
CAMILLA

The Duchess of Cornwall was born Camilla Rosemary Shand on 17 July 1947, in London, into a well-connected, though not aristocratic, family. In 1973, she married Brigadier Andrew Parker Bowles, and had two children, but this marriage was dissolved in 1995. In 2005, she married Charles in a civil ceremony, followed by a service of prayer and dedication in St George's Chapel, Windsor Castle, presided over by the Archbishop of Canterbury, followed by a reception hosted by the Queen. The Palace announced that if Prince Charles becomes King, Camilla will use the style HRH Princess Consort.

The **Launch** of the **QE2**

The construction of the *Queen Elizabeth 2 (QE2)* – the mighty new flagship of the famous Cunard Line – signalled both the end of one era and the start of a new one. The last great passenger ship to be built on the River Clyde in Scotland, it marked the beginning of cruisers replacing liners.

Just a few days before the launch of the shipping company Cunard's latest and greatest ocean liner, the previous holder of that title, the *Queen Mary*, had made her last transatlantic crossing. This marked the transition from the old era of pre-aviation passenger shipping to a new age. In the early 1950s, liners carried over one million passengers a year across the Atlantic. By 1967, sea traffic had almost halved to around 600,000 journeys, while the airlines were carrying more than five million people each year. Accordingly, the 59,000-tonne new ship was built to be quite different from its predecessors. It was equipped for cruising as an end in itself, with nearly 1,000 cabins, restaurants on the upper decks with sea views, cocktail bars, nightclubs, and a theatre. As Sir John Brocklebank, chairman of Cunard, had announced in 1962, "She must be a top flight cruise ship... with a concept in advance of any existing ship."

The great mystery to be revealed on the day of the launch was the name of the vessel, known up to that point simply as *Q4*. The presence of the Queen's sister at the launch led many to conclude it would be named the *Princess Margaret*. However, written on the slip of paper that was handed to the Queen with the name of the ship on it was simply *Queen Elizabeth*. It was she who chose, by the act of declaring it aloud, that the ship would be known as the *Queen Elizabeth the Second*.

The Queen pressed the button to release a bottle of white wine (which Cunard always use in preference to champagne) to smash against the bow. Soon the huge ship began to gather pace down the slipway, reaching 35.4 kph (22 mph) before entering the water stern-first and sending a 60 cm (2 ft) high wave washing across the Clyde.

> **"Like her great predecessors, the new liner will write a further chapter in the history of ocean travel."**
> **BRITISH PATHÉ NEWSREEL COMMENTATOR, 1967**

Ready for launch
The *QE2*, with its vast bulk of the hull and lower superstructure, is poised for its launch on 20 September 1967. Thousands of tons of drag chains – on either side of the slipway – would slow the mighty ship's descent so that she didn't crash into the far bank of the Clyde.

« BEFORE

Charles began studying at Trinity College, Cambridge, in 1967. As the day of the investiture approached, he left Cambridge and went to Wales to prepare.

LIFE AS A STUDENT
Charles spent his first year at Trinity College, Cambridge, studying archaeology and physical and social anthropology. He studied history for another year and then, in April 1969, left

CHARLES AT CAMBRIDGE IN 1969

Cambridge to **study Welsh** and the history of the Principality at the University College of Wales in Aberystwyth, in a move to improve his **appeal to the Welsh public.**

WELSH BLOOD IN HIS VEINS
At the time there was considerable controversy stirred by Welsh nationalists, who questioned the **legitimacy of an English royal being installed as their prince.** One newspaper reported that the Welsh "are sick and tired of having the skeletons of long-dead princes dug up and rattled before them." Charles responded by pointing out that he was "**descended three times over from the original Welsh princes.** My grandmother, Queen Elizabeth, is descended twice over through both sides, so I seem to have quite a lot of Welsh blood in me." Three weeks before the investiture, Charles gave **a speech in Welsh at Aberystwyth,** but it failed to dissuade militant Welsh nationalists from staging **bomb attacks** on government and military buildings.

Accoutrements of office
Charles kneels before his mother, the Queen, to receive the accoutrements of his new office. He is holding the ceremonial sword and the gold rod, and wearing the newly fashioned coronet of Welsh gold.

Charles is Invested as the Prince of Wales

Although Charles had been made Prince of Wales 11 years earlier in 1958 when he was 9 years old, it was deemed better to wait until he had grown to manhood before unleashing all the pomp and pageantry of the investiture ceremony on him.

The title of Prince of Wales, traditionally, though not always, held by the heir to the throne, has a long but contentious history. According to legend, it was Edward I who, having slain Llywelyn ap Gruffud, the last independent Prince of Wales, promised the people of Wales a prince "who spoke not a word of English". This led them to believe he would appoint a Welshman, when he actually meant his preverbal infant son. By 1301, Edward had indeed invested the title on his son, the future Edward II. This legend extends to the origin of the motto of the Prince of Wales, *Ich Dien*, usually translated as "I serve". According to one Welsh tradition, when Edward I presented his newborn son to the Welsh assembly, he proclaimed in Welsh *Eich dyn*, which means "Behold the man". The more general belief is that *Ich Dien* was the motto under the plume of John, King of Bohemia, who was slain by the Black Prince – Edward of Woodstock, Prince of Wales, eldest son of Edward III – at Crécy in northern France in 1346. According to *Brewer's Dictionary of Phrase and Fable,* when the Black Prince defeated John of Bohemia, he assumed the slain king's motto in a show of modesty, to indicate that "he served under the king, his father".

Delayed ceremony
Charles became Prince of Wales when he was only 9 years old, and it was felt that the investiture ceremony would be too much for him at that young age. Accordingly it was decided to wait until he was older, and so the investiture was planned for 1969, when he would be almost 21 years old.

Caernarfon Castle in North Wales was chosen as a suitably spectacular backdrop for a ceremony intended to entertain and impress. Lord Snowdon, husband of Princess Margaret, was appointed Constable of Caernarfon Castle and given the task of devising and arranging the ceremony, a job he took on with gusto, inventing an array of pomp and pageantry. Snowdon ordered 4,000 chairs upholstered in bright scarlet

Impressive backdrop
With its tall polygonal towers, sheer scale, and dominating presence, the 13th-century Caernarfon Castle proved to be the perfect venue for the investiture ceremony.

titles including the Principality of Wales and the Earldom of Chester. He was presented with the accoutrements of his new offices, including a sword, new coronet of Welsh gold, mantle, gold ring, and gold rod. In formal response to the Queen, he pledged: "I, Charles, Prince of Wales, do become your liege man of life and limb and earthly worship and faith and truth I will bear unto you to live and die against all manner of folks." After this the Queen led Charles to Queen Eleanor's Gate overlooking the square to formally present him to the crowd.

singers, a very memorable 'Goon', and eminent film stars. All these people have been inspired in some way by this heritage." The mention of a "Goon" is a reference to Harry Secombe, a Welsh member of the cast of *The Goon Show*, an offbeat radio comedy of which Charles has always been a huge fan.

Apart from the 4,000 guests at the castle and some 90,000 people on the streets of Caernarfon, the investiture was witnessed by a television audience of 19 million people in the UK and up to 500 million around the world. This is believed to be the largest TV audience ever gained for an event in Wales. The event was used to market Wales at a time of upheaval and change for the Welsh economy, and against a backdrop of increasing Welsh nationalism. A year-long promotional campaign called "Croeso [Welcome] '69" was built around the investiture.

for the guests – these were later sold by the Ministry of Works for £12 each in an attempt to recover some of the considerable cost of the ceremony. Snowdon devised for himself as constable a costume in Lincoln green, which he later described as a cross between "a cinema usherette from the 1950s and the panto character Buttons". This caused some controversy with the arch-traditionalist Sir Anthony Wagner, Garter King of Arms. Snowdon also modernized other aspects of the ceremony, introducing a transparent Perspex canopy for the dais where the Prince would be invested, so that TV cameras could capture the event.

Gunpowder, treason, and plot
The investiture would not have happened at all, had a plot by foreign powers been duly executed. This at least was the tale of Russian defector Major Vasili Mitrokhin, who smuggled the information out of archives in the Soviet Union during the 12 years he worked for the KGB (the Soviet foreign intelligence service), before defecting to Britain in 1992. It was revealed in 1999 that Mitrokhin's trove of smuggled documents outlined a fantastical plot to disrupt the investiture. Code-named Operation Edding, the plan called for the destruction of a

bridge on the road from Porthmadog to Caernarfon Castle a month before the ceremony. This would then be blamed on British security services (to what end is unclear). However, the unlikely scheme was aborted at

the last minute, leaving the British security services to cope solely with home-grown Welsh nationalists. In one incident, two Welsh extremists, Alwyn Jones and George Taylor, were killed when the bomb they were carrying exploded prematurely. It is believed that they were targeting the railway line that would bring the royal train to Caernarfon.

Loyal addresses
On 1 July 1969, however, the event went off without a hitch. Prince Charles was invested with

Chairs for sale
The scarlet chairs commissioned for the ceremony were emblazoned with the triple ostrich feathers of the Prince of Wales crest. The chairs, sold off by the government, are now valuable collectables.

A loyal address from the people of Wales was read out in Welsh and English by the President of Aberystwyth University, where Charles had studied Welsh. The president explained that the Principality looked forward to a period when the Prince would associate himself personally with its tradition and language, its aspirations and problems. He concluded by stating, "In this confidence and hope we greet him and declare our loyalty." In turn, Charles responded in both languages, telling the crowd: "It is with a certain sense of pride and emotion that I have received these symbols of office, here in this magnificent fortress, where no one could fail to be stirred by its atmosphere of time-worn grandeur, nor where I myself could be unaware of the long history of Wales and its determination to remain individual and to guard its own particular heritage – a heritage that dates back into the mists of ancient British history, that has produced many brave men, princes, poets, bards, scholars, and, more recently, great

"It is with… **pride** and **emotion** that I have **received** these **symbols of office.**"

PRINCE CHARLES, IN RESPONSE TO THE LOYAL ADDRESS FROM THE PEOPLE OF WALES

AFTER »

Despite nationalist opposition, the investiture seemed popular with the Welsh. On the day, a poll in the *Western Mail* newspaper reported that 74 per cent of people were glad the investiture was taking place and that Charles would be Prince of Wales.

STINT WITH DRAMATICS
Later that year, Charles returned to Trinity College, Cambridge, for the final year of his degree. A **fan of dramatics**, Charles became involved with **the college acting society,** memorably appearing during a show standing in a dustbin. In November 1969, he turned 21 and **came into the colossal income** due from his estates as the Duke of Cornwall. He was now **one of the most substantial landowners in Britain 256–57** ».

CHARLES GIVES A MOCK WEATHER FORECAST IN A DRAMATIC PRODUCTION

Royal Family

One of the television events of the post-war era, the remarkable 1969 behind-the-scenes documentary *Royal Family* changed the way the world saw the monarchy and was subsequently broadcast in 140 countries.

Traditionally, Buckingham Palace had been very wary of the media, at best keeping them at arm's length, but Philip, the Duke of Edinburgh, had long advocated a more open approach for the Royal Family. He recognized that the ever-increasing clamour for access would need a higher degree of proficiency in dealing with the media, especially in the younger royals. He was supported by a few of the more progressive Palace staff, who recognized that the monarchy itself might be threatened as young people increasingly came to see them as irrelevant and old-fashioned.

It was against this background that the idea for a documentary was planned by the Queen's new Press Secretary, William Heseltine. In the wake of the announcement of the forthcoming investiture of Prince Charles, Heseltine recalled, there was "an unsolicited rush of requests from the media for... features about the young Prince... The Queen and Prince Philip decided that a biography of such a young man was not likely to be a very interesting one." Instead it was suggested that a more general documentary would be an "icebreaker".

The then BBC Controller David Attenborough worried that a documentary of the Royal Family would "kill the monarchy" by "damaging the mystique" upon which it relied. However, the project went ahead nonetheless, with producer Richard Cawston and his team following the family at official engagements and in private from June 1968 to May 1969. The resulting film was first broadcast on 21 June 1969, when it was watched by an audience of 23 million, and repeated on commercial television eight days later.

> "A **television film designed to show** something of the role for which **the heir to the throne** was **being educated and prepared...**"
>
> **WILLIAM HESELTINE,** PRESS SECRETARY TO THE QUEEN

Filming the documentary
The Royal Family, observed by a camera, try to act natural. Princess Anne looks less enthusiastic than the others. She later said "I never liked the idea of *Royal Family*... The attention which had been brought upon one ever since one was a child... you just didn't need any more."

Born 1950

The **Princess** Royal

"Princess Anne… [is] **a formidable girl…** She is **a challenge.**"

PHOTOGRAPHER NORMAN PARKINSON, 1981

Famed for her down-to-earth manner and relentless work ethic, Anne has achieved success in sports, campaigned tirelessly for social causes, and fought to give her children as normal an upbringing as possible.

The hardest working royal

Since Princess Anne embarked on public life in the late 1960s, she has carved out a distinctive role for herself as a tireless and able advocate for charity. She has been closely associated with the Save the Children fund, the presidency of which she accepted in 1970. In the course of her work for the organization she has visited more than 70 countries, including Indonesia, China, Cambodia, Vietnam, Ethiopia, Malawi, Botswana, and Madagascar. In addition, she is associated with over 200 charities, among which she has

been particularly closely involved with the creation of The Princess Royal's Trust for Carers, Transaid, and Riders for Health. Other significant roles have included being President of the British Olympic Association and a UK member of the International Olympic Committee, and working on the London Olympics committee. Anne is often described as "the hardest working royal": she undertakes over 600 official engagements each year, both in the UK and overseas. Asked what she would have done if she'd not been a princess she said she'd like to have been a long-distance lorry driver.

Private life

Like her mother, Princess Anne takes a dim view of the public fascination with and media intrusion into her private life. So when in 1968 she met a

Wedding portrait
Princess Anne and her future husband Captain Mark Phillips, photographed before their wedding, once again by her favourite photographer Norman Parkinson.

dashing cavalryman who shared her love of equine sports – Lieutenant Mark Phillips of the Queen's Dragoon Guards – they conducted their courtship in private for some years.

By early 1973, the news had spread, leading the Palace to issue an official statement on Anne's behalf in February: "We are not engaged and there is no prospect of an engagement." However, an engagement was in fact announced just three months later; Mark had proposed in April at the Badminton horse trials, and on 29 May, the Palace released the news. Anne insisted that she wanted a quiet wedding, but on the morning of 14 November 1973, as she rode in the glass coach to Westminster Abbey, 1,800 guests waited for her there, and 500 million people watched on television.

Kidnap attempt

On 20 March 1974, a dramatic attempt was made to kidnap the Princess. Four people, including protection officers, were shot by lone gunman Ian Ball, who then attempted to drag Anne from her car on the Mall, near Buckingham Palace. According to the official investigation: "Ball then came around to the side of the car, pointed a gun at Princess Anne, and said, 'I want you to come with me… because I want £2 million. Will you get out of the car?'" The Princess replied, "[Not] bloody likely; and I haven't got £2 million." The conversation went on for some time. "It was all so infuriating," the Princess said. "I nearly lost my temper with him, but I knew that if I did, I should hit him and he would shoot me." Nearby pedestrians and policemen intervened to foil the kidnap attempt.

Kidnap survivors
Anne visits police officer Michael Hills at St George's Hospital in London. Hills was shot in the stomach while trying to intervene during the attempt to kidnap the Princess on the Mall.

In his interrogation after being arrested, Ball told the police: "There is one good thing coming out of this: you will have to improve on her protection."

No titles for children

Princess Anne and her husband went on to have two children. Peter Mark Andrew Phillips was born on 15 November 1977 at St Mary's Hospital, Paddington, and christened at a service conducted in the Music Room of Buckingham Palace by the Archbishop of Canterbury on 22 December 1977. Zara Anne Elizabeth Phillips was born on 15 May 1981, also at St Mary's Hospital. She was christened at Windsor Castle by the Dean of Windsor on 27 July 1981. Zara followed her mother in a highly successful riding career, becoming the Three-Day Event European Champion in 2005 and winning the World Championships in 2006. On 13 June 1987, the Queen created Anne Princess Royal, the title traditionally given to the monarch's eldest daughter. However, Anne decided at the start of her children's lives not to burden them with titles, which means that Peter Phillips is the first grandson of a monarch not to have a title.

Save the Children
Princess Anne at the launch of the International Save the Children campaign. The purpose of the campaign was to bring attention to the mortality of children under 5 years of age.

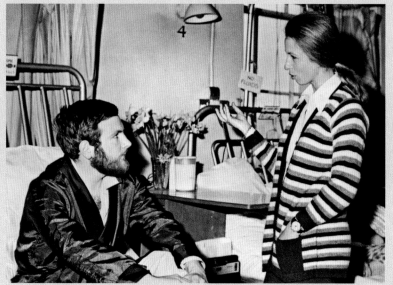

"[I'm] not everyone's **idea** of a fairy-tale **princess.**"

PRINCESS ANNE

Second time around

In April 1992, Anne's first marriage was dissolved, and in December, she married Commander Timothy Laurence – now Vice Admiral Laurence – of the Royal Navy in a private ceremony at Crathie Church (see pp.150–51), near Balmoral Castle in Scotland. The Church of England forbids the remarriage of divorcees, so Anne's second marriage was under the auspices of the Church of Scotland. She was the first British Royal since Henry VIII to divorce and re-marry (see pp.28–29).

Fantastic in fur

In this photograph of Princess Anne, taken by Norman Parkinson for *Vogue* magazine in 1973, she is wearing white fur and the Festoon Tiara, a gift from the World Wide Shipping Group.

TIMELINE

15 August 1950 Born at Clarence House, London; baptized Anne Elizabeth Alice Louise at Buckingham Palace on 21 October.

1962 Has a run-in with French paparazzi while on holiday, signalling the start of her spiky relationship with the press.

1963 Joins Benenden School, Kent, as a boarder.

1968 Meets Lieutenant Mark Phillips of the Queen's Dragoon Guards at a party to celebrate Britain's gold medal for eventing at the Mexico Olympics.

May 1969 Accompanies the Queen and the Duke of Edinburgh to Austria; this is her first state visit.

21 June 1969 The documentary *Royal Family* airs – Princess Anne has strong reservations about it.

1970 Becomes President of the Save the Children fund.

4 September 1971 Wins the individual title at the European Championship 3-day event, and is voted the BBC's Sports Personality of the Year (see pp.186–87).

29 May 1973 Buckingham Palace announces Anne's engagement to Lieutenant Mark Phillips.

14 November 1973 Marries Lieutenant Mark Phillips in the "wedding of the decade".

20 March 1974 Ian Ball attempts to kidnap the Princess, shooting four people in the process.

1975 Wins a silver medal in the individual and team events at the European Eventing Championship.

July 1976 Competes in the Montreal Olympics as part of the British equestrian team.

15 November 1977 Birth of Peter Phillips.

15 May 1981 Birth of Zara Phillips.

13 June 1987 The Queen creates Anne the Princess Royal.

1989 Announces separation from Mark Phillips.

April 1992 Divorces Mark Phillips.

12 December 1992 Anne marries Commander Timothy Laurence of the Royal Navy.

17 May 2008 Peter Phillips marries Miss Autumn Kelly.

30 July 2011 Zara Phillips marries England rugby player Mike Tindall.

WEDDING OF ANNE AND TIMOTHY LAURENCE

14 August 2020 To mark her 70th birthday, Anne is promoted to general and air chief marshal, guest edits *Country Life* magazine, and is the subject of a documentary on ITV.

The Royal Walkabout

Today it seems the most natural thing in the world for any royal visit to be marked by an informal meet and greet with a crowd of well-wishers. However, when Elizabeth II first went "walkabout" in New Zealand in 1970, it signalled a radical break with centuries of tradition.

Elizabeth II's 1970 visit to New Zealand and Australia was particularly notable for inaugurating what has now become an integral royal tradition – the walkabout, an event where royals meet and greet crowds in person. In fact, the first royal walkabout was arguably not Elizabeth's, but one led by her father and mother in Canada in 1939. On 21 May that year, they charmed the Canadian people when, after unveiling the national war memorial in Ottawa, they plunged into a crowd of over 6,000 veterans and spent 30 minutes interacting with them in person. Lord Tweedsmuir, Canada's governor general, related how: "One old fellow said to me, 'Aye, man if Hitler could just see this'. It was wonderful proof of what a people's King means."

The official story of Elizabeth II's walkabout in New Zealand was that the Queen spontaneously broke protocol on spying a group of schoolchildren waiting to greet her. However, the walkabout was in fact far from impromptu. "It didn't happen by accident", admitted William Heseltine, who had just been appointed the new press secretary to the Queen. "We were thinking, 'How can we make this a bit different so it's not just a repeat of the rather anti-climactic visit in 1963?' Out of our deliberations came the idea of closer contact with the public at large – who'd mostly been the recipients of little more than a wave or smile – rather than just mayors, councillors and politicians."

Back home in England, the Queen did her first walkabout in Coventry, and it was a huge success. A new royal tradition had been born, and soon politicians were emulating it, and have done so ever since.

> **"The most important thing of all was that it got a name – 'the walkabout'… it had a romantic aura…"**
>
> **WILLIAM HESELTINE,** PRESS SECRETARY TO THE QUEEN

Breaking traditions
The Queen, with her trademark bag on her arm, goes "walkabout" among a crowd of school children in New Zealand in 1970. The choice of a bright primary colour for her dress is very deliberate, as the Queen has always believed that part of her role is to be visible.

Full kilt
This Royal Family portrait – taken in 1972, on their annual summer holiday at Balmoral – is part of a series to mark the silver wedding anniversary of the Queen and the Duke of Edinburgh.

« BEFORE

In 1976, Charles spent nearly ten months in command of minesweeper HMS *Bronington*, following a lieutenant's course at the Royal Naval College, Greenwich.

RETIRING FROM MILITARY SERVICE
In December, Charles retired from active military service, although he continued to be promoted in all three branches of the armed forces. By 2006 he was an Admiral in the Royal Navy, General in the Army, and Air Chief Marshal in the Royal Air Force.

IN CHARGE ON HMS *BRONINGTON*

The Prince's Trust

In the early 1970s a young, idealistic prince saw the opportunity to make a real, sustained difference to the lives of young people who had not enjoyed similar advantages to his own. He set up the Prince's Trust and, more than 40 years on, it is still changing lives.

In 1972 a young Prince Charles heard something on the radio that grabbed his attention. On BBC Radio 4's *Today* programme, he listened to an interview with George Pratt, the second-ranked probation officer in London, talking about the challenges facing troubled youngsters. Prince Charles believed firmly that it was his duty to help those less fortunate than he was. He also had a strong sympathy with people of his own generation who needed support and to believe in themselves.

Enthusiastic and idealistic

Not long after the radio broadcast, Pratt received a phone call from the Prince's private secretary to arrange a meeting. Pratt later recalled how he "met this young, enthusiastic, and idealistic person". Charles told him that he wanted to do something to help young people like those Pratt had talked about.

At this point the Prince was still serving in the navy, and he started off on a small scale, channelling his efforts through Pratt, who put the word out for funding applications. These applications would be sent in a diplomatic bag to the Prince, wherever he was stationed. Charles would read nearly every one, and where he thought he could help, he would disburse, via Pratt, anonymous small gifts of cash and equipment. On one occasion, for instance, to help a group of young offenders go camping in the Peak District, Derbyshire, Charles paid for their rail fares and sent camping equipment that he had borrowed from the Armed Forces.

Birth of the Trust

This went on for some time with Charles remaining incognito but, eventually, the Prince was encouraged to come out of the shadows when it was put to him that his public involvement would help raise the

Keeping it real

Prince Charles poses for a photograph with local young people who take part in the Prince's Trust activities during a visit to Surrey County Cricket Club. The Trust helps over 100 young people a day.

profile of the scheme. Accordingly, in December 1976, Charles formally launched the Prince's Trust. Looking back in 2013, Charles explained, "The belief that every young person deserves a chance to succeed, no matter what their background, led me to set up the Prince's Trust back in 1976." The Trust started with 21 pilot projects around the UK. Examples included a grant for a 19-year-old woman to run a social centre for the Haggerston Housing Estate in east London; a grant for two ex-offenders to run a fishing club; funds to hire swimming baths in Cornwall to train young lifeguards; and money to set up a self-help bicycle repair scheme.

Since these modest beginnings the Prince's Trust has flourished, becoming one of the most important charities in Britain. Part of its success has been due to its fundraising ability, with a

1,000,000
The number of young people helped directly by the Prince's Trust since 1976.

particular emphasis on using rock music to raise money. In 1982 the Trust held its first fundraising concert, with Status Quo. The same year the first Prince's Trust Rock Gala was held at the Dominion Theatre on London's Tottenham Court Road, featuring Madness, Joan Armatrading, Phil Collins, Kate Bush, and Pete Townshend. In 1996 the Trust held a huge rock concert in Hyde Park – the first one allowed there in over 20 years.

Milestones
In 1983 a key platform of the Trust was launched with the business start-up programme for unemployed

Prince's Trust

Three feathers
The logo of the Prince's Trust is based on the Prince of Wales's badge, specifically the insignia of the three ostrich feathers, which comes from the "shield of peace" of the Black Prince in the 14th century.

young people – a scheme to help young people put together the business model and initial funding to start their own businesses. Within three years, 1,000 businesses were trading, and 80 per cent survived the first year of existence (a high success rate compared to normal start-ups). Since the launch of the start-up programme, the Prince's Trust has helped more than 90,000 young people set up in business.

"**Every young person deserves a chance to succeed, no matter what their background...**"

PRINCE CHARLES, 2013

In 1999, a reorganization saw various different Trust charities brought under one umbrella as the Prince's Trust, and the Queen granted the Trust a Royal Charter, generally regarded as the stamp of approval of a stable and successful institution embedded in public life. Since 2000, the Trust has broadened its outreach, merging with another youth charity called Fairbridge in 2011, and responding to the economic hardships of the 2010s with a programme for teenagers struggling to access education. Since 1999, the Trust has supported more than 146,000 young people who were struggling at school or were at risk of exclusion.

Standing up for young people
The personal involvement of the Prince makes a real difference to the work of the charity. Martina Milburn, the chief executive of the Trust, explains, "I've sat with him in prisons, I've sat with him on sink estates, I've sat with him in classrooms when he's been talking to young people. A

nd he really cares about making a difference to them. You talk to young people – somehow they understand it, because he has been the one person over the last 37 years that has consistently stood up for them." Charles himself reflects: "You can see how it is possible to turn young people's lives around and give them self-confidence, self-worth, and self-esteem."

Success stories
Among all the statistics of the Trust's good work, individual success stories stand out. Arnold Sebutinde was sent to jail at the age of 22, and faced a difficult path when he was released. He recalls, "I'd seen a television report about how the Trust supports young people, but I was worried it might turn me away as soon as I mentioned my criminal record. Instead, they invited me to join their Enterprise programme." Workshops, a loan, and a business mentor helped him to start a successful business capitalizing on his artistic talent. "The Trust was there for me at a time of greatest need and has opened so many doors for me". Arnold has since been invited to Clarence House as a Trust ambassador,

and reflects, "I've gone from being the guy whom society didn't think was safe to walk our streets to being a guest at one of our finest palaces. I'm proof that with the right help you can make it back from the brink. That is what the Prince's Trust has done for me."

A higher-profile Trust alumnus is Hollywood star Idris Elba, who was only able to attend theatre school thanks to a grant from the Prince's Trust. "It was the Prince's Trust that made it possible," he says. "It was a life-changing experience for me and taught me the importance of charity – of being there for people when they need it most."

Investing in the future
Prince Charles spoke on the subject of "Invest in Futures" at the Prince's Trust Gala in February 2013. In 2007, a £20 million loan was taken out from his foundation for the purchase of Dumfries House, Ayrshire, for the nation. This loan was repaid in full by 2012.

The Silver Jubilee

As with her coronation in 1953, the Queen's Silver Jubilee offered the nation a chance to forget gloomy headlines and enjoy a day of national celebration, with street parties being held across the land.

Meeting the people
The Queen on a royal walkabout in Camberwell, South London, greeting well-wishers young and old, some brandishing flags, during her Silver Jubilee year, in June 1977.

« **BEFORE**

Five years before the Jubilee festival, Queen Elizabeth II and Prince Philip celebrated another royal milestone: their silver wedding anniversary.

SILVER WEDDING ANNIVERSARY
To **commemorate** the Queen and Prince Philip's silver wedding anniversary, a special **25 pence** coin was minted, and a **thanksgiving service** was held at Westminster Abbey. In her Christmas message for the year, the Queen spoke of how, "My whole family has been deeply touched by the affection you have shown to us when we celebrated our silver wedding..."

As the Queen's reign approached its jubilee year, she might have been forgiven for wondering whether things had improved much since the start of her rule, a time of rationing, bitter winters, and grim economic news. The notorious "winter of discontent" was just a couple of years away, and Britain was riven with recession, civil strife, and the looming prospect of the weakening or break-up of the Union in the face of imminent devolution referenda. There were strikes, the oil crisis, the three-day week, runaway inflation and, by 1977, mass unemployment. The UK was in such dire economic straits that the country had to get a loan from the International Monetary Fund after the value of sterling plunged. Just as at the time of the coronation, the approaching Silver Jubilee was seen as a chance to distract the nation from its misery.

Theme of unity

The celebrations began on 6 February 1977, the anniversary of the Queen's accession to the throne. The palace and the government together had planned an ambitious series of events and tours for the jubilee year. The Queen declared that unity was the theme of the Jubilee, and that she wanted to be seen by as many of her subjects as possible, both in the UK and around the Commonwealth. On 10 February she embarked on a world tour, starting in Fiji.

On 4 May, the Queen received a loyal address from both Houses of Parliament, and in her controversial, forthright, and heartfelt reply she ignored her advisors' counsel to avoid addressing the topic of the possible break-up of the Union. Making direct reference to those agitating for devolved

Commemorative coin
This coin is unique in featuring no inscription or date on the reverse. Vast numbers were minted and issued for the Jubilee, and despite its size the coin only had a face value of 25 pence.

"The **cheerful crowd** was **symbolic** of... **people** who greeted us **wherever we went** this Jubilee year."

QUEEN ELIZABETH II, CHRISTMAS MESSAGE, 1977

national assemblies, she told the combined Houses of Parliament: "I number Kings and Queens of England and of Scotland and Princes of Wales among my ancestors and so I can readily understand these aspirations. But I cannot forget that I was crowned Queen of the United Kingdom of Great Britain and of Northern Ireland. Perhaps this Jubilee is a time to remind ourselves of the benefits which the union has conferred, at home and in our international dealings, on the inhabitants of all parts of the United Kingdom."

Home tours

On 17 May, the Queen began a series of home tours, designed, as she told Members of Parliament, to demonstrate that she was "Queen of the whole United Kingdom". In six tours, over three months, she covered all of the UK, from Scotland to Northern Ireland, clocking up 11,200 km (7,000 miles). No other sovereign had visited so much of the country in so little time. The Queen toured 36 counties, starting in Glasgow, with the biggest crowds ever

Golden miles

The Gold State Coach passing Buckingham Palace on the way to St Paul's Cathedral for the Silver Jubilee service of thanksgiving, with members of the Queen's Guard in the background.

seen there, and continued to draw vast numbers wherever she went. In Lancashire, over a million came out to see her in a single day.

Light the beacons

The climax of the Jubilee year came on 7 June, proclaimed a public holiday by royal decree, with a glorious procession to St Paul's for a thanksgiving service. The day before, the Queen herself initiated the Armada beacon chain, an homage to the beacons lit across the nation in the time of Elizabeth I to warn of the approach of the invading force of the Spanish Armada. The Queen lit a huge bonfire in Windsor Great Park, which was followed by 100 other beacons being lit from Land's End to Shetland, many on the sites of the original beacons.

On Tuesday, 7 June, over a million people watched the Royal Family progress to St Paul's Cathedral. At the Cathedral a service of thanksgiving was attended by guests, including international heads of state and current and former prime ministers of Britain. The service began with Ralph Vaughan Williams arrangement of the hymns "All People That on Earth Do Dwell", which was played at the Queen's coronation in 1953.

After the service, at a Corporation of London lunch at the Guildhall, the Queen gave another heartfelt speech, thanking "all those in Britain and the Commonwealth who through their loyalty and friendship have given me strength and encouragement during these last 25 years," and also "to the many thousands who have sent me messages of congratulations on my

Jubilee service

Queen Elizabeth II and Prince Philip, with other members of the Royal family, joined 2,700 other guests at St Paul's Cathedral during the service of thanksgiving.

silver jubilee, that and their good wishes for the future." As thousands celebrated with street parties across the nation, the Queen went on: "My Lord Mayor, when I was 21, I pledged my life to the service of our people and I asked for God's help to make good that vow. Although that vow was made in my salad days, when I was green in judgement, I do not regret nor retract one word of it." Later, the Royal Family made an appearance on the balcony of the palace, to the acclaim of a vast crowd.

Anarchy on the Thames

But not all of Britain was in a mood to celebrate. The Sex Pistols, who had burst onto the scene with their anarchic punk rock, and their iconic anti-establishment song *"God Save the Queen"* had been banned from radio stations. Their manager Malcolm Mclaren had the idea of combining a piece of "situationist" performance art with a publicity stunt, and teamed up with Richard Branson, whose Virgin label was the only one who would sign the Sex Pistols, to hire a

Family affair

The Queen and the entire Royal Family greeted the crowds from the balcony at Buckingham Palace on 7 June 1977. By contrast, 35 years later Prince Charles insisted on a "slimmed down" family group on the balcony for the Diamond Jubilee.

boat. Accordingly, the Sex Pistols tried to crash the royal party by sailing down the Thames while playing their controversial single, but they were eventually forced to shore where they were arrested.

Continued celebrations

On 9 June came the final event of the main week of the Jubilee celebrations, with a river procession along the Thames, from Greenwich to Lambeth. At Lambeth, the Queen opened the Silver Jubilee Walkway and the new South Bank Jubilee Gardens, and then, following a magnificent fireworks display, the Queen travelled back to Buckingham Palace by carriage and appeared several more times on the balcony to delight the waiting crowds.

Soon afterwards the Queen visited Wimbledon for the tennis championships, and her presence is widely credited with inspiring the British player Virginia Wade to win the ladies' singles title.

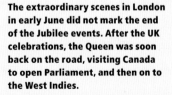

AFTER »

The extraordinary scenes in London in early June did not mark the end of the Jubilee events. After the UK celebrations, the Queen was soon back on the road, visiting Canada to open Parliament, and then on to the West Indies.

A SPECIAL YEAR

The **combined distance** of the Queen's Jubilee year itinerary is estimated at **89,600 km** (56,000 miles). But perhaps the best event of this special year, from a personal perspective, had come on 15 November, when the Queen was delayed on her way to an investiture by a phone call from her daughter Anne, telling her that she had **just become a grandmother** for the first time **296–97 »**

Party like it's 1977
Residents of Fulham, southwest London, show
their support for the Queen (affectionately dubbed
"Betty") during her Silver Jubilee year, 1977.
Street parties were held across the land.

Princess Anne's Equestrian Career

Princess Anne's grit and determination drove her to prove herself at the gruelling sport of equestrian eventing. She went on to achieve glory in Britain as well as in Europe.

Princess Anne first tasted eventing success in 1969 at age 18, riding Queen Elizabeth II's horse Royal Ocean. She had started training just a year earlier under coach Alison Oliver. Anne saw eventing as "a way of proving that you had something that was not dependent on your family, a way of being judged on what you did rather than having even more assumptions made."

In 1971, after coming fifth at the Badminton horse trials in April, Anne was selected to ride in the European championships at Burghley in September. However, her build-up to the competition was threatened by an operation on an ovarian cyst. Despite this, Anne won the three-day eventing championship on 4 September. Riding the horse Doublet, she achieved a clear round in show-jumping to win the gold.

Anne capped a year of remarkable personal achievement by winning the national press accolade for Sportswoman of the Year in November, followed by being voted BBC Sports Personality of the Year in December. She went on to win silver at the European Championships in 1975, before being selected for the British Olympic team in Montreal in July 1976. Although Anne did not win a medal at Montreal, she completed the course despite being knocked out and concussed in a fall during the cross-country.

The Princess's response to accusations that she sometimes lacked royal decorum at events was blunt: "Horses and eventing are part of my private life – that's outside working hours. If people choose to think that I'm going to behave in the same way at a highly competitive event, where the pace is fast and the hazards are testing… they expect too much." Anne's achievements would be matched 34 years later by her daughter Zara Phillips (see pp.286–87).

> **"[Eventing]** is the one thing… that has got **nothing to do** with my **position,** my **money** or **anything else."**
>
> PRINCESS ANNE

The Princess's horse
Anne crosses an obstacle on her horse Doublet at the 1972 Crookham Horse Trials. Doublet was a gift to the Princess from her mother Elizabeth II. The horse's career ended when he broke one of his legs during routine exercise in 1974 and had to be destroyed.

Born **1930** Died 2002

Princess Margaret

"The **dark princess,** if you like."

LORD CHARTERIS, ELIZABETH II'S PRIVATE SECRETARY

Margaret Rose of York was born in August 1930 in Scotland. She was christened in October the same year, in Buckingham Palace's private chapel, with her Uncle David (Edward, Prince of Wales), among others, present as a godparent.

From her earliest years, Princess Margaret was characterized as flighty and capricious (see pp.106–07). Her grandmother, the Dowager Queen Mary, told a friend during World War II that Margaret was "so outrageously amusing that one can't help encouraging her." Margaret began her public life at the age of 18 and went on to become patron of over

30 charitable and professional bodies, which spanned a diverse range of organizations, such as the Girl Guides Association, the English Folk Dance and Song Club, the Winnipeg Art Gallery, and the National Society for the Prevention of Cruelty to Children. The Princess was particularly fond of music and ballet – she became the first President of the Royal Ballet in 1957 and also headed the Sadler's Wells Foundation. Yet her dedication to royal

two children: David, born on 3 November 1961, and Sarah, born on 1 May 1964.

However, the marriage seemed to be built on a shaky foundation – Margaret had supposedly accepted Armstrong-Jones's proposal a day after discovering that Townsend was getting married to a Belgian woman. Still, Margaret and Armstrong-Jones appeared a stylish couple at the heart of the swinging sixties. They mixed with a variety of people, from aristocrats and artists to bohemians and rock stars, and were

Rock and roller
Margaret was known to keep eclectic company. Here she is seen enjoying a meal with Mick Jagger, lead singer of the Rolling Stones, at a restaurant in the West Indies in December 1976.

a senior royal since that of Princess Victoria Melita of Saxe-Coburg and Gotha in 1901.

Dark princess
By 1974, Margaret had already begun a relationship with Roddy Llewellyn, a landscape gardener 17 years her junior. As the affair became progressively public, Margaret began to drink heavily and disappeared on increasingly long jaunts to her holiday home on the Caribbean island of Mustique. Her love affair with the Caribbean can be traced back to her royal tour of the West Indies in February 1955, which inspired a calypso tribute, with lines including: "Lovin' sister of Queen Lilibet, is the Princess Margaret! Like to dance, like to sing, like to try anything!" By the 1970s, however, public opinion had turned against the Princess, with calls

"She was a **plaything... warm** and **demonstrative,** made to be **cuddled** and **played with."**

MARION CRAWFORD, GOVERNESS, DESCRIBING MARGARET AS A CHILD

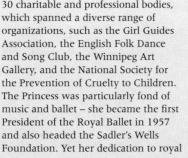

duties was often overshadowed by the intricacies of her private life, and as she grew up, she came more and more under the intense glare of media scrutiny.

Royal soap opera
Margaret's agonizing, lonely, and very public dilemma over whether to choose love for an "unsuitable" man – Group Captain Peter Townsend – over her royal status dominated headlines in the 1950s (see pp.154–55). But happiness seemed within the Princess's grasp some time later, when she became involved with photographer Antony Armstrong-Jones. The two were married in 1960, and Armstrong-Jones was created the Earl of Snowdon by the Queen a year later. The couple went on to have

Belle of the ball
Margaret attends a film premiere at the Odeon Theatre at Leicester Square in London in 1958. With her slim waist and vivid blue eyes, the Princess was considered a great society beauty.

credited with helping to break down social barriers between commoners and the aristocracy.

Sadly, the marriage started to fall apart by the early 1970s, as both partners were suspected of having frequent affairs. The couple separated by 1976, although the marriage was not formally dissolved until 1978 – the first divorce of

Happy exterior
Margaret and Antony Armstrong-Jones pose with their children in what appears to be a relaxed family portrait. There were already great tensions in the marriage at the time the photograph was taken.

to strike her from the Civil List – a list of individuals to whom money was paid by the government – and denunciations as a "royal parasite". It appeared that public preconceptions had been stacked against Margaret from the very beginning. "One of the functions of the Royal Family in the minds of the people is to be the continuing story of Peyton Place", explained Lord

> "When my sister and I were growing up, she was made out to be the **goody-goody** one. That was boring, so the Press tried to make out I was **wicked as hell.**"

PRINCESS MARGARET

Charteris, formerly the Queen's private secretary, referring to a long-running soap opera of sex, secrets, and family intrigue, "And of course in that story there is always somebody who is not actually behaving as they should be... The dark princess, if you like."

Decline and fall

In later years, Margaret's heavy drinking and smoking took a toll on her health. The Princess had a stroke while on holiday in Mustique in 1998, followed by more debilitating strokes in 2001. She suffered restricted mobility, partial paralysis of the face, as well as blindness, and finally died in February 2002, with her two children by her side. Among the tributes on her death were words from the Pope, who, "hoped the Princess would find in death the peace that had so often eluded her in life", and from one of her oldest friends, Lord St John of Fawsley, who said, "After a turbulent life she had come into port some years ago and had achieved happiness and serenity until this cruel illness struck her down."

Style icon

Margaret was known for her inventive and fashionable style. She has inspired designers such as Vivienne Westwood and Christopher Bailey, whose Spring 2006 collection for Burberry is said to have been inspired by Margaret's 1960s look.

TIMELINE

- **21 August 1930** Born at Glamis Castle in Scotland.
- **29 November 1934** First public appearance at the wedding of her uncle, Prince George.
- **20 January 1936** George V dies and Edward VIII comes to the throne.
- **11 December 1936** Edward VIII abdicates, and Margaret's father becomes King. Margaret is styled "The Princess Margaret".
- **1937** Becomes a Brownie in the 1st Buckingham Palace Brownie Pack.
- **1944** First meets Peter Townsend, Battle of Britain war hero and, later, equerry to the King.
- **8 May and 15 August 1945** Joins her sister to walk incognito among crowds on both Victory in Europe Day and Victory over Japan Day.
- **31 January–11 May 1947** Tours southern Africa with her parents and sister, chaperoned by Townsend.
- **21 August 1951** Celebrates her 21st birthday with a party at Balmoral.
- **6 February 1952** Death of her father George VI.
- **1953** Peter Townsend secures a divorce in 1952 and proposes to Margaret; her sister, the Queen, refuses to give them permission to marry.
- **31 October 1955** Renounces Townsend.
- **1957** Becomes first President of the Royal Ballet.
- **6 May 1960** Marries Antony Armstrong-Jones at Westminster Abbey.

MARGARET AND ANTONY ARMSTRONG-JONES AFTER THE ANNOUNCEMENT OF THEIR ENGAGEMENT

- **3 November 1961** Birth of son, David, Viscount Linley.
- **1 May 1964** Birth of daughter, Lady Sarah.
- **1973** Introduced to landscape gardener Roddy Llewellyn.
- **1976** Media storm after publication of photos of the Princess and Llewellyn cavorting in swimsuits on Mustique.
- **May 1978** Marriage to Snowdon dissolved.
- **1985** Has part of her left lung removed.
- **24 February 1998** Has a stroke on Mustique.
- **2001** Further debilitating strokes leave her partially blind and with mobility problems.
- **9 February 2002** Dies at King Edward VII Hospital, London.

ROYAL RESIDENCE

St James's Palace

Although no monarch has lived in St James's Palace since George III moved his family to Buckingham House in 1762, it remains the official residence of the sovereign and is the home of several members of the Royal Family. It is also used for many official functions.

St James's Palace was built on the orders of Henry VIII between 1531 and 1536, on the site of a leper hospital dedicated to St James the Lesser, one of the more obscure members of the Catholic canon. At the time, Henry was evidently much in love with his wife, Anne Boleyn – the initials "H" and "A", entwined in a lover's knot, are a common motif at the palace, carved into fireplaces.

Queen's Chapel
The Queen's Chapel at St James's Palace was the brainchild of James I, who commissioned the architect Inigo Jones to design it. The chapel, which was completed in 1626, was used by Queen Henrietta Maria, the Catholic wife of his son Charles I.

King James was also responsible for ordering the draining and landscaping of the palace grounds, now St James's Park, creating lakes, and introducing exotic animals, such as camels, crocodiles, and an elephant.

Religious conflict
Existing tensions between Catholics and Protestants in England were exacerbated when, in 1638, Charles I gave St James's Palace to his mother-in-law, Marie de Medici. She was not only the former queen of France, a recent enemy, but also a Catholic.

The gift proved deeply unpopular with Parliament and she was soon asked to move from the palace.

Charles I was tried for high treason in 1649 during the English Civil War. He stayed at St James's Palace the night before his execution in nearby Whitehall. With the monarchy abolished, the Protestant Oliver Cromwell, Lord Protector of England, turned the palace into a barracks.

Restoration
Following the restoration of the English monarchy in 1660, Charles II, who had been born in St James's Palace, had it restored. Inspired by the extravagant royal gardens he had seen during his exile in France, he had the gardens landscaped around a long canal. He also opened the park to the public, and it became a notorious rendezvous spot for secret lovers' trysts, including that of Charles and his mistress Nell Gwynn.

In 1698 the palace became the administrative centre of the monarchy after Whitehall Palace was destroyed in a fire. Years later, George I and George II found it convenient to keep their mistresses here.

Chapel Royal
The Chapel Royal at St. James's Palace, where Henry VIII married Anne of Cleves in 1540, was built between

1531 and 1536. Since then, it has been used for a number of royal weddings, including those of Queen Victoria and George V.

Both chapels have been used for the lying-in-state of members of the Royal Family – the coffins of the Queen Mother and Princess Margaret were laid in the Queen's Chapel, while the coffin of Diana, Princess of Wales, was set before the altar in the Chapel Royal, so family and friends could pay their respects in private.

Weekly Sunday services take place at either the Chapel Royal or the Queen's Chapel, which remain active places of worship. They are the only parts of the palace open to the public.

Working palace
As well as being used for a number of official functions, St James's Palace contains the London residences of the Princess Royal and Princess Alexandra. Various royal offices are also based here.

The Palace and the Chapel Royal
The exterior of St James's Palace today has changed little from the time of this illustration from 1812 (below left). A general view of the interior of the Chapel Royal, where the christening of Prince George of Cambridge took place in 2013 (below right).

ST JAMES'S PALACE

CHAPEL ROYAL

« BEFORE

Mountbatten spent decades at the very highest levels of British statecraft, involved in machinations relating to many major issues of post war British history.

PLOTS AND SCHEMES

Having served as First Sea Lord and Chief of the Defence Staff, Mountbatten was approached allegedly in the late 1960s by rogue MI5 agents plotting a right-wing coup to overthrow a possible Labour government under Harold Wilson. More pertinently to his assassination, Mountbatten was also involved in making **peace advances to representatives of Ireland,** approaching the Irish ambassador to the United Kingdom.

THE WRONG MAN?

According to papers in the National Archives in Dublin, Mountbatten told the Irish ambassador to London, Donal O'Sullivan, "that he hoped the policies of Edward Heath's government would ultimately **achieve Irish unity.**" If it is true that Mountbatten supported the policy of reunification, it makes his death at the hands of the IRA a particularly bitter irony.

EARL MOUNTBATTEN OF BURMA

LOUIS MOUNTBATTEN

Born on 25 June 1900, Mountbatten was Queen Victoria's great-grandson, Elizabeth II's second cousin, and Prince Philip's uncle. He had a distinguished naval career in both World Wars, after which he was appointed by Winston Churchill to take a lead role in Combined Operations, a special executive developing radical ideas and technologies to help the war effort. As Supreme Allied Commander in Southeast Asia, he oversaw the reconquest of Burma. After the war, he was appointed the last Viceroy and First Governor General of India.

The **Assassination** of **Lord Mountbatten**

A tragedy that rocked the Royal Family to its core, the 1979 assassination of Louis Mountbatten on his boat took the lives of one of the great figures of post-war British history, along with those of his grandson and son-in-law's mother, and a young Irish crew member.

Louis Mountbatten was a fascinating character in some of the great dramas of the 20th century, from World War II to Indian independence and the partition, but his final act would prove to be part of the grim tragedy of the Northern Irish Troubles – the period of unrest and terror attacks arising from the ongoing political and sectarian conflict in Northern Ireland.

Mountbatten had a home in Ireland (in Eire), just across the border from Northern Ireland. "I have a place in Eire, Classiebawn Castle in County Sligo," Mountbatten told the Empire Club of Canada in 1967, "and I and my family could not be treated with greater friendship by the Irish." This may have been true, but many questioned the wisdom of one of the highest grandees in the British establishment residing in a part of the country where his presence was likely to be seen as a provocation. As early as 1960, Mountbatten's estate manager, Patrick O'Grady, raised questions with the Irish police, the Garda, about the Earl's safety. "While everything points to the fact that no attack of any kind on the Earl by subversive elements

was at any time contemplated," the reply went, "it would in my opinion be asking too much to say in effect that we can guarantee his safety while in this country." Mountbatten refused to heed warnings anyway, protesting that he was used to giving orders, not taking them. But, according to his biographer Richard Hough, "Second only to his cousin, Queen Elizabeth II, there was no more attractive victim for the IRA (Irish Republican Army) – a militant

Family affair
The entire Royal Family was present for the funeral of Mountbatten. Here the Queen and Prince Philip lead the Queen Mother and Charles; behind them are Andrew in his midshipman's uniform and Edward.

organization that wanted a united independent Ireland – than this widely admired and much loved Englishman."

Attack on the boat

At the height of the Troubles, an audacious plot was hatched by the IRA. Early on 27 August 1979, Thomas McMahon – one of the IRA's experienced bombmakers – planted a huge bomb on Lord Mountbatten's 9-m (29-ft) fishing boat *Shadow V*, which was moored in the harbour at Mullaghmore, near Classiebawn Castle. Shortly afterwards, McMahon was stopped at a police checkpoint and taken into police custody on suspicion of driving a stolen vehicle. He was later found to have on his clothes flakes of green paint from Lord Mountbatten's boat and traces of nitroglycerine.

At around 11 am, Mountbatten and five others – his elder daughter, Patricia, her husband Lord Brabourne, Lord Brabourne's 83-year-old mother, the Dowager Lady Brabourne, and the 14-year-old identical-twin sons of the Brabournes, Timothy and Nicholas Knatchbull – joined 15-year-old local crew member Paul Maxwell on board the *Shadow V*. Maxwell took the helm

Happier times
Mountbatten and his family enjoy a quiet day's fishing on board his fishing boat, *Shadow V*, nine years before it would become the scene of his grisly death.

and set off round Mullaghmore Head to the fishing ground. A routine Garda police patrol followed the progress of the boat out of the harbour.

The scene
At 11.39 am, a bomb on board the boat was detonated by radio control, just as it cleared the harbour wall.

23 KG (50 LB) **The weight of explosives in the bomb.**

Richard Hough described what happened next: "The boat disintegrated in a cloud of smoke and spume, and countless fragments of timber and metal, rope and cushions, life jackets and shoes, filled the air and fell in an oval pattern of splashes in the sea." Mountbatten, his legs blown off, was pulled from the water still alive but died shortly after. Nicholas

Knatchbull and Paul Maxwell were killed instantly; Timothy was seriously injured, while the Dowager Lady Brabourne died the day after. A few hours later, two bombs went off at Warrenpoint in County Down, ambushing an army convoy and killing at least 18 soldiers, in the single worst loss of life during the Troubles. A statement from the IRA said: "This operation is one of the discriminate ways we can bring to the attention of the English people the continuing occupation of our country."

State funeral
The death of such a highly placed individual in such an appalling manner called for a show of state strength and solidarity, an opportunity amply afforded by Mountbatten's state funeral on 5 September 1979. Mountbatten had left copious notes

on the details for his funeral as many members of the Royal Family are expected to do. He had outlined everything from the roles of more than 500 Royal Navy and Royal Marines personnel to his choice of hymns. Interviewed on television not long before his death, and asked what kind of funeral he would like to have, Mountbatten replied that he would wish it to be "a happy occasion". The funeral parade, with the coffin borne on a gun carriage, was led by his horse Dolly, riderless with her master's boots reversed in their stirrups, as was tradition.

Mountbatten's daughter Patricia, who had become Countess Mountbatten of Burma on her father's death, and her husband, Lord Brabourne, were still too badly injured to attend either this funeral or that of their son, Nicholas.

"Life will never be the same now that he has gone."

PRINCE CHARLES, DIARY ENTRY AFTER LEARNING OF THE DEATH OF HIS BELOVED GREAT-UNCLE

Final journey
Mountbatten's funeral procession, with police and military escorts for the coffin, makes its way from Westminster Abbey to Waterloo Station.

The events of 27 August 1979 elicited shock and condemnation. As the world became aware of the situation in Ireland, the Royal Family reeled under the weight of their loss.

DEEP IMPACT
At a memorial service held in December that year, Prince Charles **condemned the IRA** as "the kind of subhuman extremist that blows people up when he feels like it."

In 2009, on the 30th anniversary of the assassination, **Timothy Knatchbull** published *From a Clear Blue Sky* – an account of surviving the bombing. A narrative of loss, trauma, and reconciliation, it won the **Christopher Ewart-Biggs Memorial prize** for promoting peace and understanding in Ireland.

TIMOTHY KNATCHBULL
From a Clear Blue Sky
Surviving the Mountbatten Bomb

KNATCHBULL'S BOOK

The **Decolonization** of **Africa** and the **Caribbean**

The British Empire had already embarked on a transition to something new and different when Elizabeth came to the throne – a transition that she stewarded into a Commonwealth family that she has always cherished and nurtured.

When Elizabeth was growing up her father still ruled territory that, viewed on a map, coloured a large proportion of the world pink: the lands of the British Empire. Much had changed by the time she acceded to the throne – most notably the independence of the Indian subcontinent – yet even in 1952 she could travel around the world without leaving her own territories. But this was a world in rapid transition; the Empire was transforming into a Commonwealth of nations, which, as the Queen herself said, "bears no resemblance to the Empires of the past. It is an entirely new conception..."

A bridge across the world
In the 1950s, the former empire comprised the Commonwealth – nations such Canada, Australia, and India – plus many other realms and protectorates, many of which were in Africa and the

Caribbean. The Commonwealth was vast and populous; it covered a quarter of the world's habitable surface and its population exceeded one-quarter of the human race. A large proportion of it was not yet independent. Territories that were still British colonies or protectorates included Northern and Southern Rhodesia, Malta, Malaya, Singapore, Jamaica and the British West Indies, Kenya, Nigeria, Uganda, Tanganyika, the Sudan, Nyasaland,

Zanzibar, the Gold Coast, and Somaliland. But from the very start of Elizabeth II's reign, the changing relationship between the monarch and former and current British dominions was made plain; the cabinet decided that Elizabeth's accession proclamation would not refer to the British Dominions or the Imperial Crown, and that she would not be "Queen of the British Dominions beyond the seas" but "Queen of her other Realms and Territories".

The magic of the moment
Harold Macmillan giving the "winds of change" address to the South African parliament, in which he spoke against the host country's policy of apartheid.

In its early days the Commonwealth seemed to be a successful and vibrant project. In October 1957, *Reader's Digest* magazine was able to reflect that the Queen "is as proud as her countrymen that, while the Communists have been holding 100 million foreign people

« BEFORE

The Commonwealth had existed in some form since 1924, but the independence of India meant that the former constitution of the Commonwealth would have to change.

THE LONDON DECLARATION
Issued on 28 April 1949, the **London Declaration marked the birth of the modern Commonwealth ‹‹ 64–65.** Recognizing the "impending constitutional changes in India", the Declaration stated: "Accordingly the United Kingdom, Canada, Australia, New Zealand, South Africa, India, Pakistan and Ceylon hereby declare that they remain united **as free and equal members of the Commonwealth of Nations,** freely co-operating in the **pursuit of peace, liberty and progress."**

The last dance
Queen Elizabeth II and the first president of Ghana, Kwame Nkrumah, dance the shuffle at a ball held at State House, Accra, in November 1961.

behind the Iron Curtain and giving them the treatment of Hungary, Britain has been freeing 500 million people from colonial ties, investing £100 million a year in their local industries, helping them to organise complete self-government, no strings attached." By 1957, Britain's trade with her former territories had nearly doubled and the territories' own local revenues increased by 1,200 per cent. That same year the Queen, in a speech to the young people of the Commonwealth, said, "You are growing up in a world which is as full of possibilities of

In October 1960, a few months after a tense Commonwealth premiers' conference held at Windsor in May, where apartheid was criticized, South African whites voted to jettison the Queen as head of state and the new republic left the Commonwealth.

Meanwhile the "wind of change" Macmillan had talked about in his speech was pushing over a dozen black-majority regions from across Africa and the Caribbean into nationhood. Nigeria and Somalia gained independence in 1960, Sierra Leone and Tanzania in 1961;

Fly the flag
The Commonwealth flag features a stylized globe surrounded by a crescent of golden spears making up the letter "C".

told him, "Danger is part of the job". After arriving at Accra airport, her route into town had to be lit by torches because of a power failure. Royal correspondent Audrey Russell recalled, "I was very anxious for the Queen. To carry on in those circumstances showed her enormous courage."

Contentious opinions
After Northern Rhodesia was granted independence as Zambia in 1964, the mostly white government of Southern Rhodesia pushed hard for sovereignty, a demand that was refused by Britain under its policy of "no independence before majority rule". While African premiers were strongly urging Britain to initiate immediate action against Southern Rhodesia, Prince Philip, in a speech given to students in Edinburgh, shared his personal views on the crisis: "... it is better to spin out the solution of these difficulties with patience, and with a bit of luck get a better result than risk a bloodbath by forcing a pace." The Labour Party MPs tabled a motion stating that "royalty should not give expression to contentious political opinions", and Kenyan politicians joined in the criticism.

AFTER »

In 1994, South Africa held the first free and fair elections in its history, after Nelson Mandela was freed and apartheid dismantled. That same year it rejoined the Commonwealth.

LINE OF SUCCESSION
In 2018, following the Queen's "sincere wish" that he should follow in her stead, the leaders of the member nations of the Commonwealth voted for **Prince Charles to succeed** her as **Head of the Commonwealth**. Theresa May, then UK Prime Minister, said that it was "fitting" that Prince Charles should succeed, due to his **"proud support" of the institution** for more than four decades.

The August 1979 Commonwealth conference was dominated by a row over the future of Southern Rhodesia. British Prime Minister Margaret Thatcher backed a proposal for the independence of Zimbabwe – the name Southern Rhodesia would take on after independence – under Bishop Abel Muzorewa. The proposal excluded the

29,958,050 The combined land area in square km (11,566,870 square miles) of current Commonwealth nations.

nationalists under Robert Mugabe and Joshua Nkomo, but it was argued that a lasting peace was impossible without them. The Queen played a significant backstage role in brokering a proposal for a conference in London to devise a new constitution for Zimbabwe.

" The **wind of change** is blowing... **whether we like it or not...** growth of national consciousness is a political fact. "

HAROLD MACMILLAN, SPEECH TO THE SOUTH AFRICAN PARLIAMENT, 1960

adventure as it was in the days of my predecessor, Queen Elizabeth I. What the world now needs most is a solid bridge between East and West. The British Commonwealth is surely such a bridge."

The wind of change
It was in Africa, where British dominions and protectorates covered a huge proportion of the continent, that the reign of Queen Elizabeth II would see the most profound changes. From the late 1950s onwards, a wave of newly independent nation states spread across the continent, in many cases peacefully but sometimes resulting in desperate struggles and violent upheaval. In 1957, the Gold Coast, in West Africa, became independent as the Republic of Ghana and joined the Commonwealth; it was the first majority-ruled African country to join.

The independence movement was gaining momentum across Africa when on 3 February 1960, British Prime Minister Harold Macmillan gave a famous speech to South African Members of Parliament in Cape Town. At the time, the ruling Nationalists were pursuing apartheid, and Macmillan had aroused criticism by agreeing to visit the country as their guest. But Macmillan disappointed the white politicians as he told them bluntly that a "wind of change" was blowing through Africa. "Whether we like it or not", Macmillan warned, "this growth of national consciousness is a political fact". The Nationalists were outraged; "We are the people who brought civilization to Africa", blustered South African Prime Minister Dr Verwoerd.

Jamaica, Trinidad and Tobago, and Uganda in 1962; Kenya in 1963, Malawi and Zambia in 1964; the Gambia in 1965; Botswana and Lesotho in 1966; Mauritius and Swaziland in 1968; and after a long and bitter struggle, Zimbabwe in 1980. Most of these countries immediately joined the Commonwealth.

Danger is part of the job
In 1961, the Queen defied security risks and bomb threats to visit Ghana, previously the Gold Coast, the first "black" colony in Africa to become independent. The stakes were high; a bomb blast five days before the visit cast it into doubt, but British diplomats feared that cancellation would drive the new country into the Soviet sphere of influence. The Queen reportedly said, "If I were to cancel now, Nkrumah [the Ghanaian president] might invite Khrushchev, and they wouldn't like that, would they?" When Macmillan objected that it was too dangerous, she

Honour guard
The Queen inspects an honour guard at Entebbe, on arrival in Uganda for the Commonwealth Heads of Government Meeting on 21 November 2007. These meetings are the principal policy and decision-making forum for the Commonwealth.

5
QUEEN AND GRANDMOTHER
1980–2000

QUEEN AND GRANDMOTHER
1980–2000

1980		1984		1988	

17 OCTOBER 1980
The Queen makes a state visit to the Vatican to meet Pope John Paul II.

13 JUNE 1981
A 17-year-old youth fires shots at the Queen in the Mall as she rides to the Trooping the Colour ceremony.

❯❯ Trooping the Colour

17 APRIL 1982
The Queen and Canadian Premier Pierre Trudeau sign the Proclamation of the *Constitution Act, 1982* giving Canada the power to amend its own constitution.

7–9 JUNE 1982
US President Ronald Reagan visits the UK.

30 MAY 1984
Prince Charles critiques modern architecture in a controversial speech made during the 150th anniversary celebrations of the Royal Institute of British Architects (RIBA). The speech would lead to the proposed plan for an addition to the National Gallery being scrapped.

15 SEPTEMBER 1984
The Princess of Wales gives birth to her second child, Prince Harry.

29 APRIL 1986
The Queen attends the funeral of the Duchess of Windsor, widow of the Duke, formerly Edward VIII.

23 JULY 1986
Prince Andrew marries Sarah Ferguson in Westminster Abbey. They become the Duke and Duchess of York.

❯❯ Marriage of Prince Andrew and Sarah Ferguson

3 APRIL 1987
The late Duchess of Windsor's jewels sell for £31 million at an auction in Switzerland. The entire proceeds of the sale are donated to the Pasteur Institute in Paris.

10 MARCH 1988
Prince Charles escapes an avalanche in Switzerland that kills one of his companions, Major Hugh Lindsay, former equerry to the Queen.

❯❯ Birth of Princess Beatrice

8 AUGUST 1988
The Duchess of York gives birth to her first child, Princess Beatrice.

19 SEPTEMBER 1990
RAF flypast over Buckingham Palace commemorates the 50th anniversary of the Battle of Britain.

28 NOVEMBER 1990
Margaret Thatcher resigns as Prime Minister. The Chancellor of the Exchequer, John Major, becomes the new Conservative Prime Minister.

29 JULY 1981
Prince Charles marries Lady Diana Spencer in St Paul's Cathedral.

21 JUNE 1982
The Princess of Wales gives birth to first child, Prince William, who becomes second in line of succession to the throne.

9 JULY 1982
An intruder finds his way into the Queen's bedroom in Buckingham Palace.

12–18 OCTOBER 1986
The Queen and the Duke of Edinburgh make a state visit to China. The Queen becomes the first British monarch to visit the country.

15 JUNE 1987
Prince Edward, Princess Anne, and the Duke and Duchess of York take part in TV gameshow *The Grand Knockout Tournament*.

31 AUGUST 1989
Princess Anne and Captain Mark Phillips separate after 16 years of marriage.

16 JANUARY– 28 FEBRUARY 1991
British forces join a US-led coalition army to drive Iraqi troops out of Kuwait during what became known as the Gulf War.

9 FEBRUARY 1983
The British £1 coin, with the Queen's head on the obverse, replaces the pound note.

MARCH 1983
Prince and Princess of Wales take 9-month-old William along on their official tour of New Zealand and Australia.

APRIL 1987
The Princess of Wales is photographed holding the hand of an AIDS-infected man at the Middlesex Hospital, London.

8 NOVEMBER 1987
Irish Republican Army (IRA) bomb kills 11 in a Remembrance Day service in Enniskillen, Northern Ireland.

23 MARCH 1990
The Duchess of York gives birth to her second child, Princess Eugenie.

17 MAY 1991
The Queen addresses a joint session of the US Congress in Washington, DC.

25ᴾ
29 July 1981

⌃ Commemorative stamp

The 1980s opened brightly with the marriage of the Prince of Wales to Lady Diana Spencer, followed by the birth of their sons, William and Harry. By the end of the decade, the Queen had six grandchildren, but the divorces of three of her children and the bitter quarrel between the Prince and Princess of Wales were highly damaging, as the press declared open season on the privacy of the Royal Family. At a time of economic recession, the royal finances came under fire, leading to the Queen's offer to pay income tax. Diana's tragic death was met with an outpouring of public grief. Towards the end of the 1990s, the conflict in Northern Ireland finally came to an end.

1992

7 FEBRUARY 1992
Britons become citizens of the European Union (EU) with the signing of the Maastricht Treaty.

19 MARCH 1992
The Duke and Duchess of York separate.

26 NOVEMBER 1992
Parliament is informed that the Queen will pay income tax from April 1993.

23 APRIL 1992
Princess Anne and Captain Mark Phillips divorce.

7 JUNE 1992
Andrew Morton's controversial biography *Diana: Her True Story* is published.

9 DECEMBER 1992
The Prince and Princess of Wales separate.

12 DECEMBER 1992
Princess Anne marries Commander Timothy Laurence, former equerry to the Queen.

⌃ Fire ravages Windsor Castle

20 NOVEMBER 1992
Windsor Castle is badly damaged by fire.

24 NOVEMBER 1992
The Queen gives her annus horribilis speech at London's Guildhall.

23 DECEMBER 1992
The Sun publishes the text of the Queen's Christmas Day speech two days before the event.

1993

⌃ The Green Room at Buckingham Palace

AUGUST 1993
Buckingham Palace opens its doors to the public for the first time.

3 DECEMBER 1993
Diana announces her withdrawal from public life.

12 MARCH 1994
The Church of England ordains its first women priests.

6 MAY 1994
The Queen and President Mitterrand of France formally open the Channel Tunnel.

1 JUNE 1994
South Africa rejoins the Commonwealth following the end of apartheid.

5–6 JUNE 1994
The Queen leads the national commemorations of the 50th anniversary of the D-Day landings.

19–25 MARCH 1995
The Queen visits South Africa after a gap of 48 years.

16 NOVEMBER 1995
The Queen Mother has a hip replacement operation at the age of 95.

20 NOVEMBER 1995
The Princess of Wales gives a revealing interview to Martin Bashir on BBC TV.

⌄ Diana tells all in a BBC interview

20 DECEMBER 1995
The Queen writes to the Prince and Princess of Wales urging them to divorce.

30 MAY 1996
The Duke and Duchess of York divorce.

28 AUGUST 1996
The Prince and Princess of Wales divorce.

1997

2 MAY 1997
Tony Blair becomes Prime Minister after Labour Party wins a landslide victory.

30 JUNE 1997
Prince Charles represents the Queen at the return of British-ruled Hong Kong to China.

31 AUGUST 1997
Diana is killed in a car accident in Paris.

6 SEPTEMBER 1997
Funeral of Diana takes place in Westminster Abbey after a week of mourning.

20 NOVEMBER 1997
The Queen and Prince Philip celebrate their Golden Wedding anniversary.

11 DECEMBER 1997
The Royal Yacht *Britannia* is decommissioned after 44 years in service.

10 APRIL 1998
Good Friday Agreement brings peace to Northern Ireland after 30 years of conflict.

15 JUNE 1999
Prince Edward marries Sophie Rhys-Jones. The couple become the Earl and Countess of Wessex.

⌄ Commemorative mug issued at Diana's death

"The very essence of compassion, of duty, of style, of beauty"

1 JULY 1999
The Queen opens the Scottish Parliament in Edinburgh. The parliament would look after devolved domestic matters in Scotland, such as education, health, agriculture, and justice.

6 NOVEMBER 1999
In a referendum, Australians vote to retain the Queen as monarch.

»

« BEFORE

Charles and Diana had been seeing each other for about six months before he proposed on 6 February 1981. The engagement was announced on 24 February. Charles was 33 and Diana was 19.

A SUITABLE MATCH

Prince Charles's name was linked with several possible brides during the 1970s, including Lady Sarah Spencer, Diana's elder sister. He first **met Diana in 1977**. With her connections to the monarchy – her sister Jane was married to the Queen's assistant private secretary, and Diana had spent her early childhood on the Sandringham Estate **206–207 »** – Diana seemed a **suitable wife for the future king.**

ENGAGEMENT RING

Diana chose her engagement ring from a selection at Garrard, the royal jewellers. Her engagement ring was made of **14 solitaire diamonds** surrounding an **oval sapphire** and was said to be worth £30,000.

THE ENGAGED COUPLE

> " It was an **easy decision.** I am looking forward to being a **good wife.**"

LADY DIANA SPENCER, INTERVIEWED BEFORE HER WEDDING, JULY 1981

Fairy-tale wedding
The radiant bride is seen here leaving St Paul's Cathedral on her husband's arm. Millions around the world watched the splendid ceremony unfold. The day was declared a national holiday in Britain.

The **Marriage** of **Charles** and **Diana**

The marriage of Prince Charles to Lady Diana Spencer on 29 July 1981 held the promise of a bright new future for the Royal Family. For the British public, it offered a welcome distraction from a gloomy summer of strikes, social discontent, and riots.

The question of a future wife for Prince Charles had long been a subject of speculation, but few had predicted that his choice would fall on a young English aristocrat, the daughter of an earl, rather than a suitable European princess. Press and public quickly fell in love with Lady Diana Spencer, 13 years the Prince's junior and the first British citizen to marry the heir to the throne since 1660. With her ready smile and fleeting downward glance, she was thought to bring something completely new and fresh to the Royal Family. As preparations for the "wedding of the century" got underway, Diana went to live with the Queen Mother in Clarence House, supposedly to gain an insight into royal life.

The choice of venue was a departure for a royal wedding. St Paul's Cathedral, Sir Christopher Wren's masterpiece at the heart of London's commercial centre, is the site for important national commemorations. It had never before held a royal wedding, but its long nave and magnificent dome provided a theatrical setting for the ceremony. The cathedral can house 3,500 guests, and was large enough for the wedding of a Prince of Wales, a major event attended by heads of state, Commonwealth leaders, politicians, and diplomats, as well as foreign royalty. An estimated 650,000 people lined the long route from the Mall to St Paul's, and some 750 million people worldwide watched the ceremony on television.

Nervous bride

When shortly before the wedding Diana confessed to her sisters that she was having cold feet, they are said to have replied, "Too late, your face is already on the tea towels". She later described her wedding day as "the most emotionally confusing day" of her life and that she felt "like a lamb to the slaughter" as she saw the crowds camped in the Mall.

Diana made the journey from Clarence House in the Glass Coach (from the collection at the Royal Mews) accompanied by her father, the 8th Earl Spencer. The coach proved too small to accommodate them both, and the train of her wedding dress, which was 7.5 m (25 ft) long, emerged rather crumpled at St Paul's. It took her two senior bridesmaids – Lady Sarah Armstrong-Jones (daughter of Princess Margaret) and India Hicks (granddaughter of the late Lord Mountbatten) – some time to disentangle and arrange the train before the bride mounted the red-carpeted steps of the cathedral on her father's arm. A stroke had left the Earl unsteady on his feet but he was determined to lead his daughter down the aisle.

Diana's nerves showed during the ceremony, which was conducted by the Archbishop of Canterbury, when she muddled up the Prince's names, calling him "Philip Charles Arthur George" rather than "Charles Philip Arthur George". Three of the Prince's favourite orchestras – the Philharmonia, the English Chamber, and the Royal Opera – played during the wedding, and the world-renowned New Zealand-born soprano Kiri Te Kanawa sang a Handel aria. One of the hymns, "I vow to thee my country", would be sung again on Diana's funeral in 1997.

The kiss and the honeymoon

Smiling and waving at the cheering crowds, the newly married couple returned to Buckingham Palace in an open carriage. Later they appeared on the balcony and, egged on by the crowd, exchanged a kiss. The balcony kiss has now become an established part of the ritual of royal weddings, but this was the first. After a wedding breakfast with 120 family guests, the couple were driven in a landau sporting a "Just Married" sign to Waterloo Station to travel by train to Broadlands, the Mountbatten family home in Hampshire, where the Queen and Prince Philip had also spent the first part of their honeymoon.

Mismatched couple

At the time, and for a while afterwards, Charles and Diana's marriage was seen as a true love match and a fairy-tale romance. However, the gulf between their ages and their separate interests – Charles liked classical music, Diana liked Duran Duran; Charles loved the country, Diana preferred city life; Charles liked formality, Diana rebelled against it – made them a highly mismatched couple.

> **10,000** The number of pearls sewn on to Diana's dress.

Commemorative stamp
Postage stamps featuring Charles and Diana were released a week before the wedding. The stamps were designed by Jeffrey Matthews, and the photograph was taken by Lord Snowdon.

AFTER ≫

Although the stresses in Charles and Diana's relationship did not become obvious until the late 1980s, it is clear the marriage came under strain as Diana struggled with the pressures of royal life.

COLLAPSE OF A MARRIAGE
In November 1981 it was announced that Diana was expecting a baby, and Buckingham Palace asked the press to allow her **greater privacy**. We now know she was suffering from depression and bulimia. Charles and Diana maintained a **united front** while their sons William (born 1982) and Harry (born 1984) were young, but Charles appears to have **resumed his relationship** with Camilla Parker Bowles by 1986. That was followed by Diana's affair with James Hewitt. By 1992 the marriage was to all intents and purposes over. They were divorced in 1996 **230–31 ≫**.

The balcony appearance
The Royal Couple exchanges a public kiss. Standing on either side of them are, from left to right, Prince Philip, the Queen Mother, the page boys, the bridesmaids, the Queen, Prince Edward, and Prince Andrew.

Visiting the Vatican

Following several previous visits by British royals to the Vatican, including her own as princess and as queen, Elizabeth went to Rome in 1980 for the first ever state visit by a British monarch – a trip she hoped would "support the growing movement of unity between the Christian Churches throughout the world."

One of the key moments in the history of British royalty was the break with Rome in the 16th century (see pp.28–29). For centuries the monarchs were at loggerheads – and sometimes at war – with the Papacy. Only in 1914 were diplomatic relationships re-established, and since then the Windsor dynasty has made great efforts to improve relations with the Vatican, and the Queen's 1980 state visit to the Vatican must be seen in this context.

The Queen's first meeting with the Pope as head of her own state came in May 1961. She and Prince Philip had flown to Sardinia, cruised across the Mediterranean, and visited the island of Vulcano. There they strolled incognito among the fishermen and dined on grilled shrimps, veal, and strawberries. Travelling by train to Rome, she was met by crowds cheering "Bella! Viva la regina!", while 20,000 people chanted outside the Quirinale Palace for an hour, as Elizabeth and Philip attended a state banquet and a glittering reception for 3,000 members of Italian high society. The next day the Derby Italiano horse race was run, the date having been deliberately set to coincide with her visit. After meeting with Pope John XXIII, and enjoying a rendition of "God save the Queen!" by 1,000 nuns and priests, the royal couple went on to Venice where Elizabeth won the hearts of gondoliers by declaring "I would love to ride in a gondola."

The Queen's 1980 trip to meet Pope John Paul II was marked by an exchange of gifts. The Pope presented her with a copy of Dante's *Divine Comedy* with its illustration of the Order of the Garter in the time of Edward IV. The Queen responded with a book about Windsor Castle by St John Hope and two signed photographs.

> **"Meetings** between **popes** and **British sovereigns...** serve to push back… **political** and **bilateral obstacles…"**
>
> **MARK PELLEW,** FORMER UK AMBASSADOR TO THE HOLY SEE

Heads of state and church
The Queen, dressed in black according to Vatican protocol, chats with Pope John Paul II. At this meeting she invited him to the UK to visit "the Roman Catholic community in Great Britain where some four million of my people are members of the Roman Catholic Church."

Commemorative Stamps

Although some commemorative stamps were produced in Britain's overseas territories in the 1800s, they were not issued in Britain until 1924. The first royal event marked in a British stamp was George V's Silver Jubilee in 1935.

1 **Victoria's Diamond Jubilee** Canada was one of eight Commonwealth territories to issue commemorative stamps to mark the Diamond Jubilee. 2 **George V's Silver Jubilee** Stamps featuring a portrait of the King against Windsor Castle were issued throughout the empire. 3 **George VI's coronation** A total of 57 Commonwealth countries brought out these coronation stamps. 4 **Silver wedding of George VI and Elizabeth** Initial designs for this British stamp included famous landmarks, but George VI preferred this simple portrait style. 5 **Elizabeth II's coronation** Stamps were issued in 68 countries to mark the occasion. The New Zealand set featured Westminster Abbey, the Royal Crown and Sceptre, Buckingham Palace, the Gold State Coach, and a portrait of the Queen. 6 **Elizabeth II's Silver Jubilee** This set was designed by British designer Richard Guyatt. 7 **Marriage of Charles and Diana** Various territories issued stamps to celebrate the royal wedding. This one from Australia

was also produced in red. 8 **The life of Diana** Issued a year after Diana's death, these British stamps belong to a set of five, each with a different portrait. 9 **The life of the Queen Mother** The stamps in this set show the Queen Mother's transition from young girl to royal matriarch. 10 **William's 21st birthday** Prince William was the first royal to have his 21st birthday marked with stamps and coins in Britain. 11 **Marriage of Charles and Camilla** The issuing of these stamps was widely seen as a sign of the Queen's support for the marriage. 12 **Elizabeth II's 80th birthday** This stamp is from a series of eight stamps featuring cheerful, informal photographs of the Queen. 13 **Engagement and wedding of William and Catherine** The royal wedding was featured in stamps across the Commonwealth. 14 **Elizabeth II's Diamond Jubilee** These British stamps show the Queen carrying out various royal duties during her reign.

6 ELIZABETH II'S SILVER JUBILEE, 1977

1 VICTORIA'S DIAMOND JUBILEE, 1897

3 GEORGE VI'S CORONATION, 1937

7 MARRIAGE OF CHARLES AND DIANA, 1981

4 SILVER WEDDING OF GEORGE VI AND ELIZABETH, 1948

8 THE LIFE OF DIANA, 1998

5 ELIZABETH II'S CORONATION, 1953

2 GEORGE V'S SILVER JUBILEE, 1935

9 THE LIFE OF THE QUEEN MOTHER, 2002

10 WILLIAM'S 21ST BIRTHDAY, GREAT BRITAIN, 2003

12 ELIZABETH II'S 80TH BIRTHDAY, 2006

10 WILLIAM'S 21ST BIRTHDAY, BRITISH INDIAN OCEAN TERRITORY, 2003

11 MARRIAGE OF CHARLES AND CAMILLA, 2005

13 ENGAGEMENT AND WEDDING OF WILLIAM AND CATHERINE, PITCAIRN ISLANDS, 2011

13 WEDDING OF WILLIAM AND CATHERINE, AUSTRALIA, 2011

14 ELIZABETH II'S DIAMOND JUBILEE, 2012

Born 1961 Died 1997

Diana, Princess of Wales

"Hugs can do great amounts of good – especially for children."

DIANA, PRINCESS OF WALES

Diana Spencer was the fourth child and the youngest daughter of Viscount and Viscountess Althorp. Her father, Edward John Spencer, was a former Equerry – officer attendant – to King George VI and Queen Elizabeth II; her mother, Frances Roche, was the daughter of Baroness Fermoy, Lady-in-Waiting to the Queen Mother. Diana grew up at Park House, on the Queen's Sandringham Estate in Norfolk. Diana's parents divorced when she was 8 years old.

In 1975, after the death of her grandfather, Diana's father became the 8th Earl Spencer, and the family moved into the family seat of Althorp in Northamptonshire. As the daughter of an earl, Diana became Lady Diana Spencer (she was previously the Honourable Diana Spencer). In 1976, her father married Raine, Countess of Dartmouth, daughter of the bestselling romantic novelist, Barbara Cartland.

Diana was first educated at Riddlesworth Hall near Diss, Norfolk, and later at West Heath Girls' School in Kent, but she left school without passing her O-level exams. At school, she showed a particular talent for music and dance – she was an accomplished pianist and was very keen on ballet. After a brief spell at finishing school at the Institut Alpin Videmanette in Rougemont, Switzerland, Diana moved to London, where she shared a flat with three other girls and held a variety of jobs including that of a nursery (pre-school) assistant.

English schoolgirl
Diana enjoyed sport as a girl, especially swimming, and she dreamed of becoming a ballet dancer until she grew too tall for it. This photo was taken the year after her parents divorced.

Engagement
Diana first met Prince Charles, who was older than her by 13 years, in 1977, when he was going out with her elder sister Sarah. They met again in 1980, when Diana was 19, and the affair between Charles and Sarah had been over for more than two years.

"... the unique, the complex, the extraordinary... Diana."

CHARLES, EARL SPENCER, WHEN GIVING DIANA'S FUNERAL EULOGY, 1997

Their relationship developed over the summer of 1980, and that same year the Queen invited Diana to Balmoral Castle, the Queen's private holiday home in Scotland. The Royal Family, too, approved of Diana. As the press got wind of the affair and photographers set up camp outside Diana's flat, she got an early taste of the relentless paparazzi attention she would have to live with for the rest of her life.

Prince Charles proposed on 6 February 1981, and the engagement was officially announced on 24 February. When asked by a reporter on the day of the engagement if they were in love, Diana replied in tones of mock rebuke, "of course", and Prince Charles added, "whatever 'in love' means".

Marriage and children
Charles and Diana's wedding (see pp.200–01) attracted a great deal of public interest. The couple made their homes at Kensington Palace and at Highgrove House, the Gloucestershire Estate Prince Charles acquired in 1980.

Royal bride-to-be
The shy, naive nursery assistant was about to become engaged to the heir to the throne when this famous photo was taken. Diana was always warm and spontaneous with children.

Soon after the wedding, Diana became involved in her official duties as a member of the Royal Family.

On 5 November 1981, Diana's first pregnancy was announced, and the couple's elder son, William, was born just 11 months after the wedding. She flouted tradition by deciding that 9-month-old Prince William should accompany her and Prince Charles to Australia and New Zealand rather than be left in the care of nannies.

Their second son, Harry, followed two years later in 1984. Diana was a devoted and protective mother who declared, "I live for my sons. I would be lost without them."

Divorce and death
The marriage, under strain from very early on, fell apart in the early 1990s (see pp.230–31). Diana continued to

live in Kensington Palace after her separation and divorce, and gave much of her time to her charities (see pp.208–09). In the last year of her life she used her status as an international figure to call for a ban on the manufacture and use of landmines, a move that was seen by some as being out of step with government policy. Her tragic death in a car crash at the age of 36 (see pp.242–43) shocked and stunned the world.

Sparkling princess
The Princess of Wales is seen here wearing a beautiful tiara featuring 19 fabulous pearls hanging from diamond-encrusted lover's knots. Part of the Royal Collection, it was lent to her by the Queen.

> "I'd like to be a **queen of people's hearts,** in people's hearts, but **I don't see myself** being **Queen of this country.**"

DIANA, IN BBC1 PANORAMA INTERVIEW WITH MARTIN BASHIR, 1995

THE 9TH EARL SPENCER
CHARLES SPENCER

Born in May 1964, Charles was the youngest of Diana's siblings – she had two older sisters, Sarah and Jane. Charles became the 9th Earl Spencer on the death of his father in 1992. As Diana's closest male relative, Charles gave the eulogy at her funeral in Westminster Abbey. He described her as "the very essence of compassion, of duty, of style, of beauty", and recalled how she had mothered him when, as young children, they were shunted back and forth between their parents' homes.

TIMELINE

- **1 July 1961** Born Diana Frances Spencer in Norfolk, England, to Viscount and Viscountess Althorp.

- **1969** Her parents divorce; her father gains custody of the children.

- **1970** Goes to her first boarding school – Riddlesworth Hall in Norfolk.

- **1974** Goes to West Heath Girls' School, Kent.

- **1975** Her father succeeds as 8th Earl Spencer.

- **1977** Leaves West Heath and goes to finishing school in Switzerland for a few months.

- **Summer 1977** Meets Prince Charles at a country weekend.

- **24 February 1981** Official announcement of engagement to Prince Charles.

- **29 July 1981** Marries Prince Charles at St Paul's Cathedral, London.

- **21 June 1982** Birth of Prince William.

- **September 1982** Represents the Queen at the State funeral of Princess Grace of Monaco on her first official visit overseas on her own.

- **March–April 1983** Charles and Diana take William with them on a 6-week visit to Australia and New Zealand.

- **February 1984** Attends a performance of *Carmen* by the London City Ballet in Norway, during her first solo overseas tour.

- **15 September 1984** Birth of Prince Harry.

- **9 November 1985** Dances with John Travolta at the White House (see pp.240–41).

- **19 April 1987** Shakes hands with an AIDS patient on a visit to Middlesex Hospital, London, in an effort to rid the disease of social stigma.

- **June 1992** Andrew Morton publishes her biography, *Diana: Her True Story*.

- **9 December 1992** Charles and Diana agree to separate.

- **December 1993** Announces that she will be reducing the extent of her public life.

- **20 November 1995** Appears in an interview by Martin Bashir on BBC television.

- **28 August 1996** Divorce of Charles and Diana.

- **January 1997** Backs international anti-landmine campaign on a visit to Angola.

- **25 June 1997** Auction of her dresses at Christies' New York raises money for cancer and AIDS charities.

- **21 July 1997** Visits the children's accident and emergency unit in Northwick Park Hospital, London, on her last official engagement.

- **31 August 1997** Dies of injuries sustained in a car accident in Paris, France.

- **6 September 1997** Funeral in Westminster Abbey, followed by burial at Althorp.

Princess of Wales Memorial Fund

DIANA'S SIGNATURE

BEFORE ‹‹

Royal patronage goes back a long way. Queen Victoria was the patron of many hospitals, including Great Ormond Street Hospital and Royal Free Hospital in London.

QUEEN ALEXANDRA ROSE DAY

Queen Alexandra launched the Alexandra Rose Day Appeal on 26 June 1912, to mark the 50th year of her arrival in Britain to marry the Prince of Wales, later King Edward VII **‹‹ 72–73**. The aim was to raise money for

POSTCARD FROM ROSE DAY, 11 JULY 1914

hospitals through the sale of artificial silk roses. The first appeal raised £32,000 and was such a success that it became an annual event. By 1920, Rose Days had raised more than £775,000 for London hospitals. **Rose Days still take place every year.** Princess Alexandra, great-granddaughter of Queen Alexandra, is the present royal patron. Traditionally, the **prime minister buys the first rose**.

The Caring Princess

The Princess of Wales threw herself into charity work in a very personal way. She is best remembered for her natural warmth and compassion, and for the time and energy she spent supporting humanitarian causes around the world.

> " Anywhere I see **suffering**, that is where I want to be, **doing what I can.**"
>
> DIANA, PRINCESS OF WALES, 1997

Caring for sick children
This picture from the 1996 National Heart Week shows Diana posing with young patients at a children's hospital ward in London. The Princess was known to take time to sit by patients' beds, hold their hands, and listen to their individual stories and problems.

On marrying the heir to the throne, Diana was expected to give her patronage to charities and philanthropic organizations. Visiting hospitals, opening buildings, and hosting receptions had long been seen, particularly since World War I, as a key function of the monarchy, and a means of bringing it into contact with ordinary people. Much of this work was high profile – Philip, Duke of Edinburgh, was president of the World Wildlife Fund; Charles founded the Prince's Trust and functioned as its president since 1976; and Princess Anne worked extensively for Save the Children. But, for the most part, royal charity work meant acting as a figurehead for fund-raising. To the public, it seemed that the royals' work mostly involved shaking hands, making speeches, receiving bouquets, and cutting ribbons.

Personal touch

That, however, was not Diana's style. Her natural empathy with sick people broke the mould of royal hospital visits. She had a special way of connecting with vulnerable young people, stemming from her own unhappiness during and after her parents' divorce and from her battles with bulimia and depression.

It is sometimes suggested that, after the breakdown of her marriage, Diana used her charity work to promote her own image at the expense of her husband's. There may be some truth in this, just as there is in the charge that she colluded with the press to give them the best photo opportunities. However, the individual stories that emerged after her death bear moving testimony to her ability to reach out to people in pain. She privately visited the Royal Brompton Hospital in London up to three times a week, befriending some of the sickest patients. She painted the fingernails of one little girl on a dialysis machine a different colour every week. Discovering that another was fascinated by ballet, she had a birthday cake made for her in the shape of pink ballet shoes.

Diana used her relationship with the press to help change public attitudes. In April 1987, she opened Britain's first ward for HIV (human immunodeficiency virus) infection and AIDS (acquired immune deficiency syndrome) patients at London's Middlesex Hospital, and was photographed shaking hands with someone suffering from the disease. At that time, AIDS was still greatly feared and misunderstood, and her gesture helped to break down the prejudice surrounding the disease.

Role model

Diana is regarded by many as a role model for the way she spoke publicly about her unhappy marriage and about having sought psychiatric help for her depression and eating disorders, thereby enabling other women to talk openly about these problems.

Meeting Mother Teresa
Diana meets Mother Teresa at the Missionaries of Charity in the South Bronx, New York, in 1997. The Princess's visit to Mother Teresa's hospice for the sick and dying in Kolkata, India, in 1992 left a lasting impression on her.

Chosen charities

As a working royal, Diana was patron of more than 100 charities. After her separation from Charles, she gave nearly all of them up, retaining only six. These were: the Centrepoint charity for homeless young people, English National Ballet, Great Ormond Street Hospital for Children, Royal Marsden Hospital for cancer, National AIDS Trust, and the Leprosy Mission.

Diana had become patron of the Leprosy Mission, the only international charity on the list, after visiting a leprosy hospital in Indonesia in 1989. Leprosy is easily treatable if caught early enough, but sufferers are often regarded with revulsion because of the disfiguring effects. Officials advised Diana not to make the visit but she chose to ignore them. Instead, she was filmed holding hands with leprosy patients and touching their bandaged wounds, actions that were highly influential in tackling the age-old taboos. On later tours, she went out of her way to visit the Leprosy Mission's projects in India, Nepal, and Zimbabwe.

International star

Diana used her fame to support humanitarian causes all over the world. She was photographed holding a baby with AIDS at a paediatric unit in Harlem, New York. In June 1997, she auctioned a large number of her dresses at Christie's in New York in aid of AIDS and cancer charities. In the last year of her life, she campaigned extensively to ban landmines. It was on a visit to New York to promote this cause that Diana met Mother Teresa for the second time.

Landmine victims
Diana is photographed with young landmine victims during a visit to Angola in January 1997. She visited war-torn Bosnia just two weeks before her death, calling for a ban on these weapons.

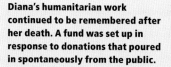

AFTER

Diana's humanitarian work continued to be remembered after her death. A fund was set up in response to donations that poured in spontaneously from the public.

The aim of the Diana, Princess of Wales Memorial Fund was to create a **lasting memorial to Diana's humanitarian work** by supporting charities for disadvantaged people. A sum of £38 million was raised from CD sales of the version of *Candle in the Wind* that singer Elton John performed at Diana's funeral. The general public gave £34 million, and the princess's brother, Charles Spencer, donated proceeds from the Diana: A Celebration exhibition, which showcased 150 objects, including dresses and mementoes. By the time the Fund closed in 2012, it had awarded 727 grants to 471 organizations and **spent over £112 million on charitable causes.**

CONCERT FOR DIANA
Hosted by William and Harry, the Concert for Diana was held at London's Wembley Stadium in July 2007. It was organized to **raise money for Diana's chosen charities,** and for those of her sons.

THE HALO TRUST

BRITISH RED CROSS

Treading carefully
In the last year of her life, Diana, Princess of Wales, campaigned actively for an international ban on landmines. This famous picture of her walking through a minefield in Huambo, Angola, was taken in January 1997.

ROYAL RESIDENCE

Kensington Palace

Originally a modest Jacobean mansion in a rural village, Kensington Palace became the Royal Family's favourite London residence for almost 70 years. It was acquired by William and Mary, who wished to escape chilly Whitehall Palace and the fogs and floods of the River Thames.

I n 1688 when William III and Mary II assumed the throne, the King was in frail health, and his asthma was exacerbated by the cold, humid rooms of Whitehall Palace. Their search for a suitable alternative ended in 1689 with the purchase of Nottingham House – a two-storey mansion in the village of Kensington – for £20,000. Christopher Wren, Surveyor of the King's Works, was hired to transform it into a palace.

The royal couple were anxious to move in, so speed was of the essence. Using bricks rather than stone to keep costs down, Wren's first step was to build a three-storey pavilion at each corner of the mansion to accommodate the monarchs and their retinue, with a series of grand rooms – the State Apartments – for audiences and state ceremonies. Wren re-oriented the house towards the west, and the north and south wings were added to flank a courtyard accessed through an archway that pierced the clock tower. The grounds were landscaped with lawns and formal gardens laid out in the Dutch fashion with geometrical paths and flower beds.

By Christmas 1689 – just six months after work began – the royal court was able to move in, although building work continued. In 1694, tragedy struck the palace when Mary died of smallpox with a devastated William at her bedside. Eight years later, in 1702, William also died at Kensington Palace after falling from his horse and then contracting pneumonia as he recuperated in the King's Gallery.

William's successor, Anne, continued to improve the palace, commissioning a staircase from Wren to link her apartments with the gardens. However, it was in the grounds that Anne made her mark: she redesigned the garden as a baroque parterre with elaborate topiary and erected a magnificent Orangery to protect her orange trees over winter. Designed by Nicholas Hawksmoor and John Vanbrugh, with carvings in pear- and pinewood by Grinling Gibbons, the Orangery served an additional purpose as an enchanting venue for royal receptions.

Georgian heydey

After Queen Anne died in 1714, the throne passed to her closest Protestant relative, George, Elector of Hanover. A survey discovered that the palace was in need of repair, but the new King "lik'd it very much" and proceeded to spend vast amounts on Kensington. Three additional state rooms – the Cupola Room, the Privy Chamber, and the Withdrawing Room – were created in the process. The existing State Apartments were given a makeover by the then unknown artist and designer,

William Kent, who undercut the expected choice – the established painter Sir James Thornhill – on price.

George II and his consort Queen Caroline presided over a glittering time for the palace. They loved to entertain, and the court attracted a fashionable set of intellectuals, politicians, writers, philosophers, and poets. Outside, the old-fashioned parterres were replaced with gardens designed in a romantic "natural" style by the royal gardener Charles Bridgeman. He created many features still seen in Kensington Gardens today, such as the Serpentine, the Round Pond, and the Broad Walk. The gardens were opened on Saturdays when the Royal Family decamped to Richmond; they soon became a centre of high society, as the great and good gathered to parade the latest fashions.

After Caroline's death in 1737, the palace declined. George II died there in 1760; his successor, George III, elected to live at Kew, Windsor, and newly-purchased Buckingham House. »

Palatial heights

The palace complex sits at the edge of Kensington Gardens. A statue of Queen Victoria by her daughter Princess Louise for the 1887 Golden Jubilee celebration marks the main public entrance, while the bronze figure of William of Orange guards the south front.

WILLIAM OF ORANGE AT THE SOUTH FRONT

KENSINGTON PALACE FROM THE SOUTH

The Sunken Garden
The 17th-century Dutch-style garden is a relatively modern development. It was created by Ernest Law in 1909 at the behest of Edward VII, to replace an unsightly cluster of greenhouses and potting sheds.

THE KING'S GALLERY

THE KING'S STAIRCASE

>> Kensington thenceforth became a home for minor royals and monarchs-in-waiting. One of the more colourful denizens was George III's sixth son, Prince Augustus Frederick, Duke of Sussex, whose menagerie of songbirds flew freely around his apartments. His brother, Prince Edward, Duke of Kent and Strathearn, also had rooms in the palace; Edward's daughter, Alexandrina Victoria, was born at Kensington nine months before his death, on 24 May 1819. Her childhood was lonely: educated under the "Kensington System" she was confined to the Palace with every move monitored by her mother and her equerry, Sir John Conroy, who strove to keep the

the palace in which she was born should not be destroyed". Eventually Parliament agreed to fund the palace's restoration. Subsequently the state rooms opened to the public on the Queen's birthday in 1899, launching the palace's dual role as a private home to royalty and public museum.

Kensington Palace was hit by a bomb in 1940, which severely damaged many of the surrounding buildings including the Queen's Apartments. The garden was full of anti-aircraft guns, sandbags, and trenches. After the war, the palace entered another period of neglect, but in the 1960s its fortunes revived when Princess Margaret and Antony Armstrong-

The King's State Apartments
Kensington was at the heart of Georgian society: well-dressed courtiers were immortalized by Kent on the staircase leading to the sumptuous rooms. William III's wind dial, connected to a weather vane on the roof, was retained when Kent redesigned the King's Gallery.

"normal" childhood, with visits to the local barbers, Kensington Odeon, and McDonalds on Kensington High Street. Kensington Palace remained the official residence of Diana, Princess of Wales until her untimely death on 31 August 1997, when the Golden Gates at the south entrance became the focus of public mourning. Over one million bouquets, reaching 1.5 m (5 ft) deep in places, were left in tribute. The Princess's coffin spent its last night in London at Kensington Palace, departing on the morning of 6 September 1997, on a gun carriage, towards Westminster Abbey.

In 2011, it was announced that the Duke and Duchess of Cambridge would move from Nottingham Cottage, in the grounds of Kensington Palace, into the former residence of Princess Margaret. The following year Prince Harry also moved back into the palace: the long-established tradition of combining private royal residences at the palace with a public space looked set to continue for years to come.

Meanwhile, the State Rooms have also seen a major renovation. They were re-opened in 2012, in time for Elizabeth II's Diamond Jubilee, as a museum with digital presentations, interactive experiences, and audio sequences bringing to life the State Apartments and the people who lived there, and making the rich collections of royal fashion, antique furniture, and other memorabilia accessible to visitors from around the world.

"I have gone through **painful and disagreeable scenes** here, 'tis true, but still **I am fond of the poor old Palace.**"

QUEEN VICTORIA, 1837

Princess under their control. Victoria's first request, when she became 18, was that she be allowed an hour by herself each day, and one of her first acts upon her accession to the throne was to banish Conroy forever from the royal apartments, and to evict her mother from the palace.

A palace for everyone
By the end of the 19th century, the State Rooms were severely neglected. With the brickwork decaying, and the woodwork infested with dry rot and rising damp, calls came for the palace to be demolished. However, Queen Victoria declared that "while she lived,

Jones, 1st Earl of Snowdon moved in. They lived in Apartment 10 – "the doll's house" as Margaret described it, while they renovated and redecorated Apartment 1A in Margaret's favourite pink and kingfisher blue with the help of theatre designer Carl Toms, adding a photographic darkroom for Lord Snowdon.

In 1981, the newly married Prince of Wales and his wife, Diana, moved into a part of the palace that George I had created for his mistress. Princes William and Harry were raised there, attending local nursery and pre-preparatory schools in Notting Hill. They were given occasional tastes of

The Cupola Room
Queen Victoria was christened in the magnificent Cupola Room, William Kent's first commission for George I. The King liked his work so much, he was commissioned to redecorate other State Rooms.

Prince Andrew in the Falklands

On 2 April 1982, Argentina invaded the British overseas territory of the Falkland Islands, a remote, windswept archipelago in the South Atlantic. Prince Andrew, a sub-lieutenant in the Royal Navy, was serving on board the aircraft carrier HMS *Invincible* as Britain set about assembling a task force to retake the islands.

The hastily assembled fleet of 127 ships that set sail in mid-April included two aircraft carriers, one of them being the HMS *Invincible*. Prince Andrew was a Sea King helicopter pilot, trained for operational flying. He was also second in line to the throne. It was widely assumed that he would be kept out of harm's way and given a safe desk job, as several members of the Cabinet urged, but Andrew, backed up by the Queen, insisted on being allowed to remain with his ship.

The battle to regain the islands began on 1 May. As a Sea King co-pilot, Prince Andrew flew on missions that included anti-submarine and anti-surface warfare. One task of the Sea King helicopters was to act as decoys against the deadly Exocet missiles launched by Argentinian jets against British warships. By hovering near the rear of the carrier, the helicopter created a large radar target that diverted the missile away from the ship. Prince Andrew co-piloted a Sea King that helped save seamen from the requisitioned merchant navy ship SS *Atlantic Conveyor* after it had been hit by two Exocets. He later described the experience as "probably the most frightening moment of my war." He also revealed that his biggest worry was being hit by friendly fire from the Royal Navy's Sea Wolf defence missiles: "It is not much fun having one of those fellows pick you out as a target."

Port Stanley, the capital of the Falkland Islands, was retaken on 14 June. When HMS *Invincible* returned to Portsmouth on 17 September, the Queen and Prince Philip joined other families of the crew in welcoming the ship carrying their son home.

> " It's **not particularly nice** being **shot** at and I can attest to that. You **look at life** in a **different way.**"
>
> **PRINCE ANDREW**, ON THE FALKLANDS WAR, AUGUST 2014

Action man
Prince Andrew, seen here with the Sea King helicopter in the background, returns to Portsmouth on board HMS *Invincible* after the cessation of the Falklands War. The first royal to see frontline action in modern times, he served 22 years in the Royal Navy.

Born 1960

The **Duke** of **York**

"I'm **not** even going to say that was **a piece of cake**. I will **never do it again**."

PRINCE ANDREW, AFTER ABSEILING DOWN THE SHARD, SEPTEMBER 2012

Naval officer
In his 22-year-long naval career, Prince Andrew participated in the Falklands War and commanded HMS *Cottesmore*. He retired from active service in 2001.

Prince Andrew is the second son and third child of Queen Elizabeth II and Prince Philip. Born on 19 February 1960, in Buckingham Palace, he was the first child to be born to a reigning monarch since the birth of Queen Victoria's youngest child, Princess Beatrice, in 1857. At the time of his birth, he was second in line of succession to the throne; he is now eighth. He was christened Andrew Albert Christian Edward, Andrew being the name of his paternal grandfather, Prince Andrew of Greece, who died in 1944.

Prince Andrew was educated at Heatherdown Preparatory School, Ascot, in Berkshire, from the age of 8 to 13, before going on to Gordonstoun School in Scotland, where both his father and his elder brother, Charles, had been educated. After taking his O-levels, he spent two terms at Lakefield College School in Ontario, Canada, before returning to Gordonstoun to take his A-levels. Unlike his brothers, he did not go to university, but entered the Britannia Royal Naval College at Dartmouth (BRNC, popularly known as Dartmouth), Devon, where he began training to become an officer in the Royal Navy.

Naval career
After passing out of Dartmouth, Andrew learned to fly Gazelle and Sea King helicopters and was appointed to 820 Naval Air Squadron, serving aboard the aircraft carrier HMS *Invincible*. Six months later, in April 1982, he sailed in HMS *Invincible* as

Farewell to Hong Kong
Prince Andrew undertook many military duties. He is seen here visiting a British army unit based on Stonecutters Island in Hong Kong as preparations are made for the transfer of sovereignty from Britain to China in 1997.

part of the Task Force sent to the South Atlantic to regain the Falkland Islands (see pp.216–17). On his return, he converted to flying Lynx helicopters. He was made a Commander in 1999, and retired with the rank of honorary Captain. In 2010 he was promoted to Honorary Rear Admiral, and five years later to Vice Admiral.

Marriage and children
Andrew was known to have had several girlfriends, including American actress Koo Stark, before his engagement to Sarah Ferguson. The redhead was a great success with the press and was soon universally known as Fergie. Prince Andrew was created Duke of York, a dukedom

traditionally reserved for the second son of the monarch – on his marriage to Sarah on 23 July 1986 (see pp.222–23). The Queen built a 12-bedroom, ranch-like house for them at Sunninghill Park, Berkshire. Andrew and Sarah have two daughters, Princess Beatrice and Princess Eugenie.

Separation and divorce
As a serving naval officer, Andrew was frequently away, and during one of his absences Sarah took lessons in helicopter flying. This experience led her to write a series of children's books about Budgie, a little helicopter, which later became an animated television series. Sarah's popularity

started to fall about this time, when the press began to publish pictures of her in the company of other men. The couple separated in March 1992, and divorced in May 1996, just three months before Charles and Diana. Like Diana, she was no longer styled Her Royal Highness.

Andrew and Sarah agreed to have joint custody of their daughters and shared Sunninghill Park as their family home until 2004, when Andrew moved into Royal Lodge, the Queen Mother's former home. Since 2008 Sarah has lived there as well. She spends much of her time in New York, where she pursues various commercial interests. In 2010 she was caught in

> ## "There is **something about** going to **sea**. A little bit of **discipline** and **humility** is required."
> PRINCE ANDREW, IN AN INTERVIEW

THE DUCHESS OF YORK

SARAH FERGUSON

Born in 1959, Sarah Ferguson is the daughter of the late Major Ronald Ferguson, polo manager to the Duke of Edinburgh and later to the Prince of Wales, and his wife Susan. After Sarah's parents divorced in 1974, her mother married an Argentinian polo player, Hector Barrantes. Sarah and Andrew knew each other as children, but their romance began after she was asked to join the royal party at Windsor Castle during Royal Ascot in 1985, reportedly at the Princess of Wales's suggestion. Sarah was working in publishing at the time of their engagement. Andrew designed an engagement ring for her consisting of 10 diamonds surrounding a ruby, chosen to complement her fiery red hair.

a newspaper sting offering access to Andrew for £500,000 and was forced to apologize. She and Andrew remain on good terms and often speak affectionately of each other.

Life after the navy
On leaving the navy, Prince Andrew was appointed Special Representative for International Trade and Investment, promoting British business interests abroad. He resigned from this role in 2011, following criticism about his friendly relations with controversial figures, including one of Libyan leader Colonel Gaddafi's sons, and a wealthy American financier convicted of sex offences.

In the wake of further scandal surrounding his relationships, and accusations of serious impropriety, in 2019 Andrew announced that he was stepping back from public life.

TIMELINE

- **19 February 1960** Born at Buckingham Palace, the first child born to a reigning monarch for 103 years. Christened Andrew Albert Christian Edward.
- **1973** Attends Gordonstoun School in Morayshire, Scotland.
- **1979** Joins the Royal Navy on a short-term commission as a Seaman Officer with the aim of becoming a helicopter pilot.
- **April 1981** Receives his flying brevet (wings) from the Duke of Edinburgh as well as winning an award as best pilot.
- **5 April 1982** Sails on board HMS *Invincible* as part of the Task Force to regain the Falkland Islands; flies several frontline missions.
- **May 1984** Promoted Lieutenant and serves as Flight Pilot in the Type 22 Frigate HMS *Brazen*.
- **1984** The Queen appoints him her personal aide-de-camp.
- **23 July 1986** Marries Sarah Ferguson at Westminster Abbey and is created Duke of York.
- **8 August 1988** Birth of first daughter, Beatrice.
- **23 March 1990** Birth of second daughter, Eugenie.
- **March 1992** Duke and Duchess of York separate; divorce follows four years later.
- **20 November 1992** Helps to rescue treasures from the Windsor Castle fire.
- **1993** Appointed Commander to command the anti-mine vessel HMS *Cottesmore*.
- **1999** Appointed Commander in the Diplomatic Directorate of the Naval Staff.
- **July 2001** Retires from active service with the Royal Navy.

PRINCE ANDREW AT CERN, GENEVA

- **2001–11** Serves as Special Representative for International Trade and Investment, promoting British business interests abroad. His tours included a trip to the European Organization for Nuclear Research (CERN), Geneva.
- **July 2005** Promoted to Captain. Appointed Commodore in Chief of the Fleet Air Arm the following year.
- **February 2010** Promoted to Rear Admiral.
- **3 September 2012** Abseils down the Shard, London's tallest skyscraper, to raise money for the Outward Bound Trust.
- **November 2019** Steps back from all royal and public duties.

Queen visiting Canada
The Queen inspects a guard of honour of the
Governor General's Foot Guards outside
the Parliament Building in Ottawa while
on a visit to Canada in 1984.

« BEFORE

In 1923, an earlier Duke of York, the Queen's father (later King George VI), was married in Westminster Abbey.

BRIDAL BOUQUETS
The bride on that day was **Lady Elizabeth Bowes-Lyon**. As a young bride in 1923, she had impulsively stopped on her way up the nave of the abbey, and in a simple gesture placed her bouquet on the **Tomb of the Unknown Warrior**, containing the body of an unknown soldier, killed on a European battlefield during **World War I**. She did this in memory of her beloved brother **Fergus**, who had died at the **Battle of Loos** in 1915.

Recalling this act, **Sarah, as the new Duchess of York,** arranged to have her bouquet placed on the tomb after the official wedding photographs had been taken. This tradition was later followed by **Catherine Middleton,** at her wedding to Prince William in 2011.

"It was the **finest moment** of my life... when I **married him.**"

SARAH, DUCHESS OF YORK,
IN AN INTERVIEW, 2015

The **Marriage** of **Andrew** and **Sarah**

On 23 July 1986, Prince Charles's younger brother, Prince Andrew, married Sarah Ferguson in Westminster Abbey. On the morning of the wedding, the Queen created Prince Andrew Duke of York, Earl of Inverness, and Baron Killyleagh.

Bridal procession
The newly married Duke and Duchess of York leave the choir of Westminster Abbey through an arch of roses and lilies. Pageboy Prince William, in a sailor-boy hat, is immediately behind the couple.

Thousands of people lined the route as Sarah Ferguson, soon to be Her Royal Highness the Duchess of York, travelled with her father, Major Ronald Ferguson, in the gilded Glass Coach from Clarence House to Westminster Abbey. Some 2,000 people, including many of the crowned heads of Europe and a number of celebrity guests, such as Nancy Reagan, Elton John, and Michael Caine, were present in the abbey to witness the traditional ceremony.

The wedding had a decided nautical theme, in keeping with the groom's occupation. The silver beadwork on Sarah's ivory satin wedding dress, designed by Lindka Cierach, had motifs of anchors and waves, and the train bore the couple's intertwined initials "A" and "S". The four young pageboys, one of whom was four-year-old Prince William, were dressed in sailor suits and boaters. Peter Phillips, son of Princess Anne, was also a pageboy, and his sister Zara Phillips, a bridesmaid. Prince Andrew, wearing the dress uniform of a naval lieutenant, had his younger brother, Prince Edward, as his best man.

The Archbishop of Canterbury, Dr Robert Runcie, conducted the service, and Prince Charles read a lesson. During the exchange of vows, the bride promised to obey her husband (a clause that Diana had chosen to omit five years before) – and was roundly rebuked by feminists for doing so.

The balcony kiss
Laughing and waving, the couple left the abbey in an open carriage for the procession along the Mall

Relaxed demeanour
Sarah Ferguson was remarkably at ease during her wedding to Prince Andrew, sharing frequent laughs with her husband. She winked to the child attendants as she walked down the aisle, and gave a thumbs-up sign to the crowd gathered outside.

to Buckingham Palace. A crowd of about 100,000 had gathered in front of the palace for the bridal party's balcony appearance. Smiling broadly, Andrew and Sarah playfully pretended not to understand the crowd's call for them to kiss. Their eventual embrace was greeted with enthusiastic applause.

Later a reception was held at the Buckingham Palace. The Duke and Duchess left for their honeymoon

1.6 The height of the wedding cake in metres (5.5 ft) made by chefs at the naval supply school HMS *Raleigh* in Cornwall.

in an open carriage adorned with a papier-mâché satellite dish and a sign that read "Phone Home" (a reference to the movie *E.T.*), placed there by Prince Edward. They shared the carriage with a king-sized teddy bear, smuggled in by the Princess of Wales and Viscount Linley, the son of Princess Margaret, Countess of Snowdon. On arriving at Heathrow Airport, they boarded a royal jet emblazoned with "Just Married" on the rear flaps to fly to the Azores. Once there, they spent their five-day honeymoon on board the Royal Yacht *Britannia*.

Popular couple
Although some critics of royalty complained about the lavish arrangements for Prince Andrew and Sarah's wedding, on the whole it was a popular event, and shops and stores were full of wedding souvenirs. Prince Andrew's public image was still positive after his experience of active service in the Falklands War. He was known to enjoy partying and had had many girlfriends, earning him the nickname "Randy Andy". In this respect, he was lucky in his timing, escaping the media censure that might have befallen him a few years earlier, or later. The

Unconventional family
Prince Andrew and Sarah have remained friends after their divorce and have brought up their daughters together. The Queen, reportedly, is still fond of Sarah and thinks she is a good mother.

press thought he had found an ideal soulmate in Sarah Ferguson. More relaxed and down-to-earth than the Princess of Wales, Fergie – as she was now universally known – was always ready with a joke and a quip. She was also, at 26 years, older and considerably more experienced than Diana had been at the time of her marriage. It was widely known that Sarah had moved into Prince Andrew's Buckingham Palace apartment ahead of the wedding, in contrast to Diana's seclusion in Clarence House. It was also common knowledge that Sarah had at least one long-term boyfriend before Andrew. No one seemed to disapprove.

Breath of fresh air
Observers suggested that Sarah would bring a welcome breath of fresh air to the stuffiness of royal life. She was said to be popular with the Queen, who enjoyed her jokes. It was also believed that Sarah would be a good and supportive friend to the Princess of Wales, and the two were close for a time.

The week before the wedding, the tabloid newspapers reported that Sarah and Diana, with Pamela Stephenson, the comedian and actress, disguised as policewomen, had tried to gate-crash Andrew's stag (bachelor) party. They had later got a case of nerves and changed their plans, and instead spent their time sipping champagne at Annabel's, a West End nightclub.

While this escapade was in keeping with Sarah's uncomplicated sense of humour, the episode also pointed to something more – a growing intimacy between the Royal Family and the world of celebrity. This association would ultimately work to destroy the mystique of royalty and make its members increasingly vulnerable to hostile press attack.

AFTER

Although Sarah and Andrew have remained remarkably devoted to one another for many decades now, their marriage could not survive the unforgiving glare of the public spotlight.

A DIFFICULT ROAD
Sarah suffered greatly at the hands of vicious press coverage, with cruel comments on her weight, an inglorious showing in the poorly received 1987 TV show *The Grand Knockout Tournament*, and invidious comparisons with her one-time sister-in-law, Diana. The relentless and spiteful campaign against her, together with missteps by both Andrew and Sarah, led to their separation in 1992, and divorce in 1996. Her refusal to stay out of the headlines afterwards frequently embarrassed the Royal Family. However, the couple's **friendship survived the vicissitudes of divorce and public disgrace**, and Andrew and Sarah frequently speak up to support one another and to reaffirm their deep bond of love and companionship. They still live together, and after a difficult period in the 2010s, were able to enjoy the weddings of their daughters in 2018 and 2020.

COMMEMORATIVE STAMP

« BEFORE

Trooping the Colour dates back to the 1700s when a battalion's flag, or colour, was carried slowly (trooped) along the ranks of soldiers so it could be seen and recognized.

BIRTHDAY PARADE

The Trooping the Colour ceremony was first used to mark the sovereign's birthday in 1748, when **George II** was on the throne. Since this time the Trooping the Colour ceremony has **celebrated the sovereign's official birthday** on a Saturday in June in the expectation of good weather.

KING GEORGE V AT THE PARADE, 1925

The Queen's 60th Birthday

The Queen celebrates two birthdays every year – her actual birthday on 21 April, and the official one in early June, when she attends the Trooping the Colour ceremony. Her 60th birthday in 1986 was marked by special tributes at home and around the Commonwealth.

The two royal events that took place in 1986 – the marriage of Prince Andrew and Sarah Ferguson in July (see pp. 222–23) and the Queen's 60th birthday celebrations – were welcome interludes in what was otherwise a challenging year for the monarchy. There was talk of differences between the Queen and Prime Minister Margaret Thatcher over Britain's stance with regard to the apartheid regime in South Africa. In July, a newspaper report claimed that the Queen was dismayed with the government's harsh social policies in the wake of the miners' strike the year before, but this was instantly denied by the palace. The Royal Family was frequently caricatured on the satirical TV puppet show *Spitting Image* – something that would have been unthinkable a few years earlier. There were also worries over security – in 1981, a pistol had been fired from the crowd as the Queen rode down the Mall for the Trooping the Colour, and the IRA (Irish Republican Army) terror campaign in mainland Britain was an ever-present threat. However, these concerns did not deter the crowds from turning out to celebrate the Queen's birthday.

Bagpipes and daffodils

Queen Elizabeth's 60th birthday on 21 April 1986 started with an early morning rendition of "Happy Birthday to You", played on the bagpipes by the Queen's Piper outside her apartment at

Say it with flowers

Radiant in springtime yellow, a smiling Queen Elizabeth collects bunches of daffodils from a group of children in the forecourt of Buckingham Palace.

Birthday procession
The band and troops of the Household Division, headed by five Drum Majors in ceremonial state dress, return along the Mall towards Buckingham Palace at the end of the Trooping the Colour ceremony in June 2014.

Windsor Castle. The Piper is a member of the royal household. His principal duty is to play under the Queen's window every morning at 9am, a tradition started by Queen Victoria. This was followed by a 21-gun salute

"We **saw your car,** Hurrah! Hurrah! We saw you **wave,** the **smile you gave,** We saw **your horse,** of course, of course."

THE QUEEN'S BIRTHDAY SONG, BY CHRISTOPHER LOGUE, 1986

in Windsor Great Park, a service of thanksgiving in St George's Chapel, Windsor, and a carriage procession through the town.

That afternoon the Queen was driven to Buckingham Palace, where she was greeted by a parade of 6,000 children from all over Britain and the Commonwealth who processed the length of the Mall in the steady rain, each carrying a daffodil. Standing on the balcony of the Palace, she listened to them sing a song specially composed for the occasion, "Happy Birthday Ma'am, God Bless You", before going down into the palace forecourt to collect bunches of daffodils from the children. She was helped by Prince Andrew and Sarah Ferguson, who were due to be married in three months' time. In the evening the entire Royal Family attended a gala at the Royal Opera House with a cast

headed by Placido Domingo. It included a ballet portraying the Queen and Princess Margaret as young girls.

Last appearance for Burmese
The Trooping the Colour parade held on 14 June was notable for being the last public appearance of Burmese, the Queen's favourite black parade horse. Burmese, a mare, had been presented to the Queen by the Royal Canadian Mounted Police in 1969 and had

Inspecting the Terracotta Army
Queen Elizabeth II visited the now world-famous excavation site of the "terracotta warriors" at Xi'an in Shaanxi province in October 1986. She was the first British monarch to set foot in China.

carried the Queen, who always rode her side-saddle, at every Trooping the Colour for 18 years. The Queen had been mounted on Burmese in 1981 when the horse reared after five blank shots were fired from the crowd. The Queen quickly brought the mare under control, winning great praise for her presence of mind. She later explained that Burmese had not heard the shots above the noise of the crowd, but was

6,000 The number of children in the Mall who sang "Happy Birthday" as part of the Queen's 60th birthday celebrations.

reacting to the movement of the Household Cavalry's horses who had immediately turned to protect the sovereign. "Burmese felt that the Household Cavalry was going to attack me, so she attacked them first", she was reported as saying. The assailant was a 17-year-old boy who did it, he said, because "I wanted to be famous. I wanted to be somebody."

Burmese was retired after the 1986 Trooping the Colour and put out to pasture in Windsor Castle's Home Park. She died in 1990. The Queen decided not to replace her. In 1987, the Queen was driven to the Trooping the Colour in a phaeton (light carriage) and took the salute from a dais, a procedure she has followed ever since.

Commemorative stamps
The Queen's 60th birthday was celebrated at home and around the Commonwealth with the issue of commemorative stamps and coins. The British set of four stamps carried portraits, three on each stamp, of the

Twenty years on, the Queen celebrated her 80th birthday with a royal walkabout in Windsor, where she was greeted by thousands of well-wishers.

SAY IT WITH EMAILS
Buckingham Palace announced that the Queen had received **20,000 cards** and **17,000 emails,** sent via her 80th-birthday website. Tributes included a visual greeting from the **500 members** of the crew of **HMS Illustrious,** on deployment in the Indian Ocean, who lined up to spell out "Happy 80th". The **Cabinet** presented the Queen with a **Spode china tea set.** In the evening **Prince Charles,** who had earlier broadcast a **tribute to his mother** on BBC Radio, **hosted a family dinner** for the Queen at Kew Palace, before fireworks and laser display over Kew Gardens in southwest London. On 25 June, a party for 2,000 children, chosen through a national ballot, was held in the garden of Buckingham Palace.

THE QUEEN'S 80TH BIRTHDAY, 2006

Queen at different times of her life, from the earliest portrait of her as a two year old to the present time. Eleven Commonwealth countries also issued commemorative stamps. However, when the Queen opened the 13th Commonwealth Games in Edinburgh on 24 July, 32 of the 59 countries that were eligible to compete stayed away in protest against the British government's policy of maintaining sporting links with South Africa, and its refusal to apply economic sanctions against the apartheid regime. The Queen rounded off her 60th birthday year with a state visit to China in October. It was the first time a British monarch had ever visited China, ending years of enmity dating back to the 19th century.

Come reign, come shine
Elizabeth rides through pouring rain on to
Horse Guards Parade for the 1983 Trooping
the Colour. The ceremony is held each year
on her official birthday in June.

Diana's Dresses

Diana was famous throughout the world for her glamorous dress-sense. Shortly before her death she selected 10 dresses to be auctioned for charity. Her other dresses occasionally feature in royal exhibitions.

1 **Victor Edelstein dress** The Princess of Wales wore this midnight blue velvet dress to a state dinner at the White House in 1985. At this event she danced with American actor John Travolta to music from the movie *Saturday Night Fever* (see pp.240–41). It became known as the Travolta dress, and raised £240,000 at an auction in 2013. Diana also wore it in her last official portrait photograph, taken by the Earl of Snowdon, former husband of Princess Margaret, in 1997. 2 **Bruce Oldfield evening dress** This dress was worn by Diana while on royal tour of Saudi Arabia in 1986. This dress was included in the "Fashion Rules" royal clothing exhibition held at Kensington Palace, London, in 2013. 3 **Murray Arbeid dress** Diana wore this dress – a midnight blue creation with diamanté stars and a

dramatic fish-tail skirt of layered tulle – to a dinner held at Claridge's Hotel for the President of Greece in 1986. A stamp issued in Togo to commemorate her charity work features the Princess of Wales wearing this dress. 4 **Catherine Walker evening gown** This sea green sequined evening gown is by one of the Princess of Wales's favourite designers, Catherine Walker. It was worn by Diana on a variety of occasions ranging from a state visit to Austria in 1989 to the premier of the film *Biggles* in 1993. 5 **Catherine Walker gown and jacket** This opulent Mughal-inspired dress was made for Diana's official visit to India in 1992. Made of pink slubbed silk, the bolero jacket and bodice are encrusted with opulent embroidery. The sleeveless dress is lined in ivory satin.

1 VICTOR EDELSTEIN DRESS

Long bodice embroidered with beads

2 BRUCE OLDFIELD EVENING DRESS

Blue tulle skirt lined with purple silk

3 MURRAY ARBEID DRESS

Gathers running
down the centre
seam at the front
of the dress

Bolero jacket with floral
embroidery in corded silk,
embellished with pink
sequins and coloured beads

Gold chain-stitched
leaves on bodice

5 CATHERINE WALKER
GOWN AND JACKET

4 CATHERINE WALKER
EVENING GOWN

Charles and Diana Divorce

The marriage of the Prince and Princess of Wales fell apart publicly in the early 1990s. Their mutual accusations – fanned by press speculation and rumour – scandalized, entertained, and divided the nation. The media came to call the divorce "the war of the Waleses".

The cracks that appeared early in the marriage of the Prince and Princess of Wales did not become obvious to the public for a few years. To the outside world, they seemed a united couple and caring parents of two young sons. But they began to appear together less frequently, and when they did, Charles often seemed peevish and unhappy that Diana was more popular with the crowds than he was, whereas in the early days of their marriage he had been proud to show her off.

Rumours about the failing marriage first broke when Charles and Diana were on a official visit to India in February 1992. When Diana went

on her own to the Taj Mahal, she was photographed sitting alone in front of the white marble mausoleum, built by the Mughal emperor Shah Jahan as a memorial to his wife and widely regarded as a monument to love. The pose was clearly intended to signal her loneliness and isolation.

Revelations

Three months later, English writer Andrew Morton published *Diana: Her True Story*. This book revealed details of Diana's bulimia and her attempted suicide while pregnant with William by

throwing herself down a staircase at Sandringham. It also exposed Charles's long-running affair with Camilla Parker Bowles (see pp.264–65). Diana undoubtedly cooperated in the writing of the biography and encouraged her friends to do so too. The book had a devastating effect on public opinion by portraying the Royal Family as cold and dysfunctional.

In the past, the Royal Family might have hoped to cover up the marital difficulties of the heir to the throne – a situation that was not without

precedent – but there was a new factor to be reckoned with: the media. Over the coming months, it proved impossible to keep the couple's increasingly bitter estrangement out of the headlines.

A series of leaked phone calls, first between Diana and a close friend, James Gilbey, and then between Charles and Camilla, horrified and enthralled the nation. Meanwhile, rumours began to surface that Diana was having an affair with her children's former horse riding instructor, James Hewitt.

In December 1992, Prime Minister John Major announced to the House of Commons that Charles and Diana

Unhappy couple
Charles and Diana attend the State Opening of Parliament in October 1991. Increasingly, photographs of the couple showed them staring in different directions, suggesting a rift in the relationship.

« BEFORE

Prince Charles and Camilla Parker Bowles, then Camilla Shand, got to know each other in the early 1970s. They frequently met at polo matches and soon began dating.

THE THIRD IN THE MARRIAGE
Charles's relationship with Camilla ended abruptly in 1973, and she **married Andrew Parker Bowles,** a cavalry officer with whom she had had an on-off relationship for some time. It is doubtful that Camilla would have been thought a suitable wife for Charles at this time, even if she had wished to marry him.

CHARLES AND CAMILLA AT A POLO MATCH, 1975

The friendship between Charles and Camilla appears to have revived in the late 1970s or early 1980s, before his engagement to Diana Spencer, who became aware of it just before or soon after their marriage. Camilla and Andrew Parker Bowles had two children. They were **divorced in 1995,** a year after Charles admitted to his relationship with Camilla in his interview with Jonathan Dimbleby.

"Well, there were **three of us** in this **marriage**, so it was a bit **crowded.**"

DIANA, TO BRITISH JOURNALIST MARTIN BASHIR, ON BBC'S PANORAMA, 20 NOVEMBER 1995

Panorama interview
Diana was able to make her controversial interview on BBC's *Panorama* by keeping the broadcast a secret from Buckingham Palace till just before the programme was aired.

AFTER ➤➤

After the separation was announced, discussion centred on whether Diana would be allowed to retain the style of Her Royal Highness, reserved for members of the royal family.

LOSS OF TITLE
In July 1996, a joint statement issued by Buckingham Palace and Diana's lawyers announced that Diana would receive a **lump-sum financial settlement**. Just before the divorce was made absolute in August, letters patent were issued **regulating royal titles** after divorce. As she was no longer married to the Prince of Wales, Diana would in future be styled "Diana, Princess of Wales", without the Her Royal Highness (HRH). She would **continue to live at Kensington Palace** and, as the mother of the second and third in line to the throne, would be "regarded as a member of the Royal Family". Upset by the loss of his mother's HRH, Prince William is reported to have said he would give it back to her when he became king.

were to separate amicably but had no plans to divorce, adding that, "there is no reason why the Princess of Wales should not be crowned Queen of England in due course".

Diana turned down an invitation to spend that Christmas at Sandringham with the Royal family, but the couple continued to attend some functions together. Decisions had to be made about their sons, now at boarding school. It was arranged that they should spend part of each school holiday at Highgrove, with their father, and part at Kensington Palace, with their mother. In December 1993, Diana announced her withdrawal from public life.

Swaying public opinion
A large proportion of the British public sided with the Princess – she was young and attractive, and a devoted mother. They could not understand why Charles should prefer an older woman, and questioned why he always seemed so glum. In June 1994, in an apparent attempt to make himself seem more appealing, the Prince gave a television interview to journalist Jonathan Dimbleby as part of a documentary on his life and work. In it he publicly admitted that he had been unfaithful to Diana "once the

> **15 MILLION** The number of people who tuned in to watch Diana's BBC interview.

marriage had irretrievably broken down". His words caused an instant furore and undid any chance the programme might have had of restoring his reputation. In November, the publication of Dimbleby's authorized biography of the Prince of Wales confirmed he was having an affair with Camilla.

A year later, Diana had her revenge by giving an hour-long interview on BBC's *Panorama*. Millions tuned in to watch ashen-faced Diana, wearing minimal make-up except for kohl around her eyes, confess to her adultery with James Hewitt, her depression and bulimia, and her hurt over Charles's affair with Camilla. Perhaps the most damaging exchanges came late in the interview when Diana said she did not think she would ever be queen, and that she doubted that Charles would adapt to the demanding role of being king. She also said she had no wish for a divorce.

Damage limitation
The Queen, however, thought otherwise. Too much harm was being done to the monarchy to allow this undignified warfare between her son and her daughter-in-law to continue. After consulting the prime minister and the Archbishop of Canterbury, she wrote to both the Prince and the Princess, advising them to seek an

The Prince's biography
For the completion of the biography, Dimbleby was given access to the Prince's own archives – more than 10,000 letters, private journals, and diaries, none of which had ever been made public before.

early divorce. Charles issued a statement saying he took the same view, and declared he had no intention of remarrying. Diana took longer to agree, but eventually announced that she had instructed her lawyers to begin negotiating a divorce settlement.

> **£17 MILLION** The amount of Diana's financial settlement.

The terms were agreed upon in July 1996, and the couple divorced on 28 August after 15 years of marriage.

Changing times
Sixty years earlier, a constitutional crisis had erupted over Edward VIII's decision to marry a twice-divorced woman (see pp.90–91). He chose to abdicate rather than give her up. Now, when Charles eventually becomes king, he will do so as a divorced and remarried man – a sign of how much public opinion, and the Royal Family have changed through the years.

Windsor Castle on fire
Perched high above its towering walls, a firefighter
tackles the flames that swept through Windsor
Castle on 20 November 1992. The blaze was
visible for miles around.

BEFORE «

The Latin phrase annus horribilis was suggested to the Queen in a letter from Sir Edward Ford, her former private secretary.

ANNUS MIRABILIS

The phrase was a rueful play on words, reversing the more common Latin phrase annus mirabilis (wonderful year). In British history, **annus mirabilis usually refers to the year 1759,** when the British won a series of decisive battles against the French in the **Seven Years' War** (1756–63). The greatest victory of all was the **capture of Quebec in Canada by General James Wolfe,** who sailed up the St Lawrence River with a fleet of 50 ships and 5,000 men to lay siege to the heavily fortified city, and was killed on the field of battle.

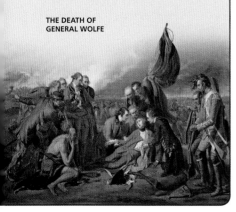

THE DEATH OF GENERAL WOLFE

The Annus Horribilis

Four days after Windsor Castle had been badly damaged by fire, the Queen referred to 1992 as her annus horribilis (horrible year). The occasion was a speech given at a lunch in London's Guildhall to mark the 40th anniversary of her accession.

The Queen's voice was noticeably hoarse as she gave her speech on 24 November 1992. She had caught a cold on the night of the fire while watching the firefighters' efforts to save Windsor Castle. This added to the bleakness of her words, making her appear more vulnerable than at any other time in her reign.

The Queen had reason to sound rueful – the year 1992 had been disastrous for the Royal Family. The separation of the Duke and Duchess of York in March had been followed by Princess Anne's divorce from Mark Phillips in April, the publication of Andrew Morton's revelations about the marriage of the Prince and Princess of Wales in May, and the release of scandalous photos of the Duchess of York in August. The leaked tapes of Diana's intimate phone conversations, followed by those of Prince Charles with Camilla Parker Bowles, kept the tabloids in a frenzy throughout the autumn. Before the year was out, Charles and Diana would

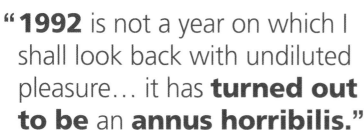

> ## " **1992** is not a year on which I shall look back with undiluted pleasure… it has **turned out to be** an **annus horribilis.**"
>
> QUEEN ELIZABETH II, 24 NOVEMBER 1992

announce their separation. The publication of Andrew Morton's book *Diana*, serialized in *The Sunday Times*, had exposed the Royal Family to public censure as never before and, for once, not even the Queen escaped the barrage of criticism. The fact that three of her children's marriages had failed so publicly was said to reflect badly on her and Prince Philip's parenting skills.

Windsor Castle fire

The fire that broke out in Windsor Castle on the morning of 20 November was a personal tragedy for the Queen, who regards the Castle as her real home. The fire started in the Private Chapel in the northeast wing of the Castle and spread rapidly through the State Apartments. More than 35 fire engines and 225 firefighters were called in to deal with the flames, which were finally extinguished after 15 hours. As night fell, the flames and smoke engulfing the Castle could be seen for many miles.

Prince Andrew, who was present in the Castle at the time, alerted the Queen, and she arrived on the scene at about 3 pm. It was her 45th wedding anniversary; Prince Philip, at a conference in Argentina, consoled her over the phone. Along with members of the Royal Household, officers and soldiers of the Household Cavalry, and policemen from the royalty protection squad, Prince Andrew took part in the human chain

Scene of desolation

Charred roof timbers dating from the 15th century litter the floor of St George's Hall. The hall was completely destroyed in the blaze, but has since been magnificently rebuilt.

Restoration in progress

A craftswoman works with skill and precision to repair a damaged stained glass window. The task of restoring the castle was completed six months ahead of schedule.

to rescue the Castle's valuable collection of works of art and furniture. Casualties of the fire included an enormous equestrian portrait of King George III – too big to remove from its frame – one large sideboard, some pieces of porcelain, and several chandeliers. The damage to the fabric of Windsor Castle was much more substantial: St George's Hall, the State Dining Room, and the Grand Reception Room were all severely damaged, with their ceilings wholly or partially collapsed.

Royal finances

In the immediate aftermath of the blaze, the Heritage Secretary Peter Brooke suggested that, since the Castle was uninsured, the government would meet the cost of repairs, estimated at between £20 million and £40 million. Although the Queen's plight had produced a wave of sympathy, it soon became clear that the public was not prepared for taxpayers'

15,000 The number of fragments of plaster salvaged from the fire.

100 The number of rooms damaged in the fire.

money to be used to subsidize repairs to what was still largely a private palace, though owned by the government. In recent months, the question of whether the Queen should lose her exemption from paying tax on her private income had been hotly debated in the press, with opinion polls suggesting that 80 per cent of the population were in favour of such a move. The government quickly backed down.

In her Guildhall speech, the Queen remarked that "no institution – City, Monarchy, whatever – should expect to be free from the scrutiny of those who give it their support, not to mention those that don't" and that this sort of questioning should act as an "effective engine for change". Two days later, on 26 November, Prime Minister John Major announced

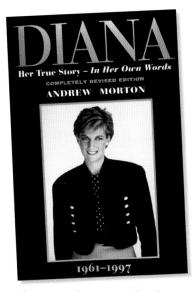

DIANA
Her True Story – In Her Own Words
COMPLETELY REVISED EDITION
ANDREW MORTON
1961–1997

Diana's biography
The controversial biography of Diana, Princess of Wales, took the Royal Family by surprise. The details of her difficult marriage to Prince Charles were made public.

reached earlier in the summer. Some elements of the press, however, were clear that credit for the change should go to them. *The Sun* newspaper, which had been campaigning on the issue, boasted, "The Queen Pays Tax and it's Victory for People Power".

The full details of the plan were released early in 1993. In addition to paying income tax, the Queen agreed to restrict Civil List payments (money

> **£36.5 MILLION** The cost of repairing the fire damage to Windsor Castle.

in the House of Commons that the Queen and the Prince of Wales had volunteered to pay income tax on their private incomes. The initiative, he said, had come from the Queen herself, and the decision had been

from the government) to herself, the Duke of Edinburgh, and the Queen Mother. She would fund the other members of the Royal Family previously on the Civil List (her

four children and Princess Margaret) herself. She offered to meet 70 per cent of the repair costs to Windsor Castle herself, and planned to open Buckingham Palace (see pp.236–37) to the public to help raise the money.

Christmas Day speech leaked
The Queen had to face one more blow before the end of her annus horribilis. Two days before Christmas, *The Sun* published the text of the Queen's Christmas Day speech across its centre pages, breaking the normal embargo rules. The Queen was described as "very very distressed" and sued *The Sun* for breach of copyright. In a rare climb-down, the newspaper agreed to pay legal costs of £200,000 to a charity of the Queen's choosing.

Reflection on the difficult year
The Queen's annus horribilis speech at Guildhall in London came just four days after the Windsor Castle fire. She expressed her sadness at her children's broken marriages and the destruction to the castle.

AFTER »

A Restoration Committee, headed by Prince Philip, the Duke of Edinburgh, and Prince Charles, was set up to oversee the task of restoring Windsor Castle.

RESTORING THE CASTLE
One of the first tasks for the team of restoration workers was drying out the walls and floors of the State Apartments, which had been soaked by the gallons of water pumped into them. The committee decided that some rooms destroyed by the fire – the Grand Reception Room, the State Dining Room, and two drawing rooms – should be restored to their former state, but others should be redesigned. This included St George's Hall, which was reinterpreted in the Gothic style. The work was completed in time for the Queen and Prince Philip to **celebrate their 50th wedding anniversary** in the restored state rooms, where they gave a reception for 1,500 contractors, workers, and firefighters.

Buckingham Palace opens to the Public

Buckingham Palace had never before been put on public show. The urgent need to raise funds to pay for the restoration of Windsor Castle after the fire prompted the Queen's decision to open the State Rooms, with their priceless collections of paintings, furniture, and porcelain, for two months each summer while she was resident in Scotland.

The decision to invite the public into the heart of Buckingham Palace came about after a period of intense soul-searching and debate within the royal household following the Windsor Castle fire (see pp.232–33) and other events that took place in the annus horribilis (see pp.234–35). Taken aback by the strength of opposition to the idea that the taxpayer should help fund the repairs, the Queen's advisors hoped that this move would help bring the monarchy closer to the people and show its willingness to modernize.

On the first day of the opening, 4,314 people paid £8 each to visit the palace's State Rooms, including the 47-m (155-ft) long Picture Gallery, the State Dining Room, the Green Drawing Room, and the Throne Room. All group visits – booked in advance – had been sold for the next three years. The scheme, originally intended to last five years, proved a huge success, regularly drawing in around 400,000 visitors a year, and the palace continued to open its doors even after the Windsor Castle restorations had been paid for.

In the early years, there was some criticism that the tour was dull and uninformative. Since then, more rooms have been opened up and visitors can now see part of the palace gardens, as well as an exhibition on a particular theme each year. Buckingham Palace, together with the Royal Mews and the Queen's Gallery, which displays items from the Queen's fabulous art collection, is now one of London's top tourist attractions. The income it generates is ploughed back through the Royal Collection Trust into the upkeep of the royal palaces and their contents.

" It is indeed **not easy to conceive** anything **more splendid.**"

ALLAN CUNNINGHAM, ART CRITIC, ON JOHN NASH'S DESIGNS FOR BUCKINGHAM PALACE, 1830

The Green Drawing Room
Visitors are given an extensive tour of the State Rooms, designed by architect John Nash for King George IV. The people enter the Throne Room, used by the Queen for state and ceremonial entertaining, through the Green Drawing Room.

ISABELLA CLARA EUGENIA AND CATHARINA.
DAUGHTERS OF PHILIP II. OF SPAIN.

Wartime Anniversaries

The Queen and the Royal Family led the entire nation in commemorating two significant 50th anniversaries: the D-Day landings of Allied troops on the beaches of Normandy on 6 June 1944, and the end of World War II in Europe on 8 May 1945.

On 6 June 1944, an Allied force of more than 150,000 American, British, and Canadian troops landed along an 80 km (50 mile) stretch of coast in Normandy, France. The operation, officially codenamed Overlord but commonly known as D-Day, was the largest amphibious assault in modern history. More than 5,000 ships and landing craft were mobilized in great secrecy to carry troops and supplies across the Channel from England. The landings marked the start of the invasion of Nazi-occupied Europe, which ended in Germany's defeat in May 1945.

Portsmouth remembers

Fifty years later, in 1994, the D-Day landings were remembered on both sides of the Channel. The main commemorative events in England took place in Portsmouth Harbour, the major departure point for the invasion fleet in 1944.

They began with a drumhead service, which is usually held on or close to the field of battle, often with an altar improvised from military drums. On this occasion, the service was held on the waterfront and several upturned drums were used to form an altar. The combined flags of the Allied nations were prominently displayed. The Queen, Prince Philip, and other

◀◀ BEFORE

Large American and British cemeteries in Normandy tell of the heavy cost of life borne during World War II. These became centres of memory for returning Allied veterans.

D-DAY REMEMBERED
The first official commemorations of D-Day were held on the **40th anniversary in 1984,** when US President Ronald Reagan honoured the heroes at **Pointe du Hoc, Normandy.** The ceremony was also attended by the Queen and other Allied leaders.

COMMEMORATIVE D-DAY STAMP

members of the Royal Family, together with heads of state from all the countries that had fought on the Allied side in Normandy, including US President Bill Clinton, French President François Mitterrand, the kings of Norway and Belgium, and the prime ministers of Canada, New Zealand, and Australia, attended the service. President Lech Wałesa of Poland, President Michal Kovác of Slovakia, and President Václav Havel of the Czech Republic were there to honour the sizeable contingents of Polish and Czech soldiers and airmen who had fought with the Allies in 1944.

Later that afternoon the Queen and her guests went on board Royal Yacht *Britannia* to watch a flypast of military aircraft before reviewing two lines of vessels drawn up offshore. These

> **54** The number of world leaders who attended the service of thanksgiving in St Paul's Cathedral.

ranged from the huge aircraft carrier USS *George Washington*, temporary home to President and Mrs Clinton, the liner *Queen Elizabeth II*, and a wartime Liberty ship that had been sailed from California for the occasion, to hundreds of small landing craft and pleasure boats. After the review, Royal Yacht *Britannia* headed the flotilla of ships that carried dignitaries and veterans across the Channel for the next day's events in France.

Events in Normandy

On the morning of 6 June, the Queen and Prince Philip attended a service of remembrance at the military cemetery in Bayeux, which contains the graves of more than 4,000 British and Commonwealth servicemen who died in Normandy. With other international leaders, the Queen was present at the international ceremony on Omaha Beach, where more than 34,000 American troops landed on D-Day. She then made her way to the small town of Arromanches, in sight of the remains of the floating Mulberry Harbour that served as the disembarkation point for troops and supplies throughout the Normandy campaign. Thousands of British veterans had returned to Normandy, many of them for

the first time since the war, to revisit the scenes of past exploits, meet up with old friends and, above all, to remember with pride former comrades who had fallen in the battle for Normandy. A large contingent of veterans marched past the Queen on the beach at Arromanches.

Celebrating the end of the war

The events that took place throughout Britain and the Commonwealth to mark the 50th anniversary of the end of the war were more celebratory in nature. A three-day holiday over the weekend of 6–8 May 1995 commemorated the end of the war in Europe. The commemorations began solemnly enough on 5 May with a ceremony in Westminster Hall at which the Queen addressed both Houses of Parliament. Recalling the memories of war, she urged her listeners to remember those who did not come back: "It is to their courage and heroic sacrifice that

Act of remembrance
The Queen walks among rows of headstones in the Bayeux War Cemetery – the largest World War II cemetery in France – on 6 June 1994.

we owe our celebrations today." A state banquet was held the next day in London's Guildhall, and on Sunday, 7 May, the Queen and the Royal Family led the nation

Flotilla of ships
The Royal Yacht *Britannia* (centre) is seen here surrounded by tiny boats in the Solent. The USS *George Washington* is on the left and the *Queen Elizabeth II* on the right.

a large festival site in London's Hyde Park, along with displays of World War II military vehicles and aircraft. The highpoint of the celebrations came on Monday 8 May, exactly 50 years after Victory in Europe (VE) Day had united the country in an exuberant outburst of rejoicing after five grim years of war. At street parties throughout Britain, people dressed themselves in 1940s' style and even replicated wartime recipes. Huge crowds gathered outside Buckingham Palace and all the way down the Mall for a concert on the forecourt of the Palace, starring the much-loved wartime singer Vera Lynn, "the forces' sweetheart". The Queen Mother, Queen Elizabeth II, and Princess Margaret emerged onto the balcony

> The Queen was not present for the 65th anniversary commemorations of the D-Day landings in 2009; French President Nicolas Sarkozy issued the official invitation to Prime Minister Gordon Brown instead.
>
> **THE LAST OF THE VETERANS**
> The Queen returned to Normandy for the **70th anniversary** in 2014. She was the only world leader in attendance to have actually witnessed the war. The 70th anniversary would be the **last official commemoration of D-Day,** as there were now so few surviving veterans. Despite her years, **the Queen carried out a full programme of events,** from the service of remembrance in Bayeux cemetery to the international ceremony on Omaha Beach. She then returned to Paris for an **official state banquet** given in her honour by Sarkozy's successor President François Hollande.

in a service of thanksgiving, reconciliation, and hope in St Paul's Cathedral. Germany's President Helmut Kohl was among the world leaders who attended the service. Similar ceremonies were held over the weekend in Paris, Berlin, and Moscow as world leaders came together to demonstrate common purpose in striving for peace.

A festive mood prevailed for most of the weekend in Britain, bringing back memories of the victory celebrations 50 years before. Most newspapers printed facsimile front pages from 1945, with grainy black-and-white photographs of Londoners revelling in the fountains of Trafalgar Square and shinning up lampposts in the Mall. Concerts and picnics took place on

"We remember the dark days of the **Battle of Britain**... We **remember** when we **stood alone** in Europe."

QUEEN ELIZABETH II, AT LAUNCH OF VE DAY COMMEMORATIONS, 5 MAY 1995

to join the crowd in singing wartime favourites, such as "We'll meet again", "There'll be bluebirds over the white cliffs of Dover", and "Roll out the barrel". It was a reprise of the Royal Family's famous balcony appearance of 50 years before, when the three of them had stood beside the King and Winston Churchill to receive the rapturous applause of the crowd, and they were visibly moved. Later that evening, a nationwide, two-minute silence was observed to remember the dead of World War II before the Queen lit the first of a chain of beacons that spread across the length and breadth of the country.

The war against Japan
While the end of the war was being celebrated in Europe in 1945, the Allies were still waging a bitter conflict against Japan in the Pacific. On 6 August 1945, the US dropped the first of two atomic bombs on Japan, with horrific consequences. Just nine

Emotional tribute
Visibly moved by the applause of the crowd, the Queen Mother wipes a tear from her eye as she stands between her daughters on the balcony of Buckingham Palace on the 50th anniversary of VE Day.

days later, on 15 August, Japan surrendered unconditionally, bringing World War II to an end.

The Queen headed the national commemorations held on 19 August 1995 to mark the 50th anniversary of these events. A large crowd gathered outside Buckingham Palace for a memorial ceremony attended by 25,000 veterans of the campaign fought against the Japanese in the jungles of Burma, in which thousands of British and Commonwealth soldiers died. Thousands more had perished in Japan's prison camps or as slave labour building railways. After the ceremony, the veterans marched past the Queen as a World War II Lancaster bomber flew low over the Palace to shower the veterans and crowds with thousands of red poppies symbolizing the sacrifice of all those who had died in the war.

Commemorative march past
Standard bearers of the Royal British Legion, the association for British veterans, march over the wet sands of Gold Beach, where British troops landed in Normandy in 1944.

Diana: A Star is Born

It was at a gala dinner at the White House that Diana took to the dance floor with Hollywood actor John Travolta. Images of the princess in a figure-hugging, dark blue velvet gown being swung around the floor by the world's most feted disco dancer announced Diana's glittering arrival on the international scene.

The dinner hosted by President Ronald Reagan and his wife Nancy came at the beginning of Charles and Diana's first visit to the US after their marriage. There was a moment of embarrassment when the President welcomed her as "Princess David... er, Princess Diane", but this was soon forgotten because, in the days that followed, Diana took the US by storm.

From the naive nursery assistant, who avoided looking directly at the camera, and the young bride and mother with an uncertain taste for frills and puffed sleeves, Diana had transformed herself into a beautiful and self-confident fashion icon, sure of her own taste. Her favourite designers were Bruce Oldfield, Catherine Walker, Victor Edelstein, and Versace. In the mid-1980s, she adopted the "Dynasty" style, named after the popular TV series, which called for wide shoulders and big hairstyles, but she later championed the slim sheath dress, stamping it with her individual style and elegance. Despite her fraught relationship with the paparazzi, no one understood the power of the image better than she did or could control the camera more effectively. Whether posing alone in front of the Taj Mahal, wearing a dazzling evening gown for a gala movie premiere or a demure white suit to meet Mother Teresa, or dressed in a crisp chambray shirt and chinos on a minefield in Angola, she filled the pages of the world press for more than a decade.

"As [Diana] matured, she was less concerned about fashion and followed her own sense of style even more."

VICTOR EDELSTEIN, DRESS DESIGNER

Iconic gown
Diana included this Edwardian-inspired gown, by the British designer Victor Edelstein, in the collection of dresses she auctioned for charity in New York in June 1997. It was bought for £137,000.

The **Death** of **Diana**

On Sunday, 31 August 1997, Britons awoke to the news that Diana, Princess of Wales, had died in Paris from injuries sustained in a car crash. They reacted with shock and disbelief as they struggled to comprehend that the life of this vibrant, beautiful woman had ended so tragically.

Diana was in Paris with Egyptian heir and film producer Dodi Fayed, her boyfriend of only a few weeks. They had just returned from holidaying on a luxury yacht belonging to Dodi's father, Mohamed Al Fayed, owner of Harrods department store in London and the Ritz hotel in Paris. Henri Paul, deputy head of security at the Ritz, was driving the couple in a Mercedes-Benz from the hotel to Dodi Fayed's private apartment. They were being pursued by photographers on motorbikes and in cars. At around 12.23 am, the car entered an underpass at an estimated speed of 105 kph (65 mph). Paul lost control of the vehicle and it hit a pillar before spinning off to crash into the tunnel wall. Fayed and the driver died at the scene of the accident. Diana died in Paris's Pitié-Salpêtrière Hospital a few hours later.

BEFORE

Diana's affair with Dodi Al Fayed is said to have started in July 1997, when the Princess and her sons holidayed on board Mohamed Al Fayed's yacht.

DIANA ON BOARD AL FAYED'S YACHT *JONIKAL*

HOLIDAY SNAP
A **photo of Diana and Dodi kissing** on board his father's yacht *Jonikal*, taken in late August, made **headline news** around the world. It was the first that most people knew of the affair. There are suggestions that Diana herself may have **alerted the paparazzi** to her presence on the yacht.

The people's princess
As news of the tragedy spread, one of the first to pay public tribute to Diana was British Prime Minister Tony Blair. Addressing the press before he entered church for the Sunday morning service in his northern constituency, he said, "We are a nation in a state of shock… she was the people's princess." His words struck an immediate chord with thousands of grieving Britons, many of whom were already laying floral tributes to Diana outside Kensington Palace (see pp.244–45). They began to ask why the Royal Family was still at Balmoral, their summer home, instead of returning to London, and why the Queen had made Princes William and Harry attend church

Coming home
Draped in the Royal Standard, the coffin containing Diana's body arrives at Royal Air Force Northolt airfield, close to London. Prince Charles and Diana's sisters were in the plane that carried her back from France.

> " There are **lessons** to be drawn from her life and from the **extraordinary** and moving **reaction** to her **death.** "

ELIZABETH II, FROM A LIVE BROADCAST, 5 SEPTEMBER 1997

straight after learning of their mother's death (the fact is that they had asked to do so). Reflecting the people's mood, the press – a portion of which had been highly critical of Diana only a short while before – joined in the attacks. These came to focus on why the Union Jack was not flying at half-mast over Buckingham Palace. According to royal protocol, the only flag that ever flies over the palace is the Royal Standard, and only when the monarch is in residence. It is never flown at half-mast. This official

Flowers for Diana
The Queen and Prince Philip examine the floral tributes outside the gates of Buckingham Palace. They were said to have been deeply moved by the expressions of love for Diana following her death.

response did not satisfy the tabloids, which judged that the monarchy was out of touch with the people.

The Queen had never before come under such direct criticism. One headline read, "Speak to us, ma'am, please speak", while another demanded "Show us you care". On 5 September the Queen returned to Buckingham Palace, stopping to look at the floral tributes to Diana outside the gates. Once inside, she made a live broadcast from the Chinese Drawing Room, in which she paid her own personal tribute to Diana as "an exceptional and gifted human being". Her dignified words were well received, suggesting that the storm of hostility whipped up by the press was beginning to abate.

Diana's funeral
Diana's funeral took place on Saturday, 6 September. Over a million people lined the 6 km (4 mile) route along which her coffin, draped with her personal standard, was carried on a gun carriage from Kensington Palace to Westminster Abbey. At St James's Palace, the Duke of Edinburgh, the Prince of Wales, his two sons, and their uncle Charles Spencer joined the procession to walk behind the coffin the rest of the way. At Buckingham Palace, the Union Jack was flying at half-mast

United in grief
Prince William and Prince Harry walk behind their mother's coffin, flanked by their father, grandfather, and uncle. The princes were aged 15 and 12 when their mother died.

on the Queen's orders. She was waiting at the gates with other members of the Royal Family and bowed her head as the coffin passed by.

Some 31.5 million viewers watched the funeral in Britain, while an estimated 2.5 billion people viewed it live worldwide. During the traditional Church of England funeral service, Elton John performed a version of his song *Candle in the Wind* dedicated to Diana. In his eulogy, Charles Spencer took the opportunity to criticize the press and, indirectly, the Royal Family for their treatment of his sister. Many in the congregation applauded. Afterwards, the coffin was driven to the Spencer family home of Althorp where, in a private ceremony, Diana was laid to rest on an island in the middle of a lake.

Cause of the accident

Immediately after the crash, the paparazzi who had been pursuing the car were blamed for the accident. However, the official French report concluded that the driver, Henri Paul,

was driving at excessive speed under the influence of both prescription drugs and alcohol. None of the photographers arrested after the crash were charged with manslaughter. Mohamed Al Fayed was not satisfied with this verdict. He claimed that Diana and his son were

£12.5 MILLION The cost of the inquiry into Diana's death.

250 The number of witnesses that were interviewed during the inquiry.

about to announce their engagement, and that they had been killed by the British secret service to prevent this happening. He even accused Prince Philip of masterminding the plot. In 2004, a British inquest was opened into their deaths, but it did not begin hearing evidence until 2007. In April 2008 the jury delivered its verdict that Diana and Fayed had been killed by the grossly negligent driving of Henri Paul and the vehicles in pursuit.

AFTER ⏵⏵

In the years that followed her death, several memorials were erected in different locations to commemorate Diana's life and work.

REMEMBERING DIANA
The **Princess of Wales Memorial Playground** in Kensington Gardens, close to her former home, celebrates Diana's love of children. It encourages children to explore and follow their imagination, and has a wooden pirate ship as its centrepiece. The playground also features toys and play sculptures.

Nearby in Hyde Park, the **Diana Memorial Fountain** is formed as a stone oval made from slabs of Cornish granite. It was opened by the Queen in 2004.

The **Flame of Liberty,** built in 1989 in Paris, stands not far from the entrance to the tunnel where Diana died. It became

an unofficial memorial when people began leaving flowers and messages there soon after the Princess's death.

Her memory is commemorated by a **classical temple** built close to the site of her island grave at Althorp. One of the most extraordinary memorials was the **bronze statue of Diana and Dodi** placed by Mohamed Al Fayed, which stood at Harrods until 2018.

DIANA MEMORIAL FOUNTAIN, HYDE PARK

Daily Mail
1961 1997

R.I.P.

Farewell to Diana

Diana's death was met with an unprecedented wave of emotion from the public. Within hours of the news breaking, people of all ages began to leave bouquets of flowers and other mementos outside the gates of Kensington Palace. In places, the pile of flowers was 1.5 m (5 ft) high.

The spontaneous outpouring of grief over Diana's death was extraordinarily intense. Many people attached heartfelt messages to the bouquets explaining that, although they had never met her, it was as if they had lost a close family member. The waiting time to sign books of condolence at St James's Palace grew to five hours, then to 11, and the Salvation Army provided free cups of tea to the lengthening queues. The displays of emotion were not confined to London – floral tributes sprang up in cities throughout the country, and people lined up to sign books of condolence all around the world, from Sydney to New York. In Paris, messages and flowers were placed at the foot of the Flame of Liberty memorial at the Pont d'Alma, close to where Diana had died. On the day of her funeral, more than three million people waited silently on the streets to watch Diana's coffin being taken to Westminster Abbey.

In retrospect, the heightened emotions that accompanied Diana's death seem inexplicable. Several commentators at the time put the reaction down to mass hysteria, but there was no doubt that Diana's projected personality had struck a chord with the public, and many people experienced genuine feelings of loss. A large number of the personal notes written by the public contrasted her warmth and spontaneity with the supposed coldness of the Royal Family. The press picked up on this theme. They helped fuel accusations that the Royal Family was uncaring by questioning why the Union Jack was not flying at half-mast over Buckingham Palace.

"I **can't understand** this feeling of **pain** for someone who **never** even **knew** my name."

ONE OF THE THOUSANDS OF HANDWRITTEN MESSAGES LEFT FOR DIANA

Floral tributes
Thousands of people left flowers outside Kensington Palace, Diana's home. It was later estimated that Londoners had spent £25 million on 1.3 million bouquets. The bottom layer had started to compost before they were cleared away.

ROYAL RESIDENCE

Balmoral Castle

Built of local granite and bristling with towers and turrets, Balmoral epitomizes the romantic vision of Scotland prevalent in Victorian England. The Aberdeenshire Estate has been the private property of the Royal Family since 1852, when it was acquired by Prince Albert.

Queen Victoria and Prince Albert first visited Scotland in 1842, two years after their marriage. Captivated by its beauty, which Albert felt was "very Germanic", it was the first of several visits. Their enthusiasm undampened by their experience of the rainy weather, they set about finding a highland retreat of their own.

A highland paradise

The search began in Deeside at the suggestion of the royal physician, who recommended the area for its gentler climate. Advised by Lord Aberdeen – who had inherited the lease on the estate from his brother – the royal couple bought the lease on Balmoral blind. Both instantly loved the estate when they arrived there for the first time in September 1848. "All seemed to breathe freedom and peace, and to make one forget the world and its sad turmoils", wrote Victoria in her diary. Albert, on the other hand, found that the landscape reminded him of his Thuringian roots, and prominent artists including Edwin and Charles Landseer were soon commissioned to paint Balmoral landscapes.

The house was deemed pretty, but it was far too small to meet the needs of their growing family and a stream of official visitors. The initial plan to extend the house was soon abandoned:

ever more enamoured of the property, they began negotiations to buy out the landowner in 1849, with a view to building a completely new house. Meanwhile, Albert came up with an interim solution to their space issue. Inspired by a display at the Great Exhibition of 1851, he ordered a pre-fabricated iron building to serve as a temporary ballroom and dining room, which remained in use until 1856.

Albert and Victoria finally managed to buy the Balmoral Estate, and that of neighbouring Birkhall, outright in 1852. On 28 September 1853, Victoria laid the foundation stone of their new house on a site just to the north of the existing building. It was designed by local Aberdeen architect William Smith with "amendments" by Prince Albert. The result was an extremely cleverly planned country house formed of two quadrangular blocks, broadly arranged on a diagonal, each with its own courtyard, and a passage linking them together. One block was devoted to the kitchen, household offices, and the ballroom (the only public room); the other provided the family and intimate guests with the privacy they craved.

The royal apartments were ready in time for the autumn visit in 1855; the old house was used by the servants until the construction finished the following year, then it was demolished.

Finally, a bridge designed by Isambard Kingdom Brunel was erected over the Dee providing a direct link between Balmoral and the village of Crathie, home to many of the estate workers.

Victoria and Albert's fondness for all things Scottish had a powerful impact on the castle interior. Tartan appeared everywhere: carpets were woven in red Royal Stewart and green Hunting Stewart; curtains and upholstery covers in Dress Stewart. They even designed their own tartans, the Queen creating Victoria tartan, and Albert, Balmoral; both are still used as royal tartans today. The decor was not to everyone's taste: visiting in 1855, the Duchess of Kent's lady-in-waiting, Lady Augusta Bruce, admired many of the ornaments, but felt "a certain absence of harmony of the whole," adding that the tartans were all "highly characteristic and appropriate, but not all equally *flatteux* to the eye." »

Holiday home

The Queen spends about 10 weeks at the castle every year, from August to October, relaxing on horseback in the seclusion of the estate. She occasionally appears at local events: here she is pictured in 1967 at the North of Scotland Gun Dog Association's Open Stake Retriever Trials – held at Balmoral – with trial judge Lord Porchester and head gamekeeper James Gillan.

THE QUEEN FOLLOWING GUN DOG TRIALS IN 1967

ELIZABETH II ON HOLIDAY AT BALMORAL IN 1971

TURRETS AND CRENELLATIONS ARE TYPICAL OF SCOTTISH BARONIAL ARCHITECTURE

Balmoral south front
The walled garden laid out by Queen Mary in the 1920s, complete with monogrammed gates, enhances the castle's fairy-tale setting at the heart of the Cairngorm National Park.

>> Balmorality

An advocate of the benefits of fresh air, Victoria revelled in the freedom of the secluded surroundings, often going for long walks while Albert hunted deer and game. The Queen observed a strict interest in country pursuits. According to Henry Campbell-Bannerman it was just like a convent: "We meet at meals, breakfast at 9.45, lunch 2, dinner 9, and when we have finished each is off to his cell." Tsar Nicholas II had hoped

> "The **weather is awful**, rain and wind every day and, on top of it, **no luck at all** – I haven't killed a stag yet."

NICHOLAS II, TSAR OF RUSSIA, IN A LETTER TO HIS MOTHER, 1896

daily routine of walking, answering State correspondence, and writing her diaries that continued after Albert's death, when she spent increasingly long periods at Balmoral. Castle guests were expected to adhere to a similarly rigid timetable – Victoria simply assumed her visitors shared the same

to enjoy some family time with his new wife (Victoria's granddaughter) and infant daughter when they visited Balmoral in 1896; instead he endured long days hunting with the Prince of Wales followed by heavy discussions on European affairs with the Queen and Prime Minister, Lord Salisbury.

Today, the 20,000 hectares (50,000 acre) estate remains the private property of the royal family, who continue to spend summer holidays there. It is a working estate, rich in wildlife, with grouse moors, forest, and farmland, as well as managed herds of Highland cattle, ponies, and deer, but the grounds, gardens, and ballroom are open to visitors at specified times of year. With landscapes ranging from the Dee river valley to lochs and open mountains including seven Munros – hills over 910m (3,000ft) – it is one of the most beautiful parts of Scotland.

Artists in residence

James Giles and James Roberts were two of many artists commissioned by Victoria and Albert to capture interiors and landscapes before and after the new castle was built. Old Balmoral was demolished in 1856; a stone in the lawn marks the position of its front door.

DINING ROOM, OLD BALMORAL (JAMES GILES,1855)

BILLIARD ROOM AND LIBRARY, OLD BALMORAL (JAMES GILES,1855)

PRINCE ALBERT'S SITTING ROOM, OLD BALMORAL (JAMES ROBERTS, c.1860)

Queen Victoria's bedroom, *c.*1880–1890
Balmoral was intended as a private house, and was fairly simply furnished. With no one to please but themselves, Victoria and Albert indulged a passion for all things tartan – from carpets to tablecloths.

Born 1964

The Earl of Wessex

"I love... show business. It's a wonderful world of fantasy."

PRINCE EDWARD, 1987

The Queen's youngest son was born on 10 March 1964 at Buckingham Palace and christened Edward Antony Richard Louis. At the time of his birth he was third in line of succession; he is currently eleventh. His first public appearance was at the age of 3 months, when the Queen carried Edward in her arms on the balcony of Buckingham Palace after the Trooping the Colour ceremony.

At the age of 13 Prince Edward went to Gordonstoun school in Scotland, following in his father's and brothers' footsteps. He was elected guardian (head boy) for his last term and left with A-levels in History, English Literature, and Economic and Political Studies. After a gap term spent teaching at a school in Wanganui, New Zealand, he went to Jesus College, Cambridge, to study history – his admission caused some controversy at the time as his A-level grades were below the standard normally required for entry. During his time at Cambridge he acted in and produced a number of student shows.

Choice of career

After leaving university in 1986, Prince Edward joined the Royal Marines as a university cadet but dropped out after completing just one-third of the gruelling 12-month training course. Some in the media criticized his decision to quit, and

Real tennis player
Edward took up real tennis at university. Also known as royal tennis, the game is much older than lawn tennis. He met his future wife Sophie at a real tennis charity competition he had organized.

Prince Philip was said to be furious with Edward for breaking with royal tradition by not following his brothers into the armed services.

Edward opted instead for a career in entertainment, but his first foray plunged him into fresh controversy when he helped stage *The Grand Knockout Tournament* – nicknamed *It's a Royal Knockout* – for charity on British television in June 1987. In the show, four members of the Royal Family – Prince Edward, Princess Anne, and the Duke and Duchess of York – each captained a team of celebrities, urging them on to greater feats in rough-and-tumble games. The press took against the show, and it is remembered as an embarrassment; however, it succeeded in raising over £1 million for charity.

Stage-struck prince
Prince Edward's decision to follow a career in entertainment rather than the army, as was royal tradition, was criticized at the time but it revealed that he had a streak of quiet determination.

Home office
At one time, Ardent Productions was housed in the stable block of Bagshot Park in Surrey, the family home of the Earl and Countess of Wessex.

In January 1988, Buckingham Palace announced that Prince Edward was joining the Really Useful Group, the theatre company founded by composer Andrew Lloyd Webber. His job of production assistant was described as being on "the very lowest rung" of the theatrical ladder. Five years later, in 1993, Prince Edward formed Ardent Productions, which produced a number of television documentaries and dramas but failed to make a profit. In 2002, not long after an Ardent film crew was alleged to have invaded

Prince William's privacy during his time at St Andrews University, Edward left the company to support the Queen during her Golden Jubilee year.

Marriage

In January 1999, Edward announced his engagement to Sophie Rhys-Jones, a public relations executive he had met in 1993. Their wedding on 19 June was a low-key event compared with those of his elder siblings. It was held in St George's Chapel at Windsor Castle, rather than in Westminster Abbey, and the guest list was much smaller – not even the then Prime Minister Tony Blair was invited. In another break with tradition, the Queen made Edward an earl, rather

than a royal duke, on marriage. Edward's choice of Wessex as his title showed his love of theatre – he is said to have borrowed the title from a fictional character in the film *Shakespeare in Love* (1998).

At first Sophie, who became Her Royal Highness the Countess of Wessex on marriage, continued to work for her own public relations agency but she resigned in 2002 in order to devote more time to her royal duties. Edward and Sophie frequently travel abroad on behalf of the Queen and the Foreign Office, and they often act as the Queen's personal representatives at events involving foreign royalty. In recent years, they have visited Canada, Malawi, Norway, Brunei, and Sri Lanka. In 2019, the Queen granted Edward the additional title of Earl of Forfar, and he and Sophie visited the town in July of that year to receive a special tartan. Edward has taken on many of his father's causes and organizations, particularly the Duke of Edinburgh's Award scheme. It is known that the Queen would like him to eventually succeed to the title of Duke of Edinburgh.

The couple have two children, Lady Louise Windsor and James, Viscount Severn. Both were born in Frimley Park Hospital, a National Health Service (NHS) hospital. They are styled as the children of an earl, rather than a royal duke, so do not use the HRH style. The family home is at Bagshot Park, a royal residence in Surrey that Prince Edward rents from the Crown. A 19th-century palatial country house of Anglo-Indian style, it was once the home of Queen Victoria's son Arthur, the Duke of Connaught.

SOPHIE RHYS-JONES

Born on 20 January 1965, Sophie Rhys-Jones is the daughter of Christopher and Mary Rhys-Jones. Her father was a businessman and she was brought up in Kent. When she met Edward in 1993, she had already embarked on a career in public relations, although she later gave this up to focus on her royal duties, advocate for causes such as women's rights, and support learning for disabled children. She represented the UK at the 2019 UN Commission on the Status of Women. In 2020, she became the first member of the Royal Family to visit South Sudan, where she advocated for the rights for women and survivors of gender-based violence.

10 March 1964 Born at Buckingham Palace; christened Edward Antony Richard Louis.

September 1972 Goes to Heatherdown Preparatory School near Ascot, Berkshire.

1977–82 Attends Gordonstoun school; elected guardian (head boy) in the last term; gains three A-levels.

1982 Spends part of his gap year teaching at a school in New Zealand.

1983–86 Studies history at Jesus College, University of Cambridge.

1987 Fails to complete Royal Marines university cadet training course.

15 June 1987 Organizes a charity fundraiser event, *The Grand Knockout Tournament*, on television.

1988 Joins the Really Useful Group, a theatre company founded by Andrew Lloyd Webber, as a production assistant.

1993 Sets up an independent television company, Ardent Productions, under the name Edward Windsor.

1993 Meets Sophie Rhys-Jones, a public relations professional, at a real tennis charity event.

19 June 1999 Marries Sophie Rhys-Jones at St George's Chapel, Windsor Castle; they become the Earl and Countess of Wessex.

2001 Sophie gives an interview to an undercover reporter, in which she appears to use her royal status to benefit her agency.

6 December 2001 Sophie is admitted to hospital with an ectopic pregnancy.

2 March 2002 Edward announces that he and Sophie will quit their respective companies, Ardent Productions and RJH Public Relations, in order to support the Queen.

8 November 2003 Their daughter Lady Louise Windsor is born prematurely.

23 April 2006 Prince Edward becomes a Royal Knight of the Order of the Garter.

17 December 2007 Their son, James, Viscount Severn, is born.

20 January 2010 Sophie is appointed a Dame Grand Cross of the Royal Victorian Order.

February–March 2012 The Earl and Countess of Wessex visit nine Caribbean countries for the Queen's Diamond Jubilee.

October 2018 Sophie and Edward tour the Baltic states.

March 2019 Edward is granted the Earldom of Forfar.

March 2020 Sophie visits South Sudan.

EDWARD AND SOPHIE WITH THEIR CHILDREN

GOD SAVE THE QUEEN

HONI SOIT MAL Y PENSE

DIEU ET MON DROIT

2012

6
TODAY'S ROYAL FAMILY
2000–PRESENT

TODAY'S ROYAL FAMILY
2000–PRESENT

2000	2003	2008

1 JANUARY 2000
Queen Elizabeth II officially opens the Millennium Dome in Greenwich, London.

4 AUGUST 2000
The Queen Mother celebrates her 100th birthday.

» Mug commemorating the Queen Mother's 100th birthday

NOVEMBER 2003
A *Daily Mirror* reporter reveals he faked references to obtain a job as footman at Buckingham Palace.

8 NOVEMBER 2003
Lady Louise Windsor, the daughter of the Earl and Countess of Wessex, is born.

23 JUNE 2005
Prince William graduates from the University of St Andrews, Scotland.

1 MARCH 2006
The Queen opens the Senedd – the debating chamber of the National Assembly for Wales – in Cardiff.

26 MARCH 2008
The Queen welcomes French President Nicolas Sarkozy and his wife Carla Bruni on a state visit to the UK.

7 APRIL 2008
The inquest into the death of Diana records a verdict of accidental death.

15–21 JUNE 2010
Princes William and Harry make their first joint tour to southern Africa.

16 NOVEMBER 2010
Prince William and Catherine Middleton are engaged.

21 SEPTEMBER 2001
The Queen's message – "Grief is the price we pay for love" – is read by the British ambassador to the US, Sir Christopher Meyer, at the prayer service for the 67 British victims of the 9/11 terrorist attack in New York.

⌄ The Queen en route to St Paul's Cathedral for a Golden Jubilee service

29 APRIL 2002
The Queen attends dinner with the five living prime ministers who have served under her.

6 JANUARY 2004
The coroner's inquest into the deaths of Diana and Dodi Al-Fayed opens on in London.

8 JANUARY 2004
The Queen names the *Queen Mary 2*, the first major transatlantic liner built in more than 30 years.

12 APRIL 2006
Prince Harry is commissioned into the Household Cavalry.

10 DECEMBER 2006
Zara Phillips, the daughter of Princess Anne, is voted BBC Sports Personality of the Year.

15 DECEMBER 2006
Catherine Middleton attends Prince William's passing out parade at Sandhurst.

JANUARY 2009
Prince William begins training as an RAF helicopter pilot.

9 DECEMBER 2010
Student protesters attack a car carrying Prince Charles and the Duchess of Cornwall in London.

29 DECEMBER 2010
The Queen's first great-grandchild, Savannah Phillips, is born.

1–4 JUNE 2002
The Queen's Golden Jubilee is celebrated with a weekend of events, including "The Party in the Palace" in the Buckingham Palace garden.

25 JULY 2002
The Queen opens the Commonwealth Games in Manchester.

6 JULY 2004
The Queen opens the Diana Memorial Fountain in Hyde Park, London.

30 JANUARY 2005
Pictures of Prince Harry wearing a swastika armband to a private fancy dress party appear in the press.

SEPTEMBER 2009
The Princes set up their own charitable foundation: Foundation of Prince William and Prince Harry, renamed the Royal Foundation of the Duke and Duchess of Cambridge and Prince Harry in 2011.

FEBRUARY 2011
Prince William makes a special visit to New Zealand following the Christchurch earthquake.

29 APRIL 2011
Prince William and Catherine Middleton are married in Westminster Abbey.

⌄ Wedding portrait of William and Catherine with the bridesmaids and page boys

DECEMBER 2001
Lucian Freud's controversial portrait of the Queen is exhibited. It is widely criticized as unflattering.

9 FEBRUARY 2002
Princess Margaret dies peacefully in her sleep, aged 71.

1 NOVEMBER 2002
Paul Burrell, former butler to Diana, the Princess of Wales, is cleared of stealing from her estate.

9 APRIL 2005
Prince Charles and Camilla Parker-Bowles are married in a civil ceremony, followed by a service of blessing in St George's Chapel, Windsor. Camilla becomes the Duchess of Cornwall.

⌄ Family photograph after Prince Charles and Camilla's wedding

⌃ Prince William and Prince Harry hosting Concert for Diana

1 JULY 2007
Princes William and Harry host Concert for Diana at Wembley Stadium to mark the forthcoming 10th anniversary of their mother's death.

30 MARCH 2002
The Queen Mother dies at the age of 101.

9 APRIL 2002
The Queen Mother's funeral is held at Westminster Abbey, followed by burial at St George's Chapel, Windsor Castle.

17 DECEMBER 2007
James, Viscount Severn, son of the Earl and Countess of Wessex, is born.

23 DECEMBER 2007
The Royal Channel, the official channel of the British monarchy, goes live on YouTube.

The first decade and a half of the 21st century saw public affection for Queen Elizabeth II soar with every milestone she passed – her Golden and Diamond Jubilees were both national celebrations. Her son Charles, the Prince of Wales, married again, and the royal grandchildren began to take centre stage, with Prince William and Prince Harry taking on greater responsibilities. Both pursued army careers. The wedding of Prince William and Catherine Middleton in 2011 was a worldwide event, as was the birth of their first son, George, two years later. In 2015, the Queen became the longest-reigning monarch in British history.

2012

6 FEBRUARY 2012
The Queen marks the 60th anniversary of her accession to the throne.

2–5 JUNE 2012
The Queen's Diamond Jubilee is celebrated with a pageant of boats on the River Thames and a pop concert outside Buckingham Palace.

JULY 2012
The Queen officially opens the Summer Olympic Games in London on 27 July. Zara Phillips wins a silver medal with the British eventing team on 31 July.

⌄ Zara Phillips competes in the London 2012 Olympics

30 AUGUST 2012
The Queen opens the Paralympic Games in London.

SEPTEMBER 2012
Prince Harry is deployed to Afghanistan as an Apache co-pilot, gunner.

17 APRIL 2013
The Queen and Duke of Edinburgh attend Margaret Thatcher's funeral in St Paul's Cathedral.

22 JULY 2013
Duchess of Cambridge gives birth to her first son, George.

17 JANUARY 2014
Mia, the daughter of Zara Philips and Mike Tindall, is born.

⌄ Commemorative collection for the Queen's Diamond Jubilee

5–7 JUNE 2014
The Queen visits France for the 70th anniversary of the D-Day landings.

23 JULY 2014
The Queen opens the Commonwealth Games in Glasgow.

10–14 SEPTEMBER 2014
The first Invictus Games for wounded soldiers are held in London.

19 SEPTEMBER 2014
Scotland rejects independence by voting in a referendum.

≫ Harry and Zara at the Invictus Games

24 OCTOBER 2014
The Queen sends her first tweet.

2 MAY 2015
The Duchess of Cambridge gives birth to her second child, Charlotte.

9 SEPTEMBER 2015
The Queen becomes the longest reigning monarch in British history.

2016

21 APRIL 2016
Elizabeth II turns 90.

20–22 JUNE 2016
A weekend of celebrations marks the Queen's official 90th birthday.

23 JUNE 2016
In the Brexit referendum, Britain votes to leave the European Union, an event with profound constitutional implications, particularly on the issue of Scottish independence.

6 FEBRUARY 2017
The Queen's Sapphire Jubilee marks 65 years on the throne.

APRIL 2017
Princes William and Harry talk about the mental anguish over the death of their mother to promote the Heads Together mental health campaign.

17 JUNE 2017
The Queen uses her birthday message to reflect on the recent tragedies of the Grenfell Tower blaze and the Manchester arena bombing.

27 JULY 2017
Prince William works his last shift as an Air Ambulance pilot, giving up his career for his royal duties.

25 SEPTEMBER 2017
Meghan accompanies Harry at the Invictus Games, their first public occasion together.

AUGUST 2017
Prince Philip retires from public life.

20 NOVEMBER 2017
The Queen and Prince Philip celebrate their 70th wedding anniversary.

2018

23 APRIL 2018
Prince Louis Arthur Charles, third child of the Duke and Duchess of Cambridge, is born.

19 MAY 2018
Harry and Meghan are married at St George's Chapel in Windsor.

14 JUNE 2018
Meghan, Duchess of Sussex, joins the Queen for their first royal engagement together, in Cheshire.

18 JUNE 2018
Mike and Zara Tindall's second daughter, Lena Elizabeth Tindall, is born.

12 OCTOBER 2018
Princess Eugenie marries Jack Brooksbank at St George's Chapel, Windsor.

17 JANUARY 2019
Prince Philip is involved in a car accident near Sandringham.

6 MAY 2019
Archie Harrison Mountbatten-Windsor, first child of Meghan and Harry, is born.

SEPTEMBER 2019
Meghan and Harry tour southern Africa, meeting Archbishop Desmond Tutu and advocating for landmine removal efforts.

7 OCTOBER 2019
William, Catherine, Meghan, and Harry lend their voices to a national mental health campaign, Every Mind Matters.

20 NOVEMBER 2019
Prince Andrew announces that he will step back from public life, in the wake of public furore over his association with a sex offender.

⌃ Harry and Meghan speak to children after attending the Commonwealth Service, their last official royal event.

9 MARCH 2020
Harry and Meghan attend their last event as senior royals, after announcing in January that they will step back from royal duties, pursue financial independence, and move to North America.

MARCH–APRIL 2020
Princes Charles and William contract Covid-19 but recover without lasting ill effects.

21 SEPTEMBER 2020
Prince Charles gives the opening video address at global Climate Week, having earlier in the year visited the Davos Conference to push world leaders to take more action on climate concerns.

JULY 2020
Meghan, Duchess of Sussex, suffers a miscarriage and speaks movingly of her and Harry's "unbearable grief".

17 JULY 2020
Princess Beatrice marries Edoardo Mapelli Mozzi in a private ceremony in Windsor.

BEFORE «

The Duchy was founded in 1337 by Edward III for his eldest son, Edward, the Black Prince, who became the first Duke of Cornwall aged just 7 years.

THE BLACK PRINCE

As an adult, the Black Prince spent much of his time in France – **fighting to reclaim the French crown** for his father. However, in Cornwall he was considered to be a **benevolent landlord.** When Cornwall and the rest of England were in the grip of the **Black Death,** he **alleviated suffering** by letting his tenants live **rent free,** and commanded that the Duchy animals grazing on Dartmoor be given to the poor.

The Isles of Scilly
The Duchy of Cornwall owns most of the Scilly Isles, and is the archipelago's port authority, based at St Mary's. Several of its properties are holiday homes, run on environmentally friendly principles.

"**My whole aim** was to **repair the damage,** to **heal the wounds,** as it were, of the countryside."

PRINCE CHARLES, MAY 2006

The **Duchy** of **Cornwall**

As well as being Prince of Wales, Prince Charles is also Duke of Cornwall. Founded as a source of private income for the heir to the throne, the Duchy of Cornwall's revenues today support the public, private, and charitable activities of Prince Charles and his immediate family.

Although Cornwall is often referred to as "The Duchy", the estate actually includes land throughout the southwest of England – only 13 per cent of the estate is in Cornwall. Since it was founded by Edward III, the extent of the estate has varied, as lands were bought and sold. Today the Duchy includes 53,134 hectares (131,297 acres) of land spread over 24 counties. Almost half of the holdings are in Devon, with others in Herefordshire, Somerset, and Wales. The Oval cricket ground in London is also part of the Duchy – dating back to the days when it was a market garden. The Duchy includes arable and livestock farms, residential and commercial properties, forests, rivers, quarries, coastline – and the new town of Poundbury, created in the 1990s.

Many of the Duchy's holdings and laws date back to the medieval era – indeed, some have their origin in ancient Celtic and Anglo-Saxon law – prompting accusations of anachronistic feudalism. The Duchy has the right of *bona vacantia* – a right to the estates of anyone in Cornwall who dies without a will or surviving relatives. This is paid into a charitable account that funds environmental and community projects. It also has the right to appoint the county's High Sheriff, is the port authority for the Isles of Scilly, and owns about three-fifths of the Cornish foreshore. The Duke has "right of wreck" on all ships wrecked on Cornish shores, as well as to any "royal fish", such as whales, porpoises, and sturgeon, washed up on its beaches.

The origins of the Duchy

In Saxon times, Cornwall and Wales were not ruled by England – indeed King Athelstan (see p.12) set the English border along the River Tamar – and their independence survived the Norman Conquest. William the Conqueror's half-brother, Robert of Mortain acquired Cornwall in 1072, and the Domesday Book, compiled 14 years later, shows that Cornish landowners owed allegiance only to Mortain, not, as in the rest of the country, to the King.

When in 1337, Edward III created the Duchy of Cornwall for his son, the Black Prince, and for all future "first-begotten" sons and "heirs apparent to the kingdom of England", its charter renounced the King's rights to tax revenues within the Duchy, and stated that royal ministers, sheriffs, or bailiffs had no right to enter the territory. Although Prince Charles has volunteered to pay income tax (see p.235), the Duchy estate is not subject to corporation tax on the grounds that it is a private estate; the Duchy retains the right to appoint a High Sheriff; and although the first-born child of a monarch – whether girl or boy – will inherit the throne, a woman cannot inherit the Duchy of Cornwall. If the monarch has no male children, the rights and responsibilities of the Duchy belong to the Crown and there is no Duke.

The Duchy today

Prince Charles is the longest-ever serving Duke of Cornwall, having inherited the Duchy of Cornwall on the death of King George VI in 1952. He became the 24th Duke of Cornwall aged just 4 years old on the Queen's accession to the throne. In 1969, at the age of 21, he became responsible

Educating the next duke
Prince William and Prince Charles check on their rare-breed Ayrshire dairy cattle on the Highgrove estate. Prince William will inherit the Duchy of Cornwall when his father accedes to the throne.

Visit to Waitrose store
Prince Charles and the Duchess of Cornwall visited the Waitrose store in Belgravia, London, on 10 September 2009. Duchy Originals was set up by Prince Charles to promote sustainable organic food and to raise money for his charities.

Heritage to manage the many ancient and historical sites and monuments on its lands. The Duchy also owns most of the land, and almost one-third of the residential buildings on the Scilly Isles, where it promotes sustainable tourism. It even has its own environmentally friendly holiday cottages on the islands, in Cornwall, and also in Wales.

The future of the Duchy
The Duchy has also given Prince Charles the opportunity to put into practice the architectural and social theories in his book, *A Vision of Britain*. In 1994 the Duchy created Poundbury, an experimental new town outside Dorchester. With houses built in a mix of traditional and classical styles, the town was designed as a "walkable community", with shops, leisure facilities, and residential areas integrated, rather than segregated as they are in many modern towns and cities. The Duchy has undertaken similar projects in Truro and Newquay, while in Kennington, London – where

When Prince Charles accedes to the throne, the Duchy of Cornwall will pass to Prince William.

DUCHY OF LANCASTER
As **King,** Charles will become **Duke of Lancaster** in succession to the Queen. Similar to the Duchy of Cornwall, the Duchy of Lancaster is **held in trust** for a Royal Family member, in this case the Sovereign. **Revenues** from its properties **provide** his or her **main source of income.**

THE FUTURE DUKE
Prince Charles has already taken measures to **prepare Prince William** to take over the Duchy of Cornwall. Since 2011, Prince William has attended the twice-yearly meetings of the **Prince's Council,** which controls the Duchy. According to a Clarence House spokesman, William "… has been learning about the Duchy for a number of years with a view to getting a greater understanding of how it all works."

the age of 21, he became responsible for the managing of the Duchy – and entitled to its income.

The Duchy of Cornwall's portfolio of land and property is valued at £763 million. In 2013 the Duchy generated

531
The total extent of lands in square kilometres (205 sq miles) held by the Duchy of Cornwall.

£28.8 million, and Charles received an income of £19 million – up 4 per cent on the previous year. The Prince pays income tax on the money left after costs – around £9.2 million in 2013 – so his tax bill was £4.4 million. The vestiges of the ancient laws defining the Duchy mean that only the Royal Family, its advisors, and HM Revenue and Customs currently know what the Prince claims as expenses before tax.

Prince Charles has silenced some critics by volunteering to pay tax, but the demand for more transparency continues. Labour MP Margaret Hodge, chairing the House of Commons Public Accounts Committee, said, "The Duchy enjoys an exemption from paying tax even though it engages in a range of commercial activities. This tax exemption may give it an unfair advantage over its competitors who do pay corporation and capital gains tax." There have consequently been calls for the Duchy's centuries-old charter, which confers it its tax-exempt status, to be reformed.

Sustainable farming
The Duchy of Cornwall has given Prince Charles the opportunity to put his passions for sustainable agriculture and organic farming into practice. The Duchy Home Farm, in the grounds of Highgrove House, has been entirely organic since 1985, making the Prince a

pioneer in the field. Managed hands-on by Prince Charles, the estate has been built and is run on the philosophy that commercial success can be balanced with environmental and social responsibility. The commercial success has been huge – with the Duchy's income doubling between 2012 and 2013. One success story is the Duchy Originals brand – set up in 1990 to market its produce. Now owned by Waitrose, a chain of British supermarkets, the brand is now known as Duchy Originals from Waitrose. It pays royalties of around £1 million each year back to the Prince's Charitable Foundation.

Home Farm is the Duchy's flagship, playing an important role in preserving rare indigenous breeds such as Tamworth pigs, Irish Moiled, Gloucester, Shetland and British White cattle, as well as Hebridean and Shropshire sheep. When British farmers complained of how hard it was to sell mature sheep, Prince Charles headed the Mutton Renaissance campaign, in the hope of encouraging British families to start eating more mutton.

The Duchy includes many areas of outstanding natural beauty and gives much support to conservation projects. It makes regular contributions to projects such as the Fishing for Litter initiative, which encourages fishermen to bring ashore litter caught in their nets at sea. It also works with English

New Highgrove Farm shop
Prince Charles and the Duchess of Cornwall opening the new Highgrove Farm Shop on the High Street, Tetbury. The shop sells gifts inspired by Highgrove or made from organic produce cultivated on the estates and farms of the Duchy of Cornwall.

Oat biscuit with the Duchy crest
Oat biscuits are part of a brand of organic food sold in Waitrose stores in Britain. The Duchy Originals company was set up by Prince Charles in 1990.

it has owned land since 1337 – rents on its properties have been frozen to make them affordable for elderly tenants. The Duchy – a complex mix of arcane ancient tradition and contemporary ecological and social responsibility – is likely to continue to cause controversy, but the commitment of Prince Charles to his estate remains unquestionable.

"I have **tried to break** conventional **moulds** because **I think** they are **mistaken.**"
PRINCE CHARLES, MAY 2006

« BEFORE

As the Queen Mother became celebrated for her longevity, well-wishers would gather outside Clarence House every year on 4 August, her birthday, to congratulate her.

100TH BIRTHDAY

More than 40,000 people were in the Mall on the Queen Mother's 100th birthday in 2000 to greet her as she stepped out onto the balcony of Buckingham Palace, accompanied by her daughters. That morning, the Queen, following her practice of congratulating all centenarians on their birthday, had a handwritten telegram delivered to Clarence House, the Queen Mother's residence. The Queen Mother was **one of 12 centenarians celebrating their birthdays that day.**

Other 100th birthday celebrations for the Queen Mother included a lunch at Guildhall, London, on 27 June. A pageant in her honour was held at Horse Guards Parade on 19 July. It included marching bands, carnival floats, choirs, race horses, Aberdeen Angus bulls, and even camels. The Queen Mother, accompanied by Prince Charles, arrived at the pageant in an open carriage. At the end of the hour-long festivities, she thanked all who had attended, saying the **parade had been "a great joy" to her.**

Mother and daughters
This portrait of the Queen Mother with the Queen and Princess Margaret was taken by celebrated fashion and portrait photographer Norman Parkinson for the Queen Mother's 80th birthday in 1980.

Two Royal Farewells

The year 2002 – the 50th of her reign – began on a sad note for Her Majesty the Queen. Within the space of eight weeks she lost her sister Princess Margaret, on 9 February, followed by her mother, the Queen Mother, on 30 March at the age of 101.

Princess Margaret, four years younger than Queen Elizabeth II, died in hospital at the age of 71. She had been ill for many years and had suffered the first of a series of strokes in 1998. To those born after 1960 Princess Margaret seemed a remote figure, but an older generation remembered the young princess of the 1950s who loved nightclubs and theatre. In the light of recent royal divorces and scandal, it was now hard to believe she had been prevented from marrying the man she loved, Captain Peter Townsend, because he was divorced (see pp.154–55). Margaret's subsequent marriage to the successful

photographer Antony Armstrong-Jones (Lord Snowdon), their stormy relationship and divorce, and gossip about her private life dominated the newspaper headlines in the 1960s and 1970s. Margaret had sometimes seemed bored by her royal duties and was judged by some to have been haughty and extravagant, but she was always unfailing in her loyalty to her sister. Despite their different lifestyles, she and the Queen remained very close.

Margaret's funeral
Princess Margaret's funeral service was held at St George's Chapel, Windsor on 15 February, which was also the

50th anniversary of the burial of her father King George VI. The mourners were headed by the Queen and Prince Philip, and by Princess Margaret's children, Viscount Linley and Lady Sarah Chatto, and Lord Snowdon, her former husband. The Queen Mother, who had had a chest infection since Christmas, attended the service in a wheelchair, having been flown by helicopter from Sandringham the day before. Princess Margaret had planned many details of the funeral herself, including the choice of hymns, and had also requested that her body be cremated. After the service, her coffin was driven by hearse to Slough

Centennial menu
The roundels on the menu for the Queen Mother's centennial lunch show four places connected with her life (clockwise from top left): Clarence House, Royal Lodge, Glamis Castle, and the Castle of Mey.

"My **mother**... had an infectious zest for living."

FROM THE QUEEN'S TRIBUTE, 5 APRIL 2002

municipal crematorium, and her ashes were later returned to St George's Chapel for interment in the Royal Vault.

Death of the Queen Mother

After attending the funeral of Princess Margaret, the Queen Mother returned to the Royal Lodge, Windsor, her country residence since 1931. Her health steadily deteriorated, and she died peacefully in her sleep at 3.15 pm on 30 March, with Queen Elizabeth II at her bedside. She was 101 years old. Prince Charles, her eldest grandson to whom she was particularly close, immediately returned to England from Klosters in Switzerland, where he was on a skiing holiday with Princes William and Harry.

On hearing the news of her death, crowds immediately began to gather outside Buckingham Palace and Clarence House, the Queen Mother's London home. Although the Queen Mother's death could by no means be described as unexpected, she was nevertheless deeply mourned. Born in 1900, she represented continuity throughout a century of change. Her popularity with the public, forged in the days of World War II (see pp.102–103), remained as strong as ever, and she was loved and admired by millions for her good spirits, ready smile, and devotion to duty. Her last official engagement had been on 22 November, only four months before her death, when she was guest of honour at the recommissioning ceremony of the aircraft carrier HMS *Ark Royal*. As

Famous for her hats
The portrait on this 100th birthday commemorative mug shows the Queen Mother wearing one of the broad-brimmed feathered hats for which she was famous.

tributes to the Queen Mother poured in from members of the public as well as national and international leaders, books of condolence were opened at locations including St James's Palace, the Palace of Holyroodhouse in Edinburgh, and Windsor Castle.

Lying-in-state and funeral

On Friday, 5 April, the Queen Mother's coffin was borne on a gun carriage in a solemn procession from St James's Palace to Westminster Hall, where it would lie-in-state for four days until the funeral. Fifty years earlier, King George VI had also lain in state in Westminster Hall, the medieval hall that is the oldest part of the Palace of Westminster.

Fourteen members of the royal family walked behind the coffin. In a break with precedent (traditionally it was only men who followed the coffin), Princess Anne, the Princess Royal, was among their number. The Queen attended a short service as the coffin, draped with the Queen Mother's personal Royal Standard and bearing the crown she had worn for George VI's coronation in 1937, was placed on a 2 m- (7 ft-)

Silent vigil
Wearing the dress uniform of a Rear Admiral, Prince Charles mounts guard at a corner of the Queen Mother's catafalque. Her three other grandsons stood at the other corners in a shared moment of solemn tribute.

high catafalque (coffin support) in the hall. Over the next three days, more than 200,000 people filed past the catafalque to pay their last respects, where soldiers stood guard at each corner throughout the vigil. On the eve of her funeral, the Queen Mother's four grandsons – the Prince of Wales, the Duke of York, the Earl of Wessex, and Viscount Linley – mounted the guard as a mark of mourning and respect.

On the eve of the funeral, the Queen made a televised speech in which she paid tribute to her mother's "resolve, dedication, and enthusiasm for life." Before the start of the funeral service on 9 April, the tenor bell of Westminster Abbey tolled 101 times for every year of the Queen Mother's life, and her coffin was carried from Westminster Hall to the Great West Door of the Abbey to the sound of 128 pipers. Over a million people crowded the area outside the Abbey and the surrounding streets, as more than 2,100 mourners, including 35 members of the British Royal Family and representatives from 25 foreign royal families, attended the 55-minute-long

service, which included two of the Queen Mother's favourite hymns, "Immortal, invisible, God only wise", and "Guide me, O thou great Redeemer".

After the service, as her coffin started on its final journey to Windsor Castle, the Royal Air Force Battle of Britain Memorial Flight of vintage Spitfires, Hurricanes, a Dakota, and a Lancaster flew over Buckingham Palace and the Mall. Large crowds lined the 37 km (23 mile) route. Later that day, in a private service of committal, the Queen Mother's body was interred next to that of her husband in the black marble vault of the George VI Memorial Chapel in the north aisle of St George's Chapel. The ashes of Princess Margaret were placed with them.

AFTER »

After the Queen Mother's death, **Prince Charles moved into Clarence House, her former London home, and Prince Andrew into the Royal Lodge at Windsor.**

WORKS OF ART
The Queen Mother left her entire **estate to the Queen,** her only surviving daughter. She had previously established a **trust fund for her great-grandchildren.** Reported to be worth an estimated £70 million, the Queen Mother's fortune came mainly from paintings, china, jewellery, and other works of art, including a valuable Fabergé collection. These now form part of the Royal Collection, and many can be seen on display in the Queen's Gallery.

MEMORIAL STATUE
In 2009, a 3 m- (9½-ft-) high **bronze statue of the Queen Mother** was unveiled beside the statue of King George VI on the steps overlooking the Mall. The statue, which cost £2 million, was paid for from the sales of the £5 coin issued to celebrate the Queen's 80th birthday in 2006.

Gun salute
Gunners of the 105 Royal Artillery Regiment fire a 41-gun salute from the walls of Stirling Castle in Scotland to honour the Queen Mother. Similar gun salutes were sounded in several other cities in the UK.

Golden occasion
Thousands of onlookers line the Mall as the Gold State Coach carrying the Queen, guarded by members of the Household Cavalry and other mounted troops, approaches Admiralty Arch.

The **Golden Jubilee**

Millions of people throughout the UK and the Commonwealth joined in celebrating the Queen's Golden Jubilee in 2002. During the year-long commemorations the Queen and Prince Philip travelled more than 64,000 km (nearly 40,000 miles) to all parts of the globe.

AFTER

As part of her Golden Jubilee celebrations the Queen founded the Queen's Award for Voluntary Service (originally known as the Queen's Golden Jubilee Award).

The Queen wanted to celebrate her Golden Jubilee year by visiting and being seen by as many of her subjects as possible – at home and around the world – to thank them for their support and loyalty during the 50 years of her reign. Although the death of Princess Margaret in February and that of the Queen Mother in March (see pp.258–59), coming so close to the 50th anniversary of the Queen's accession on 6 February 2002, cast a deep shadow over the start of the celebrations, the Queen went ahead with the programme as planned. Just nine days after the death of her sister, she was welcomed to Jamaica as its Queen, and over the course of the next few months she and Prince Philip would make extensive tours of New Zealand, Australia, and Canada.

Between May and August, the Queen visited more than 70 cities and towns in all four countries of the United Kingdom, and took part in scores of "meet the people" walkabouts. The predictions made by several British newspapers that

HELPING THE COMMUNITY
The Queen's Award for Voluntary Service is given for **outstanding achievement by groups of volunteers** who regularly give up their time to helping others in the community, improving the quality of life and opportunity for others, and providing an outstanding service. **The first awards were given in 2003.** The Cabinet Office announces the names of the winning groups on 2 June each year, the **anniversary of the Queen's coronation.** Examples of the kind of service recognized include such things as providing support to victims of crime, driving cars for the elderly, or organizing community sport projects.

Wave of affection
The Queen waves to the crowds as she rides to the service of thanksgiving at St Paul's Cathedral. She is said to have been amazed by the vast numbers who turned out to see her.

the Golden Jubilee would turn out to be a flop as the public had lost its enthusiasm for royal events proved to be very wide of the mark.

Golden Jubilee weekend
Thousands of adults and children took part in the celebrations organized in London over the Golden Jubilee weekend at the beginning of June, and millions more watched on television. Among the highlights of the weekend's events were two concerts in the gardens of Buckingham Palace. The "Prom in the Palace" on 1 June, attended by 12,500 guests, featured classical music performed by the BBC Symphony Orchestra and the BBC Symphony Choir. The "Party at the Palace" on 3 June showcased 50 years of British pop, and was led by Brian May, guitarist in the rock band Queen, playing his arrangement of "God Save the Queen" from the roof of the Palace. The concert, which included performances by Paul McCartney, Eric Clapton, Cliff Richard, and Tony Bennett, attracted over 200 million viewers around the world and was particularly enjoyed by the younger members of the Royal Family. Between two Paul McCartney numbers the Queen lit the National Beacon in front of the Queen Victoria

Memorial in the Mall. It formed part of a chain of more than 2,000 beacons lit throughout British territories and Commonwealth countries around the world and covering the length and breadth of the United Kingdom.

Jubilee Day
On Monday, 4 June the Queen rode in the Gold State Coach in a procession from Buckingham Palace to St Paul's Cathedral for a national service of thanksgiving led by the Archbishop of Canterbury. Leaders of the Roman Catholic and Methodist churches, the Church in Wales, and the Church of Scotland also took part, as did representative leaders from the Commonwealth.

After a luncheon in the Guildhall hosted by the Lord Mayor of London, the Queen and Royal

Commemorative plate
This blue-and-white Wedgwood plate was one of many commemorative items produced to celebrate the Queen's Golden Jubilee.

Family returned to Buckingham Palace for the Jubilee Parade involving more than 20,000 people. Numerous floats illustrating aspects of British life in the 50 years since the Queen's accession paraded down the Mall and in front of the Palace. Later an ocean of people, nearly all of them waving Union Jacks, packed the entire length of the Mall to cheer the Queen and the Royal Family as they appeared on the balcony of Buckingham Palace at the end of the day's celebr.ations.

People held their own street parties and events to celebrate the Jubilee, including a cricket match played on sea ice by members of the British Antarctic Survey. In New York, the Empire State Building was lit up in purple and gold on the evening of 4 June in honour of the Queen – a rare compliment to an overseas figure.

BEFORE

Vast numbers of those taking part in the Golden Jubilee celebrations were too young to remember the Queen's Silver Jubilee, or had been born after it.

TWENTY-FIVE YEARS BEFORE
The Golden Jubilee commemorations reprised many elements of the **Silver Jubilee ‹‹ 182–83,** most notably the ceremonial procession in the **Gold State Coach** from **Buckingham Palace** to **St Paul's Cathedral** for the national service of thanksgiving. The nation in 1977 was in festive mood, and street parties were very much a theme of the earlier celebrations. **Millions greeted the Queen,** who made several appearances on the balcony of Buckingham Palace. There was a **Royal Progress by boat along the River Thames** and a **fireworks display.** But worldwide television was not yet the phenomenon it became by 2002, and nothing was organized quite on the scale of the two Palace music events.

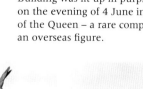

Royal salute
Concorde and the Red Arrows bring up the rear of the 22 km- (14 mile-) long flypast over the Mall and Buckingham Palace that brought the Jubilee Day celebrations to a close.

Back to School

Prince William and his fiancée Catherine Middleton returned to the University of St Andrews in Scotland, where they had met as students 10 years earlier, to launch the university's 600th anniversary commemorations. It was fitting that one of their first official engagements together was at the place where their romance began.

William and Catherine first met in September 2001 as students at St Andrews University, on the east coast of Scotland. St Andrews, home to the world-famous Royal and Ancient Golf Club, founded in 1764, is a small seaside town. Its university, the oldest in Scotland, has 6,000 undergraduates, who wear a distinctive red gown. William and Catherine lived in St Salvator's Hall (affectionately known as Sallies), the university's oldest hall of residence, during their first year. Both were studying for an honours degree in the History of Art, though William later switched to Geography.

While at university, William had reached an agreement with the media that once he had given them an interview and a photo opportunity, they would leave him alone to lead a normal student life. He enjoyed shopping in the local supermarket and going out to student pubs and bars. William captained the collegiate water polo team and represented the Scottish national universities at the Celtic Nations tournament in 2004.

Catherine is said to have caught William's eye when she was modelling at a student fashion show early in their first year of studies. They shared a flat in the centre of St Andrews with two friends during their second year, and moved into a cottage a little way outside the town for their final year. Both graduated on the same day: 23 June 2005.

Speculation that the couple were about to get engaged intensified around the time of Catherine's 25th birthday in January 2007, and caused them to split up for a time. They eventually became engaged in October 2010 while on holiday in Kenya.

"It feels like coming home."

PRINCE WILLIAM, AT THE LAUNCH OF ST ANDREWS'S 600TH ANNIVERSARY CAMPAIGN, 25 FEBRUARY 2011

First official visit as a royal couple
Wearing a scarlet coat to match the scarlet gowns worn by St Andrews's undergraduate students, Catherine waves to a crowd of well-wishers. During their visit, the engaged couple unveiled a plaque to mark the launch of the university's 600th anniversary.

« BEFORE

Following the death of Diana, Camilla was rarely seen in public. The campaign to rehabilitate public perception of her as Charles's chosen companion was carefully managed.

STEP BY STEP

Charles and Camilla's **first appearance as a couple** was at the 50th birthday party for her sister Annabel at the Ritz Hotel, London.

CHARLES AND CAMILLA LEAVE THE RITZ

The press had been informed that the Prince would be present, and 200 photographers were on hand to record them leaving the event. In 2002, in her capacity as President of the National Osteoporosis Society, **Camilla greeted Charles with a kiss** – their first in public – as he arrived at a reception for the charity. Much was made of **her commitment to raising awareness of osteoporosis**, a disease that had affected her mother and grandmother, as part of the campaign to boost her public profile.

The **Marriage** of Charles and **Camilla**

More than 30 years after their romance first began, a decade after their affair was first made public, and nearly eight years after Diana's death, the Prince of Wales and Camilla Parker Bowles finally became husband and wife on 9 April 2005.

Clarence House announced the engagement of the Prince of Wales and Camilla Parker Bowles on 10 February 2005. Charles gave his bride-to-be a ring belonging to his grandmother Queen Elizabeth the Queen Mother, as an engagement ring. The Queen immediately issued a statement expressing her and Prince Philip's good wishes for the couple's future, and Princes William and Harry were said to be delighted.

Following his divorce, Prince Charles had publicly said that his relationship with Camilla Parker Bowles was "non-negotiable", but Diana's popularity, and the swell of emotion after her death, had made it hard for him to win the public over to his side. Press opinion was uniformly hostile to the woman it blamed for causing Diana's unhappiness.

In 2000 the Queen met Camilla for the first time since the relationship had become known. This was seen as a sign that she had come to accept Camilla, who was invited to sit in the royal box at the 2002 Golden Jubilee celebrations. Camilla moved into Clarence House when it became Charles's household and official residence in 2003, though she kept (and still keeps) her own house in Wiltshire. The climate of opinion had gradually changed, making it possible for the couple to legitimize their relationship.

Constitutional questions

Camilla's divorced status raised potential constitutional difficulties in view of Charles's future rule as Supreme Governor of the Church of England, and aroused memories of the

arrangements for the remarriage were consistent with the Church of England guidelines, "which the Prince of Wales fully accepts as a committed Anglican and as prospective Supreme Governor of the Church of England." Some constitutionalists argued that the heir to the throne could not legally be married in a civil ceremony, but the Lord Chancellor, Lord Falconer, made it clear in a statement to the House of Lords on 24 February that the Human Rights Act of 1998 superseded any laws concerning royal marriages.

Two ceremonies

The marriage had originally been set for 8 April, but was postponed for one day, so that Charles could represent the Queen at the funeral of Pope John Paul II. A crowd of more than 20,000

> **"The Duke of Edinburgh and I are very happy that the Prince of Wales and Mrs Parker Bowles are to marry."**
>
> QUEEN ELIZABETH II, IN A STATEMENT ISSUED BY BUCKINGHAM PALACE

abdication crisis of Edward VIII in 1936 (see pp.92–93). A traditional Church of England wedding service was ruled out because Camilla was a divorcée with a husband still living; although Charles had been divorced, his first wife was no longer alive and so he was a widower in the eyes of the Church. It was decided that the couple would have a civil wedding at the Windsor Guildhall, the nearest register office to Windsor Castle, followed by a service of blessing in St George's Chapel, Windsor. The Archbishop of Canterbury, Dr Rowan Williams, issued a statement saying that the

Highland Games

Charles and Camilla are seen here in relaxed mood at the Caithness Highland Games in Scotland in August 2003. By now the public was becoming used to seeing them together.

people greeted the couple as they arrived for their private register office wedding at 12.30 pm. It took place in front of a small group of family guests, who were driven from Windsor Castle to the Guildhall in a hired minibus. The guests did not include the Queen and Duke of Edinburgh – the Queen had earlier announced her decision not to attend on the grounds that the couple wanted to keep it low-key and her presence would not allow that to happen. The legal witnesses to the marriage were Prince William and Tom Parker Bowles, Camilla's son.

The bride wore a cream-coloured dress and coat with a wide-brimmed, cream-coloured hat for the civil ceremony. She changed into a blue and gold silk coat and dress with a gold headdress for the televised service of blessing in St George's Chapel, which was attended

Family portrait
In this official wedding portrait, the newly wed royal couple is seen with the Royal Family (left) and Camilla's father Major Bruce Shand and her children Tom and Laura (right).

by the Queen and Prince Philip. Other guests included Charles's biographer Jonathan Dimbleby, broadcaster Sir David Frost, and actors Kenneth Branagh and Joanna Lumley.

Charles and Camilla entered the chapel arm-in-arm and stood facing the Archbishop of Canterbury to reaffirm their vows. Afterwards they walked around and chatted with the crowd gathered outside the chapel before returning to the State Apartments at Windsor Castle for a reception hosted by the Queen. In a speech at the reception, Elizabeth said how very proud she was of her son

Grand Cross of the Royal Victorian Order
The Queen created Camilla a Dame Grand Cross of the Royal Victorian Order in 2012. Admission to the Order is in the Queen's personal gift, and is given in recognition of distinguished personal service and as a sign of her affection and trust.

who "despite Becher's Brook and The Chair [a reference to the Grand National steeplechase being run that same day] and all kinds of other terrible obstacles… has come through."

Duchess of Cornwall

Camilla became Her Royal Highness the Duchess of Cornwall (the Duchess of Rothesay in Scotland) on her marriage instead of the Princess of Wales. This was out of deference to public opinion, which still associated Diana with the title. For similar reasons it was announced that Camilla would become Princess Consort on Charles's accession rather than Queen Camilla. An opinion poll taken at the time found that while 65 per cent of people were in favour of the marriage, only 7 per cent thought that Camilla should eventually become queen.

Camilla has taken on significant new duties in recent years and played a prominent part in the Diamond Jubilee celebrations in 2012.

The Duchess made her **first overseas tour** with Charles a few months after their wedding, when they visited the US in November and met with President George W Bush in the White House. She attended the **Trooping the Colour** in London, in June 2005, making her first appearance on the balcony of Buckingham Palace.

FUTURE QUEEN CONSORT?
As the Prince of Wales took on more of the Queen's public duties, Camilla appeared more frequently at State events. On 8 May 2013, dressed in full regalia, she sat beside Charles at the **State opening of Parliament**. This was taken by many as a sign that she was being seen as a future Queen Consort, a topic on which public opinion has been wavering – in a 2015 poll, 49 per cent of

people supported the idea, but in a 2017 poll, only 19 per cent did so.

As the Queen and Prince Philip have withdrawn from public life, Camilla has stepped up. In 2020, for instance, she took over from Philip as **Colonel-in-Chief** of the Rifles infantry regiment. In April of the same year, she opened one of the nation's Nightingale Hospitals, set up to help tackle the Covid-19 emergency.

CAMILLA IN REGAL DRESS, 2013

The **Diamond Wedding**

Another milestone was passed when the Queen became the first monarch in British history to celebrate 60 years of marriage. She and Prince Philip were married in 1947 at a time of austerity in Britain. Sixty years later they came together to Westminster Abbey to renew their wedding vows in a special service of celebration.

The service took place on 19 November, the day before the actual wedding anniversary. It was attended by more than 30 members of the Royal Family and 2,000 guests. Among them were five choristers who had sung in the Westminster Abbey choir in 1947 and 10 couples who had married on the same day. The music included psalms and hymns chosen by the couple for their wedding, and during the prayers the Archbishop of Canterbury, Dr Rowan Williams, asked the Queen and Duke of Edinburgh "to renew in your hearts promises you made to one another". Prince William gave a reading from the Bible, and the Oscar-winning actress Dame Judi Dench read a poem specially written for the occasion by the Poet Laureate Andrew Motion. Afterwards the Queen and Duke chatted with some of the waiting crowds in Parliament Square.

The day before the service the couple revisited Broadlands, the former home of the late Lord Mountbatten where they had spent their honeymoon 60 years before. Then on 20 November, the day of their wedding anniversary, the Queen and Duke of Edinburgh flew to the Mediterranean island of Malta where they had lived from 1949 to 1951, when Prince Philip was serving in the Royal Navy. The Queen is known to have especially fond memories of her years on the island. It was the only period of their marriage when she and Philip were able to enjoy a relatively normal life away from the "full light of publicity… and the pressure this brings." These were the words used by the Archbishop of Canterbury the day before in thanking the couple for the public character of their 60 years of service and dedication to the country and the Commonwealth.

"**Some couples** have to **live** more than others in the **full light of publicity.**"

DR ROWAN WILLIAMS, SERMON, 19 NOVEMBER 2007

Happy memories
As part of their diamond wedding celebrations the Queen and Duke of Edinburgh revisited Broadlands, the house where they spent their honeymoon. This photograph of the couple was taken while they were walking in the grounds together, remembering old times.

Born 1982

The Duke of Cambridge

"I'm pretty **normal.**"

PRINCE WILLIAM, IN AN INTERVIEW WITH NBC NEWS, 15 JUNE 2007

illiam was born on 21 June 1982 at St Mary's Hospital, Paddington, less than a year after the marriage of the Prince and Princess of Wales. Charles was present in the delivery room during the birth. The baby immediately became second in line of succession to the throne. He was christened William Arthur Philip Louis by the Archbishop of Canterbury in the Music Room at Buckingham Palace six weeks later. Among his six godparents were the former Constantine II, the former king of Greece, and Laurens van der Post, the South African writer and explorer, who was a spiritual guru to Charles.

William was nine months old and just beginning to crawl when he accompanied his parents on a six-week official visit to New Zealand and Australia. This, too, was a first – when Charles was at a similar age, he had been left behind at home when his mother, then Princess Elizabeth,

went on a prolonged overseas visit in 1949. Nicknamed Wombat, William proved a magnet for the photographers covering the tour, just as his own son George would 31 years later.

Childhood and school

Diana first began to suffer from depression and the eating disorder bulimia while she was pregnant with William, but strains in her marriage with Charles were still concealed from the outside world. Both parents were determined to protect their sons from press intrusion and to give them as normal an upbringing as possible. Diana let the boys wear casual jeans and sweatshirts and took them on outings to theme parks and fast-food restaurants so they could have a wider experience of life. Later she took them with her on visits to hospitals and homeless centres to deepen their emotional understanding.

William's schooling began at the age of four at Jane Mynors' nursery school in Notting Hill, about five minutes away from Kensington Palace. He later went to Wetherby School, London, followed by Ludgrove boarding school in Berkshire when he was eight. In 1995, William entered Eton College, just outside Windsor, founded by King Henry VI in 1440. It is often said that it was Diana who decided to send William to Eton as both her father and brother had been educated there. However,

Mother and son
Chubby baby William gurgles with joy as his mother Diana swings him high in the air. William was very close to his mother, who died when he was only 15 years old.

Prince charming
This official photo was released for William's 21st birthday on 21 June 2003. He denied having a girlfriend in an interview that he gave for the occasion, though Catherine Middleton attended his birthday party at Windsor Castle that year.

Charles, who had hated the rigorous regime of his own school, Gordonstoun, was also in favour of the choice.

William was on holiday with his father and brother at Balmoral when Diana was killed in August 1997. In the hysteria surrounding her death, the media, quite unfairly, accused the Royal Family of insensitivity to the princes in dealing with the blow. William was devastated by his mother's death, and it was at his suggestion that singer Elton John performed *Candle in the Wind* at her funeral. The agreement that had been reached earlier with the tabloid press to allow William to study at Eton free of intrusion in return for regular updates on his progress, undoubtedly helped to protect him and Harry, who joined him there the following autumn, in the difficult months that followed.

Student prince

William left Eton in June 2000 with three A-levels – in Geography, Biology, and History of Art. He had also captained the school water polo team. After a gap year travelling and working in Africa, Belize, and Chile, he enrolled at St Andrews University, the oldest university in Scotland, founded in 1413. This was another break with royal

Friend and colleague
Prince William and broadcaster and campaigner Sir David Attenborough attend the naming ceremony for the research ship RSS *Sir David Attenborough*. The two have worked together on several conservation initiatives.

tradition – every prince who had previously been to university had gone either to Oxford or Cambridge (his father's alma mater), but St Andrews, situated in a small town on the Scottish east coast, offered William the chance of greater privacy and freedom. There was only one serious

service, this was considered too dangerous for the second in line to the throne. In January 2009 he transferred to the Royal Air Force (RAF) and qualified as a Search and Rescue Sea King helicopter pilot.

Royal responsibilities

The engagement between William and Catherine Middleton was announced on 16 November 2010, and their marriage took place five months later, when they became the Duke and Duchess of Cambridge. Shortly after

> "It's not a **question** of **wanting to be [king],** it's something I was **born into,** and it's **my duty.**"

PRINCE WILLIAM, IN AN INTERVIEW WITH PETER ARCHER OF THE PRESS ASSOCIATION, 21 JUNE 2003

press intrusion while he was there. Ironically, this was by a film crew from Ardent Productions, his uncle Prince Edward's company. William met Catherine (Kate) Middleton early on during his time at St Andrews, and he shared a flat with her and two friends in their final year.

After graduating with a Master of Arts degree in Geography in 2005, William embarked on a military career, entering the Royal Military Academy Sandhurst, Berkshire, in the footsteps of his younger brother, who had gone there the year before. In December 2006, William was commissioned as Lieutenant Wales into the Blues and Royals regiment of the Household Cavalry. Although he expressed a desire to experience active combat

the birth of their first child, George, in July 2013, William announced that he would be ending his full-time military career to give more time to his royal responsibilities and charity work. Their second child was born in May 2015, and their third in April 2018.

As well as carrying out many duties on behalf of the Queen at home and overseas, William supports numerous charities and has a strong interest in conservation work, particularly projects involving countering the illegal wildlife trade. Through the Royal Foundation of the Duke and Duchess of Cambridge, William and Catherine also advocate for young people and mental health issues. Their 2017 Heads Together initiative has tried to change the national conversation on mental health.

TIMELINE

- **21 June 1982** Born to Charles and Diana, Prince and Princess of Wales, at St Mary's Hospital, Paddington, London.
- **4 August 1982** Christened William Arthur Philip Louis in the Music Room, Buckingham Palace.
- **September 1990** Starts at Ludgrove School, a boys' boarding school in Berkshire.
- **December 1992** The Prince and Princess of Wales separate.
- **September 1995** Enters Eton College, where he goes on to gain three A-Levels.
- **31 August 1997** His mother, Diana, Princess of Wales, dies in a car crash.
- **September 2001** Begins a four-year Master of Arts (Honours) degree course at St Andrews University in Scotland.
- **June 2005** Completes degree at St Andrews.
- **July 2005** Undertakes his first solo overseas tour, visiting New Zealand on the Queen's behalf.
- **September 2005** Becomes the patron of Centrepoint, the youth charity for the homeless in London.

PRINCE WILLIAM'S COAT OF ARMS

- **September 2006** Enters the Royal Military Academy at Sandhurst, Berkshire, to train as an army officer.
- **16 June 2008** Becomes a Royal Knight Companion of the Most Noble Order of the Garter.
- **January 2009** Begins training as a Search and Rescue pilot in the RAF.
- **29 April 2011** Marries Catherine Middleton at Westminster Abbey, London.
- **22 July 2013** Birth of their first child, George Alexander Louis.
- **September 2013** Active service in the RAF ends.
- **April 2014** Duke and Duchess of Cambridge tour New Zealand and Australia with Prince George.
- **2 May 2015** Birth of his second child, Charlotte Elizabeth Diana.
- **April 2017** Prince William talks openly about the impact of Diana's death on his mental health while promoting the Heads Together campaign.
- **27 July 2017** Prince William works his last shift as an Air Ambulance pilot.
- **23 April 2018** Birth of Prince Louis Arthur Charles, third child of the Duke and Duchess of Cambridge.
- **7 October 2019** William helps to front the national mental health campaign, Every Mind Matters.

State Visit to Ireland

The Queen's state visit to the Republic of Ireland, made at the invitation of its President, Mary McAleese, was the first by a British monarch since 1911. It marked a historic turning point in the troubled relations between the United Kingdom and the Republic of Ireland.

The last British monarch to visit Ireland was the Queen's grandfather, George V, when the whole of Ireland was still part of the United Kingdom. Since then, the two countries had been divided by a long history of hostilities stemming from the Easter Rising of 1916, the bloody struggle for Irish independence, and the subsequent bitter conflict over the island's partition into the Irish Free State (later the Republic of Ireland) and Northern Ireland, which remains part of the United Kingdom. The signing of the Good Friday Agreement in 1998, by which the Republic gave up its territorial claim to Northern Ireland, helped to pave the way for the royal visit, which was seen as a symbol of reconciliation.

Dublin was on full security alert throughout the Queen's visit. On the first day, Elizabeth laid a wreath in the Garden of Remembrance, which was dedicated to the memory of "all those who gave their lives in the cause of Irish freedom". She visited Croke Park, where British troops had fired on Irish civilians at a Gaelic football match in 1920. Speaking later that evening at a state banquet in Dublin Castle, the Queen delighted her audience by beginning in Irish, a notoriously difficult language: "A Uachtarain agus a chairde" (President and friends). On hearing this, Mary McAleese was seen to mouth "Wow". The Queen spoke feelingly of the troubled past and the building of bridges to a better future. Her mention of the personal pain suffered by those who had lost family members was a clear reference to the murder of her cousin, Lord Mountbatten, by the Irish Republican Army (IRA) in 1979 (see pp.192–93).

"With the benefit of historical hindsight we can all see things we would wish had been done differently, or not at all."

QUEEN ELIZABETH II, AT THE STATE BANQUET IN DUBLIN CASTLE, 18 MAY 2011

Coat of emerald green
The Queen wears Irish green for a tour of the historic Rock of Cashel in County Tipperary. Coming at the end of her visit, this was a more relaxed day, giving her time to visit the famous Coolmore Stud for racehorses.

BEFORE

William is the fourth pilot in the Royal Family, following in the footsteps of his grandfather, his father, and his uncle, the Duke of York.

LIKE FATHER, LIKE SON

William owes his **passion for flying** to his father. Prince Charles had already gained his **private pilot's licence** when he flew himself to RAF Cranwell in 1971 to start advanced training as a jet pilot. Three years later, he trained as a helicopter pilot with the **Royal Navy** at Yeovilton in 1974. He frequently took the controls when flying on aircraft belonging to the Queen's Flight – a unit that until 1995 operated aircraft for the transportation of members of the Royal Family.

4-YEAR-OLD WILLIAM STEPS OUT OF A HELICOPTER

FALKLANDS STORIES

Andrew, the Duke of York, then second in line to the throne, served as a **Sea King helicopter co-pilot** on board HMS *Invincible* during the **Falklands War.** He would have inspired William with stories of how he lured Argentinian Exocet missiles away from the ships of the British Task Force ≪ **216–17.**

The **Pilot Prince**

Flying is in the royal blood. William gained his pilot's badge, the RAF wings, during his time in the military. He went on to become a dedicated Search and Rescue (SAR) pilot. On leaving the armed forces, he planned to continue flying helicopters alongside his royal duties.

In 2007, the Ministry of Defence announced that William was to serve a four-month attachment with the Royal Air Force (RAF). Lieutenant Wales, as he was known in the army, had recently completed a training course as a troop commander in an armoured reconnaissance unit. He had signed up for a three-year army commission, but once it became clear he would not be allowed to see frontline action in Afghanistan, it was decided he should spend time experiencing life in the other two services (the RAF and the Royal Navy). Secondment to the RAF would allow him to realize his lifetime ambition of learning to fly, and familiarize him with the use of modern air power.

William underwent an intensive 12-week course learning to pilot helicopters and fixed-wing aircraft at Cranwell, the RAF's flying college in Lincolnshire. After eight and a half hours' flying time, he made his first solo flight. "It was an amazing feeling," he said afterwards. On 11 April 2008, Prince Charles, who had trained at Cranwell in the 1970s, presented William with his RAF wings. At the end of his secondment, William even made it to the frontline when he flew (though not at the controls) in a C-17 Globemaster military transport plane on a 30-hour round trip to Kandahar air base in Afghanistan to repatriate the body of a fallen soldier. The news broke after his return to RAF Lyneham in Wiltshire; he said he was "deeply honoured" to have been part of the crew that brought the body home.

William also served a short attachment to the Royal Navy. While deployed on HMS *Iron Duke* in the Caribbean, he took part in a joint operation with the United States Coast Guard to seize a speedboat carrying 900 kg (1,984 lb) of cocaine worth approximately £40 million.

Search and Rescue pilot

In 2009, William extended his commission and transferred to the RAF to train to become a helicopter pilot with their Search and Rescue (SAR) Force. This branch of the service provides round-the-clock air search-and-rescue cover throughout the UK, Cyprus, and the Falkland Islands. It developed out of the air-sea rescue squadrons formed during World War II to pick up aircrew downed in the sea. Although its role remains military, today most of SARF's operational missions are undertaken to rescue civilians from emergencies at sea or on mountainsides, which it carries out in cooperation with Her Majesty's Coastguard.

Service with the SARF would allow William to continue flying and have an active role in the armed forces without being deployed on combat operations. Promoted to Flight Lieutenant, he completed a 12-month course in advanced helicopter flying

at the Defence Helicopter Flying School based at RAF Shawbury in Shropshire. During this course he completed around 80 hours of training on the Griffin HT1 helicopter, covering advanced handling, night flying, emergency handling, and tactical and formation flying.

In January 2010, Flight Lieutenant Wales transferred to the Search and Rescue Conversion Course at RAF Valley on the island of Anglesey in North Wales. For the first six weeks he continued to train in the Griffin

1,765 The number of incidents to which William's Search and Rescue unit from RAF Valley responded in 2012.

helicopter before moving on to the Sea King Operation Conversion Unit, where he trained on a mixture of simulators and RAF Sea King helicopters.

The busiest SAR unit

In September 2010, at the end of his training, William was assigned to C Flight No. 22 Squadron based at RAF Valley – the busiest SAR unit in the country – to fly the Sea King Mark 3 helicopter. His operational tour was expected to last from 30 to 36 months.

An SAR duty shift is 24 hours. The crew must be ready for take-off within 15 minutes of receiving an emergency call (45 minutes at night). There is a morning briefing session to pass on information about weather conditions and other operational factors, and to report on the state of their aircraft. The crew is responsible for carrying out preflight checks, but much of the time on base is spent in the crew-room.

The standard SAR crew includes two pilots, one of whom is the aircraft captain. Additionally, there is a radio operator who operates the winch that is used at the rescue scene to lower the winchman on a rope, and to lift

Billy the Fish

William's RAF name badge states his name as Will Wales. He earned the nickname Billy the Fish during his training because "Wales" sounds like "whales".

SAR graduates

Along with six fellow students, Flight Lieutenant Wales (middle back row) displays his graduation certificate after completing his SAR training course at RAF Valley in September 2012.

"I **really enjoy my time** in the **Air Force.** And **I'd love to continue it.** But the **pressures** of my **other life are building.**"

WILLIAM, BEFORE LEAVING ACTIVE SERVICE IN 2013

In August 2014, it was announced that William would return to flying by training to become an air ambulance pilot.

A NEW CAREER IN THE AIR

After a period of training, William began work with the **East Anglian Air Ambulance (EAAA)**, based at Cambridge and Norwich airports, in March 2015, shortly before the birth of his second child. For two years, William fitted his new role around his royal duties, **donating his salary to charity**. During this period, he and the Duchess of Cambridge mostly lived at Anmer Hall, their country house on the Sandringham Estate in Norfolk.

In July 2017, William flew his **last mission** for the EAAA, before giving up his career to focus full time on his royal duties and charity work. His colleagues at the Air Ambulance service described him as "much-loved", "hard-working", and a "wonderful character".

At the controls
Described as "a highly professional and competent pilot", William took part in many daring rescue missions over the stormy waters of the Irish Sea and the mountains of Snowdonia in North Wales.

the injured person to safety. The winchman is normally trained to paramedic standard and supplies immediate first-aid and recovery services at the rescue site. William's first mission as co-pilot took place on 2 October 2010, when he was part of a team airlifting a casualty from an offshore gas rig to hospital. Over the next three years, the Prince would take part in a total of 156 Search and Rescue operations with C Flight, resulting in 149 saved lives. In 2012, he passed the required tests to become an operational captain, in charge of the four-man crew.

No greater feeling
William's pleasure in flying helicopters is obvious. A BBC TV documentary in 2013, *Helicopter Rescue,* showed him as the aircraft captain on a flight to rescue a boy from a quarry. In the documentary, William spoke about his role: "There's no greater feeling than when you've actually done some good and saved someone's life."

Before their marriage, William and Catherine made their first home together in a rented farmhouse on Anglesey. Catherine has spoken of the fears she had for his safety when he was flying dangerous missions. When William's period of active service in the RAF ended in September 2013, he had completed more than 1,300 flying hours.

The **Wedding** of **William** and **Catherine**

In a break with tradition, a commoner and a member of the middle class, Catherine Middleton wed Prince William. Catherine had won the public's heart and a million people turned out to cheer the couple after their wedding took place in Westminster Abbey on 29 April 2011.

Eight-tiered cake
It took cake-maker Fiona Cairns and her team five weeks to create the magnificent eight-tiered wedding cake. The groom also requested a chocolate biscuit cake made to a favourite recipe.

Comparisons with the wedding of Prince Charles and Lady Diana Spencer, 30 years earlier, were inevitable. That, too, had been heralded as "a fairy-tale wedding" and preceded by months of eager anticipation. Their wedding had been a state occasion held amid the baroque splendours of St Paul's Cathedral. Westminster Abbey, though grand enough and with closer connections to the monarchy, seats less than 2,000 people. William had insisted that he and Catherine should be allowed to have a say in who was invited. As a result, more than half the guests were family and friends of the couple, and the number of invitations traditionally issued to heads of state, politicians, diplomats, and other dignitaries was greatly reduced.

It was announced on the morning of the wedding that the Queen had created her grandson the Duke of Cambridge, Earl of Strathearn, and Baron Carrickfergus, and that Catherine (Kate) would assume the title of Her Royal Highness the Duchess of Cambridge immediately upon the marriage. William's new titles were drawn from England, Scotland, and Northern Ireland respectively.

Floral theme
The medieval nave of Westminster Abbey had been transformed into an avenue of trees, some of them standing up to 7.5 m (25 ft) high, and decorated with 30,000 flowers, including azaleas and other blossoms from Windsor Great Park. Prince William, in the full-dress scarlet uniform of the Irish Guards, and Prince Harry, his best man, in the bold blue of the Blues and Royals, stood out against this English floral background.

The bride, attended by her sister Pippa as maid of honour, four bridesmaids, and two pageboys, made the three-and-a-half minute journey from the Great West Door of the Abbey to the choir on her father's arm. Her dress, designed by Sarah Burton at Alexander McQueen, was made of ivory and white satin, and both the bodice and skirt incorporated lace floral motifs appliquéd by workers from the Royal School of Needlework. The skirt formed a Victorian-style semi-bustle at the back and finished in a short train measuring just under 3 m (10 ft) long. The veil was held in place by a tiara lent by the Queen. Catherine carried a small bouquet of white spring flowers.

The Dean of Westminster, John Hall, led the traditional Church of England service and the Archbishop of Canterbury, Rowan Williams, married the couple. Richard Chartres, the Bishop of London, gave a sermon, and the bride's brother, James Middleton, read the lesson.

The newly married couple left the abbey to a peal of bells. They returned to Buckingham Palace in the 1902 State Landau (pp.136–37) drawn by four Windsor greys. It was followed by a procession of carriages carrying the Queen and other members of the Royal Family back to Buckingham Palace.

Lunchtime reception
The Queen hosted a lunchtime reception for about 600 guests, made up of friends of the couple as well as representatives from the many organizations they are associated with.

72 MILLION The number of people who viewed the royal wedding on YouTube.

3 The number of hours the bells of Westminster Abbey were rung after the royal wedding.

William and Catherine, together with their families, appeared on the balcony of Buckingham Palace to greet the thousands of people gathered below. The crowd roared their approval as the couple exchanged the by now traditional royal marriage kiss, and then repeated it. Overcome by the noise, one of the tiny bridesmaids, William's three-year-old goddaughter Grace van Cutsem, covered her ears. The traditional Royal Air Force flypast over the palace included Lancaster, Spitfire, and Hurricane planes from World War II.

Just after 3.30 pm, William drove his bride in a classic Aston Martin convertible to Clarence House, his official residence. The couple returned to the Palace in the evening for a private dinner given by Prince Charles for close friends and family. It was followed by dancing, with a small fireworks display in the palace grounds.

Public celebrations
The wedding day, a Friday, was declared a national holiday in the UK. Millions of people watched the day's events on television. It was broadcast live to millions more around the world. More than 5,000 permits were issued to hold street parties, including one hosted by Prime Minister David Cameron in Downing Street. Union Jacks and bunting decorated the streets of London and other cities. The cost of the event was estimated at £20 million, most of which was paid for by Prince Charles, though the Middletons also made a contribution.

BEFORE

The engagement of Prince William, who is second in line to the throne, to Catherine Middleton was announced on 16 November 2010.

DIANA'S RING
William gave Catherine the sapphire and diamond engagement ring belonging to the **Princess of Wales << 200**. William told reporters that the ring was "very special to him" and was "my way of making sure my mother didn't miss out on today."

Wedding portrait
The bride and groom, surrounded by Catherine's young attendants, pose in the Throne Room of Buckingham Palace after the wedding.

Husband and wife
Catherine has a special smile for Prince William as he takes her hand as the newly married couple prepare to lead the procession out of Westminster Abbey after the wedding.

"When we go for it, **we really go for it.** "

DAVID CAMERON, BRITISH PRIME MINISTER, ON THE ROYAL WEDDING CELEBRATIONS

Leaving in style
Prince William drives his wife from the reception in a classic Aston Martin convertible belonging to his father. It was decorated with balloons, and the registration plate had been altered to read "JUST WED".

AFTER

Prince William returned to duty as an RAF Search and Rescue pilot the day after the wedding. The couple did not leave for their honeymoon in the Seychelles until 9 May.

WORKING ROYAL
The Duchess's official duties began soon after their honeymoon. In May, she and William attended a private meeting at Buckingham Palace for **US President Barack Obama** and his wife Michelle. In July the couple made their first overseas tour together to **Canada and the US 294–95 》**.

CHARITY FUND RAISER
Catherine's wedding dress was put on display in Buckingham Palace throughout the summer, where it attracted a record number of visitors. It helped to raise £8 million for the Duchess of Cambridge's own charity fund.

Two entwined "A"s – the initials of Prince Albert and Princess Alexandra

Double portrait of King Edward VII and Queen Alexandra

1 WEDDING SOUVENIR

2 EDWARD VII CORONATION BEAKER

Royal Memorabilia

Since the days of Queen Victoria, many people have shared a passion for collecting royal memorabilia, ranging from fine china commemorating coronations to mass-produced items such as sweet tins, mugs, and posters.

1 **Wedding souvenir** A rare silver gilt and enamel medal given to a Royal Entertainments committee member after the wedding in 1863 of Prince Albert of Wales and Princess Alexandra. 2 **Edward VII coronation beaker** This Royal Doulton porcelain cup was presented to guests invited to the official coronation dinners. 3 **Edward VII coronation vase** Another Royal Doulton creation, this 1902 vase has painted floral motifs on a gilt and blue ground. 4 **George V coronation cup** The Royal Crown Derby miniature loving (two-handled) cup was created to commemorate George V's coronation. 5 **George V Silver Jubilee medal** This commemorative medal was given by J J Cash, Coventry, to its employees. 6 **George V Silver Jubilee ribbon pin** Attached with a pin at the back, this embroidered ribbon was designed to be worn on a jacket. 7 **George V coronation souvenir tin** Rowntree & Sons released this unusual coronation casket containing chocolates in 1911. 8 **George VI coronation cup**

The blue and gold Coalport loving cup commemorates the coronation of George VI and Elizabeth on 12 May 1937. 9 **Elizabeth II diamond wedding anniversary presentation tin** Complete with a piece of cake inside, this cake tin commemorates the 60th wedding anniversary of Queen Elizabeth II and Prince Philip. 10 **Prince of Wales wedding cake tin** This wedding cake tin bears the crests of the Prince of Wales and the Duchess of Cornwall along with the date of their wedding. 11 , 12 **Miniature loving cups** The births of Princes William and Harry were marked by the release of a miniature loving cup. 13 **Elizabeth II Diamond Jubilee teapot** The limited edition bone china teapot is from a collection officially approved by the Queen. The proceeds from sales go towards the upkeep of the Royal Collection of art and antiquities. 14 **Royal wedding mug** This souvenir mug formed part of the official range of fine bone china commemorating Prince William's marriage to Catherine Middleton.

Edward VII's royal cypher, ERVII, standing for Edward Rex (king)

3 EDWARD VII CORONATION VASE

5 GEORGE V SILVER JUBILEE MEDAL

6 GEORGE V SILVER JUBILEE RIBBON PIN

22-carat gilding

Scenes from the King's vast empire, which includes India, and parts of Africa, and Australasia

4 GEORGE V CORONATION CUP

7 GEORGE V CORONATION SOUVENIR TIN

8 GEORGE VI CORONATION CUP

9 ELIZABETH II DIAMOND WEDDING ANNIVERSARY PRESENTATION TIN

10 PRINCE OF WALES WEDDING CAKE TIN

11 MINIATURE LOVING CUP – WILLIAM

12 MINIATURE LOVING CUP – HENRY

Royal coat of arms

13 ELIZABETH II DIAMOND JUBILEE TEAPOT

Embellishments in burnished gold and platinum

The initials of "C" and "W" for Catherine and William appear below Prince William's coronet

14 ROYAL WEDDING MUG

Born 1982

The Duchess of Cambridge

"I really hope I can **make a difference**, even in the smallest way."

CATHERINE MIDDLETON, POST-ENGAGEMENT INTERVIEW, 16 NOVEMBER 2010

Catherine Elizabeth Middleton was born in Reading, Berkshire, on 9 January 1982, the first child of Carole and Michael, who met while working with British Airways (BA). In 1984 the family moved to Jordan, where Michael continued to work for BA, and Catherine attended an English nursery school. The Middletons returned to England in time for Catherine to start at St Andrew's prep school in Pangbourne. Carole started one of the UK's first internet mail-order companies, Party Pieces, selling childrens' party supplies. It became a huge success.

Graduation day
Catherine Middleton collected her degree in 2005, graduating with an upper-second class Bachelor of Arts. There she had already impressed fellow student Prince William, who was to become her husband.

Attending the Jubilee
Catherine, seen here during the Queen's Diamond Jubilee celebrations, had become a fashion icon, her every move, outfit, and even slightest fluctuation in weight scrutinized.

Tall and shy, Catherine excelled at sport, and was among the spectators when Prince William, then aged 9, visited her school to play hockey. After leaving St Andrews in 1995, she went briefly to Downe House School, an elite girls's school in Berkshire, where it seems she was unhappy and was removed by her parents. She then went to Marlborough College in Wiltshire. Catherine did well at school, getting two As and a B at A level, and she was offered a place at Edinburgh University to study, but decided to take a gap year in Italy and applied instead to study History of Art at the University of St Andrews for the following year.

University life
Both William and Catherine went up to St Andrews in the autumn of 2001 and were placed in the same hall of residence. Despite close monitoring of the Prince by the ever-voracious press, it was not until the following spring that Catherine first attracted attention. She had agreed to model at a student fashion show, and it was discovered that William had paid £200 for a front row seat. Catherine appeared several times on the catwalk, her costumes ranging from a vibrant, voluminous sloppy Joe to a transparent black shift dress. The Prince, so the story goes, was most intrigued. A discreet romance began, and the following

Down with the kids

Catherine interacts with children during a breakfast visit to Stockwell Gardens Nursery and Pre-school, London, in January 2020. She has a passion for supporting the health and well-being of young children.

year they moved into a terraced house in the centre of St Andrews with two other students.

Leaving university

In 2006, after graduating, Catherine began to work part time for the fashion company Jigsaw. Press speculation about the future of her relationship with William was fevered. Jigsaw founder Belle Robinson remembers that there were days when the road outside the office was clogged with TV crews. "We'd say: 'Listen, do you want to go out the back way?' And she'd say: 'To be honest, they're going to hound us until they've got the picture. So why don't I just go, get the picture done, and then they'll leave us alone.' I thought she was very mature for a 26-year-old." In April 2007, William and Catherine caused a press furore by calling a pause in their relationship. Clarence House refused to comment, and press speculation was rife. But the couple soon began to be seen in public together again and there were reports that their relationship had rekindled.

Royal wedding

The couple eventually became engaged in October 2010, while on holiday in Kenya to celebrate Prince William passing his RAF helicopter Search and Rescue course. Prince William gave Catherine the engagement ring that had belonged to his mother, Diana, Princess of Wales. They married in Westminster Abbey $on 29 April 2011, and moved to a remote farmhouse on the island of Anglesey, where William worked as a Search and Rescue pilot. They had no domestic staff, and friends reported that they wanted to live as normal a life as possible, with Catherine cooking dinner, buying groceries in the local shop, and having a bath run for William by the time he came home. Their carefully guarded private life

provided much-needed respite from the constant attention of the press. Catherine had become a fashion icon, though she bucked royal tradition in selecting her own clothes – from UK high street chains as well as from exclusive designers.

> ## "The best **dressing up outfit** I ever had was a pair of **clown dungarees** my Granny made."
>
> DUCHESS OF CAMBRIDGE, IN AN INTERVIEW

It was enough for Catherine to appear in a dress for it to sell out.

New generation

After a pregnancy during which she was hospitalized for extreme morning sickness, Catherine gave birth to Prince George on 22 July 2013. For some time, the new family continued to live on Anglesey, but in October 2014 they moved into Kensington Palace. The following year, William took on a new role as an air ambulance pilot in

The new princess

In June 2016, and at the age of 13 months, Princess Charlotte joined her family on the Buckingham Palace balcony to watch an RAF flypast marking her great-grandmother's 90th birthday.

Norfolk, and for two years the family was mostly based at Anmer Hall, on the Sandringham Estate. On 2 May 2015, Catherine and William's second child, Princess Charlotte Elizabeth Diana, was born at St Mary's Hospital, London, and their third child, Prince Louis Arthur

Charles, was born on 23 April 2018. Catherine supports many charities and good causes, with particular emphasis on development in the early years of a child, physical education, and the visual arts. A keen photographer, her own photos are often used in palace press releases.

TIMELINE

- **9 January 1982** Born Catherine Elizabeth, the eldest child of Michael and Carole Middleton, at Royal Berkshire Hospital, Reading.
- **May 1984** The Middletons move to Amman, Jordan, where Michael Middleton works as a flight dispatcher for British Airways. Catherine attends an English-language nursery school.
- **September 1987** The Middletons return to England and Catherine is enrolled at St Andrew's School, Berkshire.
- **1987** Carole and Michael Middleton found Party Pieces, a mail-order company selling party supplies.
- **April 1996** Begins attending Marlborough College, a coeducational boarding school.
- **2000** Studies at the British Institute in Florence during her gap year.
- **September 2001** Enrols at St Andrews University, Scotland, to study History of Art.

COMBINED COAT OF ARMS OF THE DUKE AND DUCHESS OF CAMBRIDGE

- **2003** Begins dating Prince William. They try to keep the romance discreet in an attempt to avoid press coverage.
- **15 December 2006** Attends Prince William's Passing Out Parade at Sandhurst as an official royal guest.
- **April 2007** The couple split up for a short time.
- **October 2010** William and Catherine become engaged during a 10-day trip to Kenya.
- **29 April 2011** Marries the Duke of Cambridge at Westminster Abbey and is created the Duchess of Cambridge.
- **22 July 2013** Gives birth to first child, George Alexander Louis.
- **2 May 2015** Catherine's second child, Princess Charlotte Elizabeth Diana, is born.
- **March 2018** The Duchess becomes the first Royal Patron of the Victoria and Albert Museum in London.
- **23 April 2018** Birth of Prince Louis Arthur Charles, Catherine's third child.
- **October 2019** Catherine and William embark on a royal tour to Pakistan.
- **March 2020** Catherine and William set off on a royal visit to Ireland.
- **May 2020** Catherine launches Hold Still, a national photography exhibition to document the Covid-19 pandemic in Britain.

« BEFORE

The only other monarch in British history to have had a Diamond Jubilee was Queen Victoria, who celebrated her 60 years as Queen in 1897.

BANDANA COMMEMORATING THE GOLDEN JUBILEE OF QUEEN VICTORIA

VICTORIA'S JUBILEES

While **Queen Victoria's Diamond Jubilee** celebration was **grander than** that of her **Golden Jubilee,** the Queen kept in poor health **« 67**. Crippled with arthritis, she was unable to climb the steps of St Paul's Cathedral for the service of thanksgiving, and so it was decided to hold it outside. Dressed as usual in black, she remained seated in her carriage throughout.

The **Diamond Jubilee**

In 2012, Queen Elizabeth II celebrated her Diamond Jubilee. The event came less than a year after the excitement of the marriage of the Duke and Duchess of Cambridge, and the nation and the Commonwealth were in a mood to celebrate 60 years of her reign.

The Diamond Jubilee provided the occasion for her subjects to reflect upon the Queen's lifetime of service to her country through 60 years of change. Prime Minister David Cameron echoed these sentiments when, addressing the House of Commons on 7 March, he said, "While the sands of culture shift and the tides of politics ebb and flow, Her Majesty has been a permanent anchor… grounding us in certainty."

Weekend of celebrations

The government announced in January that the focal point of the Queen's Diamond Jubilee celebrations would be the first weekend in June. Monday, 4 June and Tuesday, 5 June were designated as public holidays, giving people throughout the country the chance to hold street parties or picnics, or to join in one of the hundreds of public events being organized.

The Queen began her Diamond Jubilee celebrations by attending the Epsom Derby horse races on Saturday, 2 June. In London, the celebrations were marked on Sunday, 3 June with a spectacular pageant on the Thames, an event inspired by a painting by the 18th-century artist Canaletto, *The Thames on Lord Mayor's Day*, depicting gilded barges and a

400,000 **The number of Diamond Jubilee medals awarded in the UK to the armed forces, prison police, and emergency services.**

flotilla of river craft against the backdrop of St Paul's Cathedral. More than 1,000 boats, old and new, from all over the country and further afield, assembled on the river. They included vessels that had taken part in the Dunkirk evacuation during World War II in 1940, an early 19th-century Maori war canoe, and a wooden gig (rowing boat) believed to have ferried Queen Victoria on a visit to Cornwall. *Gloriana*, a rowing barge specially commissioned for this event, was powered by an 18-man team of rowers, including Olympic oarsmen Sir Steve Redgrave and Sir Matthew Pinsent.

The Queen and Duke of Edinburgh, and other members of the Royal Family, were on board the royal barge – MV *The Spirit of Chartwell* – lavishly got up with

Pageant on the Thames
As scores of tiny rowing boats stream under Westminster Bridge, the high-rise buildings behind are testament to how much the London skyline has changed during Queen Elizabeth II's reign.

Diamond Jubilee china
The official range of commemorative china for the Diamond Jubilee was modelled on the Rockingham Service, first used at the coronation banquet of Queen Victoria in 1838.

AFTER ▶▶

The Queen's Diamond Jubilee was marked in many different ways to provide a lasting legacy of her 60 years on the throne.

JUBILEE TRIBUTES

Among the permanent tributes to the Queen were the **60 Jubilee woodlands planted by the Woodland Trust.** The clock tower of Westminster Palace that houses Big Ben was renamed the Elizabeth Tower, the main gate to Kew Gardens became the Elizabeth Gate and in December 2012, the British Foreign Office announced that a portion of **the British Antarctic Territory would be known as Queen Elizabeth Land.** The Queen bestowed city status on Chelmsford in England, Perth in Scotland, and St Asaph in Wales, while Armagh in Northern Ireland was granted a Lord Mayor. The borough of Richmond in southwest London became a Royal Borough.

DIAMOND JUBILEE MEDAL

Three versions of the **Queen Elizabeth II Diamond Jubilee medal** were issued, one each by the UK, Canada, and the Caribbean Commonwealth realms. It was awarded for honourable service in the armed forces, police, prison, and emergency services, or for outstanding achievement or public service.

---

gold and velvet awnings. In cold, chilly rain they watched the early part of the 12 km- (7.5 miles-) long flotilla of boats pass by before the Royal Barge joined the procession to the pageant's finale at Tower Bridge.

Concert at the palace
The next day a concert organized by singer and songwriter Gary Barlow took place in front of Buckingham Palace on a stage built around the Queen Victoria

Barge fit for a Queen
The rowing barge *Gloriana*, which was privately built as a tribute to the Queen, was modelled on the Lord Mayor's guilded barge pictured in Canaletto's painting of the River Thames.

Memorial. A total of 10,000 free tickets had been made available to the public and distributed by ballot. An afternoon picnic, with a menu designed by top chef Heston Blumenthal, was laid on for ticket-holders in the palace gardens beforehand. The concert included headline performances by Elton John, Stevie Wonder, and Paul McCartney. Prince Philip, who had been admitted to hospital earlier that day with a bladder

right around the world from Tonga and New Zealand to Sydney, New Delhi, Hong Kong, and Canada, and from John O'Groats to the Channel Islands.

On the final day of the celebrations, the Queen and other members of the Royal Family attended a national service of thanksgiving at St Paul's Cathedral. Also present were the governors general and prime ministers of the Commonwealth, together with

> # " In this special year… I **dedicate myself anew** to your service."
> THE QUEEN, ON THE 60TH ANNIVERSARY OF HER ACCESSION, 2 FEBRUARY 2012

infection, could not attend the concert. At 10.30 pm, the Queen placed a crystal glass diamond into a special pod to activate a laser that lit the last in a chain of more than 4,000 beacons stretching

representatives of many branches of national life. After a lunch with 700 guests in Westminster Hall, the Queen returned in an open-top carriage to Buckingham Palace. The celebrations ended with the customary appearance of the Royal Family on the balcony of Buckingham Palace for a flypast by the Red Arrows, the RAF aerobatic display team, and other aircraft.

Overseas tours
Ten years before, for the Golden Jubilee, the Queen and Prince Philip had visited every country of the Commonwealth, but now the 86-year-old monarch called upon the support of other members of the Royal Family. Overseas tours undertaken on behalf of the Queen included visits by the Prince of Wales and the Duchess of Cornwall to Australia, Canada, New Zealand, and Papua New Guinea; the Duke and Duchess of Cambridge to Malaysia, Singapore, the Solomon Islands, and Tuvalu; and Prince Harry to Belize, Jamaica, and the Bahamas.

Lighting the National Beacon
The Queen manipulates the crystal glass diamond into position to light the National Beacon. Seconds later, the brilliant white flare rose high into the sky in front of Buckingham Palace.

Other events held in the Diamond Jubilee year included an overseas sovereigns' lunch hosted by the Queen at Windsor Castle on 18 May. In all, 22 reigning and former monarchs attended, including the Emperor of Japan, two queens, nine kings, three princes, one grand duke, and one sultan.

Opening the Olympics

Early in the morning of 28 July, Queen Elizabeth II stepped up to the microphone to declare the 2012 London Olympic Games officially open. Her brief words came in the midst of a lavish opening ceremony – created by Oscar-winning director Danny Boyle – that had begun five hours before.

For many, the highlight of the show came at around 10.30 pm when the huge audience packed into the stadium, and the millions viewing at home, were treated to a short film showing Daniel Craig as James Bond arriving at Buckingham Palace. Followed by the Queen's corgis Monty, Willow, and Holly, he is shown into the royal study where the Queen, with her back to the camera, is writing at her desk. Is it really her? All doubts are put aside when she turns and greets the famous spy: "Good evening, Mr Bond".

The monarch and spy are then seen leaving the Palace and apparently climbing aboard a helicopter, which flies across London to the Olympic Stadium, where they leap out. At that moment, in real time, two skydivers, one dressed as the Queen, appeared above the stadium. And minutes later, the Queen, wearing the same outfit as in the film, accompanied by the Duke of Edinburgh arrived to take her seat. The Queen's starring role was one of the best-kept secrets of the night. According to Lord Coe, chairman of the Games' organizing committee, Princes William and Harry were as stunned as anyone to see the Queen in her first film part. As the skydiver started to descend, the Princes were heard to shout, "Go, Granny!"

The Queen's surprise cameo, which had taken three hours to film under Danny Boyle's direction, gave the royal seal of approval to a hugely successful summer Olympic Games, in which Great Britain finished third in the medal rankings. It crowned a triumphant regal summer, following on from the enormous success of the Queen's Diamond Jubilee in June (see pp.282–83).

> **"I declare open the Games of London,** celebrating the **30th Olympiad** of the modern era."
>
> **QUEEN ELIZABETH II,** OPENING THE OLYMPIC GAMES, 28 JULY 2012

Crown of light
Her Majesty the Queen, in a peach-coloured cocktail dress and a headpiece with handmade porcelain flowers, formally opens the London Olympic Games. Seconds later an explosion of fireworks appeared to enfold the stadium in a scintillating crown of light.

Riding for Britain
Zara Phillips took part in the showjumping final at the London Olympics in 2012. Her mother Princess Anne had competed in the Olympics 36 years earlier, in Montreal.

Born 1984

Prince Harry

"There are **three** parts of **me** – one wearing a **uniform,** one being **Prince Harry,** and the other… **private.**"

PRINCE HARRY, ON RETURN FROM AFGHANISTAN, JANUARY 2012

The people's prince
People have tended to identify more with Prince Harry than any other royal. His very public transformation from a cheeky young boy to a vociferous advocate for various charities has endeared him to the public.

P rince Harry is the younger son of Charles, Prince of Wales and Diana, Princess of Wales, and is currently sixth in line of succession to the throne – after Prince Charles, Prince William, and William's three children. Harry was born on 15 September 1984 at St Mary's Hospital, in Paddington, central London, and named Henry Charles Albert David. A good-looking toddler with striking red hair and an impish grin, Harry seems to have a developed a cheeky, happy-go-lucky attitude to life from an early age, in contrast to his shyer, more serious older brother.

Death of Diana
Harry was 12 at the time of his mother's tragic death. A diminutive figure in an unfamiliar black suit, he walked bravely behind his mother's coffin with his grandfather, father, brother, and maternal uncle, Earl Spencer, as it made its way to Westminster Abbey. As an adult, Harry has spoken openly about the pain of losing his mother – "To us, she was quite simply the best mother in the world" – and it cannot be doubted it is this experience that allows him to empathize with children in his charity work and official engagements. A trip that Harry made to Botswana and South Africa with Prince Charles in the winter after Diana's death gave him his first taste of Africa, a continent he has visited many times since.

Eton and after
In September 1998, Harry joined Prince William at Eton College – an independent secondary school in Berkshire, near Windsor. Although he did not shine academically, he excelled in sports, particularly polo and rugby union, and joined the school Combined Cadet Force (CCF), reaching the rank of Cadet Officer. He did not escape getting into teenage scrapes – when the press published reports that he had taken part in underage drinking and

Cheeky appearance
Prince Harry peers out of the garden door of Highgrove, Prince Charles's country home. Harry and William divided school holidays between Highgrove and Diana's Kensington Palace apartment.

cannabis smoking, his father arranged for him to visit a South London drug rehabilitation centre.

On leaving school in 2003, and before embarking on a military career, Harry took a gap year to travel in Australia, Argentina, and Africa. In Africa, he made a documentary about the plight of orphan children in Lesotho. He also spent part of the year training as a coach with the Rugby Football Union, visiting schools and clubs around the country to promote the sport.

Prince Harry entered the Royal Military Academy at Sandhurst, Berkshire, in May 2005 and on completing his training course was commissioned as a second lieutenant into the Blues and Royals, part of the Household Cavalry. He was deployed twice to Afghanistan and is a qualified Apache helicopter commander (see pp.290–91). In an interview to the press about life on the

For love of Africa
On a 2014 trip to Lesotho, Prince Harry shows a group of boys the photo he has just taken of them on his camera. The boys go to a night school built by Sentebale, Prince Harry's African charity.

frontline, he said "I haven't really had a shower for four days, I haven't washed my clothes for a week."

A talent for caring
As with William, the influence of Diana, Princess of Wales, is evident in many of the charities and causes that Harry supports. In 2006, he founded Sentebale with Prince Seeiso of Lesotho. Sentebale, which

> # "We're **very privileged** in the **position** that we are. But… with privilege comes **great responsibility.**"

PRINCE HARRY, INTERVIEWED ON CBS NEWS, 13 MARCH 2012

means "forget-me-not" in the Lesotho language, helps care for vulnerable children who are the forgotten victims of poverty and the HIV/AIDS epidemic. The Concert for Diana, organized by William and Harry at Wembley Stadium in July 2007, was held to aid Sentebale, along with Diana's favourite charities.

Harry's personal experience of military life has led him to take an ever more active role in supporting those injured in the line of duty, above all through his Invictus Games initiative, which he launched in October 2014 (see pp.300–301). Another personal experience that has profoundly affected him has been the mental anguish that he suffered in the wake of his mother's untimely death. This has inspired his

Prince Harry's coat of arms
The Queen gave Prince Harry his own coat of arms on his 18th birthday. The red escallops (shells) on the collars of the lions, unicorn, and shield are from the Spencer coat of arms of his maternal family.

involvement in mental health initiatives such as the Royal Foundation's Heads Together campaign, and his 2020 initiative, HeadFIT, a platform designed to provide mental support for members of the armed forces.

In his youth, Harry gained notoriety for incidents that made a splash in the tabloid press. He had to apologize after a photograph appeared of him wearing a uniform with a swastika armband to a themed costume party. He was also photographed naked in Las Vegas with an unknown woman, apparently taking part in a game of "strip billiards". His image was one of a fun-loving prince, especially during his younger days; in 2014, for example, he was voted the nation's favourite royal. But public affection for the Prince would soon face stern tests.

New direction
Harry's marriage to Meghan, and the birth of their first child, Archie (see pp.292–93), profoundly changed the course of Harry's life. An increasingly fraught relationship with both the media and the strictures of royal life led to Harry and Meghan making a break with the Royal Family in 2020. Withdrawing from his role as a senior member of the Royal Family, Harry relocated to California to forge a new, financially independent path in life. Harry continues to espouse the causes he holds dear while embracing the modern era in a way that poses profound challenges to the institution of the monarchy.

TIMELINE

- **15 September 1984** Born at 4.20 pm at St Mary's Hospital, Paddington.
- **21 December, 1984** Christened Henry Charles Albert David by the Archbishop of Canterbury in St George's Chapel, Windsor.
- **September 1992** Follows William to Ludgrove School, a boys' boarding school in Berkshire.
- **August 1997** Death of his mother Diana in a car accident.
- **1998–2003** Attends Eton College, where he gains two A-Levels in Art and Geography.
- **2004** Spends a gap year in Australia, Argentina, and Lesotho, Africa.
- **2006** Helps set up Sentebale, a charity to help orphans in Lesotho.
- **April 2006** Is commissioned into the Household Cavalry.
- **1 July 2007** With his brother, organizes the "Concert for Diana" at Wembley Stadium, London.
- **December 2007** Is deployed as a Forward Air Controller in Afghanistan.

CONCERT FOR DIANA

- **September 2012** Makes second operational tour in Afghanistan as an Apache helicopter co-pilot/gunner.
- **December 2013** Takes part in the Walking with the Wounded South Pole challenge.
- **8–14 September 2014** Attends all the events at the Invictus Games in his role as president.
- **September 2014** Appointed honorary president of England Rugby ahead of the Rugby World Cup hosted in England in August 2015.
- **March 2015** Announces his departure from the army, as from June, to start a new chapter in his life.
- **April 2017** Talks openly about his mental health issues as a result of losing his mother to help launch the Heads Together initiative.
- **25 September 2017** Attends the third Invictus Games with his new partner, Meghan Markle.
- **19 May 2018** Wedding of Harry and Meghan takes place at St George's Chapel in Windsor; they are made Duke and Duchess of Sussex.
- **6 May 2019** Archie Harrison Mountbatten-Windsor is born, first child of Meghan and Harry.
- **January 2020** Announces that he and Meghan plan to step back from the Royal Family.
- **June 2020** Harry, Meghan, and Archie move to California.

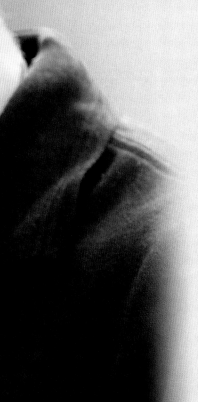

<< **BEFORE**

Harry's love of the army dates back to his childhood. Growing up in the Royal Family gave him plenty of opportunity to observe military life.

LITTLE SOLDIER

When he was 8, Harry accompanied Diana, the Princess of Wales, on an **official visit to the Light Dragoons' barracks** in Hanover, Germany, where he was photographed wearing a set of miniature army fatigues. His favourite movie was said to be the classic historical war drama *Zulu*, starring Michael Caine.

ZULU, 1964 FILM POSTER

SCHOOL CADET

Harry was an enthusiastic member of the Eton College unit of the **Combined Cadet Force (CCF),** which teaches basic military training and leadership skills in schools. Awarded the **highest rank of Cadet Officer,** he was **Parade Commander** at Eton CCF's annual inspection in 2003.

" Anyone who says they **don't enjoy the Army** is **mad...** (it is) the **best job** you could ever, **ever wish for.**"

PRINCE HARRY, IN AN INTERVIEW

Apache warrior

Prince Harry is pictured wearing camouflage fatigues at the British-controlled Camp Bastion in southern Afghanistan. Serving as an Apache helicopter co-pilot gunner, the Prince completed a four-month tour of duty on the frontline in 2012.

Harry in the Army

Prince Harry served 10 years in the army and did two tours of duty in Afghanistan – the first member of the Royal Family to fight in a war zone since Prince Andrew served in the Falklands.

Harry always wanted to be a soldier. He was not as academically inclined as his older brother, William, and achieved only two A-levels at school. However, these were enough to allow him to undertake the compulsory tests for entry to the Royal Military Academy Sandhurst – the training establishment

target and could endanger the lives of the soldiers around him. Although the Prince accepted the decision, he did not mask his disappointment.

In February the next year, the MoD revealed that Harry had secretly visited Afghanistan as a tactical air controller, calling up allied air cover to support ground forces attacking the Taliban.

Using sophisticated equipment
Harry sits in the cockpit of his Apache helicopter with a monocle gun sight mounted on his helmet. This device allows gunners to direct missiles by simply pointing their heads at a target and activating a switch.

£45 million each, Apaches are highly sophisticated and well-armed military helicopters. Designed to hunt and destroy armoured vehicles, Apaches can zero in on a specific target during day or night, and in all weather conditions. Each of these helicopters carries a mix of weapons, including rockets, 16 Hellfire laser-guided missiles, and a 30 mm (chain gun. An Apache's two-man crew consists of a pilot and a co-pilot, or gunner.

In October 2011, Harry transferred to the US Naval Air Facility at El Centro, California, for the final part of his training to fly Apaches in the war arena, including live fire training. This would qualify him for frontline action in Afghanistan. A natural pilot, Harry was top of his class at El Centro.

> "There's **no way** I'm going to put myself through **Sandhurst** and **then sit... back home** while my boys are out **fighting** for their **country.**"

PRINCE HARRY, EXPLAINING HIS DECISION TO BE DEPLOYED ON THE FRONTLINE

for officers in the British Army. Although most entrants these days are graduates, Harry was nonetheless accepted, and began training as Officer Cadet Wales in May 2005. The demanding course covered military, practical, and academic subjects, alongside tough physical training. On completion, Harry was commissioned as a cornet, or second lieutenant, into the Blues and Royals regiment of the Household Cavalry in April 2006. He then took the Troop Leaders' Course to qualify to command an armoured reconnaissance vehicle.

Disappointing decision

In February 2007, the Ministry of Defence (MoD) and the Prince of Wales' office made a joint announcement that Harry would be deployed with his regiment to Iraq as part of the 1st Mechanized Brigade. Harry had already publicly stated that he would leave the army if he were left behind while his regiment went to war. In May, General Sir Richard Dannatt, head of the British Army, reversed the decision – Harry was a high-value

The ministry, forced to make the announcement because foreign media had breached the official news blackout, immediately cut short his tour of duty. Harry returned home and commented: "Angry would be the wrong word to use, but I am slightly disappointed. I thought I could see it through to the end and come back with our guys."

Helicopter pilot

Late in 2008, Harry began learning to fly military helicopters on attachment to the Army Air Corps (AAC) based at Middle Wallop, Hampshire. In June 2009, he joined Prince William at the Defence Helicopter Flying School at Royal Air Force (RAF) Shawbury, Shropshire. The brothers lived in shared accommodation during their time together on the base. In May 2010, the Prince of Wales awarded Harry his flying brevet (wings) in a ceremony at Middle Wallop.

Harry then embarked on the long training to fly Apache attack helicopters, and was promoted to captain in 2011. Costing approximately

Blues and Royals cap badge
The Blues and Royals was formed in 1969 when two regiments of the British Army – the Royal House Guards and the Royal Dragoons – merged. Each regiment's origins can be traced back to the 1660s.

Camp Bastion

Harry arrived at Camp Bastion, the British airbase in southern Afghanistan, in September 2012 to begin a four-month combat tour as an Apache co-pilot gunner with 662 Squadron, 3 Regiment, AAC. He took part in a variety of missions over Helmand Province, from supporting NATO (North Atlantic Treaty Organization) ground troops to accompanying British Chinook and US Black Hawk medical helicopters on casualty evacuation missions. In a series of interviews and a filmed documentary, Harry made it clear how much he valued army life as an escape from the pressures and tensions of being in the public eye as a Royal: "It's very easy to forget who I am when I am in the army. Everyone's wearing the same uniform and doing the same kind of thing. I get on well with the lads and I enjoy my job. It is as easy as that." He also admitted to having fired at Taliban fighters in the course of rescuing injured personnel, but said he was only doing his job.

After Harry's attachment to the AAC ended in 2014, he worked as a staff officer, helping to organize military events in London, such as the annual Trooping the Colour (see pp.226–27). He later worked with the Defence Recovery Capability scheme, ensuring that wounded personnel have adequate recovery plans, work that led him to create the Invictus Games.

AFTER »

After completing a decade of service, Harry announced in March 2015 that he would be leaving the armed forces in June the same year.

HELPING THE WOUNDED
Harry's association with the military continued, despite his decision to quit the forces. He has worked hard to establish, as a regular feature of the sporting calendar, the **Invictus Games 300–301 »** – a competition for former military personnel, wounded in the line of duty. He also continued his work with recovery programmes and took on some of his grandfather's ceremonial roles, but his **2020 separation from the Royal Family** also meant stepping back from his military appointments.

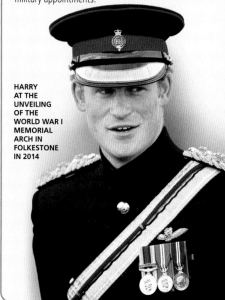

HARRY AT THE UNVEILING OF THE WORLD WAR I MEMORIAL ARCH IN FOLKESTONE IN 2014

BEFORE «

Meghan Markle had a long resumé already in place when she joined the Royal Family; she was an actress, celebrity, style icon, and humanitarian.

VERSATILE CAREER

Born in Los Angeles in 1981, Meghan grew accustomed to the bright lights of Hollywood from an early age, visiting her father, Thomas Markle, on sets where he worked as a director of cinematography and lighting. Meghan **caught the acting bug** while at university; she found global fame with a starring role in the long-running legal drama *Suits*. She also gained a reputation as an activist for equal rights and humanitarian causes. When it became known that she was dating Prince Harry, there was a widespread feeling that Meghan would bring to the royals a **heady mix** of Hollywood glamour, much-needed diversity, and a strong voice for good causes. However, even in the early days, the press was critical, referring to her earlier failed marriage and pointing out that previous liaisons between princes and American divorcees had ended badly for the Royal Family.

The **Marriage** of **Harry** and **Meghan**

What started as a fairytale romance between a handsome prince and a beautiful actress led, following an inspirational wedding, to one of the most celebrated power couples on the planet, but also to a young family who felt they were hounded out of both family and country.

In the summer of 2016, Prince Harry arrived at the hip but discreet Soho Townhouse on London's Dean Street, running late for a blind

Glamour girl
Meghan Markle, alongside fellow actors Gabriel Macht, Sarah Rafferty, and Gina Torres, is seen here attending a glitzy film-industry event in 2012. Meghan came into the Royal Family with an already high profile.

date. His first thought on catching sight of Meghan Markle was, "I'm going to have to up my game here". Just a couple of dates later, they were camping out beneath the stars on a safari in Botswana and falling deeply in love. Together, they formed a power couple with a unique blend of good looks,

glamour, and passionate advocacy for humanitarian causes. The couple would prove to be an irresistible object of fascination for the global media and, above all, the sensation-hungry British tabloid press. Harry's first public confirmation of the relationship, in late 2016, was accompanied by a broadside against reporters who, he said, had relentlessly subjected his new girlfriend to "a wave of abuse and harassment" and defamatory stories with racist overtones directed at the first mixed-race woman to join

Just married
Following their wedding, the newly married couple toured Windsor in a horse-drawn carriage, giving members of the public an opportunity to join in the celebration.

Special place
Ever since they fell in love beneath the stars in Botswana, southern Africa has held a special place in the hearts of the Duke and Duchess of Sussex. They have revisited the region since their wedding.

the Royal Family. The couple's relationship with the press would only go downhill from here.

Moving ahead
Harry and Meghan's relationship, however, continued to blossom. In September 2017, Meghan told *Vanity Fair* magazine, "Personally,

the image of the monarchy. Held at St George's Chapel, Windsor, in May 2018, and overseen by the Archbishop of Canterbury, the ceremony was noted for elements such as the inclusion of a gospel choir, an electrifying sermon from Michael Curry – the head of the American Episcopal Church – and a performance by young black cellist Sheku Kanneh-Mason. The absence of Meghan's father cast a shadow over the festivities. He had become embroiled in a series of tabloid exposés that had caused an estrangement between parent and daughter.

Duke and Duchess of Sussex
On the occasion of their wedding, Harry and Meghan were created Duke and Duchess of Sussex and offered a new home, Frogmore Cottage – a substantial residence in the grounds of Windsor Castle. By October 2018, Harry and Meghan were on their first royal tour, visiting Australia, New Zealand, Fiji, and Tonga. During this trip, Meghan revealed that they were expecting their first baby. Archie Harrison Mountbatten-Windsor, seventh in line to the throne and the Queen's eighth great-grandchild, was born on 6 May 2019.

In January 2020, they announced that they intended to "step back" from their royal duties, cut their ties to the public purse, become "financially independent", and move to North America. The Queen issued a statement in support of their wish for a more independent and peaceful life.

Archie's christening
Harry and Meghan, with the newly christened Archie, are surrounded by family members, including the Duke and Duchess of Cornwall, the Duke and Duchess of Cambridge, and Meghan's mother, Doria Ragland.

AFTER

> " **... being a dad** myself, the whole point in life, I guess, for me, is to try to **leave the world in a better place** than when you found it. "

PRINCE HARRY, IN AN INTERVIEW WITH PATRICK HUTCHINSON IN 2020

I love a great love story". Just two months later, while cooking roast chicken together at Kensington Palace, Harry got down on one knee and proposed to her with an engagement ring he had designed himself. It incorporated two diamonds that had belonged to his mother, and a central stone from Botswana. In an acknowledgement that joining the Royal Family would profoundly change her life, Meghan committed to give up acting and closed her social media accounts. The happy couple were looking forward to working together on the worthy causes close to their heart.

First, however, there was the small matter of a royal wedding to plan, and it was through their celebrated but unconventional version of this ancient ritual that Meghan and Harry really began to express their potential to transform

What should have been a happy time for the couple, however, was tainted by an increasing sensation of being under siege in the arena of public opinion. In September, in an ITV documentary about the couple's African tour, Meghan opened up about the pressure she had been dealing with since becoming a royal and the resulting effect on her mental health. "Not many people have asked if I'm OK," she said, reflecting that she had told Harry that it was not enough just to survive, "that's not the point of life – you have got to thrive".

Their battle with the press began spilling into the courts. For instance, Meghan sued the British *Daily Mail* tabloid over their publication of private letters that she had written. As things became worse, the couple dropped a bombshell or, as they put it, "a transition ... in starting to carve out a progressive new role".

Final flourish
Harry and Meghan chat with schoolchildren after attending the Commonwealth Day Service at Westminster Abbey on 9 March 2020. This was their last official engagement before stepping back from royal duties.

Striking out on their own, Harry and Meghan relocated to California but soon found that their troubles were not so easy to leave behind.

AFTER EXIT
Despite widespread speculation that the couple would move to Canada, where Meghan had spent so much time during her acting days, they actually **moved to California**, where they would be close to Meghan's mother. In July 2020, they paid a reported $14 million (£10 million) for a house in the star-studded enclave of Montecito. In the US, they planned to focus on their charitable causes, developing plans for **Archewell** – named partly in honour of their son – a foundation to support environmental and societal well-being. They recently signed a deal with Netflix to produce a range of content.

INTRUSIVE PRESS
Seeking to counter critics of their receipt of public funds for the renovation of Frogmore Cottage, the Duke of Sussex announced that he and his wife would be **paying back** the full cost out of their own pockets.

The couple are still plagued by **intrusive attention from the press**. They have complained about drones flying over their house and are mired in increasingly acrimonious court cases. In July 2020, they were struck by tragedy when Meghan **miscarried**, an event that caused, she wrote, "an almost unbearable grief".

Feeding time
The Duke and Duchess of Cambridge feed baby elephants at a conservation centre during their tour of India and Bhutan in 2016.

« **BEFORE**

Royal tours in the past used to be very different from today, both in protocol and duration.

SEASONED TRAVELLERS
Partly due to the limitations of the transport available, overseas tours for the royals used to last comparatively **longer**. The Queen's post-coronation tour of the Commonwealth famously lasted six months. Touring royals would leave their children behind for long periods. Strict observation of royal protocol imposed much greater **restrictions on public interaction** with royal travellers in the past; the public was expected to keep their distance.

THE QUEEN'S 1953-54 COMMONWEALTH TOUR

Royal Ambassadors

The 2010s and 2020s have increasingly seen younger generations of royals stepping up to take on more duties and representing the Queen and the Royal Family at home and abroad. They use all the channels available in the modern era, from personal appearances to social media.

Although the Queen has remained remarkably active in her 90s, she inevitably started to wind down her public duties and engagements, beginning with her overseas trips; she took her last long-haul flight in 2015. The younger generations of royals have stepped up to fill her shoes, moulding and evolving their approaches to meet the challenges and opportunities of the modern era. From Prince Charles and his siblings to the Queen's grandchildren and their heirs, the younger royals have acted as the Queen's ambassadors in foreign lands and on new frontiers.

Double act

As the princes, William and Harry, matured and married, their portfolios of duties and causes evolved, and they began to increasingly deputize for their father and grandmother. At first, the two princes undertook some duties in concert, such as their joint goodwill tour of southern Africa in June 2010. During this tour, their relaxed and friendly manner with the public won them admirers wherever they went. In Botswana, the brothers saw at first hand the work of Tusk – a wildlife conservation organization that William supports. They travelled on to Lesotho, where Harry showed his brother some of the projects carried out by Sentebale – the charity he cofounded with Prince Seeiso of Lesotho to help vulnerable children and orphans. At the end of the tour, both brothers watched England play in a World Cup soccer match.

Following William's marriage, William, Catherine, and Harry formed a crowd-pleasing trio, supporting causes such as mental-health charities.

In 2012, Harry made his first solo official overseas tour when he visited Belize, the Bahamas, and Jamaica on behalf of the Queen during her Diamond Jubilee year. While carrying out his public duties, he delighted his hosts by completely entering into the spirit of the celebrations – joining in dances at street parties and playing football with the local children. In Jamaica, he took part in a mock race against champion sprinter Usain Bolt. The enormous success of Harry's trips, and the popularity of William and Catherine, gave the young royals a unique and immense celebrity status, investing royal outreach with a new kind of power. This power became amplified with the addition of Harry's new partner Meghan, Duchess of Sussex. For a time, it looked as though the future pattern of core royal engagement with the public was set, with Prince Charles and the Duchess of Cornwall as the senior, more sober central players, backed by the more informal twin double acts of William and Catherine and Harry and Meghan. Their post-marriage tours Down Under, in 2014 and 2018 respectively, were hugely popular. Harry and Meghan's schedule on their 2018 tour, which packed an exhausting 76 engagements into just 16 days, showed just how gruelling these royal visits could be.

Seen to be believed

However, before long, this pattern would have to evolve once more. Harry and Meghan's decision to step back from royal duties, together with Prince Andrew's enforced withdrawal from public life and the restrictions imposed by the Covid-19 pandemic on the Queen, have forced a radical reappraisal of how the core of active royals is constituted. Charles and Camilla and William and Catherine have become more central than ever while Prince Edward and Sophie, Countess of Wessex, have stepped up to assume greater prominence alongside the always hard-working Princess Royal. Describing the outlook of what some have dubbed the New Firm, a palace source said that

671 **The number of gifts Prince George received on his visit to New Zealand and Australia.**

Embracing traditional cultures
Prince Charles and Camilla, Duchess of Cornwall, pose with traditionally attired Croatian dancers during their 2016 tour of the Balkans, which included Croatia, Serbia, Montenegro, and Kosovo.

"the family are united in exploring the possibilities in working with each other to highlight the causes dear to their hearts, helping each other and the country at the same time." The guiding hand behind this new dispensation has been the Queen herself. Her oft-repeated dictum has been that the Royal Family "needs to be seen to be believed", that is, it is through public engagement that the royals can maintain their relevance and purpose in the modern world.

To this end, Charles and Camilla undertook significant initiatives, visiting Germany for Remembrance Day in November 2020, representing the Queen at the Cenotaph memorial, meeting with Greta Thunberg to discuss the global climate crisis, and launching the Sustainable Market Initiative. Meanwhile, William and Catherine mixed telepresence through technology with old-fashioned personal visits, video-calling health-care workers and touring Wales and Scotland during the pandemic. More generally, the Palace has increasingly embraced the possibilities of digital media in the service of the Queen's mission statement about staying visible. In 2016, the new Royal.uk site – "the home of the Royal Family" – was launched, with an emphasis on compatibility with mobile devices, a factor that is of particular importance in communicating with the Commonwealth, where nearly 60 per cent of the population is under the age of 30 and mobile communication is predominant. On average, more than 12 million people globally visit the Royal website each year.

Social networking

The royals have also embraced social media. The official Twitter account of the Duke and Duchess of Cambridge and their Royal Foundation has almost 1.7 million followers, and their Instagram account boasts 7.1 million followers. The Royal Family has 3.8 million followers on Twitter, 4.5 million on Instagram, and its Facebook page has 4.8 million likes. However, neither Catherine nor Meghan have personal social media accounts. Even the Queen has modernized her communication style; in December 2020, she held her first-ever virtual diplomatic meeting, granting a royal audience to three foreign ambassadors who visited Buckingham Palace while she was at Windsor Castle. A video screen was positioned on a wooden cabinet so the Queen could be telepresent for her special guests.

"He's **cool,** very **down to earth...** you think it will be difficult but **he just wanted to laugh.**"

USAIN BOLT, ON HIS MEETING WITH PRINCE HARRY IN JAMAICA, 2012

AFTER »

New wave
The Duke and Duchess of Sussex demonstrate the less formal style of the younger royals while talking to members of OneWave, a mental-health awareness group, on South Bondi Beach in Sydney, Australia, in 2018.

Modern royal tours tend to be relatively short and densely packed, yet also much less formal, with more fun and spontaneity.

RELAXED AND CASUAL
Royal tours have got steadily **shorter** over the years. For example, while Charles and Diana's tour of Australia and New Zealand in 1983 lasted 41 days, William and Catherine undertook a trip with a similar itinerary in 2014 in just 18 days. This is partly a result of better air travel, and partly dictated by the **needs of royal children**. While the Queen left behind her infants for months, young royals now typically accompany their parents, or if this is not possible, royals sometimes undertake solo visits so that one parent can stay at home with the children. Moreover, the younger royals **interact with the public** in ways that would have been unthinkable to their grandparents, giving hugs and even posing for selfies with the public.

The Queen's Grandchildren

Queen Elizabeth II and Prince Philip, the Duke of Edinburgh, have eight grandchildren and eight great-grandchildren, with two more expected in 2021. The Queen enjoys being in their company and is said to "light up" when they are around.

Family life is very important to Elizabeth II. Each year, her children and grandchildren – now with great-grandchildren in tow – gather for summer holidays at Balmoral, where the younger cousins enjoy family picnics, pony trekking, and other outdoor activities. The family also gets together for Christmas at Sandringham and for Easter at Windsor Castle. The Queen taught all her grandchildren to ride although advancing years limit her ability to do the same for her great-grandchildren. She loves to share jokes with the younger generations and, like so many grandparents, possibly allows them more leeway than she gave her own children, to whom she is sometimes said to have been a rather remote mother.

For princes William (b.1982) and Harry (b.1984), both grandparents provided stability, support, and protection, especially during the difficult years when their parents, Charles and Diana, divorced and after the painful loss of their mother. As they grew into adulthood, the Queen became an even more important part of the princes' lives, and they both look to her for approval and advice. "My relationship with the Queen has gone from strength to strength", William has said, explaining that he sometimes found it hard to talk to her about weighty matters when he was younger but now finds it much easier. Prince Harry, too, has a good rapport with the

BEFORE

The best-known royal grandmother in British history was Queen Victoria, who had a total of 20 grandsons and 22 granddaughters, the eldest born in 1859 and the youngest in 1891.

THE GRANDMOTHER OF EUROPE

Victoria's children married into many of Europe's royal houses « 51. Her grandchildren included King George V of Great Britain, the German Emperor Wilhelm II, the wife of Tsar Nicholas II, the last ruler of Russia, and the consorts of the kings of Romania, Greece, Norway, and Spain. **Queen Victoria** was a **carrier of haemophilia,** a genetic disorder that prevents blood clotting. It is passed on by women but mostly occurs in men. Through three of Victoria's carrier daughters, haemophilia spread into many of the royal families of Europe.

VICTORIA WITH PRINCE ARTHUR AND PRINCESS MARGARET OF CONNAUGHT

The Queen and her grandchildren
This family portrait – taken on holiday in the grounds of Balmoral in 1998 – shows the Queen and Prince Philip with five of their grandchildren, left to right: Harry, Eugenie, William, Beatrice, and Zara.

Queen and has spoken warmly of her. Although he and his family have now relocated to California, even during the Covid-19 pandemic they make sure to keep little Archie in touch with his great-grandmother via video calls, such as on the occasion of her 94th birthday.

Princess Anne's children

The Queen's eldest grandchildren are Peter Phillips (b.1977) and Zara Phillips (b.1981), the son and daughter of Princess Anne and her first husband, Captain Mark Phillips. In 2021, they are 16th and 19th in the line of succession to the throne but do not have royal titles as they are the grandchildren of the monarch through the female line. Both their parents were Olympic equestrians – Mark Phillips competed

Balcony gathering
Autumn and Peter Phillips, and their children, Savannah and Isla, stand on the balcony of Buckingham Palace after watching the ceremony of the Trooping of the Colour on 8 June 2019. Sadly, the couple announced their divorce a few months later.

Catholic to succeed to the throne; the bar has since been removed by the Succession to the Crown Act of 2013. Peter and Autumn have two daughters. In 2020, they announced that they were going to divorce, a decision they described as "sad [but] amicable".

Like her parents, Zara is an accomplished equestrian. She was Eventing World Champion in 2006 and part of the British eventing team that won the team silver medal at the 2012 Olympics in London. She is nearest in age to William and Harry among the royal cousins and is godmother to William and Catherine's son, Prince George. As a young royal with a rebellious streak (aged 17, she sported a tongue piercing at Prince Charles's 50th birthday), she was frequently in the gossip magazines. In 2011, she married the former international rugby player and England captain Mike Tindall at Canongate Kirk in Edinburgh. They have two daughters and are expecting a third child in 2021.

The young Yorks

Princess Beatrice (b.1988) and Princess Eugenie (b.1990), the daughters of

Andrew and Sarah, the Duke and Duchess of York, are currently 9th and 10th in line to the throne. They are both styled Her Royal Highness as the granddaughters of the monarch through the male line. The Duke and Duchess agreed to joint custody of the daughters after their divorce and shared responsibility for their upbringing. Princess Beatrice, who is dyslexic, attended St George's School, Ascot – an independent girls' day school. She went on to study history at Goldsmiths College, University of London, and graduated in 2011. She was the first member of the Royal Family to complete the London Marathon and is patron of a number of charities and organizations, particularly those working to improve the lives of young people. She is famous for the unusual hat she wore to the wedding of Prince William and Catherine Middleton; she later offered it for auction on eBay, where it raised £81,000 for charity. Beatrice's career has included stints in the movie business and in digital services. In July 2020, she married British property developer Edoardo Mapelli Mozzi.

Princess Eugenie was a boarder at Marlborough College in Wiltshire. She graduated from Newcastle University in 2012 with a degree in English literature and history of art. She had corrective orthopaedic surgery as a girl because of a congenital spinal condition and is now closely involved with the fundraising appeal for the Royal National Orthopaedic Hospital. Eugenie works full-time as a director at a prestigious London art gallery, Hauser & Wirth. In October 2018 she married her long-term boyfriend, Jack Brooksbank,

> The Queen and the Duke of Edinburgh first became great-grandparents in 2010. In early 2021, they were great-grandparents eight times over, with two more on the way.

THE NEXT GENERATION
Elizabeth II's **eldest great-grandchild, Savannah Anne Kathleen,** the daughter of Peter and Autumn Phillips, was born in September 2010. The Queen attended her baptism at Holy Cross Church, Avening, in Gloucestershire. Their second daughter, **Isla Elizabeth,** was born to the couple in March 2012. The Queen's **first great-grandson, Prince George** of Cambridge, son of the Duke and Duchess of Cambridge, was born in July 2013. His third cousin, **Mia Grace Tindall,** daughter of Zara and Mike Tindall, was born in January 2014. George's younger sister, **Charlotte,** was born in May 2015, followed by **Louis** in April 2018. Zara and Mike Tindall's second daughter, **Lena Elizabeth,** was born in June 2018. Archie Harrison Mountbatten-Windsor, son of the Duke and Duchess of Sussex, was born in May 2019.

THE QUEEN'S GREAT-GRANDCHILDREN IN 2018

"When the **Queen** says **well done,** it **means so much.**"

PRINCE WILLIAM, IN AN INTERVIEW WITH ROBERT HARDMAN IN 2011

at Munich, Germany, in 1972, and Princess Anne at Montreal, Canada, in 1976 (see pp.186–87) – so it is not surprising that Peter and Zara both developed a strong interest in sport from an early age. They were kept out of the limelight as children and, so far, are the only grandchildren of the Duke of Edinburgh to attend his old school, Gordonstoun, in Scotland (see pp.124–25).

Peter studied sports science at the University of Exeter and pursued a career in sports sponsorship management, working for a time for the Williams Formula 1 racing team. He now works in event management. In 2008, he married Canadian-born business consultant Autumn Kelly, whom he met at the Canadian Grand Prix in Montreal. She was a Roman Catholic but became a member of the Church of England so that Peter would not have to give up his place in the line of succession. At that time, a clause of the 1701 Act of Settlement made it illegal for anyone married to a Roman

Edward and his children
Prince Edward with his children, Lady Louise Windsor and James, Viscount Severn, wait for Sophie, Countess of Wessex, to finish a gruelling charity cycle ride in September 2016, when the children were 12 and 7 respectively.

at St George's Chapel in Windsor. In September 2020, the couple revealed they were expecting their first child, who will be 11th in line to the throne.

The Earl of Wessex's children
The Queen's youngest grandchildren are Lady Louise Windsor (b.2003) and James, Viscount Severn (b.2007). The children of the Earl and Countess of Wessex, they are currently 13th and 14th in line of succession but do not have royal titles – a decision made upon their parents' marriage, when Prince Edward chose to become an earl rather than a royal duke (see p.251).

Louise was born prematurely at Frimley Park Hospital in Surrey after her mother was rushed there as a medical emergency. Louise was a bridesmaid at the wedding of Prince William and Catherine Middleton. She is frequently seen at royal occasions such as Trooping the Colour, and she attended the Diamond Jubilee river pageant with her brother. James was born by Caesarean section at the same hospital. The Queen is said to be very fond of both children and goes riding with them in Windsor Great Park.

Born 1926

Elizabeth II, the Later Years

"You can **do a lot** if you are **properly trained.**"

QUEEN ELIZABETH II

Queen Elizabeth II is said to have been taken aback by the degree of affection shown to her by the public during her Golden Jubilee year in 2002. The previous two decades had been difficult for the Royal Family, for the institution of monarchy, and for the Queen personally. She had seen three of her children's marriages fail under the glare of publicity, while she herself was subjected to an unprecedented storm of criticism after the death of Diana, Princess of Wales in 1997. At the height of these troubles, the Royal Family was held up to ridicule in the satirical puppet show *Spitting Image*, one of the most popular television comedies of the 1980s and 1990s. It even featured caricatures of the Queen as well as the Queen Mother, and Prince Philip, something that would have been unthinkable in the early years of her reign.

The Queen successfully weathered all these storms, and public respect continues to grow from year to year for the way she carries out her role as monarch, for her devotion to duty, and for her personal qualities of steadfast strength, good humour, and courtesy. In part, of course, this is due

to the Queen's longevity – she is now 95 years old, yet still carries out a punishing daily work schedule,long after the age most people have opted for retirement. However, it owes even more to the Queen's own willingness to adapt to change. She has reformed the monarchy quite substantially. In

At dinner with the Queen
Queen Elizabeth and Prince Philip welcome US President Barack Obama and his wife Michelle to a state banquet at Buckingham Palace on 24 May 2011.

1992, she offered to start paying income tax and capital gains tax on her private wealth. She opened her official residences, including Buckingham Palace, to the public in an effort to finance their upkeep. She

295 The number of the Queen's official engagements in 2019, despite being 93 years old.

Indefatigable monarch
Into her late 80s and 90s, the Queen, seen here arriving for Ladies Day at the Royal Ascot race meeting in 2014, has remained active, with a busy schedule.

supported measures to end the law of male primogeniture, which means that the eldest child of the sovereign can succeed to the throne, regardless of gender, as well as lifting the bar preventing anyone who is

Act of remembrance
The Queen pays tribute to all those who died serving their country at the national Service of Remembrance held at the Cenotaph in Whitehall in November every year.

married to a Roman Catholic from standing in the line of succession to the throne.

Personal style

The Queen has developed a personal style of dress that has served her well over the years. A two-piece suit, or dress and coat, for daytime engagements, usually in a single colour and ending just below the knees. A large hat with swept back brim to show her face, low-heeled shoes, and a handbag (no one knows what she keeps in it). She almost invariably wears a pearl necklace and has a brooch pinned to her lapel. On formal occasions, such as state banquets, she sparkles in beaded gowns, with the Garter Sash worn from the left shoulder, and diamond jewellery.

Queen Elizabeth has sometimes been accused of looking grumpy in public – she has said of herself that she has the kind of face that, when not smiling, tends to look cross. In recent years, however, she has been seen laughing and smiling more than she did formerly. She has sat for over 240 official portraits in the course of her reign.

Countrywoman

In 1986 the Queen told BBC producer Eddie Mirzoeff, who was making a documentary about the Royal Family, that she did sometimes begrudge some of the hours she has to do when she could be outdoors instead. It was a refreshingly honest admission – the Queen is at heart a countrywoman, and likes nothing

First past the post
The Queen possesses a formidable knowledge of horseracing. She is seen here congratulating her filly Estimate, winner of the Gold Cup at Ascot in June 2013.

better than going for long country walks with her dogs at Balmoral, although she stopped breeding them in 2014, and by 2020 had only one

though in later years she preferred to be mounted on sturdy fell ponies from the north of England – known for their steady temperament and sure-footedness (she is patron of the Fell Pony Society). It is public knowledge that the Queen never wears a hard riding hat, preferring a silk headscarf. Her daughter Princess Anne, her grooms, and ROSPA (the Royal Society for the Prevention of Accidents) have all remonstrated with her about it, but she takes no notice.

The Queen loves horse racing, and has a deep knowledge of breeding and bloodlines. She owns 25–30 racehorses and tries to see them run as often as she can. She is at her most relaxed at a race meeting and has won all the major Classic races, except for the

> "The **true measure** of all our **actions** is how long the **good** in them **last... everything** we do, we do **for the young.**"
>
> QUEEN ELIZABETH II, 70TH ANNIVERSARY OF D-DAY, JUNE 2014

canine companion remaining: Candy, a corgi-dachshund cross. She loves being surrounded by her grandchildren and great-grandchildren (see pp.296–97). Her passion for horses is well known. At the age of 94 she was still riding,

Epsom Derby, as an owner. In 2011, her horse Carlton House was the favourite to win the Derby, but was beaten into third place. The Queen's excitement, and disappointment at the outcome, was plain to see.

TIMELINE

- **17 October 1980** State visit to the Vatican.
- **17 April 1982** Signs the Canadian Constitution Act in Ottawa, surrendering the right of the British Parliament to make laws affecting Canada.
- **9 July 1982** An intruder, Michael Fagan, enters the Queen's bedroom in Buckingham Palace, raising questions about security.
- **1985** The Queen and members of the Royal Family are caricatured on the TV satirical puppet show *Spitting Image*.

THE QUEEN'S 60TH BIRTHDAY COMMEMORATIVE STAMPS

- **October 1986** Visits China, becoming the first British monarch to do so.
- **16 May 1991** Becomes the first British monarch to address a joint meeting of the United States Congress.
- **20 November 1992** Windsor Castle is damaged by fire at the end of the Queen's *annus horribilis*.
- **1993** Pays income tax for the first time.
- **20 December 1995** Advises Charles and Diana that a divorce is desirable.
- **September 1997** Is criticized by the media for her apparent lack of feeling on Diana's death.
- **8 November 2010** Joins Facebook with the launch of a British Monarchy page.
- **29 December 2010** Birth of the Queen's first great-grandchild, Savannah Phillips, daughter of Peter and Autumn Phillips.
- **May 2011** Visits the Republic of Ireland, a historic turning point in the troubled relations between Ireland and the UK.
- **October 2011** Carries out what is probably her last visit to Australia, the 16th of her reign.
- **2 June 2012** Starts off the Diamond Jubilee celebrations by attending the Epsom Derby.
- **28 July 2012** Opens the Summer Olympic Games in London.
- **June 2014** Makes a state visit to France on the occasion of the 70th anniversary of the D-Day landings.
- **9 September 2015** Becomes longest reigning UK monarch.
- **21 April 2016** Celebrates her 90th birthday.
- **20 November 2017** The Queen and Prince Philip celebrate their 70th wedding anniversary.

The Invictus Games

Prince Harry was the driving force behind the Invictus Games, a Paralympic-style championship for wounded servicemen and women. After attending the Warrior Games in the US in May 2013, where he witnessed the courage and determination of those taking part, he decided to bring a similar event to Britain.

Modelled on the Warrior Games – an annual sports event for injured service members and veterans in the US – the Invictus Games were organized in only 10 months. Funding came equally from the Royal Foundation – established by the Duke and Duchess of Cambridge and Prince Harry – and from the Treasury.

At the official launch in March 2014, Harry said, "I have witnessed first-hand how the power of sport can actively impact the lives of wounded, injured, and sick servicemen and women in their journey of recovery." Six months later, Prince Charles, the Duchess of Cornwall, Prince William, and Prime Minister David Cameron were there to see Harry, as founder of the Games, welcome more than 400 competitors from 13 countries to the Queen Elizabeth Olympic Park in east London. The countries taking part included eight from Europe, one from Asia, two from North America, and two from Oceania. All had fought alongside Britain in recent military campaigns. Iraq was invited to send a team, but declined to do so.

Invictus is Latin for "undefeated". At the opening ceremony, actor Idris Elba read the short poem *Invictus* by the Victorian poet William Ernest Henley, with its inspiring lines: "My head is bloody, but unbowed… I am the master of my fate, I am the captain of my soul." Over the next four days, events were held at five different venues used during the 2012 London Olympics. Serving personnel as well as veterans injured in the line of duty competed in nine different adaptive sports: archery, indoor rowing, power lifting, road cycling, sitting volleyball, swimming, wheelchair basketball, and wheelchair rugby. Prince Harry attended every single event. Further editions of the Games followed in 2016, 2017, and 2018, with more planned for 2021 and 2023.

"I have no doubt that **lives will be changed** this weekend."

PRINCE HARRY, IN HIS OPENING SPEECH AT THE INVICTUS GAMES, 10 SEPTEMBER 2014

Star-studded event
Harry and his cousin Zara Tindall, daughter of Princess Anne, compete in an exhibition game of wheelchair rugby. Other sporting stars who took part in the Invictus Games included Zara's husband Mike Tindall and British Olympic legends Dame Kelly Holmes and Denise Lewis.

The **Queen** as **Patron**

Outside the pomp of a royal ceremony or state visit, the public is most familiar with the Queen in her role as patron, visiting a hospital, school, or organization, or hosting a reception in aid of one of her many charities.

Garden party event
The Queen greets Andy Reid, an injured Afghanistan veteran, at a garden party held at Buckingham Palace for the "Not Forgotten" Association – a charity that helps ex-service personnel.

Queen Elizabeth II is patron of more than 600 organizations and charities. These range from large medical charities such as Cancer Research and the British Red Cross to smaller organizations such as the Friends of the Elderly and the Fire Fighters Charity. Many scientific and professional institutions – such as the Royal Society, the Royal Institute of British Architects, and the Royal Society for the Protection of Birds – have royal charters that ensure that the reigning monarch is always their patron, but the Queen also supports scores of small charities such as the Reedham Trust, a Surrey-based charity that cares for children who have suffered parental bereavement, the Manchester Geographical Society, which encourages geographical research in the northwest of England, and the Society for Promoting Christian Knowledge, the Church of England's earliest missionary society, established in 1698 to support Christian education.

Her Majesty is patron of the National Federation of Women's Institutes, founded in 1915 to revitalize rural communities and encourage women to play a part in food production. For many years, she attended the New Year meeting of her local branch at West Newton, Norfolk, while staying at Sandringham for her winter break. The Queen also supports a large number of animal welfare charities – from the Dog Trust and the Royal Society for the Prevention of Cruelty to Animals (RSPCA) to the Fell Pony Society and the Labrador Retriever Club.

Kinds of support

The support the Queen gives to each of her charities varies according to its type, set up, and the kind of work it does. As patron, she allows her name to be placed at the head of the organization's official communications, thereby helping to raise its public profile and promote its work. The officers of the organization may be invited from time to time to a meeting with the Queen or one of her private secretaries to report on its affairs, or she will send a representative to its annual general meeting – or even attend herself, if there is an important occasion such as a centenary to be observed. She visits national and regional headquarters, meeting staff and volunteers.

The Queen also allows individual charities to hold a lunchtime or evening reception at Buckingham Palace, Windsor Castle, or Holyrood Palace when she is in Scotland. It gives wealthy supporters of a charity the chance to meet their patron, and helps to attract donors and publicity. Sometimes the help the Queen gives a charity is of a strictly practical nature – for instance, the gift of a Land Rover to aid the work of the Leonard Cheshire Trust, which is involved with people with disabilities in Zimbabwe. She invites representatives from the many organizations she supports to the garden parties she hosts each summer at Buckingham Palace as a way of showing her appreciation for the work they do. She also gives generously as a private individual to various charities.

Raising awareness

The Queen's presence at an event or organization attracts national attention. For example, she carried out a joint engagement with the Duchess of Cornwall to open the new headquarters of Barnardo's in 2013. The Queen has been patron of the society, which supports 200,000 vulnerable children in the UK each year, since 1983 and the Duchess of Cornwall is its president. As their visit took place just before Christmas, they were invited to take part in the society's annual Giving Tree campaign by donating Christmas tree baubles. The event received newspaper and television coverage, creating favourable publicity for the charity.

£1.4 BILLION The annual amount raised by the various charities supported by the Queen.

Sharing the work

Some 14 members of the Royal Family share the work of royal patronage with the Queen, supporting a total of 2,415 organizations in the UK, and almost 3,000 worldwide. Individual members of the Royal Family support those charities that they consider to be rewarding or important, and which fall within their own areas of interest and concern. Their endorsement of a charity helps to raise public awareness of its work. At the time of his retirement, the Duke of Edinburgh alone was patron of more than 700 organizations, including more than 250 involved with sport and recreation initiatives, and 100 with the armed services. The Prince of Wales has an interest in environmental causes and the built environment, while the Duchess of Cornwall is concerned with schemes to encourage literacy and reading, such as Booktrust and First Story. She is President of the National Osteoporosis Society, which researches the brittle bone disease that affected both her mother and grandmother.

« BEFORE

The annual distribution of Maundy money by the Queen is a form of royal charity that has its origins in the Middle Ages.

ROYAL MAUNDY SERVICE

Every **Maundy Thursday** (the day in the church calendar before Good Friday) the Queen visits a **cathedral** to present local elderly people with two purses, one containing **modern** coinage, and the other, **specially minted** coins (Maundy money). The ceremony is based on Jesus Christ's command (*Mandatum*) to love one another when he washed his disciples' feet at the Last Supper and dates back to the 13th century when the sovereign would give money, food, clothing, and wash the recipient's feet.

MAUNDY MONEY OF GEORGE VI

Lifeboat naming
As patron of the Royal National Lifeboat Institution (RNLI) the Queen names a new all-weather lifeboat, RNLB *Richard Cox Scott*, in Falmouth Harbour during her Golden Jubilee visit to Cornwall in May 2002.

The number of charities supported by the Queen and the other members of the Royal Family is increasing every year.

REQUESTS FOR PATRONAGE
Charities are aware that having **a royal patron helps to attract much-needed publicity and funds,** and gives it recognition and status. Buckingham Palace receives **hundreds of requests for patronage** each year. Individual members of the Royal Family can only take on a limited number of new requests, but the younger royals in particular are championing lesser-known causes, rather than the mainstream charities.

One of the hardest working members of the Royal Family is Princess Anne, who is currently patron of more than 300 organizations. As President, and now Patron, of Save the Children since 1970, she has helped to raise awareness of the charity and its work, both at home and overseas. She makes at least two field trips a year to Africa to witness the work carried out by the charity, often venturing into remote terrain.

Prince William and Prince Harry have both inherited Diana, Princess of Wales's compassionate concern. Prince William has taken over some his mother's favourite charities, including Centrepoint, which works with homeless young people, and the Royal Marsden Hospital. He and Catherine chose to support charitable causes as part of their wedding celebrations as well.

They particularly support those causes concerned with children. The Duchess of Cambridge's growing portfolio of charities includes Place2Be, which works in schools to provide early-intervention mental health support, and sports charities such as SportsAid and the Lawn Tennis Association. Harry founded the Invictus Games and supports conservation and mental

health charities, while he and Meghan have set up the Archewell foundation, dedicated to building compassionate communities.

Traditional charity
The Queen distributed Maundy money at Blackburn Cathedral in 2014. The number of recipients is determined by her age – as she was 88 that year, she gave Maundy money to 88 men and 88 women.

The centenary of World War I
Queen Elizabeth II visits the *Blood Swept Lands and Seas of Red* display of 888,246 ceramic poppies at the Tower of London in 2014. Each poppy represented a fallen British soldier from World War I.

« BEFORE

The working life of the sovereign has changed over the centuries. Many duties the Queen carries out today have evolved in the last 100 years.

ROYAL MEDDLER
Queen Victoria « 50–55 interfered in government in a way that would be impossible now, peppering her ministers with letters of advice and admonition, especially over foreign affairs and public appointments. She did not like appearing in public and after the death of Prince Albert in 1861, hardly ever did so, attending only seven **State Openings of Parliament** « 134–35 after that.

DUTIFUL MONARCH
Although **Edward VII** « 72–73 played a more public role, opening hospitals and other institutions, the modern concept of the working monarch really developed in the reign of **George V** « 78–79. No great intellect, he emphasised the **idea of duty**, believing that the primary role of the monarchy was to maintain traditional values and customs.

The Royal Working Life

Into her 90s, the Queen continues to carry out more than 300 official engagements a year, including the ceremonial duties she performs as head of state. Although she has been increasingly stepping back from public life, she still has a varied programme of work.

On a normal day, the Queen devotes the first part of her morning to her correspondence. She receives some 200–300 letters a day. The Queen glances through this postbag, selecting some to read, and tells her correspondence secretary or ladies in waiting how she wishes them to be answered. Virtually every letter receives a reply.

The Queen then meets with her two private secretaries and goes through the official papers that are sent each day in a government red box bearing the royal cypher. They include policy papers, Cabinet documents, and letters from government ministers and Commonwealth officials. They all have to be read and, where necessary, approved and signed. She may hold audiences (meetings) with overseas diplomats, British ambassadors, senior members of the armed forces, bishops, judges, and leading figures from the fields of science or literature. She sees each visitor alone, and the meeting usually lasts 20 minutes.

Around 25 times a year, and lately decreasing in number, the Queen holds an investiture at 11 am in the ballroom at Buckingham Palace at which she invests a number of people who have been named in the Birthday or New Year's Honours List with their awards (around 2,600 are given out a year). Sometimes Prince Charles, Prince William, or Princess Anne will hold an investiture on her behalf.

50,000 The number of people who visit Buckingham Palace each year as guests of the Queen.

Public engagements
The Queen usually carries out public engagements such as visits to schools, hospitals, community centres, and places of work in the afternoon. Although sometimes she spends a whole day, in which case she would, before his retirement from public life in 2017, have been accompanied by the Duke of Edinburgh. The Queen chooses which places to visit from the many invitations she is sent each year, often by the Lord-Lieutenants – the Queen's

Royal pageantry on show
The carriage procession for the state visit of Prathiba Patil, India's first female president, climbs the steep incline to Windsor Castle. Mrs Patil was the guest of the Queen in October 2009.

The Queen has recently begun to hand over some of her public duties, particularly overseas travel, to other members of the royal family.

SCALING DOWN

That the Queen undertook no overseas visits in her **Diamond Jubilee** year ❮❮ 280–83 was a sign that she is reducing long-distance travel due to her age. Most significant was her decision not to attend the **Commonwealth Heads of Government Meeting** held in Sri Lanka in 2013, the first time in 40 years she had not attended. **Prince Charles** went in her place, amid calls to boycott the event due to human rights violations in the host country. In 2015, the Queen made what seems likely to be her **final state visits overseas**, to Berlin in June and then, revisiting old haunts, to Malta in November.

personal representatives in each county of the United Kingdom.

When she is in London, the Queen's weekly meeting with the Prime Minister takes place on Wednesdays at 6.30 pm. When Parliament is sitting she receives a report of the day's proceedings written by one of the government's whips, which she reads the same evening. Later in the evening the Queen may, on rare instances, attend a film première, concert, or reception on behalf of one of the many organizations of which she is patron. She also hosts official receptions at the Palace, such as those held annually for the diplomatic corps and those for winners of the Queen's Award

The Court Circular

A list of the Queen's engagements, and those of other members of her family, is published the next day in the Court Circular. This appears in *The Times*, the *Daily Telegraph* and *The Scotsman* newspapers, and has been in existence since 1803 when George III appointed a "court newsman". His job was to provide the newspapers with accurate

information about the court in order to counter the many false rumours in the press at that time. The Court Circular is prepared in the Queen's press office, and she always approves it before it is sent to the newspapers.

State visits

Foreign heads of state are invited by the Queen to make a formal visit to Britain on the advice of the Foreign and Commonwealth Office, with the aim of strengthening ties and building economic links. There are usually two such visits a year. The visit normally begins with a ceremonial welcome by the Queen or other senior royal. If in London, the visitor inspects a guard of honour on Horse Guards Parade, then travels in a carriage procession to Buckingham Palace. In the evening the Queen hosts a state banquet in honour of the visitor. Recent visiting heads of state have included the King and Queen of the Netherlands in 2018, and the President and First Lady of the United States in 2019.

Head of the armed forces

As sovereign the Queen is head of the armed forces, a duty she takes very seriously. Under the royal prerogative, only the monarch, acting on the advice of the Government, can declare war or peace. The Queen has never done so as there has been no formal declaration of war since 1939, though British troops have engaged in numerous armed conflicts during her reign. The Queen takes a keen interest in the armed forces of the UK and the Commonwealth. She visits army, navy,

Duke of Normandy
The Queen is known as the Duke of Normandy in the Channel Islands – self-governing territories with their own legislative assemblies that have belonged to the English crown since 1106. Here her head appears on a Jersey pound note.

for Enterprise (formerly Industry), which promotes business excellence.

Final parade
The Queen joins the Argyll and Sutherland Highlanders at their barracks in Canterbury, Kent. She was there as head of the army to witness the battalion's final parade.

"I… give my **heart** and devotion to **these islands.**"

QUEEN ELIZABETH II, CHRISTMAS BROADCAST, 1957

and air force establishments to meet servicemen and servicewomen of all ranks, and holds audiences with the Chief of Defence Staff and other senior military figures. She and members of her family hold appointments and honorary ranks in the armed forces, and she attends the Remembrance Day service in Whitehall in November.

There are many other duties, such as the State Opening of Parliament (see pp.308–309), that the Queen carries out as head of state. Many are full of symbolism, such as the annual service for the Order of the Garter, which takes place at Windsor Castle in June. The Garter is Britain's senior order of chivalry, founded by Edward III in 1348, and the service is preceded by a procession of all the Knights of the Garter in their blue velvet mantles and plumed hats.

One event the Queen always enjoys is the Chelsea Flower Show. Held in the grounds of the Royal Hospital, Chelsea, since 1913, and

organized by the Royal Horticultural Society, it has become a regular fixture in the royal calendar. Every summer the Queen hosts at least three garden parties at Buckingham Palace and one at Holyrood Palace in Edinburgh. About 8,000 people attend each one, to enjoy tea and cakes and possibly to meet the Queen. They are drawn from all walks of life and have usually contributed in some way to their community or profession.

In these, and countless other ways, the Queen fulfils her role as the head of the nation. And of course she is ready to carry out occasional tasks such as opening the Olympic Games. She has a truly formidable workload for anyone, let alone a nonagenarian.

The Order of the Garter
Four royal knights (Andrew, Edward, William, and Charles) attend the Order of the Garter service, Windsor Castle. The Queen is Sovereign of the Order, which has only 24 knights, plus the royal knights and ladies.

State Opening of Parliament
In her formal role as head of state, Queen Elizabeth II reads the Speech from the Throne at the State Opening of Parliament, a duty she usually performs once a year.

Happy birthday ma'am
The Queen accepts floral tributes from some of the hundreds of children who joined the throng of well-wishers during her birthday walkabout in Windsor.

« BEFORE

On 9 September, 2015, Elizabeth II became the longest-reigning British monarch, overtaking her great-great-grandmother, Queen Victoria.

RECORD BREAKER
The exact hour of the passing of her father, George VI, is unknown, and so it is not possible to say the precise minute at which Elizabeth II surpassed Victoria's reign. But it is known that at 17:30 on 9 September, she had reigned for at least 23,226 days, 16 hours and 30 minutes, outlasting Victoria.

TOWER BRIDGE OPENS TO THE THAMES FLOTILLA

JUST ANOTHER MILESTONE
The Queen herself insisted on carrying out her daily duties as normal, offering only a brief comment: "A long life can pass by many milestones – my own is no exception". While she and Prince Philip travelled by steam train to Tweedbank in Scotland to open a new railway, a flotilla of historic vessels, leisure cruisers, and passenger boats processed down the Thames in London.

The Queen's **90th Birthday** Celebrations

The nation, the Commonwealth and most of the rest of the world joined the festivities marking the life of a remarkable woman as she reached two significant milestones. Not long after becoming the longest-reigning British monarch, the Queen celebrated her 90th birthday.

On 20 April, 2016, the day before her birthday, the Queen started a programme of events that would stretch over the next 2 months by visiting the Royal Mail delivery office in the Royal Borough of Windsor. After meeting staff and viewing an exhibition marking the history of the service during her reign, she was serenaded by the Royal Mail choir, a group formed during a recent BBC television series. The Queen and the Duke of Edinburgh then moved on to Alexandra Gardens in Windsor to open a new bandstand, and listen to another choir: this time of children performing as part of a Shakespeare festival.

A lovely day
The Queen marked the actual day of her 90th birthday with celebrations in Windsor, beginning with one of her trademark walkabouts. She and Prince

Birthday beacon
One of the 1,000 or so beacons lit to mark the occasion of the Queen's 90th birthday, emblazoned with the royal monogram. The Queen herself lit the first beacon in Windsor on the evening of 21 April.

Philip walked from the Henry VIII Gate of Windsor Castle towards the statue of Queen Victoria at the foot of Castle Hill, where she unveiled a plaque marking the Queen's Walkway, a trail connecting 63 points of significance in the town of Windsor. The walkway was designed by the Outdoor Trust, with its length and waypoints symbolizing the record length of her reign. The Windsor walkway is one of hundreds across the Commonwealth, either planned or built. According to Hugo Vickers, chairman of The Outdoor Trust, Her Majesty "was terribly happy with the beautiful weather and the lovely occasion. She said that it was a lovely day". The Queen was also presented with a birthday cake baked by Nadiya Hussain, 2015 winner of the hit BBC television series *The Great British Bake Off*. Hussain had won plaudits for the way she represented Britain's Muslim community, and commentators noted that her role in the festivities was iconic of the changing face of Britain during the Queen's long reign. In the evening of the 21st, Her Majesty lit the first of a chain of more than 1,000 beacons, stretching across Britain and the rest of the world, ranging from specially built gas-fired structures to simple bonfires.

Lunch with the Obamas

The day after her birthday, the Queen and the Duke of Edinburgh hosted the President and First Lady of the United

thought that the President had grabbed the wheel, and later Barack Obama joked that although he had "never been driven by a Duke of Edinburgh before", he could "report that it was very smooth riding." Speaking after the two couples had enjoyed an intimate lunch, President Obama paid tribute to the Queen, calling her "one of my favourite people", and remarking, "The Queen's been a source of inspiration for me like so many people around the world... should we be fortunate enough to reach 90, may we be as vibrant as she is."

6.373 KM (3.96 miles) is the length of the Queen's Walkway and refers to the length of her reign on completion – 63 years, 7 months, and 3 days – one day more than Queen Victoria's reign.

Mr President, I presume
The Queen and the Duke of Edinburgh greet US president Barack Obama as he steps out of *Marine One*, the presidential helicopter, onto the lawn of Windsor Castle.

Katherine Jenkins, and lots and lots of horses. In one scene, Kinvara Turner, a 13-year old with a passion for horses, played the young Princess Elizabeth learning to ride on a black fell pony, one of the Queen's favourite breeds. Spectacular stunts by equine performers from Oman, Chile, Canada, and Azerbaijan culminated in a procession of some of the Queen's own horses, ridden by members of her family including her daughter Princess Anne, the Princess Royal, and her granddaughter, the Olympic equestrian Zara Tindall. One of the event's narrators, television personality and author Alan Titchmarsh, commented, "I don't think this will ever happen again, it's a real one-off occasion."

" She is an **astonishing person** and a real jewel to the world, and not just the United Kingdom."

BARACK OBAMA, 22 APRIL, 2016

States as Barack and Michelle Obama dropped in for lunch at Windsor. Arriving from London in the helicopter *Marine One*, the Obamas were greeted on the lawn of the Windsor Estate by the royal couple, and comedy ensued when Prince Philip drove the party back to the castle. First, the visiting American press pack, forgetting that in Britain the driver sits on the right,

The Long Walk pageant
In an arena set along Windsor Great Park's Long Walk, pyrotechnics, lasers, and video technology combined with human and equine performers, including the Royal Cavalry of Oman, to produce a stunning display.

The Windsor pageant

Each year the royal estate at Windsor plays host to the Royal Windsor Horse Show, and in May 2016 it culminated in a unique and dazzling celebration of the Queen's 90th birthday. Although initial omens for the gala concert were gloomy, with a scheduled preview washed out by heavy rain, on the evening of 15 May, a galaxy of stars and extraordinary equine performers combined to produce one of the most memorable spectacles of the monarch's long reign. In a purpose-built arena, thousands of spectators watched a 90-minute show featuring 900 horses and more than 1,500 participants.

The Queen, accompanied by the Duke of Edinburgh, arrived in the Scottish State Coach. She wore a sea-green dress with a lace overlay and a matching jacket, all made by her dressmaker Angela Kelly, with a turquoise diamond-surround brooch. To cheers from the 6,000-strong crowd she took her seat in the royal box, joining the Prince of Wales and the Duke of York, together with the Duke and Duchess of Cambridge and Prince Harry. They were treated to a moving and exciting journey through the story of her reign, featuring actors including Dame Helen Mirren, singing stars including Dame Shirley Bassey and

25,000 tickets for the four-night Royal Windsor Horse Show pageant sold out within hours.

17,420 pieces of post arrived for the Queen in her birthday week in April, including birthday cards and gifts.

AFTER

On 23 May, the Queen took the Duke and Duchess of Cambridge on their first visit to the Royal Horticultural Society's Chelsea Flower Show.

A TOUCH OF GREEN
It was the 51st time that Her Majesty had visited the show, a celebrated annual institution on the British social calendar. Both the Queen and the Duchess wore green, with Kate in a striking green coat by Chelsea-based designer Catherine Walker, while the Queen wore a subtle shade of peppermint, in an outfit made by Angela Kelly.

BIRTHDAY ARCH
Along with other members of the Royal Family, including the Duke of Edinburgh, the Countess of Wessex, and Prince Harry, the Queen admired the magnificent floral arch installed at the show's entrance in honour of her birthday. The Duchess of Cambridge was moved by the *5,000 Poppies* exhibit in the grounds of the Royal Hospital Chelsea, which used almost 300,000 individually crocheted poppies to create a tribute to honour servicemen and women in the armed forces.

Thanksgiving Service
at St Paul's Cathedral

On 10 June 2016, the occasion of the Queen's official 90th birthday, London's iconic St Paul's Cathedral hosted a moving and celebratory National Service of Thanksgiving for the life and service of Elizabeth II.

The Queen was accompanied at the service by the Duke of Edinburgh, the very day that he celebrated his own 95th birthday, along with 51 other family members, including the Duke and Duchess of Cambridge and Prince Harry. Dressed in one of her trademark bright dresses – this time in yellow – she arrived uncharacteristically late, having been held up by the traffic. Greeted with a fanfare of trumpets, she joined 2,000 guests including politicians, faith leaders, and members of the public nominated by the government to recognize their service.

Among the many tributes paid to her, the Dean of St Paul's, David Ison, thanked the Queen for her "gentle constancy, royal dignity, and kindly humanity". Prime Minister David Cameron read a passage from the Bible, while broadcaster Sir David Attenborough read a piece written by *Paddington Bear* creator Michael Bond, both men having been born in the same year as the Queen. Bond's piece, on "the passing of the years", reflected with humour but also gravity on the challenges experienced by those born in 1926. Lady Susan Hussey, lady-in-waiting to the Queen for over half a century, described the service as "beautiful, exactly what the Queen would have wanted". After the service, the Queen hosted a lunch at Buckingham Palace for all of her Governors-General from the Commonwealth Realms, while the Duke and Duchess of Cambridge and other royals joined 1,800 guests at London's Guildhall for a reception, where Jeffrey Mountevans, Lord Mayor of London, paid tribute to the Queen: "It is certainly with gentleness, good humour, and understanding that, against the shifting sands of societal change, Her Majesty so wonderfully exemplifies the advantages of a constitutional monarchy".

> **"**We look back on Your Majesty's **90 years** in the life of our nation with **deep wonder** and **profound gratitude."**
>
> JUSTIN WELBY, ARCHBISHOP OF CANTERBURY

View from the gallery
This bird's-eye view shows the procession coming down the nave of St Paul's Cathedral, watched by more than 2,000 guests including three generations of royals, prime ministers past and present, and hundreds selected on the basis of long public service.

BEFORE

In the period around the Queen's actual and official birthdays, tributes and messages of support flooded in from across Commonwealth, the world, and even outer space!

SERVED SO BRILLIANTLY

Her Majesty received congratulations from private individuals, institutions, and public figures including British Prime Minister David Cameron, religious leaders, and the armed forces. The Prime Minister said, "Rarely has anyone in public life served for so long, served so brilliantly", while Her Majesty's Household Division tweeted: "We would like to congratulate our Colonel-in Chief, Her Majesty the Queen, on the occasion of her 90th birthday."

A PAW-SONAL MESSAGE

There was even what Buckingham Palace called a "paw-sonal" message from Palmerston, the Foreign and Commonwealth Office cat, who tweeted, "I hope you have a lovely day". Orbiting 400km (250 miles) above Earth's surface, British astronaut Tim Peake tweeted a photo of himself floating in the International Space Station (ISS), holding a card that read "Happy Birthday Your Majesty".

TIM PEAKE ON THE ISS

The Queen's official 90th Birthday

The events marking the Queen's official birthday involved all the pomp and ceremony of the British state, from a service at St Paul's to Trooping the Colour, while a soggy Patron's Lunch street party evoked a very British response to the vagaries of the English summer.

The timing of the Queen's official birthday is supposed to boost the chances of it being attended by good weather, but British summers are fickle, and so it was to prove during Her Majesty's 90th birthday year. Events began on 10 June with a service of thanksgiving at St Paul's Cathedral (see p.312), followed the next day by a special edition of the annual Trooping the Colour on Horse Guards Parade.

Princess Charlotte and the flypast

Until she was into her 60s, the Queen rode in the parade herself, mounted side-saddle and wearing the uniform of the regiment whose colour – or flag – was being trooped. That honour she now leaves to her son, daughter, and grandson, and on 11 June, the Prince of Wales, as Colonel of the Welsh Guards, the Princess Royal, as Colonel of the Blues and Royals, and the Duke of Cambridge, as Colonel of the Irish Guards, rode in their ceremonial uniforms, joining more than 1,600 soldiers and 300 horses.

The ceremony is also known as the Queen's Birthday Parade, and has been celebrated every year of her reign but one (1955), when it was cancelled due to a rail strike. However, for the newest royal, the Queen's great-granddaughter Princess Charlotte, 2016 marked a first, as she joined her family on the Buckingham Palace balcony for the traditional culmination of the parade, the RAF flypast. Princess Charlotte held her hands to her ears as two Tornado supersonic jets flew overhead. As the ceremony came to an end, the crowds in front of the palace gave three cheers. Later that day, the royal barge *Gloriana* was rowed down

Best of British
Picnic hampers, given to guests of the Patron's Lunch, contained treats from all four corners of the UK, including "Best of British" sandwiches, mini piccalilli pork pies, and a raspberry royale dessert.

each paid £150 per ticket, but profits went to charity) being handed rainproof ponchos, owing to the poor weather. But a little light rain failed to discourage the crowds as they tucked into the delicacies in their hampers.

Members of the Royal Family walked down the Mall greeting guests, and after lunch a carnival parade showcased themes symbolizing the many eras of the Queen's reign. Alan Lloyd, the creative director of the carnival parade, described it as "affectionate and friendly".

> # "The Queen ... is the one Head of State that ... leaders can turn to for a **first-hand perspective** of the **arc of history** over the last six decades."
>
> THE DUKE OF CAMBRIDGE SPEAKING AT THE PATRON'S LUNCH

the Thames by a crew of able-bodied rowers and rowers with disabilities, leading a flotilla of boats from every decade the Queen has been monarch.

The Patron's Lunch

The climax of the official birthday celebrations was a huge street party on the Mall: the Patron's Lunch, which celebrated the work and people of the more than 600 organizations of which the Queen is patron. Organized by the Queen's grandson, Peter Phillips, the event saw 10,000 guests (who had

Pretty in pink
A day after wowing the crowds in a vibrant green outfit, the Queen again dazzled in a fuchsia pink coat by one of her favourite designers, Karl Ludwig, and a matching hat by Angela Kelly.

AFTER

According to tradition, the Queen's birthday sees honours bestowed on British and Commonwealth subjects who merit special recognition.

THE BIRTHDAY HONOURS LIST

The headline act in the Queen's 90th birthday honours list was undoubtedly Scottish singer Rod Stewart, knighted for services to music and charity, making him Sir Roderick. Up in space, Major Tim Peake received news that he had been made a Companion of the Order of St Michael and St George (normally bestowed for "serving the UK abroad") for extraordinary service to science and education. Joining the elite Companions of Honour was the "Forces Sweetheart" wartime singer Dame Vera Lynn. According to the Cabinet Office, the birthday honours list was the "most diverse" since the Order of the British Empire was founded in 1917. Women made up 47 per cent of the total, 8.2 per cent were from a black and minority ethnic background and 5.2 per cent considered themselves to have a disability.

Picnic in the park
In St James's Park, not far from the Mall, families and well-wishers enjoyed their own picnics while watching on big screens highlights from the Patron's Lunch. Drizzle did not dampen their spirits.

On the Mall
The Queen and Prince Philip travelled down the Mall in the State Review Vehicle, greeting guests at the Patron's Lunch. Their destination was a stage near Admiralty Arch, where they joined William, Catherine, and Harry for speeches.

« **BEFORE**

When Queen Elizabeth II acceded to the throne in 1952, Britain was a very different place.

WARTIME RATIONS
Food **rationing,** introduced during World War II was still in place. It **ended** with the withdrawal of the meat ration in May 1954.

SPEEDIER PHONE CALLS
Long-distance calls in the UK had to be placed by a human switchboard operator. In 1958 the **Queen publicized the new automatic telephone dialling system** (STD) by calling the Lord Provost of Edinburgh direct from Bristol.

DECIMAL CURRENCY
Pounds were divided into 20 shillings and 240 pence. On 15 February 1971, the UK switched to a **decimal currency**. New coins were introduced and the 50p coin replaced the 10 shilling note.

TEN SHILLING NOTE, 1961

45,000 The approximate number of Christmas cards the Queen had sent up to 2012.

175,000 The number of telegrams the Queen had despatched to centenarians in the UK and the Commonwealth up to 2012.

"She'll want to **hand over** knowing she's done **everything she** possibly **could.**"

PRINCE WILLIAM, SPEAKING ABOUT THE QUEEN, 2011

Elizabeth's Long Reign

Queen Elizabeth II is the longest-living and longest-reigning monarch in British history. Over a remarkable lifetime of dedication and service, she has overcome trials and transformations with dignity and grace to forge a legacy that will never be rivalled.

In many respects, the Queen's life seems to have changed little over the years. She follows the same annual routine of events – from the State Opening of Parliament to the Christmas broadcast – as she did in 1953. Her summer holidays are usually spent at Balmoral, Easter at Windsor, and Christmas at Sandringham. She still adores horses, racing, and her Corgis and Dorgis – the preferred breeds of royal canine companion. The Queen represents stability and continuity in a country that has undergone tremendous change in the years since her coronation. In 1953, Britain was a predominantly white, Christian society; today it is multi-faith and multicultural.

A unique record
Statistics issued by Buckingham Palace during the Queen's Diamond Jubilee year bear witness to her unique record of service. At that time, she had conferred more than 404,500 honours and awards and had personally held more than 610 investitures. Her experience of politics is unsurpassed. She has given the Royal Assent to more than 3,500 Acts of Parliament and attended every State Opening of Parliament except those in 1959 and 1963, when she was pregnant with Prince Andrew and Prince Edward respectively. Up until 2020, she had

been served by 14 British prime ministers. The first, Sir Winston Churchill, was born in 1874 in the age of Queen Victoria; the current, Boris Johnson, was born in 1964. The Queen has undertaken 265 official overseas visits, including 82 state visits, to 116 countries. She was the first British monarch to visit China and Russia.

Her value as a still point of calm in a world of runaway changes has won her several ardent admirers; in 2016, US President Barack Obama spoke for many when he said that she was "a source of inspiration for me like so many other people around the

The Beatles at the palace
In 1965, the Queen invested each member of The Beatles with an MBE (Member of the Order of the British Empire). Many people were outraged that the mop-haired pop stars were given the award.

world", and described her as "truly one of my favourite people… She is an astonishing person and a real jewel to the world and not just to the United Kingdom."

A changing world
According to insiders, the Queen is naturally more conservative than Prince

Wreath of laurel worn in hair, rather than a crown

PORTRAIT BY MARY GILLICK, 1952

PORTRAIT BY ARNOLD MACHIN, 1968

Philip, who is thought to have been a modernizing influence within the royal household, especially in the early years of the reign. Nevertheless, the Queen has embraced the need for the monarchy to adapt itself to a changing world. She has faced cuts in the Civil List, allowed her income to be taxed, opened Buckingham Palace to the public, given up the Royal Yacht, and even reduced the size of her household and travel costs. Some observers are of the opinion that she is more open now to new ideas than she was 20–30 years ago. Not many nonagenarians have their own Twitter account or allow their home to be used for pop concerts.

Her personal popularity, and the immense respect she commands from every generation, have helped the monarchy to endure fluctuating public opinion. A particular highpoint was the Queen's Diamond Jubilee year, in 2012, which generated enormous enthusiasm with a range of exciting events. In the same year, public affection for the monarch was boosted by her surprise starring role in the opening ceremony of the London Olympics, where she gamely played along in a James Bond spoof that showed her apparently parachuting into the stadium. The public were thus offered a rare glimpse of the sparkling sense of humour known only to those closest to her, such as her grandchildren, with whom she has always enjoyed trading jokes.

The Queen is also held in great esteem throughout the Commonwealth, although this polity has undergone a profound transformation during the historical span of her reign. In 1953, there

Generation to generation
Prince William views a portrait of his grandmother, which was part of an exhibition that he opened in Shanghai, China, to celebrate British creativity.

were only eight independent countries within the Commonwealth. Following decolonization in the 1960s and 1970s, there are now 53, but today only 15 of these recognize the Queen as head of state. In 1999, Australia narrowly voted against becoming a republic. While the Queen, no doubt, welcomed the result, she made it clear that the issue was one to be decided by the Australian people alone. Her immense tact and dignified silence on constitutional matters has been even more keenly evidenced in Britain. Despite attempts by some factions to co-opt her to their favoured views, she has maintained her silence on recent political issues such as the devolution of Scotland and Brexit.

The future of the monarchy
It is thought to be highly unlikely that the Queen will abdicate. She will not easily renounce the vow she made on her 21st birthday to devote her whole life to the service of her people (see p.130). Press speculation that the succession could bypass the Prince of

Wales and go straight to Prince William is also wide of the mark. The monarchy is hereditary and, by nature, traditional. Prince Charles is the heir apparent and has been since the age of three.

It seems beyond doubt that the monarchy will change further under Charles. He has already spoken of being a "defender of faith" rather than a "Defender of the Faith" and of his determination to slim the monarchy down. The British monarchy has survived for well over 1,000 years by adapting to change. With two generations of successors beyond Charles already in the wings, there is every reason to suppose it will continue to do so, though the relationship between the Crown and the people may come to be defined in new ways.

Literary lion
Queen Elizabeth II presents celebrated Jamaican poet Lorna Goodison with the Queen's Gold Medal for Poetry during an audience at Buckingham Palace, London, in March 2020.

AFTER »

In the British monarchy, there is never a moment when there is not a sovereign on the throne. The new monarch succeeds immediately on the death of the sovereign.

THE SUCCESSION
On the Queen's death, an Accession Council consisting of privy councillors and others will be held at St James's Palace to declare Prince Charles formally as monarch. He may choose to announce a new regnal name should he wish to do so – he does not necessarily become King Charles III. Although an Act passed in 2015 means that a first-born royal daughter may succeed to the throne, the next in line of succession after Prince Charles (Princes William and George) are both male.

THE QUEEN AND THE PRINCE OF WALES AT THE OCTOBER 2019 STATE OPENING OF PARLIAMENT

Royal Diamond Diadem crown, which the Queen wore for her coronation

The Queen's changing portrait
Five portraits of the Queen have appeared on British coins since the start of her reign. The earliest is on the left, and the latest, unveiled in March 2015, on the far right. The Latin on most of the Queen's coinage reads *Dei gratia regina fidei defensor*, which translates as "By the grace of God, Queen, and defender of the faith".

PORTRAIT BY RAPHAEL MAKLOUF, 1985

PORTRAIT BY IAN RANK-BROADLEY, 1998

PORTRAIT BY JODY CLARK, 2015

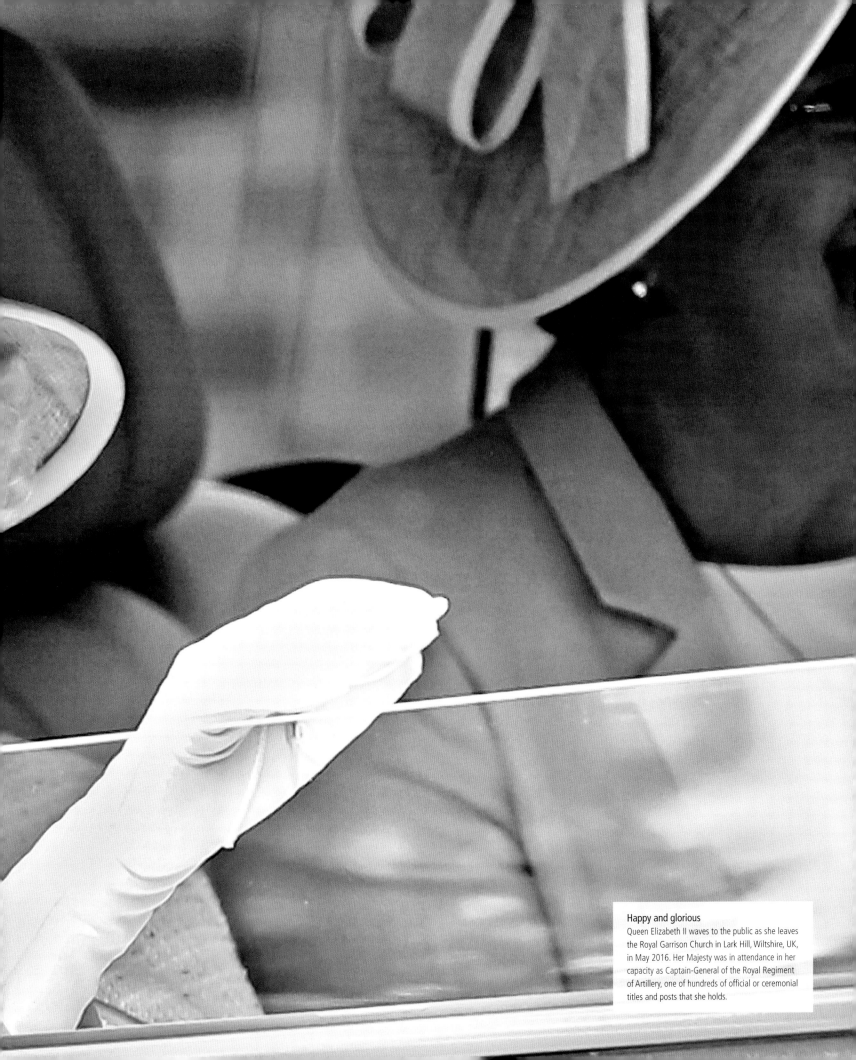

Happy and glorious
Queen Elizabeth II waves to the public as she leaves the Royal Garrison Church in Lark Hill, Wiltshire, UK, in May 2016. Her Majesty was in attendance in her capacity as Captain-General of the Royal Regiment of Artillery, one of hundreds of official or ceremonial titles and posts that she holds.

Index

A

Abdication crisis (1936) 91, 92–3
Aberdeen, Lord 246
Aberfan disaster 160
Act of Settlement (1701) 48, 297
Act of Union (1707) 35, 39
Adelaide, Queen 49
Afghanistan 254, 255, 290, 289, 291
Africa
    1947 tour 112–13
    decolonization 194–95
Agincourt, Battle of (1415) 10, 25
Airlie, Countess of 96, 97
Aitken, Max 92
Al Fayed, Dodi 242, 243, 154
Al Fayed, Mohamed 242, 243
Albert, Prince (Queen Victoria's husband) 11, 49,
    51, 52–53, 55, 57, 58, 60, 68, 72, 73, 84, 96,
    148, 246, 248, 306
Albert, Prince (Queen Victoria's son) see Edward
    VII
Albert, Prince (George V's son) see George VI
Albert Victor, Prince 72, 73, 78, 79
Albert Memorial 61
Alexander II 34–5
Alexander III 35
Alexandra, Princess 208
Alexandra, Queen 61, 72, 73, 78, 79, 86 97, 114,
    147, 208, 276
Alexandra Rose Day Appeal 208
Alexandra, Tsaritsa 76
Alexandrina Victoria, Princess 214
Alfred, Duke of Saxe-Coburg and Gotha
    (Queen Victoria's son) 55, 123
Alfred the Great 10, 12, 13
Alfred's jewel 10, 12
Alice, Princess (Queen Victoria's daughter) 55
Alice of Battenburg, Princess 114, 124
Andrew, Prince 108, 127, 131, 135, 160, 162,
    163, 198, 199, 216–17, 218–19, 222–3, 234,
    250, 272, 297
Andrew of Greece, Prince 114, 124
Anglo-Saxon Chronicle 12
Anne, Princess Royal 108, 118, 131, 153, 173,
    174–75, 183, 198, 199, 209, 223, 234, 250,
    259, 297, 299, 303, 311
    birth of 127
    childhood 162, 163
    equestrian career 161, 186–87
Anne, Queen 29, 38, 48, 212
Annigoni, Pietro 119
Annus horribilis 86, 199, 234–35, 299
Anselm of Canterbury 17
Arbeid, Murray 228
Ardent Productions 251, 269
Armills of Queen Elizabeth II 68
Armstrong-Jones, Antony 160, 161, 170–71,
    188, 189, 214, 228, 258
Armstrong-Jones, David 189, 258, 259
Armstrong-Jones, Sarah 189, 201, 258
Arthur, Prince (Henry VIII's son of) 28
Arthur, Prince (Queen Victoria's son) 55, 61,
    251
Ascot Landau 136, 137

Asquith, HH 73
Athelstan, King 12, 256
Attenborough, David 173, 312, 269
Augustine, St 10, 12
Augustus, Ernest 55
Augustus Frederick, Prince 214
Austria 175
Australia 65, 91, 92, 152–53, 161, 162,
    163, 198, 199, 255, 268, 269, 289,
    295, 299, 319
Australian State Coach 137

B

Bacon, Nicholas 29
Badminton Horse Trials 187
Bagehot, Walter 51
Bagshot Park 251
Bahamas 91, 92, 93, 289
Bailey, Christopher 189
Baldwin, Stanley 91, 92
Ball, Ian 175
Ball, John 23
Balmoral Castle 51, 60, 108–09, 115, 175, 242,
    246–49
Bank of England 11
Bannister, Roger 119
Bannockburn, Battle of (1314) 10
Barnet, Battle of (1471) 24, 26–27
Barons' War (1264–68) 21
Barry, Charles 58
Bashir, Martin 199, 207
Bayeux Tapestry 14–15
Beacon, lighting 183, 239, 261, 283, 310
Beatles, The 160, 318
Beaton, Cecil 127, 162
Beatrice, Princess (Queen Victoria's
    daughter) 55, 61, 218
Beatrice, Princess (Queen Elizabeth II's
    granddaughter) 198, 219, 223, 296, 297
    marriage to Edoardo Mapelli Mozzi 297
Becket, Thomas 10, 20, 25
Belize 289, 295
Bell, Alexander Graham 57
Benedict XVI, Pope 151
Benenden School 163, 175
Berkeley Castle 21
Berlin 164–65
Bill of Rights (1689) 11, 39
Birthday, Queen's 84, 107, 137, 144, 224–27
    21st 107, 108, 113, 130
    60th 224–27
    80th 137
    90th 310–317
Blachford, Isabella 57
Black Death 10, 21
Black Rod 134, 135
Blair, Tony 135, 199, 242
Blore, Edward 46, 84
Blumenfeld, RD 70
Blunt, Alfred 92
Blunt, Anthony 131, 161
Boer War, Second (1899–1902)
Boleyn, Anne 29, 32, 33
Bolingbroke, Henry 24

Bolt, Usain 294, 295
Bonaparte, Napoleon 14, 49
Bonnie Prince Charlie 11, 37, 41, 48
Borrallo, Maria 295
Bosworth, Battle of (1485) 10, 25
Botswana 195, 288, 294
Bowes-Lyon, Cecilia 111
Bowes-Lyon, Claude 111
Bowes-Lyon, Fergus 111, 222
Bowes-Lyon, Michael 111
Bowes-Lyon, Rose 110
Boyne, Battle of the (1690) 41
Brabourne, Lady 114, 192, 193
    Brabourne, Lord 114, 115, 192, 193
Bradlaugh, Charles 61
Branson, Richard 183
Brazil 295
Bretwalda 12
Brexit 319
Bridgeman, Charles 212
Britain, Battle of (1940) 77
Britannia, HMY 130, 153, 199, 223, 238, 299
British Empire Exhibition 76, 79, 89, 91
British Union of Fascists 77, 91, 92
Broadlands 120, 201, 267
Brocklebank, John 169
Brontë, Charlotte 58
Brooke, Peter 234
Brooksbank, Jack 297
Brown, Gordon 239
Brown, John 60–61
Brow, Louise 161
Bruce, Augusta 246
Bruce, Marjorie 35
Bruce, William 37
Brunei 153
Brunel, Isambard Kingdom 58, 246
Bruni, Carla 254
Buckingham Palace 54, 77, 80, 84–87, 97, 102–
    03, 106, 119, 123, 141, 155, 157, 162, 163,
    175, 183, 199, 212, 219, 223, 225, 236–37,
    242–43, 245, 250, 251, 255, 259, 261, 268,
    269, 274, 275, 307
Budgie (Duchess of York's book character) 219
Bunyan, John 157
Burmese (horse) 225
Burrell, Paul 254
Burton, Sarah 274
Bush, George W 265
Butler, RA 131, 135

C

Cable Street, Battle of (1936) 77
Caernarfon Castle 170–71
Cairns, Fiona 274
Calais 29
Cambridge, Duchess of see Middleton, Catherine
Cambridge, Duke of see William, Prince
Cambridge, Mary 111
Cambridge, May 111
Cambridge University 60, 97, 163, 170, 171, 250,
    251
Cameron, David 255, 274, 275, 300, 312, 314
Camp Bastian 920, 291

Campbell-Bannerman, Henry 248
Canada 65, 91, 92, 111, 119, 141, 152, 160, 161,
    162, 176, 198, 220–21, 275, 299
Cap of Maintenance 134
Cape Matapan, Battle of (1941) 125
Caribbean 194, 195
Carlton House (horse) 299
Caroline of Ansbach, Queen 212
Caron, Antoine 30
carriages 136–37
Carrington, Lord 111
Cartier 44
Cartland, Barbara 206
Catherine of Aragon 28–29
Catherine of Valois 25
Cator, Betty 111
Cavendish, Mary 140, 141
Cavendish-Bentinck, Cecilia 111
Cecil, William 29, 33
Cenotaph 76, 79, 81
Centrepoint 269
Chadwick, James 77
Chalfont, Lord 153
Châlus, Siege of 20
Chamberlain, Neville 77, 95, 111
Channel Tunnel 199
Charles I 11, 37, 38–39, 40–41, 46, 134
Charles II 11, 37, 38, 39, 41, 42–43, 46, 68, 134
Charles VI (King of France) 25
Charles, Prince of Wales 35, 118, 119, 160, 255,
    258, 259, 268, 288, 295, 307, 319
    Annus horribilis 235
    assassination of Lord Mountbatten 193
    birth of 126–27
    charity work 209, 302
    childhood 131, 162–63
    Clarence House 123
    death of Diana, Princess of Wales 242, 243
    divorce from Diana, Princess of Wales 199,
        230–31, 299
    Duchy of Cornwall 256–57
    and Duke of Cambridge 269, 272, 274, 297
    Kensington Palace 214
    life of 166–67
    made Prince of Wales 160, 170–71
    marriage to Camilla Parker Bowles 205, 254,
        264–65
    marriage to Diana, Princess of Wales 198, 200–
        01, 204, 206–07
    marriage of Prince Andrew and Duchess of
        York 223
    and Prince Harry 288, 297, 300
    Prince's Trust 161, 180–81, 209
    Royal Family 173
    royal memorabilia 276, 277
    Sandringham 148
    state visits 153, 295
    Windsor Castle 46
Charlotte of Mecklenburg 49
Charlotte, Princess (Queen Elizabeth II's great-
    granddaughter) 255, 269, 279, 297, 314
Charteris, Lord 189, 223
Chartres, Richard 274
Chatto, Sarah 189, 201, 258
Chaucer, Geoffrey 17
Cheam School 162

Chelsea Flower Show 311
Chesterfield, Lord 61
Chichester, Francis 160
Chile 295
China 198, 295, 299
Christmas messages 119, 130–31, 147, 153, 156–57, 235
Chronicles (Froissart) 21, 22–23
Church of England 29, 33, 40, 150–51, 199, 264
Churchill, John 39
Churchill, Winston 77, 91, 97, 98, 103, 118, 119, 120, 131, 133, 135, 141, 153, 160, 192
Cierrach, Lindka 223
Cipriani, Giovanni 136
Civil List 235, 255
Civil Wars (1639–51) 37, 38, 39, 40–1
Clarence House 118, 120, 122–23, 155, 175, 181, 201, 223, 259, 274
Claridge's Hotel 223
Clifden, Nellie 73
Cnut, King (c.985–1035) 10, 13, 16
coaches 136–37
Colonial Conferences 65
commemorative stamps 204–05
Common Sense (Paine) 48
Commonwealth 64–65, 92, 118, 119, 130, 131, 141, 152–53, 160, 161, 194–95, 199, 295, 307, 319
Concert for Diana 254, 289
Conroy, John 54, 214
Constantine II 268
Corfu 124, 125
corgis 98, 108, 120
Cornwall, Duchess of *see* Parker Bowles, Camilla
Coronation Chicken 141
coronation of Elizabeth II 138–45, 204
Coronation Spoon and Ampulla 68
Court Circulars 307
Coventry 176
Covid-19 pandemic 265, 280–81, 295, 297
Cranmer, Thomas 29
Crathie Church 175
Crawford, Marion 106, 114, 115, 118, 127, 130, 188
Crécy, Battle of (1346) 21
Crimean War (1853–56) 60
Croke Park 271
Cromwell, Oliver 37, 39, 40, 46
Cromwell, Richard 42
Cromwell, Thomas 29
Crookham Horse Trials 187
Crown Jewels 68–69
Cubitt, Thomas 57
Cubitt, William 58
Culloden, Battle of (1746) 41, 48
Cunningham, Allan 236
Curthose, Robert 17

D
D-Day landings (1944) 77, 103, 199, 238, 255, 299, 307
Daily Mirror 254
Dál Riata, Kingdom of 34
Danelaw 12
Dannatt, Richard 291
Dartmouth Naval College 91, 97, 114, 124, 125, 218
David I 34, 37
David II 35

de Montfort, Simon 10, 21
Dean, John 114
Deira 12
Dench, Judi 267
Dettingen, Battle of (1742) 49
Devon Loch 119
Diamond Jubilee (horse) 147
Diamond Jubilee State Coach 137
Diamond Jubilees
   (1897) 67, 70, 204
   (2012) 205, 214, 255, 282–83, 295, 299, 307
Diamond wedding anniversary (2007) 266–67
Diana, Her True Story (Morton) 199, 207, 230, 234, 235
Diana, Princess of Wales 125, 206–07, 214, 268–69, 274, 279, 288
   charity work 208–11
   death and funeral 199, 242–45, 154
   divorce from Prince Charles 199, 230–31, 299
   dresses 228–29
   marriage to Prince Charles 198, 200–01, 204, 206–07
Diana, Princess of Wales Memorial Fund 209
Diana Memorial Fountain 243, 254
Dimbleby, Jonathan 230, 231
Disraeli, Benjamin 51, 57, 61, 62
Dix, JC 70
Domesday Book 10
Dookie (corgi) 98
Doublet (horse) 186–87
Douglas-Home, Alec 135, 160
Downe House School 278, 279
Drake, Francis 33
Dublin Castle 271
Duchy of Cornwall 256–57
Duchy Originals 257
Dudley, Amy 33
Dudley, John 29
Dudley, Robert 33
Dudley Ward, Freda 91
Duke of Edinburgh Awards 119, 125, 251
Dunbar, Battle of (1650) 41
Duncan I 34
Dunnottar Castle 34
Dunstan, St 12

E
Eadred, King 12
East Anglia 12
East Anglian Air Ambulance 273
Ede, James Chuter 127
Ede & Ravenscroft 144
Edelstein, Victor 228
Eden, Anthony 119, 131, 135
Edgar, King 10, 12, 13
Edgehill, Battle of (1642) 41
Edinburgh, Duke of *see* Philip, Prince
Edmund, King 12
Edward I 10, 20, 21, 35, 170
Edward II 10, 20, 35, 170
Edward III 10, 20, 21, 24, 35, 44, 170, 256
Edward IV 10, 21, 24, 25, 27, 170, 256
Edward V 25
Edward VI 11, 29, 33
Edward VII 11, 51, 55, 57, 60, 61, 62, 64, 70, 72–73, 78, 79, 86, 97, 114, 137, 147, 148, 276, 306

Edward VIII 77, 78, 79, 81, 90–93, 94, 95, 96, 97, 106–07, 110–11, 120, 131, 161, 189
Edward the Black Prince 21
Edward the Confessor 10, 13, 16, 25
Edward the Elder 12
Edward the Martyr 13
Edward, Prince (Elizabeth II's son) 127, 131, 135, 160, 162, 162, 198, 199, 223, 250–51, 269, 307
Edward, Prince (George III's son) 214
Eisenhower, Dwight D 119
El Alamein, Battle of (1943) 103
Elba, Idris 181, 300
Eleanor of Aquitaine 10, 18–19, 20
Elizabeth I 11, 25, 29, 32–33, 38, 46, 151
Elizabeth II 29, 76, 77, 94, 118–19, 128–29, 160–61, 169, 198–99, 254–55, 295, 298–99, 318–19, 320–321
   African tour 112–13
   Annus horribilis 86, 199, 234–35, 299
   Balmoral 246
   birth of children 126, 127
   Buckingham Palace 86, 236
   childhood 98–101, 106–07
   children of 162
   Christmas messages 156–57
   Clarence House 123
   coaches 137
   coronation 138–45, 204
   death of Diana, Princess of Wales 242
   death of George VI 132–33
   decolonization 64, 65
   Diamond Jubilee 205, 255, 282–83, 295, 299, 307
   Diamond wedding anniversary 266–67
   divorce of Prince Charles and Diana, Princess of Wales 231
   early relationship with Prince Philip 114–15, 124
   early years of reign 130–31
   and George V 79
   and George VI 97
   Golden Jubilee 68, 254, 260–1, 299
   grandchildren 296–97
   great-grandchildren 296–97
   head of Church 150–51
   Holyroodhouse 37
   investiture of Prince of Wales 170, 171
   marriage of Prince Charles and Camilla Parker Bowles 264, 265
   marriage to Prince Philip 120–21, 125
   marriage of Prince William and Catherine Middleton 274
   90th birthday celebrations 310–317
   as patron 302–03, 314
   pets 108–09
   and Prince Andrew 217
   and Princess Margaret 155, 189, 259
   and Queen Elizabeth II 169
   and Queen Mother 111, 258
   Royal Family 173
   royal memorabilia 276–77
   Sandringham 147, 148
   Silver Jubilee 131, 161, 182–85, 204
   60th birthday celebrations 224–25
   social media 295
   State Opening of Parliament 134–35, 308–09
   state visits 152–53, 164–65, 202–03, 220–21, 270–71
   teenage years 106–07
   trooping the Colour 225, 226–27, 314

walkabouts 176–77
wartime anniversaries 238–39, 304–05
Windsor Castle 46
working life 306–07
World War II 103
Elizabeth, Queen Mother 76, 94, 95, 97, 98, 100–01, 106, 110–11, 118, 123, 132, 133, 176, 199, 206, 222, 239, 254, 258
   African tour 112–13
   death 254, 259
   during World War II 102–05, 111
Elizabeth of York 25
Elphinstone, Elizabeth 111
Emma of Normandy 13
Essex 12, 23
Estimate (horse) 299
Estonia 295
Ethelfleda, Queen 12
Ethelred the Unready 10, 12
Eton College 268–69, 288, 289, 290
Eugenie, Princess (Elizabeth II's granddaughter) 198, 219, 223, 296, 297
   marriage to Jack Brooksbank 297
European Union (EU) 199
Everest, Mount 119, 140

F
Fagan, Michael 299
Fairfax, Thomas 41
Falconer, Lord 264
Falkland Islands 216–17, 218–19, 272
Ferguson, Sarah 198, 199, 219, 222–23, 234, 297
Festoon Tiara 174
Fields, Gracie 157
Fildes, Luke 72
Fisher, Geoffrey 143, 155
Fitzalan-Howard, Bernard 94
Flame of Liberty (Paris) 243, 245
Flodden, Battle of (1513) 11, 35
Flores Historiarum (Flowers of History) 16
Ford, Edward 234
Forster, EM 65
Fountains Abbey 29
Franco, Francisco 94
Frecklington, WJ 137
Frederick II, Kaiser 70
Frederick William, Prince 60
French, John 80
Freud, Lucian 254
Frimley Park Hospital 297
Froissart, Jean 21, 23
From a Clear Blue Sky (Knatchbull) 193
Fulk the Red 20
Furness, Lady 91

G
Gallipoli 76
Gambia 153, 195
Gandhi, Mahatma 113, 118, 120
Garrards 200
Geelong Grammar School 60
General Strike (1926) 76, 79, 98
Geoffrey, Count of Anjou 17, 20, 21
George I 11, 48
George II 48–49, 212

George III 11, 46, 49, 50, 51, 54, 60, 84, 212, 307
George IV 45, 46, 49, 54, 84, 123, 137, 236
George V 76, 78–79, 80–81, 82–83, 86, 88–89, 90, 91, 96, 97, 110, 131, 137, 147, 148, 153, 157, 189, 204, 256, 276, 296, 306
George VI 65, 76, 77, 78, 79, 80, 81, 86, 89, 96, 97, 98, 100, 107, 108, 110, 111, 118, 120, 121, 130, 131, 144, 147, 152, 176, 189, 204, 206, 276, 277
    African tour 112–13
    becomes king 94–95
    death 132–33
    during World War II 102–05
George IV State Diadem 134, 141
George, Prince (Elizabeth II's great-grandson) 153, 255, 269, 279, 295, 297
George, Prince (son of George V) 103
George Cross 103
Germany 255, 295
Ghana 119, 153, 194, 195
Gibbons, Grinling 212
Gilbey, James 230
Giles, James 248
Gilliatt, William 127
Gladstone, William 51, 57
Glamis Castle 110, 189
Glass Coach 136, 137, 201, 223
Glorious Revolution (1688) 38, 39
God Save the Queen (Sex Pistols) 183
Godfrey-Faussett, Lady 140
Gold Cup (Ascot) 299
Gold State Coach 82–83, 136–37, 141, 183, 261
Golden Jubilees
    (1887) 61, 67–68
    (2002) 254, 260–61, 299
Goldsmiths College 297
Goon Show, The 171
Gordonstoun 114, 124, 125, 160, 162, 163, 218, 219, 250, 251, 297
Gower, George 32
Grace of Monaco, Princess 207
Grand Knockout Tournament, The 198, 223, 250, 251
Grand National 119
Grand Remonstrance 41
Great Depression 77
Great Exhibition 51, 58–59, 60
Grey, Jane 29
Gulf Wars
    (1991) 198
    (2003) 254
Gunpowder Plot (1605) 38, 39, 134
Guthrum 12

H

Haakon, King 35
Hahn, Kurt 124, 125
Haig, Douglas 80
Hair (musical) 160
Hales, Robert 23
Hall, Edward 27
Hall, John 274
Halo Tiara 144
Hamilton, Katherine 111

Hanover, Elector of 54, 55
Hardinge, Diamond 111
Hardman, Robert 297
Harold I 13, 16
Harold II 10, 14–15, 16
Harold Hadrada 16
Harold Harefoot 13, 16
Harris, Albert 64
Harry, Prince (Elizabeth II's grandson) 153, 198, 201, 206, 207, 209, 214, 231, 242, 243, 254, 255, 264, 269, 274, 276, 277, 288–89, 290–91, 294–95, 296–97, 300–01, 303
    birth of Archie 293
    marriage to Meghan 289, 292–93
    relocation to California 293
    withdrawal from the royal duties 289, 293
Harrying of the North 16–17
Hartnell, Norman 120, 140, 144
Hastings, Battle of (1066) 10, 14–15, 16
Hauser & Wirth 297
Hawksmoor, Nicholas 212
Heath, Ted 161
Heatherdown Preparatory School 163, 218
Helena, Princess (Queen Victoria's daughter) 55
Helicopter Rescue 273
Henry I 10, 17, 20
Henry II 10, 20, 21, 44
Henry III 21
Henry IV 10, 21, 24
Henry V 10, 24–25, 27, 44, 46
Henry VI 10, 24, 25, 27
Henry VII 10, 21, 25, 28–29
Henry VIII 11, 25, 28, 32, 33, 151
Henry, Prince (George V's son) 78, 79
Henry of Battenberg, Prince 61
Heptarchy, The 12
Heseltine, William 173, 176
Hewitt, James 201, 230
Hicks, India 201
Highgrove House 206, 231, 257
Hillary, Edmund 119, 140
Hill House 162
Himmler, Heinrich 14
Hitler, Adolf 77, 91, 94, 95, 111
Hodge, Margaret 257
Hoey, Brian 108
Holbein the Younger, Hans 28
Holly (corgi) 108
Holyroodhouse, Palace of 36–37, 151, 307
Hong Kong 199
Honours of Scotland 34
Horstead, James 150
Hough, Richard
Hume, Rosemary 141
Hundred Years' War 10, 21, 23, 27, 35
Huntingdon, Earl of 24
Hussain, Nadya 310–311
Hussey, Lady Susan 312
Hwicce 12
Hyde, Anne 39
Hyde, Edward 42

I

Illustrated London News 94
Imperial Federation League 65
Imperial Mantle robe 143

Imperial State Crown 134–35, 141, 143
India 62–63, 64, 79, 91, 97, 118, 192, 230
Ingelger, Count of Anjou 20
Ingrid of Sweden, Princess 188
Institut Alpin Videmanette 206, 207
investitures 306
Invictus Games 255, 289, 291, 300–01
Iran 111
Iraq 254, 291
Ireland 41, 60, 73, 76, 79, 97, 153, 192, 199, 255, 270–71, 299
Irish Republican Army (IRA) 76, 131, 192–93, 198, 224, 271
Irish State Coach 120
Isabella of Angouleme 18–19
Isabella of Mar 35
It's a Royal Knockout, see The Grand Knockout Tournament 198, 223, 250, 251

J

Jacobite rebellion 39
Jagger, Mick 188
Jamaica 160, 195, 289, 294, 295
James I (King of Scotland) 35
James I/VI 11, 28, 35, 37, 38, 46
James II (King of Scotland) 35
James II 11, 37, 38, 39, 41, 42
James III (King of Scotland) 35
James IV (King of Scotland) 11, 28, 35, 37
James V (King of Scotland) 35, 37
James, Viscount Severn 251, 254, 297
Jane Mynors' nursery school 268
Japan 295
Jarrow March 77
Jenkins, Katherine 311
Jigsaw 279
Jinping, Xi 295
Joan of Arc 25
John XXIII, Pope 203
John, Duke of Bedford 25
John, Elton 209, 243, 269
John, King 10, 20, 21, 34, 44, 68
John, Prince (George V's son) 78
John Balliol 35
John of Gaunt 23
John Paul II, Pope 202–03, 264
Jones, Alwyn 171
Jones, Inigo 46
Jones, Tom 125
Jubilee Gardens 183
Juliana, Queen 118
Junor, Penny 167
Jutland, Battle of (1916) 81

K

Karim, Hafiz Mohammed Abdul ('the Munshi') 61, 70
Kelly, Angela 311, 314
Kelly, Autumn 175, 297
Kennedy, John F 160
Kenneth mac Alpin, King 34
Kensington Palace 54, 55, 206, 212–15, 231, 242, 244–45
Kent 12, 23
Kent, William 212, 215
Kenya 132–33, 195, 262, 279
Kett's Rebellion 40

King's Evil 48
Kipling, Rudyard 89
Knatchbull, Amanda 167
Knatchbull, Nicholas 192, 193
Knatchbull, Patricia 192
Knatchbull, Timothy 192, 193
Kohl, Helmut 239
Korean War (1950–53) 118
Khrushchev, Nikita 108, 119

L

Lakefield College House 218
Lambeth Palace 151
Landseer, Charles 246
Landseer, Edwin 246
Lang, Cosmo 92, 111
Lascelles, Alan 127
Laud, Archbishop 11, 40
Laurence, Timothy 175, 199
Lawrence, Thomas 49
Lehzen, Louise 54, 55
Leo X, Pope 29
Leopold, Prince (Queen Victoria's son) 55
Leopold II (King of Belgium) 54–55
Leslie, Charles Robert 54
Lesotho 195, 289, 294
Lindsay, Hugh 198
Lister, Joseph 61
Little Princesses, The (Crawford) 118, 127, 130
Livingstone, David 51
Llewellyn, Roddy 188–89
Lloyd George, David 73, 81
Lloyd Webber, Andrew 251
Logue, Christopher 225
Logue, Lionel 102, 111
Lollards 24, 25
Londesborough, Lady 61
Longford, Elizabeth 70
Loos, Battle of (1915) 222
Louis, Prince (Elizabeth II's great-grandson) 297
Louis XIV 39
Louis Philippe (King of France) 60
Louise, Princess (Queen Victoria's daughter) 55, 212
Ludgrove School 269
Ludwig, Karl 314
Lusitania sinking 76
Lynn, Vera 314
Lytton, Lord 62

M

Macbeth, King 34
Macdonald, James 132, 133
Macdonald, Ramsay 79
Macmillan, Harold 119, 131, 135, 160, 195
Magna Carta 10, 21, 44
Major, John 198, 230–31, 234–35
Malaysia 152, 295
Malcolm II 10, 34
Malcolm III 34
Malta 103, 118, 125, 128–29, 162, 267, 295
Mandela, Nelson 113
Margaret of Anjou 27
Margaret, Maid of Norway 10

Margaret, Princess 94, 103, 108, 111, 112–13, 118, 119, 121, 124, 126, 130, 133, 141, 144, 160, 163, 169, 188–89, 214
  childhood 98–101, 106–07
  death 254, 258–59
  and Peter Townsend 152, 154–55, 188
  teenage years 106–07
Margaret, Queen of Scots 28, 34, 35, 38
Markle, Meghan 289, 292–93, 294–95, 303
  birth of Archie 293
  miscarriage 293
  relocation to California 293
  withdrawal from the royal duties 293
Marlborough College 278, 279, 297
Marlborough House 79
Marlowe, Christopher 33
Marston Moor, Battle of (1644) 40, 41
Marten, Henry 106
Mary I 11, 28, 32, 33
Mary II 11, 29, 38, 39, 48, 212
Mary, Princess (George V's daughter) 78, 79, 81, 94, 97, 111
Mary, Queen (George V's wife) 76, 78, 79, 82–83, 86, 96, 97, 119, 147
Mary Queen of Scots 11, 29, 37
Matilda, Queen 10, 17, 20, 28
Maundy Thursday 302, 303
Mauritius 195
Maxwell, Paul 192–93
May, Brian 261
May, Hugh 46
Mayer, Catherine 181
McAleese, Mary 271
McLaren, Malcolm 183
McMahon, Thomas 192
McNicoll, Alan 152
McQueen, Alexander 274
Melbourne, Lord 49
Mercia 12
Messines, Battle of (1917) 80
Meyer, Christopher 254
Middle English 13, 17
Middleton, Carole 279
Middleton, Catherine 222, 262–63, 278–79, 280–81, 303
  Kensington Palace 214
  marriage to Prince William 205, 254, 255, 268, 274–75, 276, 277
  and Prince George 269, 279, 295, 297
  and Princess Charlotte 279
  Sandringham 147, 148
Middleton, James 274
Middleton, Michael 279
Mirren, Helen 311
Milburn, Martina 181
Millennium Dome 254
Mirzoeff, Eddie 299
Mitrokhin, Vasili 171
Mitterrand, President 199
Monck, Richard 42
Monty (corgi) 108
More, Thomas 30–31
Morrah, Dermot 95, 151
Morris, Charles 148
Mortimer, Edmund 25
Mortimer, Roger 21
Morton, Andrew 199, 207, 230, 234, 235
Mosley, Oswald 77, 91
Motion, Andrew 267
Mountbatten, Lord 95, 97, 108, 120, 124, 125, 167
  assassination of 131, 161, 192–93, 271

Mountbatten, Pamela 133
Mountbatten, Patricia 115
Mountbatten-Windsor, Archie Harrison 293, 297
Mozzi, Edoardo Mapelli 297
Mugabe, Robert 195
Munich Agreement (1938) 77
Muzorewa, Abel 195

N

Naseby, Battle of (1645) 41
Nash, John 84, 123, 236
National Gallery 167, 198
National Relief Fund 77
Neville, Richard 24, 27
New Model Army 41
New Zealand 65, 91, 119, 131, 152, 153, 176–77, 198, 255, 268, 269, 294
Newcastle University 297
Nicholas II, Tsar 51, 76, 79, 81, 248, 296
Nigeria 195
Nixon, Richard 161
Nkomo, Joshua 195
Nkrumah, Kwame 194
Nonsuch Palace 33
Norman conquest 13, 14–15, 16
North Atlantic Treaty Organization (NATO) 103
Northern Ireland 76, 79, 152, 160, 199, 271
Northumbria 12

O

Obama, Barack 95, 275, 298, 311
Obama, Michelle 275, 298, 311
Odo of Bayeux, Bishop 14, 17
Offa, King 12
O'Grady, Patrick 192
Oldfield, Bruce 228
Oliver, Alison 187
Olympics
  (1976) 187
  (2012) 255, 284–87, 297, 299, 300
Omdurman, Battle of (1898) 70
Osborne House 51, 56–57, 60, 70, 91, 97
O'Sullivan, Donal 192
Outlawries Bill 135
Outward Bound Trust 219
Oxford, Edward 51, 60
Oxford University 91

P

Paine, Tom 48
Pakistan 97, 118
Panorama 231
Parker, Mike 133
Parker Bowles, Andrew 230
Parker Bowles, Camilla 201, 205, 230, 231, 234, 254, 255, 264–65, 276, 277, 295, 300
Parker Bowles, Laura 265
Parker Bowles, Tom 264, 265
Parkinson, Norman 174, 175
Parliament 21, 41, 42, 48, 134–35, 175, 306, 308–09
Parr, Catherine 32, 33
"Party at the Palace" 254, 261
Patil, Prathiba 306
Patron's Lunch 314, 315, 316–17
Paul, Henri 242, 243

Paxton, Joseph 58
Peak, Major Tim 314
Peasant's Revolt (1381) 10, 21, 22–23
Peel, Robert 57
Pellew, Mark 203
Pepys, Samuel 46
Percy dynasty 24
Persimmon (horse) 147
Petition of Right 11
pets 108–09
Pets by Royal Appointment (Hoey) 108
Philip, Prince 77, 124–25, 130, 131, 134, 160, 161, 195, 199, 209, 217, 258
  accession of Queen Elizabeth II 132, 133
  Annus horribilis 234, 235
  children of 126, 127, 162, 167
  Clarence House 123
  at coronation of Queen Elizabeth II 141, 144
  death of Diana, Princess of Wales 242, 243
  Diamond wedding anniversary 266–67
  early relationship with Queen Elizabeth II 114–15, 118
  later years of Queen Elizabeth II's reign 298, 299, 319, 312, 316–17
  in Malta 103, 118, 125, 128–29, 162, 267, 295
  marriage of Prince Charles and Camilla Parker Bowles 264
  marriage to Queen Elizabeth II 120–21, 125, 119
  pets 108
  Royal Family 173
  Sandringham 148
  Silver Jubilee 182
  state visits 152, 153, 203
Philip II (King of Spain) 29, 33
Philip Movement 124
Phillips, Isla 297
Phillips, Mark 161, 175, 198, 199, 234, 297
Phillips, Peter 161, 175, 223, 297, 314
Phillips, Savannah 297, 299
Phillips, Zara *see* Tindall, Zara
Picts 34
Pilgrimage of Grace 40
Pilgrim's Progress (Bunyan) 157
Poitiers, Battle of (1356) 21
Popes
  Benedict XVI 151
  John XXIII 203
  John Paul II 202–03, 264
  Leo X 29
Poundbury 257
Powell, Enoch 160
Pratt, George 180
Prayer Book Rebellion 40–41
Prince's Foundation for Building Community 167
Prince's Trust 161, 180–81, 209
Princess Royal *see* Anne, Princess Royal
Princess Royal's Trust for Carers 174
Princess of Wales Memorial Playground 243
Privy Council 55
Profumo, John 160
"Prom in the Palace" 261
Provisions of Oxford 21

Q

Queen Elizabeth 2 (QE2) 160, 168–69
Queen Mary 2 254
Queen Victoria's small diamond crown 68, 69

Queen's Award for Voluntary Service 261
Queen's Work for Women Fund 76
Queen's Walkway, Windsor 310

R

Rainborough, Thomas 41
rationing 120
Reagan, Ronald 198, 238
Really Useful Group, The 251
Reform Bill (1832) 11
Regency Act (1830) 51
Reid, Andy 302
Reith, John 89
Representation of the People Act (1918) 76
Restoration, The (1660) 42–43
Rhodes, Cecil 65
Rhodesia 152, 160
Rhys-Jones, Sophie 199, 251
Richard I 10, 20, 21
Richard II 10, 17, 21, 23, 24
Richard III 10, 21, 25
Richard of Gloucester 25
Richard of York 21
Riddlesworth Hall 206, 207
Riders for Health 174
Rising of the North 33, 40
Rizzio, David 37
RJH Public Relations 251
Robe of Estate 140
Robert I (the Bruce) 10, 35
Robert II 35
Robert III 35
Robert of Mortain 256
Roberts, James 248
Robinson, Belle 279
Roche, Frances 206
Rockall 119
Roger of Salisbury 17
Rolle, Lord 55
Roman Britain 10, 12
Roosevelt, Franklin 77, 95, 106
Royal Ballet 188, 189
Royal College of Music 73
Royal College of Needlework 140, 274
Royal Family 160, 163, 172–73
Royal Lodge 219
royal memorabilia 276–77
Royal Military Academy Sandhurst 269, 289, 291
Royal National Orthopaedic Hospital 297
Royal Ocean (horse) 187
royal walkabouts 131, 176–77
Royal Windsor Horse Show 311
Rozavel Golden Eagle (corgi) 108
Runcie, Robert 201, 223
Rupert, Prince 41
Russell, Lord 58
Russia 51, 76, 79, 81, 153

S

Sadler's Wells Foundation 188
St Andrews University 254, 262–63, 269, 278, 279
St Edward's Crown 68–69, 141, 143, 144, 145
St George's School 297
St James's Palace 55, 242, 245, 259
St James's Park 162, 315

St Paul's Cathedral 161, 183, 200, 207, 238, 239, 261, 312–13
St Paul's Waldenbury 110
Salisbury, Lord 65, 248
Salote Tupou III, Queen 141
Sandringham 78, 79, 89, 96, 97, 118, 132, 146–49, 200, 206, 230
Sarkozy, Nicolas 239, 254
Save the Children Fund 174, 175, 209, 303
Sceptre with the Cross 68, 69, 143
Sceptre with the Dove 143
Scotii 34
Scotland
 Act of Union 35
 Alexander II 34–35
 Alexander III 35
 Battle of Bannockburn 10, 35
 Battle of Flodden 11, 35
 Bonnie Prince Charlie 11, 41, 48
 and Civil Wars 39, 40–41
 David I 34, 37
 David II 35
 Duncan I 34
 early history of 34
 Elizabeth II 151
 George IV 49
 Holyroodhouse 36–37, 151
 Jacobite rebellion 39
 James I 35
 James II 35
 James III 35
 James IV 11, 35, 37
 James V 35, 37
 James VI 11, 28, 37, 38
 John Balliol 35
 Kenneth mac Alpin 34
 Macbeth 34
 Malcolm II 10, 34
 Malcolm III 34
 Margaret, Maid of Norway 10
 Mary, Queen of Scots 11, 29, 35, 37
 Queen Victoria 51
 Robert I (the Bruce) 10, 35
 Robert II 35
 Robert III 35
 Wars of Independence 10, 35
 William I 34
Scottish State Coach 315
Sea Bird II (horse) 130
Sebutinde, Arnold 181
Secombe, Harry 171
Seeiso, Prince 289
Sentebale 289
Seven Years' War (1756–63) 49
Sex Pistols 183
Seymour, Jane 29
Seymour, Thomas 32, 33
Shadow V (boat) 192–93
Shakespeare, William 33
Shand, Bruce 265
Sheridan, Lisa 108
Sierra Leone 153, 195
Sigismund, Emperor 44, 46
Silver Jubilee Walkway 183
Silver Jubilees
 (1935) 77, 79, 204
 (1977) 131, 161, 182–85, 204
Simnel, Lambert 28
Simpson, Ernest 91
Simpson, Wallis 91, 92–93, 95, 110–11, 120, 198

Singapore 161, 295
Smith, William 246
Snowdon, Lord 160, 161, 170–71, 188, 189, 214, 228, 258
Solomon Islands 295
Somalia 195
Somme, Battle of the (1916) 76
South Africa 65, 112–13, 115, 152, 153, 160, 161, 195, 199, 288, 294
South Korea 153
Sovereign's Orb 68, 69, 143
Spanish Armada 11, 29, 33, 183
Spencer, Charles 207, 242, 243
Spencer, John 201, 206, 207
Spencer, Raine 206
Spencer, Sarah 200, 206
Spenser, Edmund 33
Spitting Image 298, 299
Spry, Constance 141
Stalin, Joseph 94
Stamford Bridge, Battle of (1066) 16
Stark, Koo 219
State Landau 136–37, 274
state visits 130, 152–53, 202–03, 220–21, 270–71, 294–95
Statute of Labourers (1351) 23
Statute of Westminster (1931) 77
Stephen, King 10, 17, 28
Stephenson, Pamela 223
Stephenson, Robert 58
Stewart, Rod 314
Stewarts (Royal House) 35
Stewart, Walter 35
Stirling Castle 259
Stoke, Battle of (1487) 27
Stone of Scone 118
Stuart, Charles Edward 11, 37, 41, 48
Succession to the Crown Act (2012) 297
Sudbury, Simon 23
Suez crisis (1956) 119, 131, 135
Sullivan, Arthur 61
Sun, The 199, 235
Sunninghill Park 219, 223
Susan (corgi) 108, 120
Sussex 12
Sussex, Duchess of see Markle, Meghan
Sussex, Duke of see Harry, Prince
Swaziland 195
Sword of State 134

T
Taj Mahal 230
Tanna 124
Tanzania 195
Taylor, George 171
Te Kanawa, Kiri 201
Tenzing Norgay 119, 140
Teresa, Mother 209
Tewkesbury, Battle of (1471) 27
Thatcher, Margaret 50, 111, 113, 161, 195, 198, 255
Thornhill, James 212
Thunberg, Greta 295
Thynn, Mary 111
Timbertop 163
Tinchebrai, Battle of (1106) 17
Tindall, Lena 297
Tindall, Mia 255, 297

Tindall, Mike 175, 255, 297
Tindall, Zara 175, 187, 223, 254, 255, 287–87, 296, 297, 300–01, 311
Tobruk, Battle of (1942) 77
Toms, Carl 214
Tower of London 17, 23, 25, 68
Townsend, Peter 118, 119, 130, 152, 154–55, 188, 189, 258
Transaid 174
Travolta, John 207, 228
Trinidad and Tobago 195
Trooping the Colour 224, 225, 226–27, 314
Tusk Trust 269
Tuvalu 295
Tweedsmuir, Lord 176
Twelfth Night (Shakespeare) 33
Tyler, Wat 23

U
Uganda 195
Uhtred, Earl of Northumbria 34
United Nations (UN) 103
United States of America 49, 64, 91, 95, 119, 275, 299
University College of Wales, Aberystwyth 170, 171
University of Exeter 297

V
van Cutsem, Grace 274
van Cutsem, Hugh 148
van der Post, Laurens 268
Vanburgh, John 212
Vatican City 198, 202–03
VE Day 77, 97, 103, 189, 239
Verwoerd, Dr 195
Victoria, Princess (Queen Victoria's daughter) 51, 55, 60, 188
Victoria, Queen 11, 29, 46, 49, 50–51, 52–53, 57, 58, 64, 68, 72, 73, 84, 86, 96, 114, 137, 214, 215, 246, 248, 276, 296, 306
 after death of Albert 60–61
 death of 70–71, 97
 Diamond Jubilee 67, 70, 204
 early reign 54–55
 Empress of India 62
 Golden Jubilee 67–68
Victoria of Saxe-Coburg-Saalfeld, Princess 50
Victoria and Albert Museum 58
Victoria Terminus (Mumbai) 62–63
Vision of Britain, A (Prince Charles) 257
Vogue 174

W
Wace, Master 14
Wade, Virginia 183
Wagner, Anthony 171
Walker, Catherine 228, 229
Walking With the Wounded 289
Wallace, William 35
Walpole, Robert 49
Walsingham, Francis 29
War of Austrian Succession (1740–48) 49
Warbeck, Perkin 28
Wars of the Roses 10, 21, 25, 26–27

Wells, HG 70
Wentworth, Thomas 38, 41
Wessex 12
West Germany 164–65
West Heath Girls' School 206, 207
Westminster Abbey 32, 33, 55, 68, 73, 76, 79, 94, 97, 111, 118, 119, 120, 140–41, 175, 182, 207, 219, 222–23, 254, 255, 267, 274, 279
Wetherby School 288
White Lodge 91
Wilhelm I, Kaiser 147
Wilhelm II, Kaiser 51, 60, 70, 79, 80, 81, 296
William I (the Conqueror) 10, 14, 16–17, 44
William I (King of Scotland) 34
William II 11, 17
William III 38, 39, 48, 212
William IV 11, 49, 51, 54, 84, 123
William, Prince (Elizabeth II's grandson) 198, 201, 205, 223, 251, 267, 278–79, 280–81, 296, 297, 307
 charity work 209, 303
 childhood 206, 207, 288
 death of Diana, Princess of Wales 242, 243
 Duchy of Cornwall 256, 257
 education 206, 207
 flying career 272–73, 291
 future of monarchy 318, 319
 Invictus Games 300
 Kensington Palace 214
 marriage to Catherine Middleton 205, 254, 255, 268, 274–75, 276, 277
 marriage of Prince Andrew and Sarah Ferguson 223
 marriage of Prince Charles and Camilla Parker Bowles 264
 at St Andrews University 262, 269, 278, 279
 Sandringham 147, 148
 state visits 153, 294–95
William, Prince (Henry I's son) 17
William of Malmesbury 16
Williams, Rowan 264, 267, 274
Willow (corgi) 108
Wilson, Harold 160, 161, 192
Windlesham Moor 120
Windsor, Louise 251, 254, 297
Windsor Castle 44–47, 60, 70, 106–07, 133, 175, 199, 219, 225, 232–33, 234–35, 251, 258, 264, 299, 310–11
Winterhalter, Franz Xaver 50
Wolsey, Cardinal 28
Women's Land Army 76, 81
Woods, Robin 151
Woodville, Elizabeth 25
Worcester, Battle of (1651) 41
World War I 55, 76, 79, 80–81, 90, 91, 97, 110, 255, 304–05
World War II 77, 97, 102–05, 106–07, 111, 114–15, 123, 192, 198, 238–39
World Wide Fund for Nature (WWF) 125, 209
Wren, Christopher 212
Wright, Clara 130
Wyatt's Rebellion 33, 40

XYZ
York 12
York, Duchess of see Ferguson, Sarah
York, Duke of see Andrew, Prince
Zimbabwe 195

Acknowledgments

Dorling Kindersley would like to thank: Stefan Podhorodecki and Paul Self for photography, Sneha Sunder Benjamin, Arpita Dasgupta, Helen Bridge, Suefa Lee, Isha Sharma, Fleur Star, and Sonia Yooshing for editorial assistance, Devika Awasthi, Paul Drislane, Parul Gambhir, Roshni Kapur, Shahid Mahmood, and Amit Malhotra for design assistance, Monica Byles for proofreading, Colin Hynson for indexing, and Gill Pitts, Karen Self, Helen Spencer, and Sharon Bartlett for allowing us to photograph their royal memorabilia.

Special thanks go to Agata Rutkowska, Picture Library Assistant, Royal Collection Trust; Chris Barker, Assistant Curator, Royal Mint; and John Loughery for help and advice.

The publisher would also like to thank James Grinter at Reeman Dansie Auctioneers for allowing us to photograph their collections.

Reeman Dansie Auctioneers
No. 8 Wyncolls Road
Colchester CO4 9HU
www.reemandansie.com/

For the second edition, DK would like to thank Esther Ripley for planning the revisions and Joel Levy for updating the text. DK India would like to thank Rakesh Kumar, Priyanka Sharma, and Saloni Singh for jackets assistance.

Picture Credits
The publisher would like to thank the following for their kind permission to reproduce their photographs:

(Key: a-above; b-below/bottom; c-centre; f-far; l-left; r-right; t-top)

1 Royal Mint Museum.
2–3 Corbis: Reuters / Luke Macgregor.
4 Corbis: Hoberman Collection (cra).
5 Corbis: Bettmann (br); Hulton-Deutsch Collection (tr). **Dorling Kindersley:** Reeman Dansie Auctioneers (cla, bl). **Getty Images:** Hulton Archive (tl). **The Royal Collection Trust © Her Majesty Queen Elizabeth II 2015:** (cra). **6 Alamy Images:** Holmes Garden Photos (ca). **Corbis:** Ralf-Finn Hestoft (br). **Getty Images:** Hulton Archive (bl); Central Press (tl); Chris Jackson (tr). **Royal Mint Museum:** (cra). **7 Corbis:** Chris Ison / epa (br); Pool Photograph (tl). **Getty Images:** WPA Pool (tr). **The Royal Collection Trust © Her Majesty Queen Elizabeth II 2015:** (cla) **8–9 Corbis:** Hoberman Collection. **10 Bridgeman Images:** National Archives, UK (ca); Alecto Historical Editions, London, UK (bc); The Trustees of the Weston Park Foundation, UK (cr). **By permission of The British Library:** (cla). **Dorling Kindersley:** Ashmolean Museum, Oxford (cl) **11 Corbis:** The Gallery Collection (clb); Leemage (bc). **Dorling Kindersley:** Reeman Dansie Auctioneers (cr). **The Art Archive** Ashmolean Museum (cla). **12 Dorling Kindersley:** National Maritime Museum, London (b); Ashmolean Museum, Oxford (tr). **13 By permission of The British Library:** (cr). **The Art Archive:** Musée de la Tapisserie Bayeux / Gianni Dagli Orti (c). **14–15 The Art Archive:** Musée de la Tapisserie Bayeux / Gianni Dagli Orti. **16 Bridgeman Images:** Chetham's Library, Manchester, UK. **17 Bridgeman Images:** Alecto Historical Editions, London, UK (crb). **Corbis:** The Gallery Collection (t). **Photo SCALA, Florence:** British Library board / Robana / Scala, Florence (bl). **18–19 Getty Images:** DeAgostini. **20 By permission of The British Library:** (tr). **Dorling Kindersley:** The Trustees of the British Museum (b). **21 Alamy Images:** travelibUK (bl). **Bridgeman Images:** National Archives, UK (cr); Bibliothèque Nationale, Paris, France (tc). **22–23 Bridgeman Images:** Bibliothèque Nationale, Paris, France. **24 Alamy Images:** Mary Evans Picture Library (bl). **24–25 Bridgeman Images:** The Trustees of the Weston Park Foundation, UK; National Portrait Gallery, London, UK (Henry V). **25 Corbis:** Leemage (tr). **26–27 Bridgeman Images:** De Agostini Picture Library. **28 Alamy Images:** The Art Archive (cl). **Corbis:** Gianni Dagli Orti (r). **29 Corbis:** Hoberman Collection (bc); Miles Ertman / All Canada Photos (tl); Leemage (cr). **30–31 Bridgeman Images:** Musée de Blois, Blois, France. **32–33 Corbis:** The Gallery Collection. **33 Bridgeman Images:** Hoefnagel, Joris (1542–1600) / Private Collection (cb). **Corbis:** (tl, bc). **34–35 Corbis:** Farrell Grehan (b). **34 National Museums of Scotland:** (tr). **35 Bridgeman Images:** His Grace The Duke of Norfolk, Arundel Castle (tr); National Library of Scotland, Edinburgh, Scotland (cl); Scottish National Portrait Gallery, Edinburgh, Scotland (cb). **36–37 The Royal Collection Trust © Her Majesty Queen Elizabeth II 2015**. **37 Alamy Images:** Realy Easy Star / Giuseppe Masci (bc); Rolf Richardson (crb). **Corbis:** Andrew Milligan / PA Wire / epa (br). **38 Corbis:** Gianni Dagli Orti. **39 Alamy Images:** Mary Evans Picture Library (bc). **Corbis:** The Gallery Collection (cl). **Getty Images:** DEA / G. Nimatallah (tr). **40 Corbis:** (cra). **40–41 Bridgeman Images:** Cheltenham Art Gallery & Museums, Gloucestershire, UK (b). **41 Alamy Images:** The Art Archive (tl). **42–43 The Royal Collection Trust © Her Majesty Queen Elizabeth II 2015**. **44–45 Corbis:** Jason Hawkes (t). **44 Rex Features:** Jonathan Hordle (bl). **45 Corbis:** Philip Craven / Robert Harding World Imagery (bc). **Dreamstime.com:** Aagje De Jong (br). **46 Alamy Images:** Steve Vidler (b). **Getty Images:** Tim Graham (tr, cra). **47 Rex Features**. **48 Alamy Images:** GL Archive (b). **Getty Images:** Apic (tr). **49 Corbis:** The Gallery Collection (r).**50 Corbis:** The Gallery Collection (bl); Hulton-Deutsch Collection (r). **51 Dorling Kindersley:** Royal Green Jackets Museum, Winchester (crb); Thackray Medical Museum (cl). **The Royal Collection Trust © Her Majesty Queen Elizabeth II 2015:** (bc); (t). **52–53 akg-images:**Archie Miles. **ley:** Reeman Dansie Auctioneers (cra). **54–55 The Royal Collection Trust © Her Majesty Queen Elizabeth II 2015**. **55 The Royal Collection Trust © Her Majesty Queen Elizabeth II 2015:** (br); (tl). **56–57 Bridgeman Images:** De Agostini Picture Library / W. Buss. **57 Alamy Images:** Graham Prentice (cb). **Bridgeman Images:** Historic England (br) **Corbis:** Corrie: Nigel / Arcaid (bc). **58–59 Corbis:** Historical Picture Archive. **60 Corbis:** (r). **Getty Images:** Universal History Archive (bl). **61 Getty Images:** Davide Cioffi (c). **The Royal Collection Trust © Her Majesty Queen Elizabeth II 2015:** (cra). **62–63 Bridgeman Images:** Haig, Axel (1835–1921) / British Library, London, UK. **64 Alamy Images:** The Art Archive (cl). **Bridgeman Images:** Harris, Albert E (fl.1917) / Roy Miles Fine Paintings (b). **Getty Images:** Arkivi (ca). **65 Alamy Images:** David Coleman (br). **Getty Images:** Popperfoto (cb). **Mary Evans Picture Library:** Illustrated London News Ltd (t). **66 Dorling Kindersley:** Reeman Dansie Auctioneers (t, bl, cr, br). **67 Corbis:** (tr). **Getty Images:** Hulton Archive (b). **68 The Royal Collection Trust © Her Majesty Queen Elizabeth II 2015:** (cl, clb, bl). **68–69 The Royal Collection Trust © Her Majesty Queen Elizabeth II 2015**. **69 The Royal Collection Trust © Her Majesty Queen Elizabeth II 2015:** (tl, bl). **70–71 The Royal Collection Trust © Her Majesty Queen Elizabeth II 2015**. **72 The Royal Collection Trust © Her Majesty Queen Elizabeth II 2015:** (l). **V&A Images / Victoria and Albert Museum, London:** (br). **73 Dorling Kindersley:** Reeman Dansie Auctioneers (tl, tc, cla, cr). **Getty Images:** Elliott & Fry (bc). **74–75 Dorling Kindersley:** Reeman Dansie Auctioneers. **76 123RF.com:** Scott Clarke (cb). **Dorling Kindersley:** Reeman Dansie Auctioneers (cla, cr). **77 Dorling Kindersley:** Reeman Dansie Auctioneers (cl); The Wardrobe Museum, Salisbury (ca). **Getty Images:** Keystone (bc). **Press Association Images:** Topfoto / Topham Picturepoint (crb) **78 Alamy Images:** (l). **Corbis** Hulton-Deutsch Collection (cr). **79 Corbis:** Hulton-Deutsch Collection (br). **Getty Images:** Hulton Archive (bl). **The Royal Collection Trust © Her Majesty Queen Elizabeth II 2015:** (tc). **80 Getty Images:** The Print Collector (cla); Central Press / Hulton Archive (tr). **80–81 Getty Images:** Popperfoto (b). **81 Alamy Images:** Universal Art Archive (bc). **Mary Evans Picture Library:** (tr). **Royal Artillery Historical Trust:** (c). **82–83 Corbis:** Hulton-Deutsch Collection. **84 Getty Images:** Tim Graham (b). **84–85 The Royal Collection Trust © Her Majesty Queen Elizabeth II 2015**. **86 Press Association Images:** Fiona Hanson (b). **The Royal Collection Trust © Her Majesty Queen Elizabeth II 2015:** (tr, cra). **87 The Royal Collection Trust © Her Majesty Queen Elizabeth II 2015**. **88–89 Getty Images:** Hulton Archive. **90 Bridgeman Images:** Look and Learn / Elgar Collection (r). **The Art Archive:** Private Collection MD (bl). **91 Alamy Images:** Hilary Morgan (bc); Ivan Vdovin (crb). **Getty Images:** Keystone (tc). **92 Corbis:** Hulton-Deutsch Collection (br). **Dorling Kindersley:** Reeman Dansie Auctioneers (tr). **The Art Archive:** Mondadori Portfolio (bl). **93 Alamy Images:** Keystone Pictures USA. **Getty Images:** Hulton Archive (crb). **94 Dorling Kindersley:** Reeman Dansie Auctioneers (tl, tc). **Getty Images:** Fox Photos (cra). **95 Getty Images:** Topical Press Agency (tc); Keystone. **96 Corbis:** (r). **Getty Images:** The Print Collector (bl). **97 Dorling Kindersley:** Reeman Dansie Auctioneers (tl). **Royal Mint Museum:** (bc). **The Stanley Gibbons Group plc:** (cr). **98 Getty Images:** Lisa Sheridan / Studio Lisa / Hulton Archive (cl). **Press Association Images:** (br). **The Royal Collection Trust © Her Majesty Queen Elizabeth II 2015:** (ca). **99 The Royal Collection Trust © Her Majesty Queen Elizabeth II 2015**. **100–101 Corbis:** Hulton-Deutsch Collection. **102 Corbis:** Hulton-Deutsch Collection (tr). **102–103 Getty Images:** Fox Photos / Hulton Archive. **103 Alamy Images:** Pictorial Press Ltd (tc). **Press Association Images:** Topfoto / Topham Picturepoint (br). **104–105 Mirrorpix**. **106 Getty Images:** Topical Press Agency / Hulton Archive (bl). **The Royal Collection Trust © Her Majesty Queen Elizabeth II 2015:** (cra). **107 Getty Images:** David E Scherman / The LIFE Picture Collection.**108–109 Corbis:** Hulton-Deutsch Collection. **110 Corbis:** Bettmann (r). **Getty Images:** Rita Martin (bl). **Mirrorpix:** (bc). **111 Alamy Images:** Heritage Image Partnership Ltd (bl). **Corbis:** Matthew Polak / Sygma (tc). **Dorling Kindersley:** Reeman Dansie Auctioneers (tl). **112–113 Getty Images:** Popperfoto. **114 Getty Images:** Popperfoto. **115 Getty Images:** Popperfoto (bc). **Mirrorpix:** (cr). **Press Association Images:** AP Photo (tl). **116–117 The Royal Collection Trust © Her Majesty Queen Elizabeth II 2015**. **118 Dorling Kindersley:** Reeman Dansie Auctioneers (ca). **Getty Images:** Central Press (br); E Round / Fox Photos (cr). **Mirrorpix:** (cl); NCJ – Kemsley (bl). **119 Alamy Images:** Vintage Image (cla). **Corbis:** Bettmann (bl). **Getty Images:** Topical Press Agency (cl). **Press Association Images:** AP (cr). **120 123RF.com:** tommroch (cl). **Mirrorpix:** NCJ – Kemsley (bl). **Rex Features:** Associated Newspapers / Daily Mail (cr). **121 123RF.com:** © Stamp Design Royal Mail Group Ltd (br). **Rex Features:** Daily Mail. **122–123 Alamy Images:** Arcaid Images. **123 Alamy Images:** Arcaid Images (bl); Prixpics (bc); worldthroughthelens-UK (br). **124–125 Getty Images:** Central Press. **124 Christopher Hogue Thompson:** (bl). **125 Getty Images:** Central Press (crb). **Leo Reynolds:** (c). **Victor Kusin:** (tc). **126 Dorling Kindersley:** Reeman Dansie Auctioneers (bl).**126–127 Dorling Kindersley:** Reeman Dansie Auctioneers. **127 Dorling Kindersley:** Reeman Dansie Auctioneers (br). **128–129 Press Association Images:** AP Photo / Max Desfor. **130 Corbis:** Henri Bureau / Sygma (br). **Getty Images:** Lisa Sheridan / Studio Lisa (tr). **131 The College of Arms:** The royal arms (the arms of Queen Elizabeth II). Reproduced by permission of the Kings, Heralds and Pursuivants of Arms (cr). **The Royal Collection Trust © Her Majesty Queen Elizabeth II 2015**. **132 Dorling Kindersley:** Reeman Dansie Auctioneers (br). **Mirrorpix:** NCJ – Topix (t).

133 Dorling Kindersley: Reeman Dansie Auctioneers (tl). **Getty Images:** E. Round / Fox Photos (br). **134 Getty Images:** Central Press (bl). **134–135 The Royal Collection Trust © Her Majesty Queen Elizabeth II 2015. 135 Corbis:** Pool Photograph (br). **Press Association Images:** Barratts / S&G Barratts / EMPICS Archive (tr). **136 The Royal Collection Trust © Her Majesty Queen Elizabeth II 2015:** (tl, cra, tr). **136–137 The Royal Collection Trust © Her Majesty Queen Elizabeth II 2015. 137 The Royal Collection Trust © Her Majesty Queen Elizabeth II 2015:** (t, c). **138–139 Corbis:** David Boyer / National Geographic Creative. **140 Dorling Kindersley:** Reeman Dansie Auctioneers (clb, bl). **Getty Images:** Topical Press Agency. **141 Corbis:** Bettmann (ca). **Dorling Kindersley:** Paul Self. **142–143 Alamy Images:** V&A Images. **144 The Royal Collection Trust © Her Majesty Queen Elizabeth II 2015:** All Rights Reserved (cla, bl, r). **145 The Royal Collection Trust © Her Majesty Queen Elizabeth II 2015:** All Rights Reserved (tl, tr, r). **146 Alamy Images:** Justin Kase (bl). **Getty Images:** Max Mumby / Indigo (bc); Picture Post (clb). **146–147 Alamy Images:** The Print Collector (bc). **Rex Features:** Peter Richardson / Robert Harding (tl). **147 Alamy Images:** Krys Bailey (bc); The Foto Factory (cb). **148 Bridgeman Images:** English Photographer, (20th century) / Museum purchase with funds donated by Michael D Wolfe (br). **The Royal Collection Trust © Her Majesty Queen Elizabeth II 2015:** (bl). **The Art Archive:** Victoria and Albert Museum London / V&A Images (cl).**149 Bridgeman Images:** English Photographer, (20th century) / © Country Life. **150 Getty Images:** Cornell Capa / The LIFE Picture Collection. **151 Dreamstime.com:** Creativehearts (c). **Getty Images:** WPA Pool / Arthur Edwards (br). **The Art Archive:** Ashmolean Museum (clb). **152 Alamy Images:** Vintage Image (cl). **152–153 Getty Images:** Central Press (c). **153 Corbis:** Bettmann (tc); Gideon Mendel (br). **154 Rex Features. 155 Corbis:** Bettmann (bl, tr). **Getty Images:** Popperfoto (cl). **156–157 Press Association Images:** AP. **158–159 Royal Mint Museum. 160 Alamy Images:** V&A Images (ca). **Bridgeman Images:** Armstrong-Jones, Antony (b.1930) / Private Collection / Photo © Christie's Images (cr). **Press Association Images:** PA / PA Archive (bc). **161 123RF.com:** © Stamp Design Royal Mail Group Ltd (c).**Corbis:** Norman Parkinson / Sygma (bl). **Rex Features:** Mike Hollist / Associated Newspapers (crb). **Royal Mint Museum:** (cra). **162 Alamy Images:** V&A Images (cl). **Corbis:** Teresa Dapp / dpa (tr). **TopFoto.co.uk:** (bc). **163 Corbis:** Norman Parkinson / Sygma (tr). **Rex Features:** Joan Williams (bl). **164–165 Getty Images:** Jim Gray. **166 Getty Images:** Mark Cuthbert (l); Tim Graham (cr). **167 The College of Arms:** the arms of HRH the Prince of Wales. Reproduced by permission of the Kings, Heralds and Pursuivants of Arms (cr). **Getty Images:** Mark Cuthbert (bl); WPA Pool / Pool (c). **Rex Features:** Reginald Davis (tl). **168–169 Press Association Images:** PA / PA Archive. **170 Corbis:** Adam Woolfitt (cb). **Rex Features:** Joan Williams (cla). **171 Bridgeman Images:** Armstrong-Jones, Antony (b.1930) / Private Collection / Photo © Christie's Images (bl). **Corbis:** Bettmann (crb). **TopFoto.co.uk:** PA (tl). **172–173 Getty Images:** Hulton Archive. **174 Corbis:** Norman Parkinson / Sygma (t) **Getty Images:** Central Press (bl). **Press Association Images:** Khan Tariq Mikkel / Polfoto (cr). **175 Corbis:** Norman Parkinson / Sygma (c). **176–177 Rex features:** Reginald Davis. **178–179 Getty Images:** Lichfield. **180 Getty Images:** Central Press (cla); WPA Pool / Pool (b). **181 Rex Features:** (br). **The Prince's Trust:** (tc). **182 Getty Images:** Graham Wiltshire (t). **Royal Mint Museum:** (br). **183 Getty Images:** Serge Lemoine (bl); Central Press (tr); Fox Photos / Hulton Archive (c). **184–185 Corbis:** Hulton-Deutsch Collection. **186–187 Rex Features:** Reginald Davis. **188 Corbis:** Norman Parkinson / Sygma (br). **Getty Images:** Jacques Gustave (tr); Popperfoto (bl). **189 Alamy Images:** Trinity Mirror / Mirrorpix. **Getty Images:** Hulton Archive (b). **190 Getty Images:** Guildhall Library & Art Gallery / Heritage Images (bl). **Press Association Images:** John Stillwell / PA Archive (br). **190–191 Corbis:**Stapleton Collection. **192 Alamy Images:** Robert Estall photo agency (bc); Keystone Pictures USA (cra). **Corbis:** Hulton-Deutsch Collection (bl). **193 The Random House Group Ltd:** (cr). **Rex Features:** Mike Hollist / Associated Newspapers (b) **194 Rex Features:** Associated Newspapers (tr). **TopFoto.co.uk:** Topham / AP (br). **195 Corbis:** Stephen Morrison / epa (br). **196–197 Royal Mint Museum. 198 123RF.com:** © Stamp Design Royal Mail Group Ltd (bl). **Alamy Images:** Trinity Mirror / Mirrorpix (c). **Corbis:** Bettmann (cr); Quadrillion (cl).**199 Getty Images:** Tim Graham (clb). **Rex Features:** (cb). **The Royal Collection Trust © Her Majesty Queen Elizabeth II 2015** (ca). **200 Corbis:** Atlan-Bureau-Dejean-Graham-Guichard-Karel-Melloul-Nogues-Pavlovsky-Rancinan. **Getty Images:** Tim Graham (cl). **201 123RF.com:** Andy Lidstone / © Stamp Design Royal Mail Group Ltd (tr). **Corbis:** Douglas Kirkland (br). **202–203 Getty Images:** Anwar Hussein. **204 123RF.com:** © Stamp Design Group Ltd (8). **Dorling Kindersley:** © Stamp Design Royal Mail Group Ltd (t). **The Stanley Gibbons Group plc:** (14, 15); (1, 2, 3, 4, 5, 6, 7, 9, 10, 11, 12, 13). **205 Dorling Kindersley:** © Stamp Design Royal Mail Group Ltd (1, 2, 3, 4, 5, 6, 7, 8, 9, 12, 13, 15). **Dreamstime.com:** © Stamp Design Royal Mail Group Ltd (10, 11, 14). **206 Getty Images:** Central Press (bl). **Rex Features:** (tr). **207 Getty Images:** Sion Touhig (bl). **Press Association Images:** PA Archive (br). **Rex Features:** David Levenson. **208 Alamy Images:** Trinity Mirror / Mirrorpix (c). **Rushden Research:** (cla). **209 Mirrorpix:** Gavin Kent (tr). **Press Association Images:** Bebeto Mattews / AP (bl). **210–211 Getty Images:** Tim Graham. **212 Getty Images:** Jason Hawkes (br); DEA / W. BUSS (bl). **213 SuperStock:** Steve Vidler / Steve Vidler. **214 Alamy Images:** Prisma Bildagentur AG (tl). **Press Association Images:** David Jensen / EMPICS Entertainment (tc). **215 Getty Images:** Samir Hussein / WireImage. **216–217 Getty Images:** David Levenson. **218 Rex Features:**Glenn Harvey. **219 Corbis:** Denis Balibouse / Reuters (crb); Michel Setboun (t); Hulton-Deutsch Collection (bc). **220–221 Corbis:** Quadrillion. **222 Alamy Images:** Trinity Mirror / Mirrorpix. **223 Getty Images:** Tim Graham (tr). **Rex Features:** Glenn Harvey (bl). **224 Rex Features:** Associated Newspapers (cla); Illustrated London News (b). **225 Getty Images:** Chris Jackson (tl). **Rex Features:** Mauro Carraro (bc); (cr). **226–227 Corbis:** Quadrillion. **228 Rex Features:** Nils Jorgensen (l, c, r). **229 Rex Features:** Tim Stewart News (tr, r). **230 Rex Features:** (clb). **230–231 Press Association Images:** Tony Harris / PA Archive. **231 Rex Features:** (tc, cr). **232–233 Getty Images:** Tim Graham. **234 Alamy Images:** Heritage Image Partnership Ltd (bl). **Bridgeman Images:** National Gallery of Canada, Ottawa, Ontario, Canada / Phillips, Fine Art Auctioneers, New York, USA (cl). **Press Association Images:** Anthony Devlin / PA Wire (ca). **235 Alamy Images:** Terry Fincher (b). **Rex Features:** Simon & Schuster US (tl). **236–237 The Royal Collection Trust © Her Majesty Queen Elizabeth II 2015. 238–239 Rex Features:** Steve Back / Associated Newspapers. **238 123RF.com:** © Stamp Design Royal Mail Group Ltd (bl). **Rex Features:** Jeremy Selwyn / Associated Newspapers (tr). **239 Rex Features:** (tl, cr). **240–241 Corbis:** Courtesy of Ronald Reagan Library. **242 Getty Images:** Anwar Hussein (cra). **Mirrorpix:** (bl). **Rex Features:** SIPA Press (cl). **243 Corbis:** Jason Hawkes (br). **Getty Images:** AFP (t). **244–245 Corbis:** Ralf-Finn Hestoft. **246 Alamy Images:** Dennis Hardley (bc). **Getty Images:** Cowper / Central Press (cla); Lichfield (bl). **247 Corbis:** Roger Antrobus. **248 Mary Evans Picture Library** (b). **The Royal Collection Trust © Her Majesty Queen Elizabeth II 2015:** (cl, c). **249 Bridgeman Images:** English Photographer, (19th century) / Private Collection. **250 Getty Images:** Tim Graham (l, cr). **251 Getty Images:** UK Press / Mark Cuthbert (br). **Rex Features:** Glenn Harvey (tl); Tim Rooke (bc). **252–253 The Royal Collection Trust © Her Majesty Queen Elizabeth II 2015. 254 Corbis:** Pool Photograph (cl, bl). **Dorling Kindersley:** Paul Self (tl). **Getty Images:** Stephen Hird / AFP (c). **Rex Features:** Hugo Burnand / Clarence House (br). **255 Alamy Stock Photo:** PA Images / Yui Mok (tr). **Getty Images:** Alex Livesey (l). **Mirrorpix:** Phil Harris / Daily Mirror (bc). **The Royal Collection Trust © Her Majesty Queen Elizabeth II 2015:** (c). **256 Alamy Images:** Skyscan Photolibrary (cl). **Corbis:** Michael Crabtree / Reuters (br). **257 Corbis:** Demotix / Amer Ghazzal (tc). **Getty Images:** Matt Cardy (br). **Rex Features:** (tl). **258 Corbis:** Norman Parkinson / Sygma (t). **Dorling Kindersley:** Reeman Dansie Auctioneers (br). **259 Corbis:** Jeff J Mitchell / Reuters (bl); Reuters (tr). **Dorling Kindersley:** Paul Self (cla). **260 Rex Features:** Tony Kyriacou. **261 Corbis:** Pool Photograph (ca). **Rex Features:** (br). **262–263 Getty Images:** Carl De Souza. **264 Corbis:** Reuters (bl). **Photoshot:** UPPA (cl). **265 Corbis:** Dave Evans / Demotix (br); Pool Photograph. **266–267 Getty Images:** AFP. **268 Getty Images:** Tim Graham (bl). **268–269 Corbis:** Reuters (c). **269 Getty Images:** UK Press / Mark Cuthbert (tc). **270–271 Corbis:** POOL / Reuters. **272 Corbis:** Phil Noble / Reuters (crb). **Getty Images:** Tim Graham (cl). **Rex Features:** SAC Faye Storer (bl). **273 Corbis:** POOL / Reuters. **274 Corbis:** John Stillwell / PA / POOL / epa (tr). **Rex Features:** Hugo Burnand / Clarence House (bl). **275 Corbis:** Chris Ison / epa (cr). **Press Association Images:** Dave Thompson / PA Archive (l). **276 Dorling Kindersley:** Reeman Dansie Auctioneers (tl, cla, cl, bl, bc, fbr, br). **276–277 The Royal Collection Trust © Her Majesty Queen Elizabeth II 2015. 277 Dorling Kindersley:** Reeman Dansie Auctioneers (tl, tc, tr, ca, cra, br). **278 Getty Images:** Tim Graham (bl). **278–279 Getty Images:** Max Mumby / Indigo (c). **279 The College of Arms:** The conjugal arms of the Duke and Duchess of Cambridge. Reproduced by permission of the Kings, Heralds and Pursuivants of Arms (cr); **Getty Images:** Max Mumby / Indigo (bc). **280-281 Getty Images:** WPA Pool / Pool / Aaron Chown. **282 Corbis:** (tl); Kerim Okten / epa (b). **283 Corbis:** Rune Hellestad (crb). **Rex Features:** Vickie Flores / LNP (bl). **The Royal Collection Trust © Her Majesty Queen Elizabeth II 2015:** (t). **284–285 Getty Images:** WPA Pool / Pool. **286–287 Getty Images:** Alex Livesey. **288 Getty Images:** Tim Graham (bl). **288–289 Getty Images:** Chris Jackson (c). **289 The College of Arms:** The arms of HRH Prince Henry of Wales. Reproduced by permission of the Kings, Heralds and Pursuivants of Arms (bc). **Getty Images:** AFP (cr); Chris Jackson (tc). **290 Alamy Images:** AF archive (cla). **Corbis:** John Stillwell / PA Wire / epa (r). **291 Getty Images:** Max Mumby / Indigo (br). **Press Association Images:** John Stillwell / PA Archive (tr). **Roland Smithies / luped.com:** (clb). **292 Alamy Stock Photo:** PA Images / Kirsty O'Connor (b). **Getty Images:** WireImage / George Pimentel (cla). **293 Alamy Stock Photo:** PA Images / Yui Mok (cb); REUTERS / POOL New (tr). **Getty Images:** AFP / David Harrison (tl). **294 Getty Images:** AFP / Adnan Abidi (t); Rolls Press / Popperfoto (bl). **295 Getty Images:** Chris Jackson Collection (tr, bl). **296 Alamy Images:** Globe Photos / ZUMA Press, Inc. (br). **Getty Images:** Hulton Archive (bl). **297 Getty Images:** Indigo / Max Mumby (cr, bc); WireImage / Anwar Hussein (tl). **298 Getty Images:** Anwar Hussein (cr); Samir Hussein (l). **299 Dorling Kindersley:** © Stamp Design Royal Mail Group Ltd (tr). **Getty Images:** Chris Jackson (tl). **Rex Features:** Tim Rooke (bc). **300–301 Mirrorpix:** Phil Harris / Daily Mirror. **302 Dorling Kindersley:** Reeman Dansie Auctioneers (bc). **Getty Images:** WPA Pool / Pool (tl). **302–303 Getty Images:** WPA Pool / Pool (br). **303 Getty Images:** Tim Graham (tl). **304–305 Getty Images:** Chris Jackson. **306 Getty Images:**WPA Pool / Pool (b). **307 Dorling Kindersley:** Bank of Jersey (clb). **Getty Images:** WPA Pool / Pool (tl, br). **308–309 Corbis:** Pool Photograph. **310 Alamy Stock Photo:** Amer Ghazzal (clb). **Getty Images:** John Stillwell - WPA Pool (t); Samir Hussein / WireImage (bc). **311 Getty Images:** Alastair Grant - WPA Pool (tc). **Rex by Shutterstock:** Ben Cawthra (b). **312–313 Getty Images. 314 ESA:** NASA (cl). **Getty Images:** Danny Martindale / WireImage (bl); Jeff Spicer (cra). **315 Getty Images:** Oli Scarff / AFP. **316–317 Getty Images:** Toby Melville - WPA Pool. **318 Corbis:** Hulton-Deutsch Collection (cra). **Royal Mint Museum:** (br, bc). **319 Getty Images:** WPA Pool / Pool (tr). **Rex Features:** Royal Mint (br). **Royal Mint Museum** (bl, bc).**320–321 Getty Images:** Chris Jackson Collection.

All other images © Dorling Kindersley

For further information see: www.dkimages.com